The United States and the Caribbean
in the Twentieth Century

The United States and the Caribbean in the Twentieth Century

REVISED EDITION

Lester D. Langley

ersity of Georgia Press

© 1980, 1982, 1985 by the University of Georgia Press
Athens, Georgia 30602
All rights reserved

Set in 10 on 13 point Mergenthaler Baskerville

The paper in this book meets the guidelines for
permanence and durability of the Committee on
Production Guidelines for Book Longevity of the
Council on Library Resources.

Printed in the United States of America

89 88 87 86 85   5 4 3 2 1

The first edition of this book was published in 1980 under
the title *The United States and the Caribbean, 1900–1970.*

Library of Congress Cataloging in Publication Data

Langley, Lester D.
The United States and the Caribbean in the twentieth
century.
Enl. ed. of: The United States and the Caribbean,
1900–1970. c1980.
Bibliography: p.
Includes index.
1. Caribbean area—Foreign relations—United States.
2. United States—Foreign relations—Caribbean area.
3. United States—Foreign relations—20th century.
4. Caribbean area—Politics and government. I. Title.
F2178.U6L38 1982   327.730729   81-18521
AACR2
ISBN 0-8203-0775-0
ISBN 0-8203-0776-9 (pbk.)

For
Wanda D. Langley

Contents

Preface

In an earlier study,* I related the history of United States antagonism to the European presence in the Caribbean in the nineteenth century; in this work, my intent is to tell the story of American involvement in the political, economic, and cultural lives of the Caribbean republics in the twentieth century. The perspective is the view from the United States, but I have incorporated enough of the internal histories of the republics to provide background and a more balanced perspective. My approach is chronological and episodic, for successive American leaders in the twentieth century have looked at the Caribbean differently from their predecessors, and each has encountered problems in some of the republics which, though exhibiting similarities to issues elsewhere, are nonetheless deserving of individual attention. Thus, Woodrow Wilson's perceptions of Caribbean politics differed from those of Theodore Roosevelt; and Roosevelt's handling of Cuban and Panamanian affairs revealed still more distinctions and qualifications of policy toward separate portions of what contemporaries called the American empire.

Portions of the Prelude and Chapters 7, 8, and 10 have appeared in *The Americas, Intercambio Internacional,* and the *Journal of Inter-American Studies and World Affairs.* My cumulative debts for assistance in the research and writing of this work would require several pages to enumerate, but I can at least acknowledge some: Leila Oertel, Cartographic Services, University of Georgia; Gloria Davis, Nancy Heaton, Wanda Snyder, Yvonne Ivie, and Linda Green, who typed and retyped what became a long manuscript; Charles Wynes, who tried to improve the style; my students in American diplomatic history and inter-American problems, who have listened to my stories of the turbulent Caribbean; and Dana Gardner Munro, whose studies of American policy in the Caribbean I have referred to again and again.

The index was prepared with the assistance of Jonathan Jay Langley.

Struggle for the American Mediterranean: United States–European Rivalry in the Gulf-Caribbean, 1776–1904 (Athens: Univ. of Georgia Press, 1976).

Havana •

CUBA

JAMAICA

MEXICO

**BELIZE
(BRITISH
HONDURAS)**

Belmopan •

GUATEMALA

HONDURAS

Guatemala City •

San Salvador
**(EL
SALVADOR)**

• Tegucigalpa

C A R I B

NICARAGUA

Managua •

COSTA RICA

• San José

PANAMA

Panama City •

*The
Caribbean*

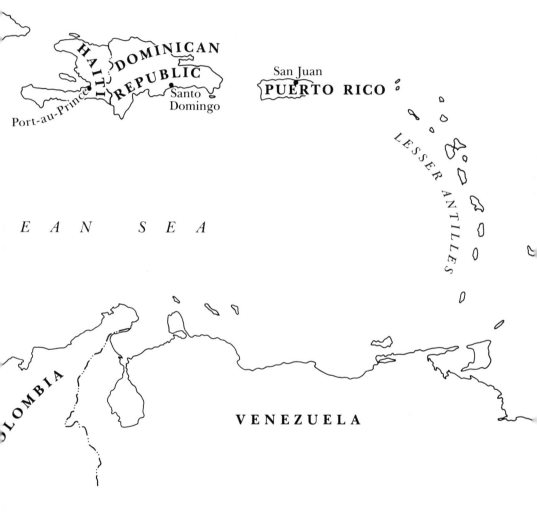

HAITI
DOMINICAN
REPUBLIC
San Juan
PUERTO RICO
Santo
Domingo
Port-au-Prince

LESSER ANTILLES

E A N   S E A

OLOMBIA

VENEZUELA

Prelude: A Vision of Empire

In the sweltering heat of August 1898 the president at last received Spain's reply to his peace proposal. The response of that old but still proud empire, whose fleet had suffered in early July a humiliating defeat in a fierce naval battle off Santiago de Cuba, sounded cocky and defiant. He had expected a compromising and submissive tone. Where he had suggested that America would "guide" Cuban independence, out of deference to its anticolonial traditions and a prewar Congressional resolution abjuring annexation, the Spanish, perhaps doubting his resolve, had noted their concern for the fate of the island's loyalists. The proposed acquisition of Puerto Rico as indemnity was met with indignation and protest. His insistence on territorial rewards in the Philippines prompted even more objections, with the Spanish arguing that the crown had no intention of renouncing sovereignty over the archipelago.

William McKinley viewed himself as a reasonable man, and he appeared visibly annoyed with Spain's counterproposal. He informed the French ambassador, Jules Cambon, who was acting as Madrid's intermediary, that Spain must immediately relinquish and evacuate Cuba and Puerto Rico before any cessation of hostilities. Such an agreement would not be a formal treaty but a protocol, and in accepting the protocol the parties were to understand that a final treaty could be thrashed out in Paris by five commissioners from each side.

Monsieur Cambon recommended acceptance, and to McKinley's relief Spain acquiesced. The document was signed at half past four on the afternoon of Friday, 12 August 1898, in the cabinet room of the White House. McKinley disliked publicity, and he had forbidden any newspapermen or photographers to witness the fall of one empire and the birth of another. The only preparations for the ceremony had been the hasty assembling of Secretary of State John Day, three of his assistants, McKinley, four of his staff, and Monsieur Cambon and his associate. No Spaniard was present. A summer rainstorm lashed the city, and heavy rain pelted the windowpanes. When everything was ready, Day went to the adjoining room where the Frenchmen waited and beckoned them to join him in signing the four copies of the protocol. The others, including McKinley, remained standing, watching silently. When Cambon finished, the president shook his hand, thanking him for mediating between two enemies. After the French departed, Day and George Cortelyou, McKinley's secretary, walked over to a huge globe. "Let's see," Day muttered, "what we get by all this."[1]

As McKinley and Day had anticipated, the Spanish renewed their protests when formal discussions began in Paris. To Spain the territorial demands were more a matter of pride than economics. But its representatives could not weaken the resolve of McKinley's commissioners, and in mid-November, after learning of the latest Spanish vacillation, Day decided to force the issue by threatening to break off discussions. Spain received the ultimatum on the twenty-second. On the twenty-eighth Montero Rios, an aging, dignified servant of the Spanish crown, capitulated. When the Spanish commissioners entered the negotiating room for the final session, the Americans motioned them to the side of the table facing the windows. The weather was cloudy, but the sun broke through just as the Spaniards were signing. One of the Americans, Whitelaw Reid, noting the sudden illumination, observed it was doubtless a good omen. No, came the Spanish response, "everything is gloom around us."[2]

The United States in 1898 was not considered, nor did it consider itself, an imperial power, but the nation lived in a world of competing, dynamic empires. Great Britain, which the year before had celebrated the Victorian Jubilee, reigned as the supreme power in the world. Her most important European rivals, France and Germany, had joined with Britain in partitioning Africa. Even in the New World, proclaimed safe for republicanism by President James Monroe in 1823, outposts of British, French, Dutch, and Spanish empires lay near the United States.

In some minds the fear was not of European encirclement nor of further European encroachment against weak Latin American states but of American unwillingness to stake out its own empire. Until the Civil War the territorial expansion of the United States had been largely acquisition of contiguous lands—Louisiana, Florida, Texas, California, and Oregon. In the Caribbean especially, antebellum American leaders had rejected annexation and disdained revolution

—annexation because that meant incorporating alien cultures, Caribbean revolution because that might unleash disruptive social and political forces. Thomas Jefferson's generation witnessed the Haitian revolution against French rule and was horrified at the racial conflict accompanying the extinction of a slave society. Years later, Secretary of State John Quincy Adams observed that the preservation of Spanish Cuba was preferable to Cuban rebellion because the rebels lacked the ability to create a stable republic. Their overthrow of Spanish rule would only invite British occupation. After the Mexican War, the question of American expansion into the Caribbean reflected mostly Southern dreams of a tropical slave empire, as in Yucatán, where separatist elements appealed for annexation to the United States in 1848; in Cuba, which, after Spain crushed a rebellion in 1851, the pro-Southern Franklin Pierce administration advocated seizing if Spain refused to sell; and in Nicaragua, where American filibusters under William Walker ruled in the mid-1850s.[3]

Postwar American leaders, of course, rejected any notion of territorial expansion to advance slavery, but they did not reject the idea of American hegemony over the Caribbean. For one thing, the Navy wanted a Caribbean naval base, preferably in Hispaniola; and to this end the Grant administration, after negotiating with a larcenous Dominican chief executive, presented the Senate with a treaty of annexation of the entire republic. A phalanx of senators, led by Charles Sumner of Massachusetts, marshalled sufficient votes to kill the scheme. At the high point of the debate Sumner, alluding to the story of Naboth's vineyard in the Old Testament, argued that acquiring the Dominican Republic was morally wrong because it meant incorporation of an alien culture into American domain. Twenty years later, naval enthusiasts advocated acquisition of a naval base at Môle Saint-Nicolas in Haiti, but Haitian suspicions over American designs destroyed the scheme.

Though the Navy acquired no West Indian bases until after the war with Spain, it experienced the modern influences of naval technology and the new doctrines of naval strategy. The American ships which sank one Spanish fleet at Manila on 1 May and another off Santiago two months later were no match for the finest British ships, but they were far more advanced in design and armament than the Spanish ships. As the United States had acquired a modern navy (which it would expand considerably under Theodore Roosevelt), so it had absorbed modern theories of naval power, brilliantly articulated by such naval philosophers as Stephen Luce, founder of the Naval War College, and Alfred Thayer Mahan, who not only read the latest books on naval history but wrote prolifically on the subject. Mahan became more than a philosopher; he emerged a prophet, spreading the faith that would be known in the 1890s as the "large policy." By its teachings, the United States must "look outward" to the new frontiers beyond its own national boundaries. Historical destiny, as exemplified by the role of sea power in British history, and internal pressures, particularly the tendency of an industrial system to saturate the domestic market with its products, compelled the nation to undertake expansion.

Mahan anticipated the military and commercial necessity for American construction and control of an isthmian canal. European rivals, he argued, would thwart American commercial expansion by seizing strategic places along the major trade routes or by extending their political influence over weak Caribbean and Asian nations. The sensible solution to such a challenge, Mahan contended, lay in a vigorous policy that looked to the acquisition of naval bases in the Caribbean and in the western Pacific. Influenced by Mahan's thinking, the General Board of the Navy, chaired by the war hero Admiral George Dewey, recommended in 1900 acquisition of bases at four sites in Cuba; the development of a base at Culebra, Puerto Rico; and, in the likelihood of European threats to the Dominican Republic or Haiti, seizure of sites in those countries.[4]

Just as outspoken as the promoters of naval expansion were the political champions of a new Caribbean empire. Appeals on behalf of manifest destiny and empire were reinforced by Social Darwinist credos and the nation's tradition of moral paternalism. It was, according to the latest doctrine, America's duty to rid Cuba of despotic Spanish rule and then remain to tutor Spain's former colony in the art of progressive democracy and civic morality.

McKinley himself had stressed this theme in a speaking tour of the Midwest and South in the fall of 1898. In his speeches he equivocated, occasionally uttering anti-expansionist thoughts but quickly following with imperialist sentiments. Attentive aides noted the louder applause for the latter. He talked continually about duty and destiny—how duty determined destiny—and the obligation of the country toward "uncivilized peoples." Mahan echoed McKinley's imperialist theme by pointing out the danger to national interest if the country, having defeated Spain, failed to carry through with a policy of regeneration and beneficence in order to uplift backward societies.

By such a combination of altruism and self-interest, expansionists argued, the United States would achieve the enviable international respectability previously attained by Great Britain. British writers such as James Antony Froude and Benjamin Kidd had already articulated a philosophy of the white man's burden. A decade before the war with Spain, Froude had produced a widely read treatise on the West Indian nonwhites. Like other tropical peoples, Froude claimed, West Indians were incapable of comprehending freedom without guidance. Weaker societies required tutelage from stronger ones or their future would be disrupted by internal anarchy and external aggression. In Kidd's *Control of the Tropics*, which appeared in 1898, this theme of imperial duty had been elaborated with somewhat differing conclusions. Where Froude talked about uplifting backward peoples, Kidd argued that superior, white cultures confronted novel problems in the tropics. Heretofore, the most intense rivalries had been for control of territory suitable for white peoples; in the future, however, imperial contest lay in the tropical zones of the globe. In part, this struggle would be economic, for the white societies, lying in the temperate zone, produced different products from the nonwhite tropical societies. The more advanced nations would thus compete in the tropics.

But when venturing into the tropics, said Kidd, whites risked physical debilitation and cultural degradation in a region where the body slowed from the enervating effects of humidity and the will slackened before the easy mores of nonwhite peoples. Kidd's solution was to raise the political, economic, and moral level of tropical cultures. This required direct guidance by a dedicated cadre of trained, God-fearing civil servants dispatched from the civilizing nations to the outlying domain of tropical empires. A rotation of the bureaucrats would ensure against physical and moral degeneracy. In a later article, Kidd applied his theories to the United States and its prospects of Caribbean empire. *The Control of the Tropics* was widely reviewed and heatedly debated, and it particularly elicited comment on the author's point about the white man's need to supervise and control but his inability to colonize the tropics. Technology and modern medicine, it was contended in rebuttal to Kidd, could provide a means for white survival in a nonwhite environment. Generally, those Americans who read and expounded on Kidd's thesis accepted his premise about the white man's duty in the tropics but optimistically modified his grim conclusions about survival there.[5]

Belief in the inferiority of tropical peoples was reinforced by the average American soldier's experience in the war. Hispanophobia historically permeated American thought and literature. In the American recounting of Cuba's nineteenth-century revolutionary struggles against Spanish rule, the counterrevolutionary politics of Madrid had been interpreted as the inevitable consequence of Spanish cowardice, treachery, and perfidy. Little wonder that the president of the University of Wisconsin confidently announced to the class of 1897 that Spain had contributed nothing to civilization; or that a political confidant told McKinley about Spaniards intriguing even in the mundane act of purchasing eggs; or that for Spain the brutal and treacherous became acceptable and commonplace.

Cubans, by contrast, may have been different from Americans in their political beliefs and ethnic makeup, but they were also different from Spaniards, as the conduct of the war illustrated. They waged a valiant struggle for liberty against Spanish imperialism and cruelty. Viewed through the prism of American values and beliefs, their actions interpreted by a biased American press, Cuban rebels had appeared braver—and whiter—than American soldiers found them to be on initial encounter. In making war the rebels practiced the 1898 version of modern guerrilla technique: they stole, burned, pillaged, and retreated in the face of superiority. To Americans who read of their exploits in the press, they fought bravely, defying a merciless, oppressive foe with much the same determination as Washington's Revolutionary army had faced the British. Some journalists, dispatched to cover the war after American entry, simply could not reconcile their earlier visions with the reality of a ragtag soldiery subsisting on meager rations and avoiding conventional military confrontation. Take away their guns and cartridges, wrote one correspondent, and Cuban rebels looked like tramps. On close inspection they were also darker-skinned than their American allies. Theodore Roosevelt believed the entire Cuban army was composed of blacks and mulattoes. Leonard Wood equated their ethnic origin with a natural affinity for savagery, an inherited trait which the war exacerbated. American troops generally concluded that skin color explained the lack of competence.

American soldiers expected effusive gratitude from their Cuban patriots, but instead they encountered indifference. Cuban rebels, generously offered American rations, merely angered their benefactors by returning several times, to be fed again. Benevolence soon became perplexity, which eventually turned to contempt. Those who often had read of Cuban bravery in the face of Spanish cruelty, as had Captain Robley D. ("Fighting Bob") Evans, were shocked at the sight of Cubans calmly picking off Spanish sailors swimming away from their burning vessels during the battle of Santiago Bay.

Not only did the Cuban fight unfairly, American troops believed, but he would not pull his weight behind the lines. He lounged about, feigned illness, refused to perform dirty work, and seemed generally indifferent to labor of any kind. Even in the critical landings at Guantánamo and Daiquirí, wrote Stephen Crane, Cubans joined the fight only to get food and a little sleep. Americans had come to Cuba, Crane complained bitterly, to struggle alongside a Cuban ally; instead of fighting valiantly with their American comrades, Cubans preferred to stay behind, eating army rations and manifesting unconcern for their cause. Crane, like other American observers, had little understanding of the meaning of rest and respite to a guerrilla involved in a long struggle.[6]

This harsh view of Cubans boded ill for the future of Cuban-American relations, for it seemed to confirm the prejudicial notions Americans had long held about other Caribbean peoples. For all their ability to survive, for all their cunning, the Cubans had been judged and found wanting. With such a harsh personal indictment it was not illogical to presume that they were unfit to run their own country.

Though American forces occupied Cuba for four years after their victory, the only Caribbean territory the United States acquired as a result of the war was Puerto Rico, and a debate soon ensued as to the status of Puerto Ricans within American domain. Were the Puerto Ricans entitled to all the benefits of American citizens, though they spoke another language and represented another culture? Former president Benjamin Harrison, waiting until the debate subsided before he condemned the imperial venture, argued cogently that the Constitution followed the flag; thus "subjects" of American rule possessed the same constitutional rights as ordinary American citizens. But in 1901, in a series of decisions called the "insular cases," the Supreme Court ruled differently. In one case, *Downes* v. *Bidwell*, the Court, in deciding whether customs officials could collect duties on goods shipped from Puerto Rico to New York, felt constrained to point out that Congress might decide what laws shall govern the "American empire," and added: "In the annexation of outlying and distant possessions grave questions will arise from differences of race, habits, laws, and customs of the people."[7] The Puerto Ricans, like other Caribbean people, were different and thus were to be governed differently.

In the evolution of a "large policy" in 1898, economic considerations played a powerful role. The great political debate of the decade had revealed widespread uncertainties over the vitality of the American economy and, in fact, over the future of American capitalism. From 1893 the country was caught in the grip of the worst depression in American history. A feeling of economic crisis pervaded. Attitudes hardened, panaceas abounded, class divisions sharpened, and, in 1896, the two major parties fought the battle of the standards.

In searching for an explanation of the economic crisis, Andrew Carnegie, the steel magnate, and David Wells advanced the "glut theory." Simply stated, this theory of economy presumed the nation could always produce more than its inhabitants were able to consume, a situation causing the boom-bust cycles of the nineteenth century. Socialism was unacceptable, so the pragmatic solution to the dilemma of a glutted economy was a dynamic export economy. American agricultural producers had long been advocates of a more aggressive export policy. Now, in the economic crisis of the 1890s, it was the industrial manufacturers who stumped for an expansionist economic policy as a palliative to the depression and a cure for the social discontents of the age. From 1776 the rebellious thirteen colonies and later the United States had pursued commercial treaties as a central feature of American diplomacy, but for the first time, the search for foreign markets had been integrated into American strategic thought.

The new markets, it was generally agreed, lay, not in Europe, which then received 80 percent of American exports, but in Latin America and East Asia. Africa and Southern Asia, two potential markets for industrial goods, were already being closed off to American trade. The United States, then, must pursue a variety of measures on the economic front: it needed to rehabilitate its shipping, encourage international branches of American banks, sign new commercial treaties, and instill in the diplomatic and consular corps an enthusiasm for promoting American economic interests. (In Argentina, the former salesman and promoter William Buchanan typified the new breed. A Democrat, Buchanan was retained by the McKinley administration. Later he became a diplomatic troubleshooter in Latin America for Theodore Roosevelt.) In 1895, when the National Association of Manufacturers was chartered, one of its first resolutions encouraged an expansionist export market. In the following years the NAM championed virtually every cause of the new economic strategists and, to cite one example, vigorously supported American construction and control of an isthmian canal.

An ambitious program for expanding American trade with the Caribbean had existed as far back as the abortive Dominican annexation scheme of the Grant administration. James G. Blaine's Pan American venture, which called for closer economic relations with Latin America, was momentarily thwarted in 1881, but his successor, Frederick Frelinghuysen, negotiated reciprocity treaties with Spain (for Cuba and Puerto Rico), Great Britain (for the British West Indies), the Dominican Republic, and El Salvador. In defending these treaties in a letter to the Senate, Frelinghuysen averred that they provided, in effect, all the advantages of annexation. In 1884 the ambitious secretary of state signed a canal treaty with Nicaragua, creating in the process a protectorate over the republic. The incoming Cleveland administration withdrew the treaty on the understandable grounds that it violated the 1850 Clayton-Bulwer Treaty with Great Britain, but Cleveland did not reject Frelinghuysen's economic theories.

Cuba before 1898 offered a special example of the American economic approach to the Caribbean. Cuban-American commerce steadily increased from 1878, when the disastrous Ten Years' War ended. In the 1880s, Leland Jenks estimated in his classic work *Our Cuban Colony* that commerce with Cuba constituted one-fourth of American trade with the entire world. American technicians and entrepreneurs moved in to build railroads and operate sugar plantations. In 1895 Secretary of State Richard Olney, assessing the impact of the rebellion on American interests, calculated the value of American capital invested in Cuba at $50 million. When the United States entered the conflict three years later, it did not do so primarily for economic reasons, but McKinley cited the disruption to commerce as a major justification for going to war. Certainly he believed that Spanish colonialism retarded Cuban economic development and that only free trade could provide the island with the economic sustenance it needed for the twentieth century. At war's end American investors saw in the island another market for their capital and manufactures, an "open door" ninety miles from home.[8]

If in 1900 the United States did not consider itself an imperial power in the European tradition, it looked upon the Caribbean as the new "American Mediterranean," and American policy expressed beliefs about the Caribbean that reflected an imperial outlook. Such a view had been forcefully advanced by Secretary of State Olney in his famous 20 July 1895 analysis on the Venezuela–British Guiana boundary dispute. Venezuela's cause against what it decried as British imperialism had previously attracted Congressional sympathizers. One publicist for Venezuela, a former American diplomat, William L. Scruggs, publicized the matter in a pamphlet with the engaging title *British Aggressions in Venezuela: The Monroe Doctrine on Trial*.

When Olney took up the fight, however, he concentrated on American, not Venezuelan, interests, though his analysis seemingly upheld Venezuela's claim. In adversarial language Olney advanced the preposterous argument that the Monroe Doctrine, a policy statement of the Monroe administration, was hemispheric public law. In ringing phrases he declared: "Today the United States is practically sovereign on this continent, and its fiat is law upon those subjects to which it confines its interposition." Believing bellicose language and secret diplomacy would prompt the British to accept arbitration, Olney and Cleveland were taken aback by the equally bracing British response, which rejected not only Olney's interpretation of the facts but also the relevance of the Monroe Doctrine to the dispute. In December Cleveland sent a ringing message to Congress, asking for a settlement according to American criteria and stating that if Britain did not accept, then the United States might be compelled to resist British "aggression" against the territory of a hemispheric republic.

The British government drew up a list of priorities: a menacing Germany on the European continent, setbacks in South Africa, and Russian pressure against India. In the Cabinet the mood of early 1896 was alternately combative and somber; a few, such as prime minister Lord Salisbury, wanted to teach the arrogant Americans a lesson; but others, not fully informed as to the military unreadiness of the American Navy, were for accommodation. Public opinion in Britain condemned Anglo-American conflict over Venezuela as fratricidal war.[9]

In the settlement of the crisis Britain lost control of the mouth of the Orinoco River but retained most of the disputed territory. America had won the diplomatic victory. Venezuela became the stepchild of American diplomacy. Effectively exploiting the Monroe Doctrine, Olney had declared that henceforth Europe must deal with Latin American republics according to American rules. More than any other state paper of the decade, Olney's note provided a rationale for empire, an empire composed, not of colonies (except for Puerto Rico), but of small, politically unstable republics with fragile economies.

And in the years following the American victory over Spain, the Caribbean, which for so long had fascinated American political theorists, would serve as laboratory for an American imperial experiment. The empire was not created by the triumph of 1898; rather, the experience of war and the exultation of victory seemed to sweep away doubts about America's special role in the Caribbean.

Expressed in idealistic terms, the vision of Caribbean empire in the American mind consisted not of colonies, as European powers had carved out in Africa, but of small republics with honest governments and stable economies. If they lacked republican traditions, as did Cuba, then a republic must be created, by Cubans but with proper consideration for those republican credos cherished by Americans. If they suffered from factious political rivalries, as did Central America, then rules of behavior must be established, by Central Americans but with proper deference to the United States to identify—and, if necessary, to penalize—the rule-breakers. If they were heavily indebted to foreign creditors, as was the Dominican Republic, then a financial reordering was necessary, by Dominicans but with proper respect for American recommendations about government expenditure. If their financial future depended more and more on their relationship to the American economy—and in the twentieth century such dependence became more apparent as wars cut commercial and investment links with Europe—then the Caribbean republics must offer the United States and American creditors the economic arrangements most compatible with the American economy. If the location of the republics on the globe gave them immense strategic value, then their governments must ultimately realize that national sovereignty was, of course, important, but not so crucial as the fact that most of the republics lay along the sea approaches to the Panama Canal.

The destiny of the Caribbean in the twentieth century would be, then, that of an empire, an empire without colonies. In its empire the United States, on occasion for genuinely unselfish, and at other times, for blatantly selfish, motives, would impose political order, economic tutelage, and civic morality.

Part I
The Protectorate Era
1900–1921

1 • Theodore Roosevelt and the Big Stick

Theodore Roosevelt brought to the presidency a keen mind and an ebullient personality, two traits particularly suitable for directing the course American policy would follow in the Caribbean in the early years of the century. As did most of his generation, he believed in the degeneracy of tropical peoples, yet he shared with other observers the conviction that Caribbean political and social structure, however defective, was amenable to improvement. Before leaving office in 1909, he had undertaken for the United States a major role in reducing European influence in the Caribbean, laid the political foundation for an American-constructed and American-controlled isthmian canal, established a Cuban protectorate, installed a customs receivership in the politically troubled Dominican Republic, and, with the support of Mexican president Porfirio Díaz, created a treaty structure in Central America presumably guaranteeing political tranquillity. In a personal manner he had shaped the early-twentieth-century Caribbean policy of the United States.

The Platt Amendment

The character of American policy in the Caribbean was shaped in large part by the postwar experience in Cuba. In the war debate of April 1898, a Senate motion to recognize the Cuban republic—a motion which McKinley believed would seriously hamper American authority in the island—failed; instead, the Senate passed another resolution, the Teller Amendment, denying any intention to annex Cuba. The American presence, then, rested on the right of conquest rather than on a formal understanding with Cuba's leaders. Postwar supervision could thus be directed by McKinley himself, as commander-in-chief, through his field commanders.[1]

Cuba's revolutionary leaders soon found out what this meant. When the Spanish formally surrendered Havana on New Year's Day 1899, they turned over the city to an American general, John R.

Brooke, not to a small group of rebel commanders watching the ceremony. Spain's formal surrender invested the United States, not the Cuban republic, with formal custody of the island. As the Spanish retired to their waiting ships, an American regimental band struck up a patriotic tune, and the head of the American Evacuation Commission spoke briefly to Brooke, naming him military commander of the island. For the last time Spanish colors were raised atop Morro Castle, to receive a gun salute from American warships in the harbor. As the flag came down a solitary voice in the throng rang out, "Viva España." The weary Cuban generals, deprived by their ally of the honor of receiving the Spanish capitulation, watched the proceedings in humiliation.

For all their previous fulminations against Spanish misrule in Cuba and their unqualified boasting about American political and cultural values, the conquerors were ill-prepared for the task ahead. Brooke had as yet been given no special instructions. He proceeded on the assumption that he must first care for the most basic requirements of a people whose lives had been disrupted by a civil war that had destroyed a tenth of the population. Between 1 January and 30 November 1899, Brooke distributed 5.5 million rations of food to the Cuban people. Farmers, driven from the land by Spanish orders and the *reconcentrado* system, returned to their plots and, surprisingly, began feeding both themselves and city dwellers in a short time.[2]

Having condemned Spain for its backward colonialism, Brooke as Cuban ruler accepted the Spanish characterization of Cubans as a people incapable of self-rule who required enlightened guidance. McKinley's initial directive authorized an orderly, transitional rule until Congress passed superseding instructions, or until the Cubans created a viable government. Brooke and his subordinates interpreted this to mean that before the Cubans could govern themselves, they must be taught not to live in filth. Sanitary brigades, composed of soldiers who had exchanged rifles for mops, were dispatched with disinfectants to public buildings. Brooke prohibited city dwellers from disposing of their garbage by the ancient expedient of tossing it into the streets and allowing their animals to roam freely about town eating it. In Santiago, General Leonard Wood, Brooke's rival and eventual successor, established the character of American rule by a paternalistic regimen which included, among other punishments, public whippings for those who violated his civic code.

In assuming power, Brooke retained much of the Spanish administrative structure, modifying it to meet current requirements; he even kept a number of Spanish bureaucrats. The Spanish had published no uniform code of laws, and instead of writing a new one, the American proconsuls merely adapted the existing regulations to meet their special needs. Brooke reformed the judiciary because Spanish judges were notoriously corrupt, but in other branches of government he simply used the bureaucracy and Spanish jobholders he inherited. Cubans waiting expectantly to obtain public employment were obviously offended at not being assigned niches in the occupation government, just as their leaders had chafed at Brooke's prohibition, for fear of rioting, of a rebel celebration on New Year's Day 1899.

Most Cubans, tired and wasted by the long struggle, did not rebel against American authority, as did Filipinos on the other side of the world. They did refuse to disband until they were paid. The amount of compensation precipitated an acrimonious debate among rebel leaders. One, Máximo Gómez, was virtually read out of the inner circle of heroes when he reluctantly acquiesced in accepting $3 million for the rebel army. Those who could prove they had fought ultimately received about $75 each. The Cuban assembly finally accepted this proposal, but it did so reluctantly and with considerable resentment.[3]

Brooke not only antagonized the Cubans with his moderate treatment of Spaniards; he also alienated Wood in Santiago. Wood's rise in the army had been spectacular. Trained as a medical doctor, he saw his mission in the tropics as that of a medical missionary, eradicating disease, demanding cleanliness, and inculcating virtuous public behavior. His break with Brooke came when the American commander tried to get control over Santiago revenues, thus depriving Wood of cash for his operations. Wood resented the interference and appealed to Secretary of War Elihu Root over Brooke's head. Wood had powerful allies in Theodore Roosevelt and Henry Cabot Lodge, both of whom pressed McKinley to end the brouhaha. Though McKinley did not move immediately to settle the feud, it soon became obvious that the backstairs intrigue against Brooke was working. McKinley spoke more often about preparing Cubans for responsible self-government, and Brooke's well-intentioned but politically damaging policy of working with leftover Spaniards hardly served the cause of Cuban self-government. In mid-December 1899 the axe fell, and Leonard Wood became military commander of Cuba.

Wood began his service as American commander with a generally favorable assessment of conditions. He retained his predecessor's military staff but named a new civilian cabinet, composed of Cubans. As for the burning question of Cuba's future, Wood noted privately that responsible elements preferred annexation. In any event the Americans, he believed, should remain until a stable government could be formed.[4]

In the interim the American proconsul insisted on firm but enlightened rule. The inherited educational system, consisting mainly of private academies, ill fitted Wood's progressive notions; he replaced it with a public school system, supervised by an ambitious pedagogue, Alexis Frye. Frye turned all kinds of old buildings into 3,000 citadels of learning. He loved numbers, and in spite of initial quarreling with Wood he managed to increase the public school population to 140,000 pupils by the time Wood's tenure ended in 1902. The inherited curriculum, which exalted Hispanic culture, was scuttled in favor of the "Ohio plan," with its emphasis on nationalism and vocational skills.[5]

Later generations of Cuban historians have treated Wood's work with a combination of reverence for his benign but authoritative manner and criticism for his innate distrust of Cuban capability. He employed Cubans in the bureaucracy but always placed American supervisors over them. He replaced corrupt judges with honest men, then arbitrarily moved them about the country to prevent favoritism. When thefts in the post office were discovered, Root told him to expel the offenders, and the general went after the culprits with missionary zeal. He built roads and bridges in Matanzas, Cienfuegos, and Guantánamo, and dredged Havana harbor. To maintain order he created a rural guard. He even tolerated new political parties—three were eventually created—which were permitted to participate in municipal elections and to voice their views about the island's future.[6]

Encouraged, Wood moved ahead with plans for a constitutional convention, which began its deliberations on 5 November 1900. He soon discovered that the Cuban-American relationship, the nature of which was still not fully spelled out, disturbed many members of the convention. The United States had forsworn annexation, as Root reminded Wood, yet its interests in Cuba were of such vital strategic importance that a special definition of Cuba's ties to the United States seemed imperative. By liberating the island the United States had incurred a special obligation to protect it against foreign aggressors. That obligation, Root believed, would continue long after the departure of American troops.

The solution lay in the various provisions of an amendment to the Army Appropriation Act of 1901, sponsored by Senator Orville Platt of Connecticut. The Platt Amendment, which embodied Wood's and Root's prescription for postoccupation Cuban-American relations, pledged the republic to maintain a low public debt; to refrain from signing any treaty impairing its obligation to the United States; to grant to the United States the right of intervention to protect life, liberty, and property; to validate the acts of the military government; and, if requested, to provide long-term naval leases.

Among anti-imperialist senators the Platt Amendment provoked considerable criticism, but unexpectedly it received the support of Henry Teller, whose name had been attached to the self-denying ordinance of 1898. In Havana it precipitated widespread, though not universal, disapproval; when a Cuban group presented Wood with a formal protest, he privately characterized its members as ungrateful. The Cuban convention resolved to oppose the amendment as a violation of national sovereignty and dispatched a delegation to Washington. It arrived only to discover that McKinley had already signed the act into law. Root mollified the Cubans with a sumptuous dinner and a soothing explanation that the amendment would be interpreted narrowly and would not be exploited to impair Cuban sovereignty. Six hours of discussions ensued, during which Root reminded them that the Monroe Doctrine already gave the United States the right to intervene in Cuban affairs. The delegation returned to Havana with Root's reassurances, but when their colleagues tried to modify the amendment, they were brusquely informed that American troops would remain until the Platt Amendment was incorporated into the fundamental law of the land. In the future American policymakers would often cite the Platt Amendment as legal precedent for interfering in Cuban affairs. Root's qualifying remarks went unrecorded and were soon forgotten.[7]

The Roosevelt Corollary

Though the United States won a decisive victory over Spain in the summer of 1898, none of the European powers except Great Britain expressed sympathy with the American condemnation of Spain's Caribbean rule. Europe's imperial powers believed the United States was simply bullying its way into membership in the imperial fraternity. In France, America's proclamation of intervention in the Cuban rebellion, in phrases redolent of the concept of mission, was condemned as little short of piracy. Even Germany, which like the United States came late in its quest for empire, decried the Monroe Doctrine, rejuvenated by American expansionists in the 1890s, as a device for keeping Germany out of the Western Hemisphere. For a few weeks before the war the Kaiser considered a vigorous rebuttal to America's declarations of imperial ambitions. Informed by advisors that such rhetoric might inflame German-American relations, Wilhelm II backed down, but the German press was almost uniformly critical of the American cause.[8]

In Great Britain, by contrast, the peculiarly American moral conviction that decrepit Spain deserved to be booted out of the Western Hemisphere won influential converts. The Foreign Office looked with obvious concern on the creation of an American empire so close to Britain's West Indian possessions, and the British press showed its undisguised contempt for Yankee diplomatic boorishness in offending an aging Spanish monarchy. Yet it was equally apparent, as the London *Daily Chronicle* editorialized, that Britain must exhibit neutrality in this war but remember its sanguinary bond with one of the belligerents.[9]

During the war Salisbury, distrustful of American expansionism, deferred to the more pro-American position enunciated by Arthur

Balfour, a devotee of Anglo-Saxon mission. As Balfour interpreted the course of the future, the American war against Spain stood as symbolic evidence of the extension of Anglo-Saxon rule over backward societies. The Victorian press amplified this theme by running long articles on divine mission and the similarity between Pax Britannica and what would later be styled Pax Americana.[10]

British naval strategists were acutely aware of the implications of America's rapid naval growth in the Caribbean. In annexing Puerto Rico and in creating a Cuban protectorate, the United States not only gained sites for naval bases but acquired control of the major sea approaches to a future isthmian canal. At the turn of the century Britain still held isthmian canal rights by virtue of the 1850 Clayton-Bulwer Treaty with the United States, which stipulated that any canal would be jointly constructed, jointly supervised, and kept neutral. American presidents and secretaries of state had been condemning this arrangement for a generation. In December 1898 British military intelligence correctly reasoned that joint control was doomed. American domination of an isthmian canal would upset the Caribbean balance by giving the United States an incalculable advantage in any Anglo-American conflict.

In a practical, immediate sense Britain stood to gain by acquiescing in American determination to control any isthmian canal. Thus, the first Hay-Pauncefote Treaty (of 5 February 1900) amended the 1850 treaty by allowing American construction of an isthmian canal but pledging the neutrality of the completed waterway. John Hay's Anglophilia was of no small consequence in granting to London what Theodore Roosevelt, then governor of New York, called the folly of building a canal but not fortifying it. The Senate, under Lodge's guidance, attached amendments which permitted defensive measures and declared the 1850 treaty superseded, both unacceptable to London. Hay was taken aback, and the British government dourly concluded that the only solution lay in allowing the Americans to build a canal and fortify it. Hay proposed another convention, called the second Hay-Pauncefote Treaty, which abrogated the 1850 arrangement. It contained nothing about fortifications, thus leaving the United States with implied authority to defend the canal.[11]

These military concessions were of profound consequence in the postwar reevaluations of Europe's role in the Caribbean. In the nineteenth century, European powers had been accustomed to dealing with weak Caribbean governments without fear of reprisal from an America arrogantly asserting a doctrine of Pax Americana over the tropics. Now, in the stunning victory over Spain, the United States emerged as a decisive force in the international politics of the Caribbean.

Fluctuations in British policy in the years after 1898 also had a profound impact on the Anglo-American relationship in the Caribbean. In the first Venezuelan crisis of 1895, the British had been compelled to take more seriously American pretensions in the Western Hemisphere. In the war with Spain, London had demonstrated fraternal sympathy with American expressions of mission. Lord Salisbury, British prime minister during the war, felt little sentimental attachment for the concept of Anglo-American fraternity, but he was surrounded by more determined men—among them Balfour and Lord Lansdowne—who believed that the days of "splendid isolation" were over and that Britain needed alliances. In their view Britain must cultivate the Americans and, on the European continent, promote a closer relationship with Germany.

A succession of disturbing events supported their contention. In South Africa the British had still failed to suppress the Boers, whose defiance of imperial authority embarrassed Britain among the other imperial powers and excited the American public. Britain had participated, with America and Germany, in crushing the Boxer rebellion in China but was soon challenged by Russian penetration into Manchuria. Apprehension over Russian ambitions in Asia prompted the British in 1902 to sign an alliance with Japan, the first formal departure from splendid isolation. And in the New World Britain was pressed by an aroused Canada to support the dominion's claims in the Alaskan boundary dispute and by Roosevelt to make concessions in the spirit of Anglo-American harmony.

The reliability of British policy was severely tested in 1902–3 in a confrontation between Britain and Germany on the one side, and the financially destitute and politically troubled Venezuelan republic on the other. Venezuela was remiss in repaying its foreign creditors and, after the 1899 revolution catapulted to power the vain but nationalistic Don Cipriano Castro, had dared to respond to British and German pressures with both obstreperous tactics and sharp communications. In London and Berlin the consensus was that Castro was not only a wastrel but also a thief who must be taught a lesson by civilized countries. Germany, particularly, became annoyed when Castro's government cavalierly dealt with the claims of the Diskonto Gesellschaft, a German firm responsible for the construction of the Great Venezuelan National Railway.

Britain dared not allow Berlin to undertake unilateral chastisement of Castro; nor did London want to intrude without assurances from the United States. In December 1901 the German foreign office drew up a list of grievances against Venezuela and presented its complaint to Roosevelt and Hay, informing them that Germany intended to blockade the Venezuelan coast. The president and his secretary of state, sympathetic to the plight of a creditor trying to squeeze payment from the wastrel debtor, warned only that the blockade must not lead to permanent occupation of Venezuelan soil, a patent violation of the Monroe Doctrine.[12]

Presumably with Roosevelt's blessing, the two governments—in due course supported by Italy, also a Venezuelan creditor—proceeded by sending to Caracas threatening memoranda and upon receipt of Castro's chauvinistic replies instituted reprisals. On 20 December 1902, after sinking several Venezuelan gunboats and neutralizing a fort at the port of Puerto Cabello, Germany and Britain proclaimed a blockade, each assuming responsibility for half the republic's coastline. Already Castro had involved the United States by requesting the American minister to Caracas, Herbert Bowen, to mediate. Bowen pressed for arbitration and found Hay agreeable; Roosevelt himself was suggested as arbiter, but he wisely deferred to the Hague Court.

During the following weeks Roosevelt undertook a searching reexamination of the implications of the Anglo-German blockade for American interests in the Caribbean. The American press speculated about German motives, and in Britain newspapers questioned the wisdom of endangering Anglo-American harmony by joining forces with Germany. Roosevelt was attentive to the rising anti-German feeling among the American public when news came of German shelling of the fort at Maracaibo. In 1916, when his Germanophobia reached its zenith, he stated that as president he had forced Germany to back down during this crisis. Though in this later account he doubtless exaggerated his forcefulness during the critical negotiations of early 1903, he nevertheless played a significant role in compelling the European powers to terminate their blockade and accept arbitration.

Under American pressure Castro promised to give initial preference in the settlement of claims to the blockading powers. On 13 February 1903, a protocol containing these concessions was signed, and a week later the blockade was lifted. In his boastful 1916 version of this episode, Roosevelt claimed he had threatened Germany with war. This seems implausible, given Roosevelt's contempt for Latin American governments and his expressed sympathy for Venezuela's creditors. Yet he had demonstrated, in a hesitant but effective manner, his apprehension about European, particularly German, maneuvering in the volatile Caribbean world. No one has discovered a copy of any ultimatum, but there can be little doubt that Roosevelt informally let both London and Berlin know that, while he respected the more advanced cultures of Europe, he also respected the Monroe Doctrine.[13]

The second Venezuelan crisis revealed the depth of anti-German feeling in both Britain and America. Rudyard Kipling published a venomous anti-German poem to commemorate the event. From the United States, Sir Michael Herbert, the British ambassador, reported that prominent American Anglophiles were upset over Britain's cooperation with Germany. Within the British cabinet there was also a deep division as to the wisdom of the Anglo-German venture. The British realized that in the Far East the interests of Germany and Britain diverged, and that the British alliance with Japan and the British approach to Asian problems coincided with American policy. Britain had foolishly jeopardized Anglo-American goodwill. After the Venezuelan imbroglio, Britain sensed even more keenly that American pretensions in the Caribbean served to protect British possessions against an expansionist Germany.

Roosevelt's firmness during the Venezuelan crisis reassured the American public that European powers would not be allowed to intimidate a Caribbean republic and thus endanger the nation, but his actions also meant that thereafter European creditors would expect the United States to guarantee Caribbean fiscal prudence in order to assure payment of debts. Financial situations similar to Venezuela's existed in other Caribbean republics. Another confrontation might not be so easily resolved.

In the midst of the controversy the Argentine foreign minister, Dr. Luís M. Drago, advanced what was at the time a proposal inimical to the interests of creditor states: that public debts should not justify the use of force or territorial occupation. This was of course at variance with Roosevelt's famous injunction about Europeans "spanking" misbehaving Latin American republics, but at the Hague Peace Conference of 1907, the Drago doctrine won the support of the United States, provided arbitration was used as a first alternative. Roosevelt was more disturbed by the arbitral decision on the Venezuelan claims at the Hague in the winter of 1904. The representative of the United States argued that all claimants should receive equal compensation, following the method of settlement after the Boxer Rebellion of 1900. The arbiters ruled unanimously that the blockading countries were entitled to preferential consideration for indemnity.

Increasingly, then, the force of events—and Roosevelt's own predilections—dictated a policy aimed at preventing another confrontation between a European creditor and a Latin American debtor.

One country already plagued with a heavy foreign indebtedness was the Dominican Republic. In the years after President Grant's aborted ambitious annexation scheme, the republic had attracted foreign investment in sugar and transportation, but the financial improvidence of its executives brought inevitable and mounting indebtedness. In 1893 a New York corporation, the San Domingo Improvement Company, became the republic's banker and collector of customs, and in the intervening years kept its governments from foundering by selling depreciated Dominican bonds among European investors.

The financial situation worsened in 1899 with the assassination of the Dominican dictator Úlises Heureaux. His successor turned against the company and dismissed its representatives from the customshouses. Negotiations to settle the impasse ensued but broke down in 1902. The American government, mindful of the difficulties of an American firm's doing business in hostile territory, urged arbitration. Talks were resumed, and in July 1903 the two sides reached an agreement.

Roosevelt's interest initially lay in protecting the rights of the San Domingo Improvement Company, but he soon grew apprehensive about the presence of European war vessels in Dominican waters, dispatched at the repeated urgings of German, Spanish, and Italian nationals in the republic for support of their claims against the government. Late in 1903 the republic was plunged into civil war; in early February 1904 its harassed president, unable to quell the rebellion, requested American guarantee of Dominican independence and sovereignty, payment of its foreign obligations, and a supply of arms and munitions. In return the Dominican chief executive promised lower import duties and coaling and naval leases at Manzanillo and Samaná.

In 1869 the United States had eagerly sought a naval lease at Samaná, but now it already possessed sites in Puerto Rico and Cuba. Roosevelt believed a Dominican protectorate unnecessary. When a special arbitral commission settled the claims of the San Domingo Improvement Company (in July 1904), the republic's European creditors prevailed upon Roosevelt to collect on their behalf. If he refused, then there existed the possibility of another "Venezuelan crisis." Faced with this possibility, Roosevelt proposed that an American appointee collect Dominican customs, segregate a portion for settlement of the foreign debt, and transmit the remainder to Santo Domingo. Though suspicious of American intentions, the Dominican president seemed even more worried about European actions.

Even before the Dominican troubles of 1904, Roosevelt had considered the implications of the Platt Amendment and the Venezuelan crisis for America's new role in the Caribbean. In his 1901 State of the Union message, Roosevelt restated the traditional interpretation of the Monroe Doctrine but added an important qualification: the United States might not be able to guarantee the territorial integrity of a Latin American state that misbehaved or neglected to fulfill its international obligations. Elihu Root, analyzing the nation's strategic goals, argued in early 1902 for American military and political domination of the Caribbean approaches to the Isthmus.

The Platt Amendment and the Venezuelan blockade provided Roosevelt with further argument for justifying a policy of interference in the internal affairs of the republics. Though the Platt Amendment technically referred only to Cuba, it expressed general principles concerning American aims, particularly the requirement for American supervision of Cuba's external relations, that applied to the entire Caribbean. And the Anglo-German punishment of Venezuela, though undertaken only after American blessing, held up the dangerous prospect of American-European confrontation. If the United States could not permit the "civilized" European states to "spank" miscreant Caribbean governments, then it must take up the burden of ensuring that the republics fulfilled their international obligations. Roosevelt officially announced the new doctrine in his 1904 State of the Union message: "Chronic wrong-doing, or an impotence which results in a general loosening of the ties of civilized society, may in America as elsewhere ultimately require intervention by some civilized nation, and in the Western Hemisphere the adherence of the United States to the Monroe Doctrine may force the United States, however reluctantly, in flagrant cases of such wrong-doing or impotence to the exercise of an international police power."

The protocol establishing the customs receivership was signed in January 1905. The Senate, wary of the implied powers granted to the United States, was alarmed at the actions Roosevelt was taking and presumed the United States was creating another Caribbean protectorate. By cleverly using a *modus vivendi* which was in fact a variation of the executive agreement, Roosevelt circumvented the constitutional restrictions on treaty-making. He was determined to keep American warships in Dominican waters to protect the customshouses from revolutionary disturbances until the Senate, mollified by Root, finally approved the Dominican customs treaty in 1907. The contention that the receivership was in fact a guise for a protectorate was seemingly borne out by the events of 1916, when the Wilson administration occupied the republic by military force. Roosevelt, in fact, had no such motive; he genuinely believed the limited role the United States played would be sufficient to stave off financial calamity and allow the republic to repay its European creditors.[14]

"I Took the Canal Zone"

No venture in American diplomacy in the Caribbean brought more discredit to Roosevelt nor precipitated more acrimony than his interference in the Panamanian revolution of 1903. The affair exhibited all the characteristics of political tragicomedy—heroes, villains, plots, subplots, ploys, and counterploys. In the course of events, the United States, presumably committed to a Nicaraguan canal, would, under Roosevelt's guidance, suddenly and suspiciously switch to a Panamanian site, sign a canal treaty with a troubled Colombian government, and then, failing to win Colombian approval of the treaty, abet a revolution in Panama. America's crowning technical achievement in cutting the Isthmus would be forever overshadowed by the unseemly manner by which the United States acquired the right to construct the canal.

In the nineteenth century most Americans believed an isthmian canal eventually would be constructed through Nicaragua, though in 1846 the United States had obtained right of passageway across Panama. In return, and in an unusual departure in foreign policy, it had guaranteed to Colombia the nutrality of the transit. After the de Lesseps venture in Panama failed, proponents of the Nicaraguan route were strengthened in their resolve. In the 1890s American engineers favored Nicaragua over rival routes, despite the 1894 reorganization of the French company and the tireless efforts of two men in its service—Philippe Bunau-Varilla and a New York lawyer, William Nelson Cromwell—to convert the canal commissioners and Congress to the Panama route. At stake were millions of dollars in equipment, rights-of-way, and plans.[15]

In March 1899 Congress authorized the Isthmian Canal Commission and empowered it to investigate possible sites in Nicaragua, along the de Lesseps route in Panama, and at both San Blas and Darien, also in Panama. The commission began by going to Europe to study the Kiel Canal and to inquire about plans and records of the French company. Cromwell sailed from New York and intercepted the commission at Paris. Bunau-Varilla, acting independently, concentrated on the more pliable members of the American entourage. In January 1900 the commission set out for Nicaragua and, in mid-1901, completed its field work.

In three reports the commission presented the arguments for each proposed route. The Panama site chosen by de Lesseps was not rejected, though the initial report discredited it because of legal complications surrounding the French canal company's commitments to Bogotá. San Blas and Darien were virtually eliminated because of expected costs of excavation. After setting minimum standards for the canal, the commission estimated that the Nicaraguan route would cost $190 million and the Panama site, $144 million, but to the latter had to be added the price of the French concession. In October 1901 the French company had asked $109 million for its assets, a sum the commission considered outrageously high. It concluded with a favorable assessment of the physical features of the Panama route but recommended Nicaragua on the understandable logic that it would be much cheaper. Its suggestion that the French assets were worth only $40 million was not lost on Bunau-Varilla or Cromwell. In December 1901 the company's board reduced the asking price for the French concession to that figure. A month later the Isthmian Canal Commission inexplicably reversed its recommendation, submitted in two earlier reports, and came out in favor of Panama.[16]

Still, the battle of the routes had not been resolved. Roosevelt had not yet announced his preference. In the Senate the Nicaraguan option had the formidable backing of Alabama's John Tyler Morgan, who was determined to quash any Panama proposal. But the advocates of Panama had time, money, and talent on their side. They had Cromwell, who exuded innocence but talked fast and, when he wished, never to the point. In the 1912 investigation of the revolution, one congressman called Cromwell as dangerous as Aaron Burr. Bunau-Varilla, by contrast, was imaginative, ebullient, and totally dedicated to vindicating de Lesseps's feat by selling the new French canal company's interests to the United States. These two could ultimately rely on another ally, Senator Marcus Alonzo Hanna, Ohio political kingmaker, confidant of William McKinley, and admittedly self-educated on the subject of canals. After Hanna committed himself to the Panama route, both Cromwell and Bunau-Varilla, who personally detested one another, claimed credit for the senator's conversion.[17]

It is too facile a conclusion to claim that the triumph of the Panama route owed its success to the machinations of these three and the intensely partisan anti-Nicaraguan campaign they conducted—though Bunau-Varilla's famous ploy of circulating among senators Nicaraguan stamps showing an active volcano did irreparable damage to Morgan's pleas on behalf of that country. After all, the final judgment of the Isthmian Canal Commission had favored Panama, principally because a Panamanian canal would be shorter by 134 miles than one in Nicaragua. Disease would be more prevalent in Panama, but Panama offered technical advantages and would be more accessible to labor forces. In anticipation of a change of mind, an American agent had signed a canal protocol with the Nicaraguan president José Santos Zelaya, later the avowed enemy of American intrusion into the internal affairs of Central America, but the State Department considered it unacceptable, mostly because it did not allow American courts total jurisdiction in the proposed canal zone.[18]

Roosevelt's timing in these matters was not above reproach. In early January 1902 the Hepburn bill, calling for a Nicaraguan route, passed the House of Representatives. Before the Senate voted, the French company lowered its asking price to $40 million, and Roosevelt quickly reconvened the Isthmian Canal Commission, which dutifully rendered its recommendation for Panama. When the Hepburn bill came before the Senate, Senator Spooner proposed an amendment authorizing funds for constructing a canal across Panama, provided the United States could make arrangements with both the French company and Colombia. If unable to do so within a reasonable time, the president might proceed with negotiations in Nicaragua. The fight over the Spooner amendment was bitter and prolonged, but the amendment passed in late June.

In negotiating a canal treaty with Colombia, Roosevelt would display unusual, and in fact unforgivable, insensitivity to the political and economic dilemmas of another hemispheric republic. In the treaty of 1846 the United States had pledged to protect the isthmian transit. On that authority it had landed troops in Panama thirteen times between 1856 and 1902, on most of these occasions at the request of Colombia. But in order to build a canal, the United States required a new treaty and Bogota's approbation for the transfer of the French company's concession to the American government. For these privileges Colombia expected a generous financial settlement.

Colombia's need for additional funds had been made more desperate by the tremendous drain on the country's resources during the Thousand-Day War, from 1899 to 1902. Rival Colombian politicians, however much they disagreed on the country's internal politics, were unanimously of the opinion that a favorable arrangement with the United States must be negotiated; such a settlement would bring into the national treasury much-needed financial resources to develop the republic but would not impair Colombian sovereignty. Unfortunately, the Colombian negotiators dealt with an American government dominated by a chief executive determined to obtain a canal treaty granting the United States considerable latitude and with a nationalistic Colombian assembly just as adamant about preventing any concessions of sovereignty or betrayal of national honor.

Under Cromwell's scrutiny the Colombian minister to the United States began negotiations in earnest in the spring of 1902. In May he presented a draft to Hay. It was unsatisfactory from the American viewpoint but exhibited, Hay believed, Colombian good faith; and talks were continued through the summer. In Colombia the civil war dragged on, distracting the government's attention during a period when its representatives in Washington sorely needed counsel. Late in the year the liberal opposition threatened to take the war to the Isthmus of Panama, historically alienated from Bogotá's control; and the Colombian government, dominated by conservatives, invoked the 1846 treaty by requesting American aid to safeguard the transit. The presence of American troops prompted the liberals to call off their projected attack, and on 21 November 1902, the two sides signed a truce aboard the U.S.S. *Wisconsin*. Colombia's call for American military support in its hour of need would be, in view of the events of the following November, an ominous portent.

With the war terminated, the way seemed clear to sign a treaty. To avoid misunderstanding, and in anticipation of possible criticism, the Colombian president, José Manuel Marroquín, recommended submitting the entire canal question to the national assembly; but that body could not be quickly convened, and besides, Roosevelt was threatening to move ahead with negotiations with Nicaragua, an alternative which the Spooner amendment had provided if Colombia tarried. With this in mind, Marroquín instructed his minister to Washington, José Vicente Concha, to obtain the best possible agreement under the circumstances. Concha demurred, but his more confident assistant, Tomás Herrán, acting on Cromwell's advice, moved ahead, and on 22 January 1903 signed the Hay-Herrán Treaty.

The treaty stipulated that the United States would have exclusive rights to build and defend a canal in a ten-kilometer-wide zone and provide order and maintain public health in that zone—with these concessions being made in spite of a reaffirmation of Colombian sovereignty—for a payment of $10 million and an annuity of $250,000. In general, these terms seemed fair, though in view of the technical and medical problems later encountered in Panama, it could be argued that the United States might have asked for even wider authority.

Where Roosevelt erred was in his inability to comprehend why the document was so vigorously assailed in Bogotá for being unfair. When the Colombian assembly debated the treaty, the smallness of the financial compensation constituted only one—and not the most important—factor in prompting the assembly to denounce the pact. More critical, apparently, was the diminution of Colombian sovereignty, the almost supine bequest of control over the canal zone to a foreign power. In a society still torn by the divisions of civil war and endless political bickering, the issue of sovereignty served as reinforcement to feelings of national unity, perhaps not achieved but nonetheless sought.

Neither Roosevelt nor Hay helped matters much by their arrogant instructions to Bogotá prohibiting Colombia from obtaining financial compensation from the French canal company for transferring its rights to the United States. In a technical sense the Hay-Herrán Treaty prohibited compensation to Colombia from the French concern, but Hay added further injury by the manner in which he conveyed his objections, as if to say Bogotá wanted American approval to squeeze a helpless company. Going further, Hay warned that Colombia's rejection of the treaty might have drastic repercussions; the inescapable inference, in view of later events, was Panama's secession.

During the assembly debate Marroquín tried to extract some kind of collective statement of responsibility for the treaty, but his opponents gave no quarter. Harassed, he suggested that the United States pay Colombia $15 million instead of $10 million and stand aside while Bogotá collected another $10 million from the French company. Piqued over Colombian dalliance, Roosevelt refused. When the treaty came up for a vote in the assembly, some of the more offensive American notes were read. Their contents doomed the treaty. Marroquín's friends and enemies, united by Washington's opprobrious commentary, overwhelmingly defeated the treaty.[19]

Colombia's peremptory rejection infuriated Roosevelt, who characterized Colombians as "damned dagoes" and "Bogotá lot of jack rabbits." Yet, for all his fury, there is still lacking persuasive evidence that, from that moment, Roosevelt plotted to seize the Isthmus and proceed with the grand work of building a canal. It is true that in August, as Colombian legislators savagely assailed the Hay-Herrán document, Roosevelt obtained what appeared to be a legal undergirding for his opinion that under article 35 of the 1846 treaty the United States possessed the right to construct a canal without Colombian permission. This view had been advanced by John Bassett Moore, third assistant secretary of state and international legal scholar, who contended that the United States had never really achieved full benefit of the 1846 arrangement. What Moore argued was our legal right to require Colombia to grant permission to dig a canal; Roosevelt and Bunau-Varilla, who wrote an article on the subject for the Paris newspaper *Le Matin*, came to a more expansive conclusion.

On 9 October Bunau-Varilla, who had already met in September with the Panamanian conspirator Manuel Amador, interviewed Roosevelt himself. By now the Frenchman had virtually given up exploiting the 1846 stipulation to provoke American action. Instead, he spoke guardedly about isthmian revolution. For Roosevelt's reactions one must rely on Bunau-Varilla's biased account, because the Roosevelt (and Hay) papers are curiously silent on Panamanian affairs from 10 October to 3 November, when the revolt occurred. Bunau-Varilla carried the conversation, talking about how Roosevelt already had authority to act, and about Panama's historic defiance of Bogotá's authority. The president, in response, had little to say. He did not have to say much, for Bunau-Varilla guessed exactly what Theodore Roosevelt, confronted with a declaration of Panamanian independence, would do.

So the Frenchman hurried back to New York for another round of plotting with Amador. Then he returned to Washington to talk with Hay and emerged from the conference convinced that the United States would protect a Panamanian revolution against Colombian counterattack. Hay had offhandedly remarked that some Panamanian commotion would come as no surprise and in anticipation of trouble naval vessels were currently underway to the Isthmus. In mid-October two army officers had returned from Panama with reports of discontent, collection of arms, and the creation of a revolutionary party—information which doubtless Hay had in mind when he talked with Bunau-Varilla.

In Panama the conspirators counted on American intervention to sustain their cause, for their revolutionary army consisted solely of the fire brigade, the local police, and a small contingent of Colombian soldiers whose commanding officer had been conveniently bribed. But the plan almost backfired for lack of gumption to start things. In late October the Colombian government, alert to reports about Panama's perennial conspiracies, made plans to send reinforcements to its isthmian garrison. Amador, having returned from New York, sent a frantic wire to Bunau-Varilla, who in turn informed Francis Loomis, his contact in the State Department, that the isthmian situation was rapidly deteriorating and the transit would be, doubtless, imperiled. The Frenchman then wired back reassurances to his Panamanian accomplices.

On 2 November orders were sent, via the American consul in Panama City, to the commanding officer of the U.S.S. *Nashville* to protect the transit by preventing the landings of either Colombian or rebel troops. The commander did not receive this order until the fourth. Already Colombian troops had disembarked at Colón, but the railroad supervisor, warned of their imminent arrival, had alertly dispatched the available cars to Panama City.

There was little fighting. The Panamanian rebels, their conspiracy secured by the tactics of the railroad supervisor and by the added protection of the *Nashville* in Colón harbor, simply arrested the provincial governor, then lodged at Amador's house, and ordered the fire brigade to seize strategic points in Panama City. By six o'clock on the evening of the third Panama City was reported as quiet. That night a Colombian gunboat shelled the town, killing Wong Kong Yee, a Chinese resident peacefully eating his supper, and a jackass in the local slaughterhouse. The following morning in Colón a rash Colombian officer, infuriated by the turn of events on the other side of the Isthmus, threatened to burn the town and kill every American in it if his superior, arrested in Panama City by the conspirators, was not released. He was soon quieted by the landing of American sailors and a bribe of $8,000. Both ends of the transit were now controlled by the rebels. On 6 November an American officer unfurled the Panamanian banner at Colón.[20]

Not quite two weeks later, on 18 November, Hay and Bunau-Varilla, Panama's first representative to the United States, signed a canal treaty granting to the United States virtually every concession it wanted.[21] In the following years, despite the marvel of American technology, French brains, and West Indian sweat that fulfilled four centuries of man's dreams to connect the oceans, the Panamanian affair continued to embarrass the United States. In 1911 Roosevelt surprised no one by announcing that he had taken the canal zone while Congress debated. The next year Congress undertook an exhaustive study of the events of 1903 and published a report entitled *The Story of Panama*.[22] In retrospect Roosevelt's utterances and maneuverings looked even more suspicious, and Cromwell's and Bunau-Varilla's, damnable. Roosevelt had had reason to be irritated with Colombia's assault on the Hay-Herrán Treaty, but had he demonstrated more patience with those "damned dagoes" and practiced a more statesmanlike diplomacy, Colombia's leaders, well aware that only the United States could construct the vital isthmian waterway, might have reconsidered. As things turned out, Bogotá eventually got its apology in the form of another treaty and a $25 million emolument—this despite the price of alienating one hemispheric republic and the burden of fathering another, which, in the course of time, has never forgotten the disreputable circumstances of its birth and how its most precious geographical asset was squandered by a shrewd Frenchman pretending to be its friend.

The Cuban Protectorate, 1902–1909

The Panama affair occurred more than a year after American troops departed Cuba. Americans believed that the new Cuban republic, safeguarded by American paternalism, was entering an era of peace and prosperity unknown to Spanish Cuba. The American economic intrusion, which nineteenth-century American observers had believed vital for Cuban advancement, was already felt in virtually every area of Cuban life.

Earlier promises about limiting American business activities in Cuba were quietly forgotten. During the occupation Senator Joseph Foraker had proposed a resolution denying to private American firms the opportunity of doing business on the island. American citizens nevertheless built an impressive stake in the new Cuban republic. Wood had opposed the Foraker amendment but had supported it in spirit by lashing out against economic adventurers who emigrated to Cuba to despoil his work. Clearly, Cuba needed development and capital. One American eager to supply both was Percival Farquhar, an indefatigable, audacious exponent of venture capitalism who arrived in Havana in the summer of 1898. He bullied his way into electrification projects, then turned to the ambitious task of constructing a railroad from Havana to Santiago.

When old Dom Tomás—Tomás Estrada Palma, former schoolmaster and Cuba's first president—took over in 1902, American capital in the island totalled $100 million, twice what Richard Olney had calculated in 1895. Most of this investment was in tobacco ($45 million) and sugar ($25 million). One of the biggest American operations was the United Fruit Company, created in 1899 by the shrewd Minor Keith, who purchased for a pittance 200,000 acres on Nipe Bay.

The reciprocity treaty, negotiated in 1902 but not ratified until late 1903, fulfilled American dreams of drawing the Cuban economy closer to that of the United States. It was also compensation to the Cubans, who wanted tariff reciprocity, for accepting the Platt Amendment. The treaty extended to Cuban sugar a 20 percent tariff preference in American ports for a 25–40 percent reduction on American products entering Cuba. It laid the basis for even greater investment and ultimately transformed Cuba into a marketplace for American goods.

Estrada Palma seemed disinterested in politics. He had served heroically in the rebel cause as early as the Ten Years' War, had languished in a Spanish jail, and had been exiled to the United States; but he rarely spoke of having lived "inside the monster," as had José Martí, his martyred compatriot, who had lived in New York City and died in the first months of the 1895 rebellion. Almost compliantly he accepted America's intrusion into Cuban affairs. During the years of Wood's occupation he methodically constructed a political following. His reward for loyalty was the presidency. But the politics that sprang up after his inauguration was typified by rival gangs of old generals whose consuming passion was division of what public spoils existed, not the creation of a vigorous young republic. Fraud characterized the first elections for the national Congress in 1904. In one province, a former rebel general, it was learned, received more votes than had actually been cast. The next year party leaders began squabbling over the presidential elections. The likeliest candidate was José Miguel Gómez, a Liberal; his enemies closed ranks and concluded that the only potentially successful rival was Don Tomás. Estrada Palma feared Gómez would ransack the treasury if elected, so he tolerated sporadic violence against Gómez's followers by the rural guard and police. Neither element, it was clear, was very interested in American-style democracy.[23]

When Estrada won, Gómez descended on New York and spoke darkly about American responsibility for ensuring Cuban democracy. His supporters back home raised the flag of revolt. Sporadic fighting followed. Estrada remained firm, but in September 1906, as his position became more precarious, he hurriedly requested American support. Roosevelt expressed dismay and skepticism about dispatching troops or establishing a protectorate. One hundred twenty-five marines were landed, but they were quickly withdrawn. Instead of polic-

ing the country with more marines, Roosevelt decided to send Secretary of War William Howard Taft and Undersecretary of State Robert Bacon to investigate.

Taft and Bacon met with Estrada and with the president's adversaries. The Cuban president, proud of his efforts to implant American constitutional principles in the young republic, refused to treat with the Liberal opposition until its adherents laid down their arms. The rebel spokesman, Alfredo Zayas, refused, arguing that all of Estrada's subordinates should first resign. Taft wrote a pessimistic report for Roosevelt and a dreary analysis for Mrs. Taft. Estrada, Taft observed, was obstinate and uncooperative. The Liberals now spoke openly of their hopes for American intervention, which would give them political power. Demoralized, Estrada suddenly resigned and compelled his subordinates to do likewise, leaving the country without a functioning government. On 29 September, two thousand marines disembarked, and Taft formally announced American occupation. Cuba's first experiment in republican government ended ignominiously, four years after its glorious inception.[24]

The second Cuban intervention occurred after Roosevelt's announcement about undertaking a policeman's role in the unstable Caribbean to prevent habitual misdeeds and to ward off European penetration. But very little in his public statements or private comments about Cuba in the fall of 1906 indicated that he interpreted the occupation as a prelude to annexation or to a radical alteration in the Cuban-American relationship. Rather, he expressed his annoyance with the Cubans for botching their first efforts at self-rule, while he looked upon the second occupation as an unfortunate but necessary measure.

This time the destiny of the republic would not be in the hands of a stern doctor turned soldier, but instead would be shaped by a competent and unimaginative former real estate tycoon, Charles Magoon. He had won his spurs in government service by rising in the Bureau of Insular Affairs to become governor of the Canal Zone, where he had triumphantly mollified the more nationalistic Panamanians, who were chagrined over the rapid expansion of American power on the Isthmus and the erosion of Panamanian sovereignty, by well-intentioned gestures and innate goodwill. He brought these skills to Havana, yet Cuban historians have remembered Magoon as, alternately, a buzzard and a leech who devoured the national treasury and opened Cuba to Yankee adventurers. These calumnies were never ascribed to Leonard Wood.

Such character traits as Magoon possessed ill suited Cuban, and American, needs. He was guilty, not of personal dishonesty, but of standing by while Liberal factions infested the bureaucracy and built a native spoils system that would plague Cuba for generations. Magoon had an excellent opportunity to create a permanent civil service. His record was marred by his attentiveness to the complaints of Estrada's enemies, especially Zayas and Gómez, who were now given their share of government positions as compensation. When in the closing days of the occupation a civil service law was finally promulgated, it came too late and with insufficient support. Magoon, condemned by later Cuban historians for the corruption that followed his rule, did not teach Cuban bureaucrats how to steal; graft they learned without American inspiration.[25]

Magoon ruled by civil authority, but most of the work of the occupation was carried out by the Army of Cuban Occupation. The army not only guaranteed peace but also, in the words of its commander, exercised a kind of moral suzerainty, a mission it had undertaken previously in the Philippines and in the first Cuban occupation. It intimidated rural populations, prevented the resurgence of another revolt against central authority, collected political data for use in controlling guerrilla activities, prepared detailed maps of the island, and, as in other portions of the American empire, built roads.

The government began paying off claimants who had suffered during the violence of 1905–6. It also inaugurated, under the astute guidance of Enoch Crowder, a study of Cuban law, which in 1905 was a hopeless jumble of Spanish codes, Wood's military orders, and the republic's first decrees. The Advisory Law Commission penetrated the morass of conflicting statutes at the municipal level and rewrote rules governing the judiciary, implanting an occasional Anglo-Saxon precept. The resulting electoral law was hardly perfect, but the creators hoped to leave Cubans with electoral machinery to prevent fraud by creating electoral boards, composed of rival political representatives, sitting in every municipality. The elections of 1908, conducted under the new rules, were probably the fairest in Cuban history.[26]

The electoral law and the refurbishing of the Cuban military into an apolitical instrument for keeping order constituted the occupation's most ambitious programs. Unfortunately, in the years that followed, the electoral code suffered continual abuses as Cuban politicians learned how to manipulate the system to perpetuate their rule. By a similar corruptive process the Cuban military was eventually politicized.

2 • Roosevelt, Taft, and the Search for Central American Stability

Despite Roosevelt's spirited defense of the Monroe Doctrine in the Venezuelan and Dominican crises, his ardent championing of the Panamanian revolution, and his acquiescence in the second Cuban occupation, his goals in the Caribbean were more circumscribed than contemporaries believed. The Roosevelt Corollary to the Monroe Doctrine, a justification for the exercise of American police power in the Caribbean to prevent chronic wrongdoing and to guard against European intrusion, was not really intended as the legal foundation for creating protectorates or establishing de facto colonies. In the Dominican customs receivership, Roosevelt wanted to safeguard the republic from internal bankruptcy and external pressures from its European creditors; when the foreign debt was paid, he argued, the receivership would be terminated. In the Canal Zone, Roosevelt wanted sufficient authority for American technicians to build the canal and to provide basic social services for its employees, but he also wanted to avoid creating an American colony. (The astute Panamanian diplomat Ricardo Alfaro, who negotiated two canal treaties with the United States, remarked years later that Roosevelt treated the republic fairly.) The Cuban occupation of 1906 he reluctantly sanctioned after persuasive evidence that Estrada Palma's government had ceased to function and that civil strife would continue unless American troops were landed. He correctly sensed that the American public would not tolerate a prolonged military occupation of Cuba.

How, then, was the United States to carry out its self-proclaimed mission of instilling democratic virtues, insuring against financial bankruptcy, and safeguarding its own military interests in a disorderly Caribbean world? The most direct method—outright military intervention—had produced limited results in Cuba and had simultaneously provoked considerable opposition. In 1906 Roosevelt and Secretary of State Elihu Root exploited still another method—benign political guidance through the application of treaty law—in the politically turbulent and volatile climate of Central America.

The Central American Treaties of 1907

In his first years in the presidency Roosevelt had taken personal charge of Caribbean policy. When Root became secretary of state in 1905, he assumed a much larger role than Hay had exercised in Caribbean affairs. As secretary of war Root had already shaped American policy toward Cuba in the critical years of Wood's reign, and he had directed the second occupation of 1906. Root, like Roosevelt, often expressed the view that American policy was directed, not toward acquisition of territory, but toward discouragement of European encroachment into the strategically vital Caribbean world. More than Roosevelt, he emphasized cooperation rather than coercion in the attainment of this goal. And, to his credit, there exists some evidence that he even liked Latin Americans.[1]

In Central America, Root wanted to bring about political tranquillity among five republics, most of which had never allowed themselves to fall into the rut of political stability. The means, he believed, lay in reviving the spirit of the nineteenth-century experiment in federation and a system of treaty law, whereby each would respect the governments and boundaries of its neighbors. Though well-intentioned and even humane, such a policy entailed a considerable risk, for the Central American republics, despite their common origin in the Spanish empire, had been historically envious of one another, resentful of domination by any one republic over the other four, and ordinarily squabbled over issues which appeared, to the outside observer, trivial. Unless threatened by an outside force, as they had been in the 1850s when filibustering expeditions descended upon the Isthmus, the republics rarely cooperated or found a common identity. The parties represented less political principles than family feuds, and bitter personal rivalries exacerbated political struggles within each country and, often, between political leaders in neighboring states.[2]

For example: In June 1906 El Salvador's powerful but unpredictable minister of war, Tomás Regalado, defying the orders of his superior, got drunk and invaded Guatemala. Regalado hated Guatemalan President Manuel Estrada Cabrera, a cruel, despotic man who had somehow convinced American observers that his rule was progressive and enlightened. Estrada suspected his neighbors of giving sanctuary to Guatemalan rebels. Regalado was killed in the initial assault. Though El Salvador found an ally in Honduras, the three combatants were persuaded to sign an armistice (on 20 July) aboard the U.S.S. *Marblehead*.[3]

In settling the Guatemalan-Salvadorean clash, Root had broached the possibility, with Mexico's joint sponsorship, of convening a general conference to resolve the outstanding grievances between the isthmian republics. The conference met at San José, Costa Rica, and, following ten days of sessions, produced a general treaty of peace and established a Central American Bureau and Pedagogical Institute.

Nicaragua boycotted the conference. Its absence was explained mostly by the xenophobic and nationalistic politics of its outspoken president, José Santos Zelaya. A Liberal, Zelaya had assumed power following the revolution of 1893. Two years later he had defended national honor by his vigorous assertion of Nicaraguan sovereignty over the Mosquitía, an area lying along the east coast, for centuries neglected by the Spanish and informally ruled by the Mosquito Indians and their British benefactors. Over the years Zelaya gained a reputation outside the country and among foreigners on the eastern coast for cruelty and oppression. American leaders disliked him for his unswerving opposition to foreign meddling in isthmian affairs. He wanted to rebuild the Central American union, the grand design of the 1820s that had come undone in the following decade, but was disinclined to achieve his goal by force. His economic prescription for the Mosquitía led him to favor foreign concessionaires, but in extending to them certain privileges he demanded in return a respect for Nicaraguan sovereignty, something which grated on foreigners accustomed to having their own way in the tropics. Unlike some of his improvident neighbors, Zelaya generally saw to it that installments on Nicaragua's international obligations were regularly paid. Zelaya's business dealings with concessionaires on the Honduran border required a government in Tegucigalpa that was friendly to him. His efforts in this direction led him to meddle in Honduran affairs, bringing Nicaragua into conflict not only with Honduras but also with El Salvador, Honduras's erstwhile ally. Zelaya's ambitions to dominate

GUATEMALA

BRITISH HONDURAS (BELIZE)

Guatemala City

Puerto Cortés

La Ceiba

EL SALVADOR

HONDURAS

San Salvador

Tegucigalpa

Gulf of Fonseca

Corinto

Jinotega

León

Matagalpa

Lake Managua

Managua

Granada

NICARAGUA

Lake Nicaragua

Bluefields

COSTA RICA

San José

Central America

PANAMA

CANAL ZONE

Colón

Panamá City

Central American politics also made him the mortal enemy of Estrada Cabrera of Guatemala.[4] When war erupted in early 1907 between Nicaragua and El Salvador, American officials moved quickly to mediate the conflict, with peace talks at Amapala in mid-April. The truce came apart momentarily after Zelaya got the mistaken impression (from an American president of a large mining company in Honduras) that Washington agreed with his Honduran policies. But the Nicaraguan dictator decided not to press the war for fear of a combined Salvadorean-Guatemalan assault on his country.

Circumstances now seemed favorable for another round of conferences. After considerable wrangling, the five republics finally agreed to convene in Washington, under the benign scrutiny of the United States and Mexico. The treaties of 1907 constituted the high-water mark of Rooseveltian diplomacy in Central America. On the assumption that isthmian troubles were traceable to mutual jealousies, the continual rise and fall of revolutionary governments, and the blatant disregard for Honduran sovereignty, the signatories dealt with these problems by (1) requiring disputes to be settled by a Central American Court of Justice, (2) forbidding revolutionaries from using national territory as a base for striking against a neighboring state, (3) agreeing to withhold recognition from any government that seized power by unconstitutional means (generally referred to as the Tobar Doctrine), and (4) neutralizing Honduras, whose succession of weak governments and whose location between Guatemala and Nicaragua had precipitated several conflicts. Root, with his legal frame of mind, viewed the treaties as the only logical fulfillment of his quest for isthmian peace and the basis for a revived Central American union.[5]

Within the year there occurred renewed bickering and sporadic fighting that jeopardized the treaties and the fragile neutrality of Honduras. In Tegucigalpa, Miguel Dávila ruled, with constant plotting against him. His enemies were sustained by Estrada Cabrera, Zelaya's avowed foe. Zelaya and Dávila thus enjoyed a tenuous political alliance. Dávila was also confronted in early 1908 by a threat from Lee Christmas, a soldier of fortune whose penury had prompted departure from New Orleans for Central America in 1894.[6] Over the years Christmas's natural bravado and fearlessness had elevated him to the status of General de Brigada in the forces serving Manuel Bonilla, Dávila's most persistent political enemy. Root also suspected that the United Fruit Company, which was expanding into Honduran fields, was behind the anti-Dávila agitation.

A ceasefire was arranged in July 1908, when Costa Rica, the only isthmian republic not directly involved in this conflict, requested arbitration by the newly created Court of Justice. The court, morally sustained by a stern statement from Roosevelt and Porfirio Díaz of Mexico, ordered the belligerents to withdraw from Honduran soil. Though Root disavowed any intention to use force to uphold the court's decision, he insisted that Mexico and the United States, as sponsors of the 1907 treaties, had an obligation to do so. In the course of this brief war Nicaragua and Honduras had charged Guatemala and El Salvador with violating the treaties. The court was now faced with rendering a decision on what constituted an obvious political matter. When the vote was taken, the judges were lenient with both El Salvador and Guatemala, leaving the impression that they were merely following the dictates of their respective countries rather than basing the decision on the merits of the case. The court's prestige suffered. Roosevelt's policy, dependent in large part on the willingness of Central Americans to settle their disputes according to treaty law, received a severe blow from which it never recovered.[7]

Taft, Knox, and the Nicaraguan Civil War

Roosevelt's departure and William Howard Taft's inauguration brought a subtle but significant change in the Caribbean policy of the United States. Historians have argued that Taft and Secretary of State Philander C. Knox merely substituted "dollars for bullets." In this interpretation the president, his secretary of state, and their allies, mostly large New York banks, manipulated the politics of fragile Caribbean economies so as to bring recalcitrant political leaders into line.[8] It is true that Taft and Knox, more than Roosevelt and Root, emphasized the role played by large banks in the internal economies of Caribbean nations. Yet, in a more important manner, Taft and

Knox altered the rules so as to allow for a more expanded role in the internal politics of the Caribbean countries. They scrutinized the internal finances of Caribbean governments more closely than Roosevelt and Root had done. Under Taft and Knox, Caribbean policy was bureaucratized. Increasingly, career officials in the State Department undertook policy decisions that would have far-reaching impact in the Caribbean world.

Zelaya's overthrow in 1909 embroiled Taft and Knox in Nicaraguan internal affairs and damaged the tenuous peace established by the 1907 treaties. Nicaragua's leader had continued to meddle in the affairs of neighboring states and had continued his enmity toward Estrada Cabrera. He had further alarmed Knox by contracting a £1,250,000 loan with the Ethelburga syndicate, a British investment firm. Nicaragua's default, Knox feared, might precipitate European interference. What antagonized Zelaya's opponents and prompted the revolt against him was his policy of granting monopolies to favored concessionaires to sell liquor, tobacco, and other products, a practice which particularly angered private businessmen, including some foreign entrepreneurs on the eastern coast.[9]

The revolt began when the governor of Bluefields district, Juan J. Estrada, abetted by prominent Nicaraguan Conservatives, declared against Zelaya. The center of the rebellion, Bluefields, isolated from Managua, boasted an influential foreign population. As befitted its importance as a major port, Bluefields had a customshouse, a lucrative source of revenue. It also had an American consul, Thomas Moffat, and was frequented by American naval vessels. As Moffat later told the story, American officers milling about town had urged Zelaya's enemies to strike a blow against the tyrant. Foreign entrepreneurs were delighted as tariff rates declined and monopolistic concessions ended in the wake of Estrada's rebellion. Moffat became something of a local celebrity by professing sympathy for Estrada and declaring against the hated Zelaya. The State Department cabled instructions ordering strict neutrality, but no matter—the damage had been done. The anti-Zelayistas surmised they could count on American support.[10]

And they judged correctly, for the hostility against Zelaya in the

State Department was so intense that American policy actually sustained Zelaya's Conservative opponents—all this in spite of the fact that the rebellion patently violated the treaties of 1907![11] When Zelaya counterattacked, penetrating the eastern regions to quash the defiant Estrada, the rebel leader retreated into the protective embrace of Moffat, the foreign community, and a contingent of marines, landed earlier to protect American citizens and their property. Estrada's wounded soldiers received care at the expense of the American consulate. Financial support in the amount of $200,000 had been contributed to the cause by Adolfo Díaz, a salaried employee of an American mining company. Local gossip had it that Díaz merely acted as a compliant intermediary between foreign businessmen and the rebels.

In any event, Zelaya, in prosecuting the war, committed an act that brought down upon him the moral wrath of Taft and Knox. Two Americans, Lee Roy Cannon and Leonard Groce, professional dynamiters in Estrada's service, laid charges in the San Juan River, causing the death of several loyalist Nicaraguans when the charges blew up one of Zelaya's ships. Captured by vengeful Zelayistas, Cannon and Groce begged for mercy, and Moffat appealed on their behalf. The story was that Zelaya pledged clemency, then unconscionably ordered their execution. Knox was furious. On 1 December 1909 he informed the Nicaraguan chargé, in a bitterly condemnatory note, that Zelaya was a "blot on Nicaraguan history" who menaced republican institutions and threatened Central American peace. The revolution, Knox averred, had the obvious support of the Nicaraguan people.[12]

American hostility to Zelaya also upset the tentative efforts at Mexican-American cooperation in Central America. President Díaz, like Roosevelt, wanted political peace in the Isthmus but, unlike Taft and Knox, regarded Zelaya with favor. Díaz and Zelaya had a common enemy in Estrata Cabrera of Guatemala. If Zelaya fell, then Guatemala might reassert its influence over isthmian affairs, a policy Mexico had always opposed. When the United States broke off relations with Zelaya, Díaz became alarmed and, in November 1909, proposed a new plan for Nicaraguan peace. The essence of the proposal was that Zelaya step down in favor of a pro-American Liberal. Zelaya was willing to go along, naming Dr. José Madriz, a former political opponent then representing Nicaragua on the Central American court. But Knox, suspicious of Mexican intentions and of Zelaya's choice, rejected it.

Invigorated by the sudden championing of its cause in Washington, the revolution was renewed. Zelaya, now portrayed as a bandit by the United States, soon recognized the futility of struggle and, partly in self-interest and partly in the interest of peace, resigned, investing his authority in Madriz. (Zelaya left Nicaragua aboard a Mexican warship and made his way to New York City, where he was arrested by federal officers who wanted to send him back to Nicaragua to face murder charges. Released when the charges were dropped, he went to Spain, invested heavily in Belgian bonds, lost everything, and, it was rumored in Managua, died a pauper in New York City in 1919. Across the street from his deteriorated mansion his political adversaries, backed by American financiers, installed the National Bank of Nicaragua.) Madriz wanted diplomatic recognition. But Knox, determined to rid Managua of all Zelayista influence, refused, saying that Nicaragua was really ruled by two competing forces, Madriz's and Estrada's. The implication was that they should fight it out. Madriz raised an army, took to the field, and won several victories; but when his makeshift navy pressed in against Bluefields, the Estrada stronghold, both combatants were warned by the ranking American naval officer that he would not tolerate any fighting in the town. This action was not unprecedented, but it understandably antagonized Madriz elements. When Madriz's ships blockaded Bluefields, American officials declared the action to be interference with American commerce, and marines were stationed on board incoming vessels to protect them from Nicaraguan intimidation. Their sanctuary in Bluefields safeguarded and their finances sustained by customs collections, the Conservatives turned inland and marched on Managua. Harassed by two enemies, Madriz gave up the fight and left the country. In late August 1910 Estrada triumphantly entered the capital. He immediately appealed for American recognition, pledged elections and rehabilitation of national finances, and requested a loan, to be secured by a portion of the customs collections. In short, he proposed an internal auditing, political and economic, in accordance with American prescriptions.[13]

Dollar Diplomacy

The policy that came to be called "dollar diplomacy" represented, in the private sphere, the efforts of American bankers to obtain adequate safeguards from the United States government for loans made to Caribbean republics. Banks considering such financial ventures ordinarily expected the State Department to render an official assessment of the financial and political trustworthiness of the recipient. In the department's view, approval of loans was a device for ensuring political respectability and financial prudence. In 1910 the most appealing form of financial guarantee was the customs collectorship, exploited successfully in the Dominican Republic. In analyzing the Central American situation, Taft and Knox believed that financial rather than strictly military measures provided the most agreeable means for achieving the goals established by the 1907 treaties.[14]

Of the five Central American republics Nicaragua, in Knox's opinion, most desperately required political and financial rehabilitation. The strife during Zelaya's last years and the subsequent struggle for control had left the nation bitterly divided. Knox believed the situation was not entirely hopeless. In his first year of office he had received loan proposals from Honduras and in the fall of 1910 anticipated a similar request from Estrada in Nicaragua. Before any loan would be approved, he would insist on a purge of Zelayistas from government and a reversal of Zelaya's policies. To ensure compliance he dispatched to Managua a special agent, Thomas C. Dawson (who would soon become first chief of the newly created Latin American division in the department), to placate the competing political chieftains and to prepare Nicaragua for new elections.

The Dawson agreements, signed by Estrada, Díaz, and Generals Emiliano Chamorro and Luís Mena, stipulated abolition of Zelaya's monopolies, which had been condemned by foreign businessmen; a special commission to adjust claims for damages to foreign property committed during Zelaya's years in office; and American assistance in the creation of a customs receivership. Estrada, it was agreed, would assume the presidency of the republic, and Díaz would become vice-president.[15]

His labors completed, Dawson left the country. The signatories to the pact bearing his name soon fell to quarreling. Mena, the new minister of war, controlled the army; Chamorro had gone to Honduras, where, Estrada speculated, he was plotting a rebellion. The president took to drinking heavily and openly recommended an American protectorate as his, and Nicaragua's, salvation. In a bold maneuver he ordered Mena's imprisonment and distributed weapons to Managua's Liberal faction, but later lost control when the army refused to obey his orders. On the evening of 8 May 1911 he appeared at the American legation, intoxicated, with Díaz in tow. The next day Estrada resigned and, like his old nemesis Zelaya, left the country.

The new president, who in the next twenty years would be disdainfully called "our" Nicaraguan, was not a familiar figure to the State Department in 1911. In Bluefields, Adolfo Díaz had proved useful in raising funds for Estrada's cause, but he had not occupied a prominent position among the inner circles of the Conservatives. On becoming president he was immediately compelled to placate Mena's followers by releasing the general from confinement. Outflanked by his political enemies, Díaz importuned Knox for support, declaring his belief that Nicaragua's destiny—and, by implication, his political future—lay in a harmonious relationship with the United States.

Within the State Department the main concern centered on Nicaraguan financial reform, which was now the staple tenet of Knox's rehabilitation scheme for the troubled isthmian republic. Accordingly, in June 1911, the two countries signed the Knox-Castrillo convention. By its provisions Nicaragua would, with the department's assistance, obtain a loan to settle its financial obligations and develop the country. In return, the United States would establish a customs receivership to guarantee repayment. Unlike the Dominican arrangement, which Knox had earlier extolled as the model for American policy in Central America, the Nicaraguan receivership placed no restrictions on the public debt.

The Senate already had under consideration a similar treaty with Honduras. A week after the signing of the Knox-Castrillo convention, Taft learned that Democratic opposition had successfully stalled the Honduran treaty in committee, despite Knox's fervent contention that the document was critical to America's search for peace in the

Isthmus. Notwithstanding the gloomy prospect for approval, Taft sent the Nicaraguan treaty to the Senate anyway, and requested reconsideration of the Honduran treaty; but Congress adjourned without senatorial action on either.

Already several New York banks had expressed interest in a Nicaraguan financial venture. One institution, Speyer and Company, had agreed to float $15 million in Nicaraguan bonds at 5 percent interest. Two others, Brown Brothers and J. and W. Seligman, also broached similar proposals. None seemed dissuaded by the Senate's dilatoriness in approving the treaties. The loan proposed by the Knox-Castrillo convention also provided for the banks' assistance in developing Nicaraguan railroads, stabilizing the currency, and establishing a national bank. Since the bankers did not anticipate speedy Senate action on the convention, they agreed to issue the financially strapped Nicaraguan government a $1.5 million loan, with repayment to be secured by the customs receipts. In March 1912 the Nicaraguan assembly, acting on the recommendation of two American financial experts, reorganized the national monetary system. In December Colonel Clifford D. Ham became customs collector. The following summer the National Bank of Nicaragua, the creation of New York bankers, opened for business.[16]

These arrangements had been undertaken despite the Senate's dissatisfaction with the Knox-Castrillo convention and its Honduran twin. In later accounts of this episode the manner by which the banks operated in Nicaragua and the State Department's protective consideration for Díaz's well-being would culminate in a damning indictment of dollar diplomacy. The 1912 Nicaraguan constitution forbade special concessions to foreigners and disavowed contracts that compromised national sovereignty, yet the bankers confidently organized a corporation, chartered in the United States, for operating Nicaragua's rail and steamship lines, acquiring in the process 51 percent of the stock, with an option to purchase the remainder. In Nicaragua's name the banks also obtained the old Ethelburga bonds from the London syndicate, negotiated originally by Zelaya. In this instance, it should be noted, the assumption of a portion of Nicaragua's external debt enhanced the republic's financial respectability.

While these financial negotiations were underway, Díaz's political strength was rapidly deteriorating. Mena, his old enemy, campaigned openly against him, proclaiming that the president was selling out Nicaragua to the State Department and to Wall Street. The national assembly supported General Mena and, despite some adroit political maneuvering by Díaz, forced the president to accept a constitutional proviso naming Mena as chief executive. When Mena's supporters stole a copy of the new constitution that Díaz had signed but not published, Knox angrily ordered the American minister, George Weitzel, to summon Mena to the legation and to inform the general that such tactics violated the Dawson agreements. The acrimony subsided when Weitzel tactfully decided not to denounce Mena but merely to wait for his adherents to calm down.

In the midst of all this, Knox hit upon the idea of a goodwill tour, with Nicaragua included on his itinerary. He arrived in Managua on 5 March 1912, amid reports of his imminent assassination. A hundred anti-American demonstrators were jailed. The papers were censored, and two Liberal editors incarcerated. Díaz's hospitality, however, was elaborately contrived and impressively expressed. Knox talked casually about his dream of bringing order and prosperity to Nicaragua. Even in the national assembly, a hotbed of anti-Díaz sentiment, the secretary was greeted politely, though his introduction (by a Mena disciple) contained subtle barbs at American expansionism. Knox assured the delegates that his country desired no territorial conquest south of the Rio Grande. With that pledge he took leave of the republic.[17]

As soon as Knox left, the fighting resumed. Mena had been secretly stashing munitions at critical places in the country. His adherents held Granada, the old Conservative stronghold, and Masaya. On 29 July the conspirators planned to take the capital. In the fighting, however, Mena's forces got the worst of it, and the general—still technically minister of war—took refuge in a military barracks connected to his office by a secret tunnel. In desperation Díaz prevailed on Weitzel to intercede. The American minister drove through a torrential rainstorm to visit Mena and, after an hour's cajoling, persuaded him to resign. His mission of peace presumably a success, Weitzel returned to the legation—but Mena continued his revolution, cutting off Managua's electric power and escaping in the darkness to Masaya to rally his followers and continue the fight.

The revolt brought Mena into direct confrontation not only with Díaz but, more importantly, with the United States. Under pressure from Weitzel to guarantee public order and the safety of foreigners, Díaz responded with a request to the United States to make such guarantees. The U.S.S. *Annapolis*, then stationed off the west coast of the republic, landed ninety marines to protect the legation. Another battalion was summoned from Panama.

Intercepted correspondence hinted that Mena was conspiring with Zelayistas. Fighting erupted in León and Chinandega, threatening the rail route leading out of the capital; and Mena's troops, in defiance of a hastily arranged truce, began shelling Managua. The Hotel Lupón, patronized by foreigners, received three hits. Many residents, including the British vice-consul, fled into the surrounding countryside. When the firing stopped, a tally of casualties showed 132 women and children killed. No American died, but the bombardment caused considerable damage to foreign property.

Their attack completed, the rebels retired, just as Major Smedley ("Old Gimlet Eye") Butler (who would in time become a seasoned veteran of the banana wars) arrived with 360 marines from the Canal Zone. In outlying towns sporadic fighting continued, often accompanied by xenophobic outbursts. A train carrying forty sailors and ten marines from Managua to León was halted by rebels, who forced the Americans to walk back to the capital.

The presence of American troops brought criticism from neighboring governments and inspired the president of El Salvador to call for mediation, a proposal that Taft arrogantly rejected in favor of a military solution to protect foreign lives and property and, not incidentally, to keep Díaz in power. American warships landed marine reinforcements, who took León and marched on Granada, where, it was reported, Mena's troops starved the populace and assaulted women. En route Butler and one hundred marines drove rebels from their strongholds in the hills and took Masaya. By the time the force arrived at Granada, Mena, sick and beaten, had taken sanctuary in the Convent of San Francisco. He surrendered and, for punishment, was sent into exile in Panama.[18]

Nicaragua had suffered a thousand casualties, but American policy was enforced. In November the promised elections took place. A few

Conservative stalwarts urged General Chamorro to run, and he sought out the American minister for advice. Weitzel, in a pleasant but firm tone, objected to his candidacy, pointing out Chamorro was a military man, and what the country needed was civilian rule. Chamorro acquiesced and withdrew from the race. Adolfo Díaz, whose unstinting faith in American guidance had sustained him through troubled days, became president of the republic. Fittingly he was feted in a sumptuous reception aboard the flagship of the Pacific fleet, the U.S.S. *California*.

The Limitations of Dollar Diplomacy

The use of marines to quell the Nicaraguan rebellion of 1912 had, in at least one respect, a therapeutic effect. For years afterwards political aspirants remembered how Mena's revolt had been crushed, and not until 1919, if one excepts the Costa Rican case of 1917, was a Central American government overturned by force. Those politicians in power learned how to perpetuate themselves: at the first sign of political restiveness they would send frantic messages to the American minister requesting the visit of an American warship. In Nicaragua the apparently unmistakable determination to snuff out any rebellion was reinforced by the presence of a one-hundred-man legation guard.

Yet, in a deeper and more profound way, the ultimate resort to force discredited Taft and Knox's optimistic view of the benefits of dollar diplomacy. By arguing that financial rehabilitation eventually brought political stability, the president and his secretary of state assumed that Central America's perennially warring factions would cease quarreling in their common desire to encourage foreign investment when, in truth, their bickering often had little to do with promoting national development or achieving currency stabilization. As evidence of the feasibility of dollar diplomacy, Taft cited the example of the Dominican Republic, where, after 1907, the economic prospects of the nation brightened considerably and were accompanied by an unsurpassed degree of political peace. This was due less to the economic arrangements made with the United States than to the firm rule of Ramón Cáceres. When Cáceres fell to assassins in November

1911, the political serenity lauded by Taft and Knox quickly faded.[19]

In Guatemala and Honduras Taft and Knox's pursuit of debt re-funding and financial rehabilitation succeeded in doing little more than alienating the British. The Honduran situation especially ag-gravated Anglo-American relations. Of three Central American re-publics—Honduras, Costa Rica, and Guatemala—with outstanding foreign debts in 1909, Honduras was burdened with the oldest obliga-tions. In 1867, following forty years of defaulting on the original indebtedness, Honduran authorities floated new loans with London investors, including three substantial railroad ventures. Only sixty miles of track were laid, and by 1872, predictably, all the loans were in default. By 1908 the interest alone amounted to £17 million, roughly triple the original indebtedness. To cover the original debt Honduras had mortgaged its rail system, but in 1908, despite British protests, the railroad was leased to Washington S. Valentine, an American. To protect British bondholders Sir Lionel Carden, the British minister to Central America, proposed to Honduran president Miguel Dávila that the external debt be reduced to £450,000, to be repaid over forty years, with the railroad and a wharf at Puerto Cortés as collateral.

Carden's scheme irritated Taft and especially Knox, who soon in-formed the British Foreign Office that the United States would not tolerate any European readjustment of the Honduran debt. London was mollified by a subsequent statement from J. P. Morgan's British agent that an American group was preparing a general settlement of the Honduran debt in a manner similar to that employed in the Dominican Republic. If successful, the Morgan syndicate promised to purchase the British bonds at 15 percent of face value. Despite Car-den's protestations the Council of Foreign Bondholders, representing British investors, decided to cooperate. In December 1909 Morgan's group announced that it was buying $10 million in Honduran bonds, to be guaranteed by proceeds from the railroad and a customs re-ceivership, modeled on the Dominican scheme. The loan would be contingent on an American guarantee of Honduran sovereignty.

For months Dávila, unsure of his political position, hesitated in negotiating the treaty that Knox believed vital to the success of any financial reform. When the treaty was finally signed, on 10 January 1911, it provided for the same measures that American negotiators incorporated into the Nicaraguan treaty signed several months later: a customs receivership, an American collector, and a refunding plan. In submitting the treaty to the Senate, Taft argued that it strengthened American peace efforts in Central America.[20]

Just as these negotiations were in their final stages, Honduras was plunged into civil war, with Dávila facing his archenemy, Manuel Bonilla, patron of the filibuster Lee Christmas. The revolt was plotted in New Orleans, chosen as headquarters by Bonilla after the State Department had sent stern warnings to Estrada Cabrera about allowing Honduran rebels to use Guatemalan territory as a staging ground. On 10 January 1911—the same day the treaty was signed—Bonilla and his party, aboard the *Hornet*, landed at Trujillo. Rumors of the involvement of Samuel Zemurray's Cuyamel Fruit Company circulated, to be resurrected years later (after Cuyamel merged with United Fruit) in a controversial *Fortune* magazine article. Zemurray wanted to import railway supplies into the country duty-free, something which a customs collector would have prevented.

Bonilla surrendered the *Hornet* to a patrolling American warship, but his followers took La Ceiba. In Tegucigalpa Dávila tried to push the loan treaty through the Honduran assembly but lost in a humiliatingly lopsided vote. He was further undermined when American naval authorities, determined to prevent fighting in Puerto Cortés, decreed that the combatants must confine their fire to a particular zone. Faced with American restrictions Dávila's commanders decided to withdraw. The president was doomed. Though a New Orleans jury indicted Bonilla and Christmas for violation of the neutrality laws, in Honduras Bonilla's influence predominated. In early March Dawson thrashed out a compromise whereby a Bonilla follower would become provisional president, pending general elections.[21]

When the new Honduran government took form, Bonilla assumed the presidency. He grew cool to the loan treaty, despite earlier pledges to support it in the assembly, and initiated financial discussions with Zemurray. Morgan's syndicate, wearied by the vicissitudes in Honduran politics and the Senate's unpredictability, acquiesced in Zemurray's efforts and, on 3 February 1912, withdrew its financial proposals. Bonilla seized Valentine's railroad and, in mid-April, declared the loan treaties null. The State Department's enthusiasm noticeably declined after Knox learned that Zemurray's plans made no provisions for a customs receivership.[22]

The dismal record of dollar diplomacy in Honduras discouraged Carden in his work on behalf of British bondholders, who had pinned their hopes on Morgan's plan. Frustrated in Honduras, Carden opened negotiations with Guatemala, where British bondholders had also invested heavily, with a determination tempered by cynicism. Like Honduras, Guatemala had entered the twentieth century with a heavy foreign debt traceable to indiscriminate borrowing in the era of the Central American federation of the 1820s and 1830s. Over the years Guatemalan governments periodically scaled down the bonds and rarely paid interest. In 1904 the republic's European creditors assaulted Estrada Cabrera with renewed protests, which the president met with renewed promises.

In 1909 several American syndicates broached a plan for reducing the foreign debt and refunding the currency, a proposal which attracted Knox's attention. Knox wanted any loan contingent on protection of American interests in the country. But, with the exception of Minor Keith, who wanted to consolidate Guatemala's railroads, the bankers shied away from a close relationship with the State Department, fearing it would demand a supervisory role. At the same time Carden pressed Estrada to resume payments on British-held bonds. From 1903 to 1908, Carden pointed out, Guatemala had used its coffee duty, originally pledged for serving the debt owed British bondholders, as collateral in obtaining loans from a San Francisco banking syndicate. With these revenues Estrada had also made periodic payments to the republic's German and American creditors. The negotiations with the American syndicates in 1909–10 convinced Carden that Estrada could not settle with Guatemala's British creditors.

At first the British Foreign Office appeared persuaded that the American refunding plan might result in more favorable treatment for its nationals. Carden soon found out differently. From Knox, he received vague reassurances about protecting British interests in the republic. But Knox really wanted to reduce British influence. When Guatemala announced its intention of signing an agreement with one of the New York syndicates, the British Foreign Office evinced skepticism that the bondholders would obtain a settlement of their claims.

Its pessimism was soon justified. Having played the Americans and British against one another for more than three years, Estrada proceeded to kill the financing scheme with crippling amendments.[23]

The frustrating experience in Central America during these years defied Taft's and Knox's most ambitious plans to substitute "dollars for bullets" in achieving America's stated goal of ensuring political and financial stability. Even in sophisticated Costa Rica, where a Europeanized culture dominated, Minor Keith's labors to rehabilitate national finance through American bankers faltered, largely because the Costa Rican congress, learning that liquor revenues were pledged as collateral for the proffered American loan, did not want to turn over its distilleries to the National City Bank of New York in the event of default.

Where American policy succeeded it did so not by dollars but by bullets. In Nicaragua Americans on the Caribbean coast had joined forces with Zelaya's enemies and had driven from power the only dedicated nationalist of the Isthmus. Zelaya had been hounded from Nicaragua, and the ultimate inheritor of his office ruled safely in Managua under the benign authority of the United States and a legation guard.

3 • The Apogee of Caribbean Empire

In Caribbean minds the most repugnant aspects of Yankee meddling would eventually be identified with a stern Presbyterian, Thomas Woodrow Wilson, who inherited an empire and then proceeded to expand it in a righteous spirit of missionary diplomacy. His Mexican policy alone would have earned him the badge of infamy among Latin critics of American expansionism. In eight years in office he and his subordinates responsible for Caribbean affairs would reinforce existing American attitudes about the need for American tutelage, and in Haiti and the Dominican Republic they would modify inherited policies to justify the occupation of two sovereign republics. A professed noninterventionist, Wilson easily exceeded his two Republican predecessors in the degree of interference in the Caribbean. His was a politics of morality which, when extended into the tropics, would inspire and uplift Caribbean governments in their presumed quest for financial respectability and an honest ballot. One of Wilson's earliest official pronouncements on Latin American problems revealed his annoyance at unprincipled politicians who sought office for personal gain rather than for public good. Later, in an important address in Mobile, Alabama, in October 1913, he chastised foreign economic exploitation in Latin America.[1] Like other Democrats who had condemned Knox's treaties with Honduras and Nicaragua, Wilson excoriated dollar diplomacy. His first secretary of state, William Jennings Bryan, an ardent enemy of Wall Street, even concocted a scheme for lending public funds at modest interest to bankrupt Caribbean governments, so they might free themselves from the shackles of New York bankers. The proposal, Bryan boasted, would advance the national interest, prevent revolutions, further education, and advance the cause of political stability. Wilson vetoed Bryan's plan even though he approved of its ultimate objectives.[2]

The Caribbean Empire, 1912: Two Outposts

On the eve of Wilson's election the Caribbean empire of the United States had developed a character that distinguished it from European imperial ventures. Yet this empire exhibited an internal diversity that could not easily be accounted for: there was the intensive American intrusion into Cuba, which had not been annexed, compared with the seemingly calculated neglect of Puerto Rico, which had become American territory, or the subtle ways by which bureaucrats Americanized the Canal Zone.

Of these three outposts of empire, Cuba perhaps felt most strongly the impact of American political and material values. The first intervention had acquainted Cubans with the intrinsic values of disinfectant, sewage systems, and public schooling. The second intervention, under Magoon, had presumably reinforced these earlier notions with a much-needed electoral reform that would, if dutifully followed, provide Cubans with honest, nonviolent political change.[3]

Magoon had been escorted to the dock by an affable politician, José Miguel Gómez, the new president, who took office a financial destitute in 1909 and left it four years later a millionaire. Cubans, on the whole, did not blame him for thievery, for the times were prosperous, and President Gómez, with his perpetual grin beneath a huge Panama hat, generously spread the graft to his friends. American entrepreneurs who had settled in Cuba to build its telephone system, lay its sewage lines, and organize its public schools savored the good life by playing bridge at the American club. The American minister was the second most powerful figure in the country.

Fewer than 10,000 Americans lived in Cuba in 1912, but their impact on Cuban society was everywhere. They not only showed the Cubans how to string electric wire and pave streets; more often than not they owned the companies that provided these services. In the countryside they purchased sugar plantations and signed contracts with soft drink and candy companies. On the Isle of Pines the Americans looked like veritable pioneers founding new towns—one was named McKinley—and they believed, until a treaty stipulating the territory as legitimately Cuban was finally ratified in 1925, that the island would be theirs.[4] Economically Cuba was fast becoming an appendage of the United States, a fulfillment of what earlier policymakers had styled its "special relationship" to its northern neighbor. Cubans sent sugar to the United States and received foodstuffs and consumer goods in return. In 1895 the American investment in the island had been calculated (by Secretary of State Richard Olney) at $50 million; in 1911, that amount was invested in sugar mills alone. Americans had pumped $25 million into railroads, another $25 million into mining and manufacturing, $20 million into public utilities, $5 million in banking, and $5 million in shipping. They also held some $30 million in obligations of the Cuban government.

American influence was more resented by the average Cuban than in the days after the war with Spain.[5] Leonard Wood had given Cubans firm but undeniably honest and, if one accepted his values, enlightened rule. The second intervention had occurred, one could argue, because of squabblings among Cuba's first political leaders and their refusal to provide a viable government. After Magoon left, the State Department decided that the American public would not tolerate another Cuban occupation, so Taft and Knox contrived the so-called preventive policy. This meant that an elastic interpretation would be applied to the Platt Amendment permitting the United States to act before the republic slipped into another political morass similar to the confusion of 1905 that had triggered the second occupation.

In 1901 Root had promised a delegation of inquisitive Cubans that the Platt Amendment would never be used to justify interference in Cuba's internal affairs. Under the new interpretation, Cubans soon learned, the island's domestic troubles became a matter for close scrutiny by the American minister. One of his important functions was to oversee the government's operation. When Gómez signed a decree permitting a private company to cut timber in the Zapata swamp in 1912, the American minister condemned the concession as a giveaway of the island's natural resources. He protested to Knox, who wired his disapproval of the concession. Gómez, without a whimper, cancelled the contract. After further investigation, the American consul-general declared the swamp worthless; American objections were withdrawn, and the contract was renewed. In the meantime the Cuban president had dutifully heeded the word of the American minister.[6]

When the island appeared threatened by revolutionary disturbances, as in the 1912 "colored revolt," the intention of the preventive policy was unmistakable. The Independent Colored Party wanted repeal of a law forbidding political groups organized along racial lines. Its activities were largely confined to Oriente province, where American landholdings were extensive. Curiously, its leader wanted American intervention on the specious logic the United States would recognize his group. No violence was directed against whites, but Americans living in Oriente were fearful of a racially motivated revolt. Gómez, more determined than Estrada Palma in dealing with internal threats, dispatched 2,000 soldiers to Oriente. After there had been five days of fighting, Knox decided to supplement Cuban forces by sending marines ashore at Daiquirí to protect the Spanish-American Iron Company. Five hundred American troops landed at Guantánamo City and fanned out to guard the sugar mills along the Guantánamo and Western Railroad. Two battleships anchored in Havana harbor. These measures were justified, Knox pointed out, by the size of the American population, especially the presence of American women, and the threat to American-owned property. These actions, he affirmed, did not constitute intervention.[7]

Cuba lay on the northern rim of the empire; Panama, on the southern periphery. Just as a generation of dedicated engineers, officers, and doctors had sallied forth to reclaim Cuba, their colleagues fanned out into the Panamanian jungle, to divide the land and connect the oceans.

In 1912 the canal, from all estimates, stood only a few years from completion. Already the Americans had dramatically altered the topography and living conditions on the Isthmus since that day in 1904 when an American officer had received the keys to locked warehouses and buildings from a French official. In the early years, from 1904 to 1907, the American invaders had bickered over procedure, organization, and medical problems. In the beginning the Canal Commission had tried to run things from Washington, with disastrous results. The first laborers arrived to discover an uninhabitable world plagued by impenetrable foliage and ravaged by disease. By early 1907 the first battles had been won by two superb organizers: William C. Gorgas, chief sanitary officer, sent to deal with yellow fever and malaria; and John F. Stevens, chief engineer, who provided more comfortable quarters and better food for the first generation of grumblers. Gorgas sanitized and paved Panama City and Colón. Bunau-Varilla had seen to it that the United States would receive in the treaty of 1903 all the authority it needed to build, protect, and service the canal. Sanitation came under that sweeping mandate, and Gorgas's edicts were holy writ. A generation of early Zonians learned to live by the manifestoes of the Sanitary Commission as medieval monks lived by the creed of Holy Mother Church. Gorgas made the Isthmus a fit place to live and work; Stevens inspired men to stay and work.[8]

In their zeal to make the Zone a more inviting place to work and live, the first Americans tried to provide many of the amenities of home and, in so doing, laid the foundation for an American colony. The Zone's gradual transformation from simply a canal area with a minimum of American authority into a separate legal entity derived in part from concessions in the 1903 treaty, and in part from day-to-day practice. The treaty, for example, gave the United States the power of eminent domain within the Zone, a necessary grant, it was contended, in order to purchase private holdings that would be flooded or would become necessary for maintenance. In short, the treaty provided the United States with the power to act in the Zone "as if it were sovereign."[9]

In practice the successive bureaucracies responsible for zone operations went far beyond the early estimates of Hay, Roosevelt, or even Bunau-Varilla in carrying out their duties. The Zone government collected revenues, established prisons, hired police, provided fire protection, and built schools. Its court system meted out Anglo-Saxon justice. It imported English-speaking black West Indians because its American foremen knew how to "work niggers" and were disinclined to learn Spanish. It provided rent-free quarters because turnover was high and inducements had to be provided to keep qualified personnel.

In 1906 a visiting senator complained of not seeing the American flag flying over what he believed was American soil. It was dutifully raised, and over the years the Panamanian banner gradually disappeared from Zone flagpoles, not to reappear until the 1960s. Class barriers were reinforced by the commission's practice of paying white, skilled Americans on the "gold roll" and black (and Panamanian) unskilled laborers at tropical rates on the "silver roll." Racial segregation, imported from the United States, came early to Zone life and remained years after racial barriers crumbled in the States. Zone schools, created to encourage married men to work in the tropics, were taught in English and by 1913 were as typically American as public schools in small Southern towns. The commissaries, inherited from the French establishment in the nineteenth century, satisfied the Zone laborers' daily needs for foodstuffs, furniture, clothes, and sundries. When Panamanian merchants complained in 1905 about unfair competition, Roosevelt issued an executive order forbidding "silver roll" employees from patronizing the commissaries; but the Canal Commission, arguing that Panamanian businessmen overcharged or failed to satisfy demand, circumvented the ruling. After Roosevelt left office, officials paid less attention to Panamanian protests about the Americanization of the Zone.[10]

Roosevelt had originally offended Colombia, not Panama. In 1913 the United States was virtually reconciled with Bogotá, though the atoning treaty was not to be ratified until after Roosevelt's death. Panama had become, as Knox once commented, "our vest pocket republic."

The Haitian Intervention

By far the most systematic and extensive intrusion into the internal processes of Caribbean countries in these years came in Haiti and the Dominican Republic. When the United States entered the world war in 1917, Hispaniola was an American base. A client government ruled in Port-au-Prince, at the behest of American naval officers; and in Santo Domingo the navy ran Dominican officials out of town and installed a military government to rule, as official phraseology put it, "on behalf of the Dominican government."[11]

The origins of the Haitian intervention lay in American racial fantasies, economic interests, and strategic requirements in the Caribbean.

Haiti was the second independent nation in the Western Hemisphere, but its birth had been, in the minds of American whites, a racial and social calamity that could only endanger slave societies. For that reason its governments went unrecognized by the United States until the Civil War—despite the existence of a Haitian-American trade dating from the 1790s. In 1891 the Benjamin Harrison administration, represented by the former slave Frederick Douglass, tried to obtain a naval cession at Môle Saint-Nicolas, on the isolated north coast, but a suspicious Haitian assembly killed the project. By 1910, when American interest in Haitian finances increased, the United States had experienced a half-century of regular diplomatic interchange with Haiti, but the relationship had produced little cordiality and even less understanding. On eight occasions between 1867 and 1900 American naval vessels had landed marines to protect foreign lives and property. Alvey A. Adee, the State Department's perennial assistant secretary of state, contemptuously referred to the republic as a "public nuisance." The ultimate insult came from William Jennings Bryan, who, after listening to a long discourse on Haitian culture and politics from an American connected with the Banque Nationale, commented: "Dear me, think of it. Niggers speaking French." [12]

Haiti's elite not only spoke French; they lived in European style and referred disdainfully to the black and mulatto masses who spoke a Creole patois and practiced voodoo. In the nineteenth century, French influence dominated the upper political and social strata—the ties strengthened by Haitian leaders who exchanged their coffee for French tobacco—who educated their children in French schools, worshipped under French priests, and, incorrectly, looked to France as tutor of the black race. After 1900 a German business community flourished in Port-au-Prince; German merchants married into the Haitian elite. In the politically volatile years preceding American intervention, the Germans found it profitable to finance revolutions and to lend money, at notorious rates of interest, to unstable Haitian governments.

American economic penetration lagged behind that of France and Germany, but by 1910 the United States controlled about 60 percent of the republic's import market, a remarkable increase from the McKinley era. American entrepreneurs began constructing a railroad, the Plaine du Cul-de-Sac, though the company was later absorbed by German interests. A second rail project, started by James P. McDonald, proceeded so slowly that an impatient Haitian government foreclosed. In 1911 McDonald's holdings were acquired by a New York banking syndicate represented by W. R. Grace and Company, which planned to construct a national rail line from Port-au-Prince to Cap Haïtien on the north coast. Because of the mountainous terrain and the frequent political disturbances, the company completed only three sections of track totaling some 108 miles. Much of the work was poorly done, and in 1914 the Haitian government ceased payment. The company demanded some $33,000 per mile in compensation for the track already laid. This project soon became a national scandal, but following the American intervention in 1915, a compliant Haitian president authorized payment.

A more serious matter was the predicament of the Haitian banking system, which in 1910 seemed perilously close to domination by European interests. In that year American, French, and German interests fought a fierce battle for control of the Banque Nationale. In late 1909 Speyer and Company and National City Bank had tried to take over the Banque but had lost out to a shrewd German consortium, which soon allied with the Banque's French managers in a bold proposal to obtain domination by reorganizing the bank and floating a

65-million-franc loan. The State Department condemned the exclusion of American banks from this scheme in such vigorous manner that the Europeans acquiesced in a move to allow National City Bank and Speyer and Company to acquire a 50 percent share. One provision permitted the Banque to collect Haitian customs duties. Americans replaced Frenchmen as managers in the Banque and, because of the government's dependence on the Banque for monthly expenses, gained a powerful influence over Haitian executives.[13]

For the Wilson administration the immediate source of Haitian problems lay in the republic's political turbulence. Since 1911 seven Haitian presidents had been assassinated or forcibly removed from office. One had been blown up in the national palace. Though harassed Haitian executives somehow managed to pay on the external debt, the growing consensus in the State Department in these years was that more direct American involvement would be necessary to stave off European powers' pressing their advantage in a country weakened by internal discord.

In their assessment of the Haitian situation Wilson and Bryan depended heavily on American officers of the Banque Nationale, particularly Roger Farnham, who also ran the Haitian National Railway. Farnham was well ahead of the State Department in his advocacy of a customs receivership and, by virtue of his position in the national bank, exercised a considerable power over financially harassed Haitian executives. When they resisted, he increased his pressure, as in 1914 when the bank ceased making monthly payments to the governments, compelling it to borrow for operating expenses until the end of the year when it received a lump-sum payment. To Bryan, Farnham was the helpful, concerned American banker trying to educate an irresponsible Haitian president in the art of fiscal responsibility. To the Haitians, he was a veritable Shylock, circulating scare stories about Franco-German intrigue, hoisting a financial sword of Damocles over the heads of Haitian bureaucrats. Ultimately he told Bryan that American business would leave the republic unless the United States intervened to protect it.

By the summer of 1915 department thinking had come to the view that what was necessary was a customs receivership, settlement of claims, protection of foreign lives and property, and a guarantee that

Môle Saint-Nicolas would not come under German control. No lesser demands seemed realistic. The Navy had already drawn up contingency plans for landing marines in the probability of violence and threats to foreign interests. No Haitian government, observed Robert Lansing after becoming secretary of state, could provide such protection. His observations on the political incapacities of American blacks and his reading of Haitian and Liberian history led him inevitably to this conclusion. The African, Lansing wrote, was politically incompetent and, in the midst of crisis, reverted to animal savagery.[14]

And on 28 July 1915, Lansing's derogatory comment about Haitian character appeared justified by a gruesome event in Port-au-Prince. President Vilbrun Guillaume Sam had been in power only five months when, it was alleged, he ordered the arrest and execution of 167 political prisoners, many from the Haitian elite. Some had been mercilessly tortured. Rumors of his implication in the killings circulated throughout the capital. A vengeful mob roamed the streets. The president sought sanctuary in the French legation, but his pursuers dragged him outside and there, to the horror of the American chargé dutifully describing the terrible event, dismembered him.[15]

American marines had already begun to disembark. The decision to intervene had been arrived at earlier in the month when it had been determined that a force loyal to Dr. Rosalvo Bobo, an outspoken critic of American influence in the republic, was prepared for battle with Guillaume Sam's forces. Admiral William Banks Caperton had arrived from Veracruz to assess a deteriorating situation. He had informed Guillaume Sam that he was ready to land troops if fighting broke out in Port-au-Prince; on the twenty-eighth, the day the president was butchered, both the French and British legations requested warships. After landing five companies of troops, Caperton informed prominent Haitians of his actions, requesting their cooperation. The elite was outwardly acquiescent, though rumors quickly circulated about American designs on Haitian sovereignty. Lansing and Wilson, in their private exchanges on Haitian affairs, seemed unsure of the legality of what they had ordered or, now that American troops were taking over in Port-au-Prince and coastal towns, what they were going to do with Haiti. Should they follow Secretary of the Navy Josephus Daniels's advice and institute a military government? Or function through a compliant Haitian administration? One thing was certain: Bobo would not be president. Caperton saw to that by disarming and disbanding his 1,500-man caco force.[16]

What emerged was both a system of martial law and a client government ruled nominally by Haitians. The month following Guillaume Sam's killing, as marine contingents occupied the coastal towns, the Navy chose a new Haitian president, Henri Dartiguenave, the only candidate acceptable to the United States after Bobo had defiantly rejected American demands. Under Caperton's orders a revolutionary committee pledged to Bobo was disbanded. In early September the admiral proclaimed martial law and forbade the press to publish incendiary material. Until 1929, when Haitians rioted in defiance of such restrictions, American military tribunals meted out justice for political offenses.

Already the State Department had composed a Haitian-American treaty authorizing American control of customshouses, construction of roads and schools, organization of a constabulary—in short, the demands advanced in the months preceding the occupation. With marines in control of Port-au-Prince, Lansing believed, the Haitians would become more compliant. Instead, he encountered further resistance, particularly to demands for American supervision of the customshouses, which, in the minds of American policymakers, had worked so well in the neighboring Dominican Republic that it had to be tried in Haiti. When Dartiguenave's ministers of foreign affairs and public works strenuously objected to the proposal for an American financial advisor, the Haitian president fired both, then discussed their replacements with the American chargé d'affaires. Haitian deputies known to oppose the treaty received personal visits from Caperton's staff. Caco bands in the mountainous interior had already begun harassing marine patrols, making imperative, Caperton argued, the speedy approval of the treaty and the creation of a constabulary. When the Haitian assembly procrastinated, Caperton appeared before Dartiguenave's cabinet, reinforcing his appeal with threats that American troops would remain to pacify the country even if the treaty remained unratified. The assembly soon approved the document.

Through various drafts the meaning of the treaty had become

muddled, leaving no clear impression as to the exact powers of the financial advisor or the right of the United States to build schools or train a national guard. Much of what the occupiers undertook, then, derived largely from inference. Having obtained the assembly's approval of the treaty, Caperton recommended release of a $1.5 million pending loan by the Banque Nationale to Dartiguenave's government. Years later, during the senatorial investigation of the occupation, Caperton disavowed charges that the treaty had been forced upon the Haitian government, and declared that his presence and persuasion were "more moral than military."[17]

In early 1916 the admiral left Port-au-Prince. Despite the unorthodox manner by which he had persuaded the assembly to approve the 1915 treaty, he had in his personal relationships with Haitians conveyed a sense of acceptance and social equality. His courtesy had derived partly from inner conviction and partly from Daniels's orders to naval officers to comport themselves so as not to offend Haitian sensibilities. When Caperton departed, the policy of conciliation, such as it was, went with him. The ruling American officer was now Colonel Littleton W. T. Waller, a proud Virginian, commander of marine forces in Haiti, who deplored Caperton's ostentatious display. Waller could practice the social graces in the presence of Dartiguenave and the upper-crust Haitians, but he was privately disgusted at "bowing and scraping to these coons." His fellow officer, Major Smedley Butler (who in the 1930s would deliver a spirited self-flagellation for his role in the banana wars), shared Waller's contempt for the Haitian elite, but Butler did exhibit some sympathy for the masses. The Haitian aristocracy, accustomed to public and even personal deference from white Europeans, was soon disillusioned by the thinly disguised racism of its benefactors. The elite believed in two Haitis, the rulers and the ruled. So did the American occupiers, but to them the "two Haitis" were the 99 percent of the "niggers" who went barefoot and the 1 percent of the "niggers" who wore shoes.[18]

From the beginning the occupiers confronted sporadic resistance. In the mountainous interior caco bands, which historically had mobilized to bring down Haitian governments, formed to drive the marines out of Haiti. At first the Americans tried bribery, paying five dollars for every surrendered weapon—a handsome sum to people who lived mostly outside the money economy—plus larger amounts to caco chieftains. Those who rejected such offers were captured or killed. In one pursuit, called the Fort Rivière battle, a contingent under Butler killed fifty-one cacos. In the heat of battle the confused Haitians had thrown their rifles aside and begun hurling rocks at their adversaries. The sole American casualty in the engagement was a marine who lost two front teeth. For his bravery at Fort Rivière, Butler was awarded the Congressional Medal of Honor. When Assistant Secretary of the Navy Franklin D. Roosevelt visited the site and heard a stirring account of the fighting, the Haitian body count had, inexplicably, escalated to two hundred.[19]

Butler's labors extended also to organization of a Haitian constabulary, presumably an apolitical national police, composed of Haitian peasants and commanded initially by marine officers. As in the Dominican Republic and in Nicaragua, the guard's function was maintenance of order and the suppression of caco resistance. But in the beginning results were disappointing. The recruits, though well paid by Haitian standards, suffered from typical tropical maladies, lacked even rudimentary education, and of course had difficulty comprehending the staccato instructions of officers. When the European war drained the contingent of officers, noncommissioned men were upgraded and assigned to guard units. Appointment of Haitian aristocrats in the upper echelons of the guard proved disappointing, for the French-speaking elite knew as little Creole patois as the Americans. In later years guard officers rose from the ranks.[20]

American entry into the war intensified the occupation and brought the occupiers into direct confrontation with the small but influential German population. In Haiti the German element had acquired considerable influence in the past by subsidizing revolutions and had attained social respectability by marrying into the Haitian elite. After 1917, marine officers eager to be shipped to the European front resented their Haitian assignment and took out their frustrations in petty harassment of German residents. Little evidence of a German conspiracy in Haiti was uncovered, but the American occupiers interned prominent Germans and seized their property.

One of the more controversial acts in the early years of the occupation involved the writing and promulgation of the new Haitian constitution. (It was the document Franklin Roosevelt later bragged about having personally written.)[21] The supreme law of 1889 gave the national assembly authority to alter the constitution, but soon after the American intervention and Dartiguenave's inauguration the assembly received an American-approved draft. In defiance it refused to approve it and substituted a more nationalistic version. Infuriated, Butler obtained a decree, bearing Dartiguenave's signature, dissolving the assembly. As one marine officer later testified, the assembly refused to appreciate what the Americans intended to do in Haiti.

Haiti's constitution was written mostly by the State Department, though several agencies, including Roosevelt's office, submitted suggestions and alterations. In Haiti a plebiscite on the document was carefully arranged. The guard, which hosted public barbecues to attract public attention, supervised the voting. Five percent of the Haitian population flocked to the polls to cast ballots, 98,000 in favor and 768 opposed.

The new constitution allowed foreigners to own property, a provision Americans considered vital to the republic's agricultural development but something which Haitian law had historically forbidden. It also validated the acts of the occupation. Butler was particularly interested in the interior, which desperately needed a road system and agricultural modernization. He soon discovered that Haitian law enabled him to build a road system at relatively low cost: an 1864 law provided that local population, in lieu of paying a road tax, might be conscripted to work on roads, an ancient principle known as the corvée.

With this statute working on his behalf Butler inaugurated an ambitious roadbuilding program. Like the public service programs in Cuba and in the Dominican Republic, the achievements in Haitian road construction were, in terms of material accomplishment, impressive. With peasants doing most of the work, the marines performed the herculean task of connecting Port-au-Prince with Cap Haïtien, 170 miles to the north. But the forced labor program aroused widespread resentment among country people, its alleged beneficiaries, for it took them from their homes to labor under harsh and often brutal conditions. In October 1918 the corvée was officially abolished, but the damage had been done. In the remote districts the practice continued illegally. Conscripted peasants ran away to join caco armies, and the national guard became more brutal in its determination to prevent runaways and instituted, it was alleged, a policy of selective executions. From Port-au-Prince came orders to cease the killing of prisoners.[22]

The most terrible violence occurred in 1919. Charlemagne Peralte, who at one time had worked with the occupation, created a provisional government in the interior. It possessed, he claimed, a 2,000-caco army capable of driving the Americans into the sea. Peralte himself was killed when two marines, with smeared faces and wearing caco clothes, penetrated his camp. As a lesson to other Haitians, the marines stripped him, leaving only a cloth tied around the loins. They tied his body to a wall and leaned beside it a flagpole bearing his caco banner. Then they photographed the corpse and disseminated the pictures. The grisly photograph, which to some suggested Christ crucified, only heightened his reputation as a martyr. The insurrection he had begun continued through the year and into the next. The guard—ill-equipped, poorly trained, and frankly not trusted by the Americans—could not suppress it. Before the revolt ran its course, the marines would kill 3,250 Haitians, in a manner unpleasantly reminiscent of the suppression of Filipino rebels a generation before.[23]

The Military Government of the Dominican Republic

The origins of the Dominican occupation of 1916 lay in the customs receivership established by Roosevelt in 1905, which was formalized in the Dominican-American convention of 1907. That agreement presumably satisfied the republic's European creditors by obligating the United States to segregate 55 percent of the customs duties in order to reduce the external debt. In the ensuing years the financial and political prospects in the republic improved, but after Roosevelt's departure from office and the shooting of President Cáceres in 1911, the Dominican situation deteriorated. Intensely rival political elements vied for office, and with each short-lived presidency the national treasury was gutted to pay bribes, suborn political enemies, and purchase loyalty.

The problem worsened when Taft and Knox—both of whom looked on the republic as an example of an American-guided, enlightened society—interpreted prior commitments as justification for interfering in the republic's internal politics. When the Wilson administration inherited Taft's policy, it expanded American responsibility to include, among other things, a requirement that the ensuing Dominican presidential election be conducted under American rules and that the new Dominican executive accept specified financial and military reforms. In May 1916 troops were landed to protect the legation from disorderly elements and to prevent General Desiderio Arias, whom the Department of State had identified as a troublemaker, from seizing power. Marine detachments also moved against Arias sympathizers in the north. When the Dominican president persisted in his refusal to acquiesce in all the American demands for internal reform, Wilson accepted Lansing's recommendation for military occupation.

Even in the most generous assessments the society over which Captain Harry Knapp proclaimed martial law in late November 1916 would have been called "backward." Though twice the size of neighboring Haiti and five times larger than Puerto Rico, the Dominican Republic in 1916 had only 750,000 people, approximately half the population in each of the other two. Yet its obvious potential prompted Otto Schoenrich, a perceptive critic of the occupation, to title his history of the republic *Santo Domingo: A Country with a Future*. Its commercial prospects, for example, had improved every year since 1905, but a history of disorderly politics, Schoenrich concluded, had impeded economic progress. Even the national capital of Santo Domingo had become a monument to neglect and vandalism amidst the scars of battle.[24]

Initially the American proconsuls were concerned about the practical difficulties of assuming power over a government that continued to function, albeit haphazardly. Knapp's proclamation reaffirmed Dominican sovereignty, recognized most Dominican laws, and stated that administration of law would continue under "such duly authorized Dominican officials as may be necessary," subject to the military government's approval. By Knapp's characterization those Dominican leaders who protested the occupation were "unpatriotic" and therefore unfit to serve in the military government. His prohibition of any Dominicans serving as ministers in War and Marine or Interior (which were both assigned to marine officers) further antagonized leading Dominican politicians, for it denied Dominican nationals high-level participation in the two most sensitive and, in view of the goals of the occupation in the countryside, the two most important posts in the government. When the Dominican president abandoned his office, his associates left with him. Their abrupt departure, though at first irritating, proved fortuitous for Knapp's 1917 governmental reorganization and made easier his decision to suspend elections for the national assembly.[25]

The first Americans brought with them a sense of dedication coupled with dismay at Dominican conditions and at Dominicans who had allowed such conditions to exist. Samuel Guy Inman toured both Haiti and the Dominican Republic on behalf of a missionary society and returned to the United States convinced that practically everything was wrong. The Dominican Republic, he wrote, had virtually no public sanitation; the population was 90 percent illiterate; the lack of roads allowed for little overland communication, so as to create, in effect, "two countries." Disease, especially venereal disease, was epidemic. American observers tended to blame these conditions on the inequities between town and country. In Cuba, Leonard Wood had concentrated on cleaning up the cities, but his counterparts in the Dominican Republic concentrated on rural areas. Dominican urbanites, a naval intelligence officer wrote, had all the money but were fascinated with politics and the pursuit of office for gain. In the countryside lived the truly needy, the illegitimate progeny of Spanish, Indian, Negro, and French parentage. Ignorant but kind, the Dominican peasant desperately needed social and educational guidance, modern roads, and justice.[26]

Of all the republic's troubles, the one that made an orderly life the most difficult for its rural citizens was the existence of bandit gangs. These armed bands, usually numbering a few dozen men, operated mostly in the remote eastern districts; since the death of Cáceres in 1911, they had increased rapidly. In American eyes these bands constituted a social scourge; when not employed by some political malefactor, they harassed the sugar plantations, compelling owners to hire their own private armies. A few, such as the bandit leader Vicentico Evangelista, were romanticized as folk heroes and dedicated nationalists defending the country against a foreign invader. The fact that rural people were reluctant to offer information about bandit activities gave credence to their image as popular defenders of the republic's sovereignty. Marine assessments did not portray banditry as necessarily and solely a criminal activity; rather, they were *gavilleros* (highwaymen), disenchanted politicians, unemployed workers, forcibly recruited country people, and common criminals.

The military government, which looked upon banditry as symptomatic of the republic's political malaise, was not content with dispersing the bandits or arresting their leaders. On his first day in office Knapp issued an executive order prohibiting the carrying of firearms or other lethal weapons. In most military occupations such decrees were common, but in the Dominican Republic the rule had a special significance, for the carrying of a firearm had historically been looked upon as a rite of manhood and a necessity for personal safety. ("Two revolutions ago," went an old proverb uttered by a Dominican woman, "my son took a gun and went into politics.") As one marine commented, the country seemed "virtually an armed garrison." By mid-1922, when the provisional government took over, the marines and the Dominican National Guard had collected 53,000 firearms, 200,000 rounds of ammunition, and 14,000 "cutting" weapons from a population of 750,000.[27]

A reformed and independent judiciary represented in American assessment a fundamental prerequisite to a free society. Similarly, fair enforcement of the law could be guaranteed only if the old, politicized Guardia Republicana were replaced by a modern, efficient, and apolitical national police force, the Guardia Nacional. The order creating the Dominican National Guard was issued in April 1917 and called for the expenditure of $500,000, a considerable portion of the annual budget, to equip and maintain a constabulary to replace the old military. Dominicans were welcome if they had "clean records," but Knapp emphasized that commanders would be "Americans of strong character." By October the guard had 21 American and 17 Dominican officers, and 691 enlistees, though it should be pointed out that the European war drew so heavily on officer contingents in both the

Dominican Republic and Haiti that these American officers were in most cases corporals and sergeants granted officer status in the guard.

The government assigned the guard considerable authority and declared that resistance to it would be viewed as a hostile act meriting trial before a military tribunal. It is clear from the record that Knapp was concerned not only with the preservation of order but with instilling in the guard a sense of professionalism and "unimpeachable conduct." As he explained to Colonel Joseph H. Pendleton, marine commander in the republic until 1918, the guardsmen "will not hold their positions because the Dominicans want them but rather in spite of that, and . . . tact and courteous though firm treatment will help, while roughness and strong-armed methods will hinder their immediate usefulness and . . . will cast discredit upon their own country."

Once created, however, the organization became something of a problem to manage; by 1919, for example, cost of recruitment and maintenance annually siphoned off more than 25 percent of the occupation budget. Training of recruits, especially of officers, proved woefully inadequate, though this problem was mitigated by the creation in 1921 of Haina Military Academy. (Within a year it graduated 800 Dominican officers and enlisted men, including Rafael Leonidas Trujillo, Jr.) Training was also impeded by American determination to make the guard something of a social experiment. American supervisors saw the guard as a socially equalizing body, giving a Dominican recruit a sense of status and social advancement and at the same time educating him in the larger, national needs of the republic. For this reason, the guard intentionally stationed recruits in unfamiliar parts of the country, away from their own villages.[28]

More lasting achaievements came in the public sector. After ratification of the convention of 1907 the United States had insisted on the creation of a Dominican department of public works, which would expend a stipulated portion of revenue on public improvement. Its activity had declined considerably during the political troubles of the post-Cáceres years. Knapp decided to revive it.

The road system was a national disgrace. In 1916 the republic possessed only about 65 kilometers of good roads; the remainder were little more than wagon trails, impassable in the rainy season, yet these offered the only overland communication between interior towns. By 1921 the military government had macadamized 150 kilometers of first-class highways and had graded 450 kilometers of second- and third-class roads. Another major carrier, a government-owned railroad from Puerto Plata to Moca, had fallen on hard times. Knapp ordered the track repaired and the rolling stock overhauled; after mid-1917 it functioned superbly and ran on time. In another move, the military government took telephones and telegraph communication from private companies and operated both as government enterprises.

The American proconsuls found the education system in deplorable shape and soon began to reform it. On the eve of the occupation the number of pupils in school was 18,000; for their education the Dominican government had failed to provide a single public schoolhouse and had instead rented space in privately owned buildings. The elite sent their children to private academies.

In early 1917 Knapp named a committee of Dominicans to study the state of education; its report recommended a radical overhaul. The Dominican superintendent of education was fired for being "without proper balance, full of theoretical ideas [and] grandiloquent conversation." As Wood had stressed in Cuba in 1900, an educational structure patterned on cultural traditions rather than on basic academic and vocational skills hardly suited a people not yet ready for the twentieth century. So, the military government suppressed one of the two so-called universities and concentrated on primary and secondary schools, and especially on education in rural areas. The reformers used the American model and curricula, requiring attendance from ages seven through thirteen, prohibiting religious instruction, political propaganda, or the "teaching of doctrines contrary to good morals or patriotic traditions." In the 700 elementary schools established by 1918, pupils went to class four hours a day, five days a week, ten months a year. This was followed by a two-year course in a "superior elementary" program. Two public high schools, boasting a curriculum in languages, mathematics, physical and natural sciences, history, social science, commerce, and drawing, were established in Santo Domingo and Santiago. Two normal schools supplied the republic's teachers. At the apex stood the Central University and its faculty of law, medicine, pharmacy, mathematics, dentistry, obstetrics, and notaries. Compared with previous efforts, the educational mission looked impressive on paper and even excited some of the occupation's severest critics. There were few frills. The mission was the eradication of illiteracy, as one observer wrote, for "a democracy can be maintained only on an intelligent public opinion."[29]

At the same time the military government moved to clean up the cities, disinfect public places, and inoculate the masses. The initial measures of 1917 called for street cleaning, garbage removal, and installation of latrines. The next year the government removed sanitary supervision entirely from the old Dominican boards of health and created a Department of Sanitation and Beneficence charged with the enforcement of a new sanitary law. The agency exercised jurisdiction over disease control; regulated food, drink, and drugs where they affected public health; approved for habitation all public places, hotels, boarding houses, and private dwellings; inspected all waste disposal facilities; required vaccination; and outlawed prostitution. To enforce its mandate, the department organized forty local health councils and twelve sanitary brigades.

The military introduced fiscal integrity to a degree unknown to previous Dominican governments, accustomed to playing politics with the national treasury. Knapp went so far as to pay back salaries to deserving employees of the preceding government. A claims commission was established to deal with $12 million in claims against preceding governments. Since the military government viewed itself as acting for the legal government of the republic, the payment of such claims was considered an act of faith. In 1918 the commission scaled down the claims to $5 million, then proceeded to sell bonds, guaranteed by customs receipts, to cover payment. (This created a legal problem, for the 1907 convention forbade the republic from unilaterally altering the document to extend the life of the customs receivership. After months of wrangling with the legal advisor in the State Department, the military government finally released the bonds, though it had to cover payment by increasing the public debt.)[30]

Such problems endangered the military government's mission to instruct Dominicans in the fine art of balancing budgets. Its work was hampered further by the postwar depression, which severely curtailed public works projects, forced the closing of some schools, and compelled the government to fire 60 percent of its employees. By 1920 the dispute between the Navy and the State Department over extension of the occupation had already flared into open quarreling between two bureaucratic elements. Daniels, for the Navy, argued that the rehabilitation begun in 1916 must continue and that State should be more liberal in approving financial assistance to a government led by American military personnel carrying out a mission planned by civilians. Secretary of State Bainbridge Colby contended that the occupation would probably terminate much sooner than anyone had foreseen and, therefore, it would be unwise to saddle future Dominican governments with new debts. In the senatorial investigation of 1921–22, both Dominican and American critics charged that deficits under the military government were higher than those of pre-1916 governments. This was believable if one looked at those budgets in the last years of the occupation, when the military government worked frantically to complete several important public works projects. In 1917 and 1918, however, the budget was balanced and the treasury had a surplus.

Though Knapp censored the press and forbade the selling of "incendiary" literature, the censorship restrictions did not become an embarrassing issue until about 1920, after the Wilson administration had indicated its willingness to terminate the occupation. This naturally encouraged Dominican and American critics to step up their activities. The outcome was a tragicomic series of press problems; Knapp's successor responded with an unnecessarily restrictive decree forbidding publication of anything advocating Bolshevism, counseling the violent overthrow of the military government, containing phrases designed to inflame or incite the public, or misrepresenting conditions in the republic so as to "incite unrest, disorder, or revolt." A supplementary clause guaranteed the right of assembly and free speech. In one confrontation the government ordered the arrest of a prominent Dominican poet and editor, Fabio Fiallo, for allegedly inciting riot by writing and publishing abusive antioccupation verse. Fiallo was eventually released on bail, but the photograph of one of the republic's most distinguished literary figures clothed in striped prison garb was a source of national shame and distress. Even Daniels thought the military had overreacted, and he tried to temper its pol-

icy. Generally, the idiotic censorship rulings of the military government damaged its reputation, not only in the republic but throughout
the hemisphere.[31]

Nicaragua: Client State

In 1912 the determination of the United States to quell General
Mena's revolt assured Adolfo Díaz that he would continue as president of the republic. The arrangements designed by Knox and a
gaggle of New York bankers to redeem Nicaragua's financial condition had run afoul of senatorial suspicion. Wilson and Bryan inherited a Nicaraguan policy shaped by Roosevelt and Root and
modified by Taft and Knox. They could repudiate, modify, or continue it.

For all their complaints about dollar diplomacy, Wilson and Bryan
chose not to scuttle that policy in Nicaragua. From the beginning, they
were confronted with importunate pleas from Díaz for money. To
this end the Nicaraguan president had negotiated in the closing days
of Taft's presidency a treaty (the Chamorro-Weitzel Treaty) providing $3 million to the distressed country and a guarantee of its inde-
pendence in return for an option to construct a canal. Weitzel had
defended the pact as a means of securing the Panamanian canal
route, as well as of guaranteeing the peace of the Isthmus. In acquiring the canal option, the United States gained the right to build a
naval station on the Gulf of Fonseca and the cession of the Great and
Little Corn islands. On one of the islands it might build still another
base.[32]

Nicaragua desperately needed that $3 million and more; it had out-
standing debts estimated at $11.5 million. It owed to the Ethelburga
syndicate of London an additional $6.2 million and to New York
bankers, $750,000. It had to meet $1.5 million for salaries, supplies,
and miscellaneous expenses and another $3 million in accumulated
claims for property damage.

As Bryan studied Nicaragua's financial conundrum, he was also
made aware of two troublesome political realities. The first was the
joint protests of El Salvador and Costa Rica against the proposed

treaty. Costa Rica shared a portion of the San Juan River, which would be one section of the canal route, as its border with Nicaragua; El Salvador contended that the proposed naval site in the Gulf of Fonseca, though lying in Nicaraguan national waters, endangered its security. The second problem involved Díaz's unceasing insistence that the two countries move quickly in ratifying the treaty despite the legal question and the more unsettling political problems created by its negotiation. To facilitate matters he suggested incorporating into the treaty a provision similar to the Platt Amendment. Bryan agreed, to the chagrin of Nicaragua's neighbors and to the dismay of the Senate. This feature, so quickly introduced by Díaz, was quietly dropped.

Another treaty (the Bryan-Chamorro Treaty) was drawn up in August 1914, but it contained no Platt Amendment. With it the United States obtained its canal option, and Nicaragua, presumably, its money, but in the process Root's labors to build Central American harmony and mutual respect between the two republics were destroyed. The former secretary of state, now in the Senate, expressed incredulity that the United States would sign a pact with a government hardly representative of its people and most certainly unmindful of the wishes and interests of its neighbors. For a year and a half the Bryan-Chamorro Treaty languished in the Senate. It finally received approval in February 1916 with the stipulation that the rights of El Salvador, Costa Rica, and Honduras, which also protested the naval cession on the Gulf of Fonseca, were not to be affected by the treaty's provisions.

In Nicaragua the treaty received the expected approval of the national assembly. Costa Rica, Honduras, and El Salvador took their case to the Central American Court of Justice, which, in two decisions, declared against Nicaragua but also stated that it possessed no jurisdiction over the American government. Neither Nicaragua nor the United States appeared troubled by the court's announcement, though the American Peace Society condemned its own government. The court soon disbanded, its prestige irreparably damaged by the very country which, a decade before, had presided over its creation.[33]

Concurrently the bankers had expanded their influence over Nicaraguan finances. One purpose of the Knox-Castrillo convention had been the transfer of the bulk of Nicaragua's external debt from European to American bankers, so as to avoid political complications if default occurred. At least this was Taft's reasoning. When the Senate failed to pass the treaty, the bankers went ahead with a $1.5 million loan, pending further consideration. At the same time the bankers lent their services to sorely needed currency reform, to be carried out by the newly created National Bank of Nicaragua. Madriz and Estrada, in their desperation to survive politically, had flooded the country with paper money. Counterfeit bills also circulated. In 1912 the bank hired two financial experts to work out a scheme whereby the national monetary unit, the *córdoba*, would be assigned a value equal to one American gold dollar. This conversion was honestly handled, but a few knowledgeable Nicaraguans made a killing by buying the old, cheaper currency, then selling it to the government at a higher rate.

The banks also renegotiated Zelaya's infamous debt to the Ethelburga syndicate at a rate favorable to Nicaragua. A customs collectorship guaranteed repayment. In December 1911 Clifford Ham, Manila port surveyor, became collector-general of Nicaraguan customs and instituted an austere, paternalistic supervision. His function was simple: he collected revenue at the source and transferred the money to American bankers, who in turn paid off Nicaragua's creditors.[34]

The degree to which Nicaraguan politics reflected American values was never more evident than in 1916 when the country "chose" a new president. Díaz, admittedly, had stayed in power because of the marine legation guard. Four years after the troubles of 1912, the prevailing opinion in the Latin American division of the State Department was that the marines hurt the American image in Nicaragua. The republic deserved free elections. Díaz frankly opposed this course, for he feared the triumph of his opponents. (In an effort to undermine them he had declared a state of siege, which discouraged political gatherings.) When the American minister raised old objections over participation in the elections by Zelayistas, Lansing, with Wilson's presumed blessing, decided that the most expedient plan lay in supporting Emiliano Chamorro for president.

In 1912 Chamorro had been dissuaded from running by the American minister, George Weitzel. Now Chamorro appeared to be the most popular Conservative in Nicaragua, and as minister to the United States, he had acquitted himself well with the Department of State. In Managua the leading candidates busied themselves trying to discern American attitudes. When Chamorro returned from Washington aboard an American warship, their question was answered; but Díaz, having already given his blessing to a subordinate, was at first annoyed. The American minister of 1916 momentarily appeared to lose his customary control over Nicaraguan political affairs, but the arrival of two warships in Corinto restored his prestige: Díaz declared in favor of Chamorro; the Liberals virtually retired from the contest and exhorted their adherents to abstain from voting. Chamorro won in what the American minister officially described as a "quiet" election.

Chamorro inherited a virtually bankrupt government, with some $500,000 in back salaries due immediately. As he bemoaned his country's financial plight in the afterglow of political triumph, the State Department and interested New York investors wrangled over the republic's economic condition. At a meeting in mid-December 1916, they decided the financial fate of Nicaragua. It could not meet its external nor its internal obligations; its debts had to be scaled down and refunded, and it needed a new financial advisor. To soothe Chamorro the department authorized an advance of $250,000 from the canal treaty payment. This would allow Chamorro to survive a few months. But to Lansing's consternation, Chamorro became defiant, instigating violent anti-American newspaper accounts about the bankers' alleged shenanigans in the country. He vowed to take over the customshouses unless the republic received its canal money. After his anger cooled, he acquiesced in the plan for an American commissioner who would cooperate with Nicaragua's minister of finance and an umpire (chosen by the American secretary of state) who would supervise the budget. After providing a stipulated amount for government services, the commissioners would allocate equal portions of the remainder to debt retirement and public works. With these reforms the State Department obligingly released the $3 million of the treaty, but five-sixths of the sum went to the republic's creditors and to payment of claims. Nicaragua, for all its strenuous efforts to exact these funds, got exactly $500,000, to meet current obligations and pay back salaries.[35]

The Protectorate Era: An Assessment

One ironic characteristic of Wilsonianism often noted by contemporary critics and scholars was Wilson's adherence to republican philosophy even though he was unable to tolerate the often violent means by which republican governments obtained power. In Mexico particularly, he failed to perceive how, ultimately, an orderly, progressive rule might emerge from chaos. In the Caribbean world his policies represented a distortion of the measures initiated by Roosevelt—measures designed to ensure against European encroachment into the American Mediterranean by the use of limited financial controls, as in the Dominican Republic, or the application of treaty law, as in Central America. Theodore Roosevelt may have been a Protestant contemptuous of Catholic societies, but he certainly was no Protestant missionary bent on reforming them.

The case of the Tinoco revolt in Costa Rica is illustrative of the protectorate system's limitations. Costa Rica had enjoyed the most stable political rule in the Caribbean. In 1917, following three years of political wrangling and public commotion over the unorthodox manner by which the president had been selected, the minister of war, Federico Tinoco, suddenly overthrew his president in a coup d'état. Though he had gained power in obvious violation of the 1907 treaties, Tinoco was undoubtedly a popular leader. But the Department of State, shocked by the suddenness of Tinoco's seizure of power, rejected any notion of accommodation to a popular government and hinted darkly that the coup might have been instigated by the United Fruit Company. The company duly received warnings emphasizing Wilson's disapproval and implying that any cooperation with Tinoco would be viewed disfavorably. Tinoco's pro-Allied sentiments apparently counted little in Wilson's judgment, though Lansing, in this instance, disagreed with the president.

The other Central American republics were told that recognition of Tinoco would incur United States disapproval, but all save Nicaragua did so. Lacking American recognition, however, Tinoco stood little chance of survival. In Costa Rica his policies became more heavy-handed as he suppressed the inevitable revolutionary movements. In the summer of 1919 the entire country was swept with violent demonstrations, and other isthmian governments were now willing to countenance intervention. On 12 August, following the assassination of his brother on a San José street, Federico Tinoco quickly resigned and left the country. Wilson remained uncompromising to the end, and in the aftermath of Tinoco's precipitate resignation, insisted that prescribed constitutional procedures be followed in naming Tinoco's successor.[36]

An obvious flaw in American policy was the ineffectiveness of non-recognition as a device for discouraging revolutionary activity by preventing the successful revolutionary, once ensconced in power, from enjoying international acceptance. Since 1907 the United States had supported the Tobar doctrine, which called for nonrecognition of coup d'état governments, to achieve political order in Central America. Yet it had been the United States, in its zeal to purge Nicaragua of Zelaya's influence, which had so severely damaged the Tobar doctrine as to render it ineffectual. Thus in Honduras, in the political turbulence of 1919, a determined and powerful revolutionary movement gained control by ousting an ineffective constitutional government, in defiance of the 1907 treaties. In the end the State Department recognized the new regime, following its qualified endorsement of free elections. In the elections the provisional president won a decisive victory and, in the analysis of the department, thereby legitimized his rule.

Similarly, in neighboring Guatemala, the aging and enfeebled dictator Manuel Estrada Cabrera confronted increasingly more outspoken and defiant opposition in 1919. When he threatened to suppress unionist adversaries by the simple expedient of executing them, the department condemned his arbitrariness while simultaneously professing disinterest in Guatemala's internal affairs! As the president moved to crush the opposition, a defiant national assembly declared him insane. A new government was quickly installed, technically in accord with constitutional precepts though, as in Honduras, in an irregular manner.[37]

If the policy of ensuring political stability proved in time to be ineffective unless backed by force or the threat of force, American policy had unquestionably altered the thinking of a generation of Caribbean politicians. In the two decades spanning Roosevelt's accession to office and Wilson's retirement, Caribbean political figures matured and acclimated themselves to the realities of American power. They became attuned to, and in some cases anticipated, American wishes and judgments. If out of power, like the Cuban rebels in 1905, they learned how to exploit American sentiment and precipitate American action by condemning the party in power and openly championing American intervention. If in power, like the Nicaraguan Conservatives after 1912, they learned how to plant in impressionable minds the fear of disorder and disruption, which required a statement of support or, better, a show of force by American naval vessels to perpetuate what was casually called constitutional government. In later years, following the repudiation of the Roosevelt corollary, Caribbean dictators learned well the art of ruling firmly while soliciting the goodwill of the United States.

The economic impact on these societies over two decades cannot be precisely measured. Contrary to Marxian analysis the dollar did not automatically follow the flag. In Cuba, doubtless, the intrusion of American capital served to create what could properly be called a marketplace economy, but in other Caribbean countries where the United States exercised considerable political influence, the amount of private American investment was significantly less than American capital in Cuba. It is true that New York bankers virtually ran Nicaragua by their control of the National Bank and the railroad, but by 1920 both were returned to Nicaraguan supervision. Still, these banks, by virtue of existing loans, continued to wield influence over their operation.

In a material way the United States left its mark in the Caribbean in public works, particularly in the impressive accomplishments in road construction, sanitary improvements, and public health measures. Dilapidated railroads, sometimes unused for years or poorly managed, were taken over by American supervisors and repaired. The roads constructed by conscript Haitians, while being cursed and maltreated, linked the republic's towns and villages and permitted, for the first time in Haitian history, unimpeded highway travel from Port-au-Prince to Cap Haïtien. The health codes instituted by the Americans brought a modicum of relief to peoples long accustomed to annual bouts with one debilitating tropical malady after another. The suppression of banditry in Haiti and the Dominican Republic, though accomplished with occasional brutality, inaugurated peace in the countryside unknown to generations of farmers.

Yet for all these accomplishments the protectorate system failed to instill democratic virtues or to commit Caribbean governments to orderly, progressive rule. In not a few instances the legacy of American rule was unmitigated hatred of the United States. A vitriolic anti-Americanism flourished in Caribbean literature. In Cuba, American materialism prevailed, reinforced daily in newspaper and magazine advertisements for an array of American goods and in the tawdry atmosphere of Havana night life. Later generations of idealistic young Cubans would feel, alternately, admiration for American technical and material achievements and shame at their reliance on the United States. Therein lay the problem: the Americans came to democratize and uplift, yet in the process they expressed their contempt for Caribbean politics, economic systems, and culture.

Part II
Between Two Wars

4 • A Reassessment of Empire, 1921–1925

Warren Gamaliel Harding was not inclined to profundity, but during the campaign of 1920 he commented on the hypocrisy of seeking to instill democratic values among Caribbean societies by bayonet rule. His observation had been provoked by an impromptu boast of the Democratic vice-presidential nominee, Franklin D. Roosevelt, who stated, erroneously, that as assistant secretary of the navy he had contributed to Caribbean political development by his authorship of the 1918 Haitian constitution.

In such divergence of views one might have anticipated that Harding and Secretary of State Charles Evans Hughes would repudiate intervention and the protectorate system. Harding and his two Republican successors did not reject the doctrine of intervention, but they subtly modified Caribbean policy. They privately questioned the utility of the Roosevelt Corollary, the political and legal basis of the protectorate system, yet proudly reaffirmed the Monroe Doctrine. In Central America they sought stability by promoting cooperation and a new treaty system, only to witness the disintegration of that system and the resurgence of political violence. But, unlike the Wilsonians, who believed in teaching by example, the Republicans proved more skeptical of military governments established in the Dominican Republic and Haiti, though the Haitian experiment, for special reasons, endured the decade. Hughes emphasized more than his Democratic predecessors his conviction that American intentions must be explained in the Pan American conferences.[1] The decade witnessed two such conferences in the regular series, at Santiago de Chile in 1923, and at Havana in 1928. At both, the United States entered its classic defense on behalf of peace, stability, and political order, which in Hughes's mind were principles firmly based in international law. In the course of the twenties the United States would sign numerous arbitration and conciliation treaties with hemispheric republics, by which, it was hoped in Washington, perennially explosive disputes could be peacefully settled.

In their reassessment of policy the Republicans would increasingly interpret private loans to Caribbean governments as economic rather than political matters. In the ten years since Knox's misadventures in dollar diplomacy in Central America, the Department of State had played a critical financial role by its aggressive promotion of lending schemes. During the war American investors had replaced their European counterparts as lenders to Caribbean governments, with the Wilson administration alert to the impact this policy would have on American political interests. After the war, when money was more plentiful and resulted in a borrower's market, the department's interest in private loans to Caribbean governments waned. In March 1922 it announced that henceforth it would not assess the merits of those private contracts. American bankers continued to lend money to harassed Caribbean countries, but dollar diplomacy now became, to borrow Herbert Feis's apt phrase, the "diplomacy of the dollar."[2]

But diplomacy of the dollar and the 1922 statement on loans did not mean the United States would relinquish its self-appointed role as tutor of impoverished and improvident Caribbean governments. It continued to impart advice and strove, wherever possible, to discourage private loans for what it considered inappropriate ventures, such as expenditures for armaments or for balancing budgets in countries lacking sufficient revenue. Similarly, the department discouraged loans to unrecognized governments or to governments which had not fulfilled their obligations to the United States.[3]

Thus, what occurred was not a reversal but a shift in policy. In any event the department angered both lenders and recipients. Private funds poured into the Cuban sugar industry and into a corrupt public works system sustained by Cuban president Gerardo Machado despite the Platt Amendment's provision for close supervision of the Cuban budget by the United States. In 1922 the American government, in an act of unappreciated paternalism, antagonized both Guatemalan borrowers and their New York creditors by blocking a loan designed for questionable financial reforms. As the decade progressed, and as bankers and their Caribbean debtors grew increasingly resentful of meddling, the department's commitment to benevolent oversight of private loans diminished.[4]

The Dominican and Haitian Protectorates

On the island of Hispaniola in 1915 the United States had undertaken two interventions which culminated in an outright military government in the Dominican Republic and a civilian regime closely supervised by American naval officers in Haiti. At the close of the war opposition to both occupations increased, sustained by Caribbean nationalistic political enemies and publicized in the United States by such magazines as the *Nation*, the *New Republic*, and *Current History*.[5] In mid-1921 a special Senate committee began investigating charges of atrocities against Haitian peasants and Dominican political prisoners.

Plans for withdrawal from the Dominican Republic were initiated in the closing months of the Wilson administration. In 1919 the State and Navy departments had thrashed out their differences over the length of the occupation, with Daniels and the Navy losing in their contention that the military government should continue. As Secretary of State Colby explained, the process of Dominican withdrawal would be in graduated steps, beginning with the military governor's appointment of a Dominican commission to study those pre-1916 problems that had brought about the occupation and also to propose corrective legislation. Lamentably, this plan failed to generate much enthusiasm among prominent Dominicans, who, understandably, simply wanted the Americans to leave their country.

Following Harding's inauguration Dominican critics of the occupation, aware of the president's campaign jibes at the military government, anticipated a speedy dismantling of the protectorate. Their expectations proved premature, for Harding and Hughes moved slowly. In April 1921 Sumner Welles, who more than anyone in the State Department could be called the architect of America's Caribbean policy during the next two decades, presented Hughes with a plan for Dominican withdrawal similar to Colby's scheme of 1920. In it, Welles requested Dominican approval for the acts of the military government, continued American training of the Dominican national guard, American financial supervision over customs collections and government expenditures, and the right to intervene to insure orderly government. Striking out the clauses pertaining to American intervention or supervision of the Dominican budget, Hughes then accepted Welles's draft. In June the plan was announced in Santo Domingo.[6]

Despite Hughes's modifications the plan was greeted in the republic by a scathing denunciation from the more outspoken Dominicans. The furor stemmed partly from the natural inclination to demand complete evacuation with no restrictive clauses and partly from the hostility between leading Dominican politicians and the military governor, Admiral Samuel S. Robison. The Navy had not remained silent during these deliberations over Dominican affairs; and Robison had worsened things by casual comments about grumbling, ungrateful, and trouble-making Dominicans. A new election was postponed. Henríquez y Carvajal, something of a martyr since his ouster in 1916 by Captain Knapp, circulated in Washington during 1921 discussing Dominican affairs with American officials. Rumor had it that he told Dominican confidants to hold out for an agreement free of restrictions.

Dominicans also awaited revelations from the special Senate investigating committee to both Port-au-Prince and Santo Domingo. In the Dominican capital it had listened to a succession of Dominican politicians and supporters of the deposed Henríquez relate the details of the 1916 takeover and had also heard disquieting stories of marine atrocities. In the eastern portion of the island, especially around Hato Mayor, marine patrols had encountered fierce resistance from bandits. In exasperation, and in some instances in retaliation, they had become heavy-handed in dealing with captured bandits or gun-toting young Dominicans. One marine officer, a noncom promoted to captain, had been charged with particularly cruel acts, but while awaiting trial he had killed himself with a revolver left in his cell by two interrogators. Little detail of these atrocities, however, appeared in the Senate hearings or in its published report. Most of the testimony related to Haiti, where stories of marine brutalities had been much more widely circulated.[7]

Dominican rejection of the 1922 proclamation left the State Department somewhat disheartened. Among military officers in the republic, it confirmed pessimistic presumptions about working with local politicians in the transfer of power; and with slightly concealed satisfaction, Robison announced, in early March 1922, continuation of the military government until July 1924. Two more years of the occupation would provide, the military believed, ample time for completion of public works programs, particularly the much-publicized north-south highway. (It opened in May 1922.) The military government issued $6.7 million in bonds, underwritten by Lee Higginson and Company, permitting the settlement of outstanding debts. (Significantly, the 1918 bonds, whose issuance had aroused Dominican condemnations about financial burdens in the republic's future, were not redeemed.)

Matters might have been left thus for some time had it not been for informal discussions between Welles and Francisco Peynado, a prominent Dominican attorney and member of the defunct Dominican commission. Both Welles and Hughes were convinced that the occupation should be ended as soon as possible. Peynado made clear what Dominicans would and would not settle for in any withdrawal agreement. The postoccupation republic would tolerate a customs receivership and even assume the financial burden of the most recent loan, but it wanted neither a military mission nor a legation guard on the Nicaraguan model. With subtle persuasion, Hughes argued, Dominicans might be willing to accept the Guardia Nacional, which, though an American creation, stood nonetheless as the one element preventing the resurgence of two old maladies in the republic's troubled history, banditry and private armies.[8]

Once more Welles proposed a plan of evacuation. This time he insured participation by leading Dominican politicians representing various political alliances and obtained their approval of the plan before any formal announcement. Under the new arrangement a provisional government would be created to assist the military government during transition to the new order. The military would relinquish various executive departments to Dominicans, but the military governor would still supervise expenditures. American military forces would regroup in three encampments, leaving to the Dominican national guard the policing of the country. Following a constitutional convention (which had to ratify the acts of the military government), new elections for the presidency would be held. After the new president's inauguration, American troops would depart the country.

Welles arrived in Santo Domingo anticipating a prolonged argument with the Dominicans. He soon discovered his most outspoken critic was Admiral Robison, who resented not being consulted about the provisions before the proclamation and disliked limiting his forces to not more than three camps. Other than this minor brouhaha, things went smoothly. The Dominican commission, working with a career State Department official and not with an American naval officer, proved cooperative. In October 1922 a provisional president was sworn in. To impress upon Dominicans that the military was not closely supervising political affairs, the admiral left town two weeks before the inauguration. Censorship of the press was lifted. As if to signal a new day in Dominican-American relations, Robison relinquished the governorship to Harry Lee, a career marine officer, who became the fourth and final American military governor of the republic.[9]

No sooner had Welles departed the capital than the old political animosities, which had plagued the pre-1916 republic, were revived in an acrimonious race for the presidency. Reports about smuggled arms, imported for a showdown, circulated. Peynado closeted himself with that old bête noire of the State Department, Desiderio Arias. The bickering disturbed Welles, who momentarily silenced the rivals with a warning that such behavior would only prolong the occupation. He soon wearied watching Dominican politicians quarrel over spoils of office, and sadly concluded that few, if any, were really fit for office. Given such somber judgments about the politics of a Caribbean society, it is easy to see how, later, even thoughtful and knowledgeable American observers, tired of the internal commotions and self-seeking opportunists that they believed infested the banana republics, would accept and even tolerate a Trujillo, Batista, or Somoza.

At last the maneuvering factions quieted, and a coalition settled on sixty-four-year-old Horacio Vásquez, assassin of the dictator Heureaux in 1899 and patron of the *horacistas*, as its presidential choice. Under the agreement the acts of the military government were ratified, and the remaining troops departed. Plans for keeping some officers to train the guard went awry when the Americans announced they would not take orders from a Dominican. In a new treaty the republic formally agreed to continue the customs receivership instituted two decades before by Theodore Roosevelt.

Of the two occupations, Haiti provoked more journalistic and political interest, and in the senatorial inquiry of 1921–22 the Haitian experiment received far more attention. This imbalance was explainable partly by the Senate's desire to avoid embarrassing the Harding administration in its negotiations with Dominican leaders. It was also partly due to the notoriety surrounding American rule in the black republic, a subject that was injected into the 1920 campaign. After Marine Corps commandant George Barnett alluded to "indiscriminate killings" in a published report, charges of American atrocities against helpless Haitians spread. Tinged with a racist theme, these accusations were picked up by the press, which, paradoxically, had supported both occupations at first, quietly forgotten them during the war, and then rediscovered the story of American imperial rule in the Caribbean in the aftermath of the Versailles peace conference and the fight over the League of Nations. Most marine officers serving in Haiti, it was charged, were white Southerners who enjoyed torturing and even killing Haitians. In tones less than strident but certainly zealous, Ernest Gruening and Oswald Garrison Villard reported Haitian horror stories in the columns of the *Nation*. James Weldon Johnson, the black literary figure, visited Haiti in early 1920 to urge Haitians to organize against the occupation.[10]

Yet, for all the attention focused on Haiti during and after the campaign of 1920, the senatorial investigation proved anticlimactic and failed to serve the cause of Haitian withdrawal. Three members of the special committee—Medill McCormick, the chairman; Tasker Oddie; and Atlee Pomerene—actually went to Port-au-Prince, heard the litany of charges, and returned to hear even more condemnations of American imperialism from the Union Patriotique, organized to restore Haitian sovereignty. What McCormick wanted was not termination but reform of the occupation. In his opinion, the United States had blundered in Haiti; the solution, he believed, lay not in leaving but in a thorough reorganization. The committee's report called for a continuation of American rule despite the damning testimony of the hearings.[11]

One new feature in the occupation was the naming of a high commissioner for Haiti, an administrative change that the State Department hoped would mollify the more outspoken Haitian critics. Hughes's first choice for this politically delicate post was none other than Smedley Butler, but the secretary was apparently dissuaded from naming Butler by Dana Gardner Munro, then of the Latin American Affairs Division. The post went instead to John Russell, who, like Butler, thought Haitians inferior but comported himself gracefully with the Haitian elite. A die-hard Georgia segregationist, Russell maintained a color line in Port-au-Prince, but for political reasons occasionally crossed it himself. Under his rule the occupation settled into a somber routine characterized by American manipulation of the treaty services—customs, finance, police, public works, and health. As before, American overseers ruled with compliant Haitians. When President Dartiguenave became obstreperous, he was replaced with the more accommodating Louis Borno, an admirer of the occupation and of Mussolini's fascist experiment in Italy. An elitist, Borno willingly accepted Russell's classification of the ordinary Haitian as ignorant and incapable of self-rule. Withdrawn and acquiescent, Borno rarely failed to perform as Russell expected; when he occasionally resisted American strictures about how to operate the government, the financial advisor straightened out his thinking by the simple expedient of withholding the president's paycheck.[12]

Haiti's foreign debt was now controlled almost exclusively by Americans. During the war the republic had sought loans from several New York bankers, but the proposals fell through when the banks demanded as security American supervision of the republic's finances during the life of the loan. Dartiguenave realized that any refunding scheme would mean a concomitant diminution of Haitian sovereignty. He grew obstinate, defying the financial advisor's warning about sloppy administration; he really wanted to embarrass his American overlords. At one point the military considered approving a loan by decree, but Borno's assumption of the presidency obviated such a severe course. Once the new president consented to the proposed loan, financial reorganization of the country was completed.[13]

As befitted American social standards, the occupiers introduced racial segregation and routinely prohibited or at least discouraged social mixing of the races. The first generation of Marine officers, who had not brought along their wives, had mingled freely with the Haitian elite. At the 1916 ball in the National Palace white American marine officers had danced with Haitian women. The arrival of white women from the United States abruptly changed the more relaxed racial atmosphere of the occupation's early years. Jim Crow edicts flourished. The American Club was declared off limits to all blacks, including the president of the republic. A few white women defied color barriers, and one, Edna Taft, wrote of her experiences in *A Puritan in Voodoo Land*.[14] One marine married Borno's niece and of course "disgraced" the Corps. Proud and sensitive Haitian elitists acquired marked anti-American feelings during these years. So critical were racial factors that diplomatic appointments, until then routinely assigned to blacks, were given only to whites.

Thus, during the occupation the old ruling classes underwent what a modern sociologist would describe as culture shock. The American occupiers despised upper-class Haitians for their antidemocratic, privileged ways; the latter suppressed their hatred of the Americans for the countless racial slurs, the social slights, and the imposition of segregation. They resented being resented. The Haitian commoner acquired, at least for a short time, a certain respect in American eyes, for it was the average Haitian, the American occupiers contended, who was being uplifted and tantalized by gestures of philanthropy and the promise of a better life. The Haitian generation maturing during these years rejected the mulatto elite and its French-like ways but did not adopt the culture of the American newcomers. Instead, it would find its identity in its African heritage, its negritude.[15]

Rejecting American racial beliefs, the generation of the occupation also eschewed such pragmatic values as self-help or faith in material progress. Haitians could admire American technology and engineering as they were applied, for instance, to road construction or sewage disposal, but they seemed unimpressed by "go-getter" exhortations. Peasants lacked proper nutrition, went barefoot, and were deemed sexually promiscuous. Before receiving the vote, wrote the American financial advisor Arthur Millspaugh, Haitians had to be taught the difference between able and incompetent political leaders. Such a view was typical among both Americans and the Haitian elite.

As in the Dominican Republic, the goal of public services during the occupation of Haiti aimed not only at improving the quality of urban life but at uniting city and country in a common support of effective government. The health service, for example, struggled manfully to eradicate malaria, hookworm, and yaws. Naval physicians trained Haitian subordinates to treat tropical maladies. By 1929 Haiti boasted 12 hospitals and 147 rural clinics, which together treated more than one million patients, a tremendous achievement considering the state of medical care in 1915. School children were routinely vaccinated, water supplies chlorinated, streets cleaned, trash collected, slaughterhouses inspected, and latrines constructed.

The occupiers fostered agricultural modernization, prompted fishing and forestry, and encouraged light industry. The agricultural advisor, working with the Service Technique, observed that Haiti imported products Haitian farmers could be taught to grow at home. The main goal was diversification and self-help: Haitians smoked incessantly, so the Service Technique launched a patriotic crusade for more tobacco cultivation. To aid agriculture, the Americans pushed large-scale farming. In the north enormous tracts were leased to the Haitian-American Development Corporation and the Haitian Agricultural Corporation. In one sector, wrote Millspaugh glowingly, an American company, with a thousand Haitian laborers, grew sisal on land which had been uncultivated for a century. To promote rural education the government created sixty-five agricultural schools and a Central School for Agriculture. These were complemented by industrial schools.[16]

The value of these endeavors is still questionable. Doubtless the miniscule Haitian agricultural plots of the old days were unsuitable for modern agricultural techniques. Haitian farmers persisted in tilling the soil with the same crude tools used by their ancestors a century earlier. American technicians in the Service Technique promoted agricultural modernization with religious fervency, but the policy, whatever its economic benefits for Haitian productivity, had an unanticipated impact on the common people. Russell, the high commissioner, claimed in defense of American-sponsored agricultural development that only 470 acres were transferred to American developers; but Suzy Castor, using American sources of information, says that the total was more than 270,000 acres. In the north, where most of the large development companies operated, thousands of Haitians were removed from their small farms and compelled to work on these tracts for twenty cents a day. Some fled across the unpatrolled border into the Dominican Republic, living a tenuous isolated existence until, it was later rumored, they were mercilessly exterminated on Rafael Trujillo's orders in 1937.[17]

In virtually every phase of occupation reform, the American overseers encountered either stoic indifference or fierce opposition. Haitian peasants, the presumed beneficiaries of agricultural modernization, resisted land consolidation and application of modern technology. The elite, accustomed to enjoying the spoils of office, chafed at their inferior social position under the Americans and suppressed their contempt for the American exhortation of self-help through industrial education and manual labor. To induce some of the Haitian aristocracy to attend industrial school, the Americans provided financial assistance equivalent, in some instances, to the salary of a Haitian physician. Yet the statistical evidence of accomplishment, which adorned the pages of the high commissioner's annual reports, told a different story: one thousand miles of roads, a telephone system, a public health service, a technical service, and a national guard to maintain order.[18]

Central America: A New Treaty System

In the troubled world of Central America in 1907 the United States had sponsored a treaty system designed to reconcile disputes, but in subsequent years the United States, by its obsessive determination to rid Nicaragua of José Santos Zelaya, destroyed the principles it had earlier espoused. In succeeding, it became the guarantor of Nicaraguan stability.

One means of achieving isthmian accord after World War I lay in reaffirmation of federalism. In each of the five republics there were parties and political spokesmen who still believed in a federal political

structure and were willing to accept a diminution of national sovereignty in the interests of isthmian peace. In 1920 a unionist element
won power in Guatemala; from El Salvador came a request for an
isthmian conference to reconsider the 1907 treaties with the aim of
creating another federal union.

The conferees gathered in San José in December. From the start
the old antagonisms resurfaced. The Nicaraguan delegate, irritated
by criticism of his country's canal treaty with the United States, stalked
out; the Costa Rican assembly debated the final document and peremptorily rejected it. This left Guatemala, Honduras, and El Salvador as supporters of the new federation. In mid-1921 Honduras
hosted the premier meeting of the federal assembly.

Once installed, with little money and no support from Nicaragua
and Costa Rica, the unionists looked north for support from the United States. It never came. Within the Department of State a detached
cynicism prevailed. Hughes had told Harding the union ought to be
recognized but had added several pointed observations about Central
America's lamentable history of cooperation. Some weeks later a Central American delegation arrived in Washington, pleading for American approval of the new experiment, or, rather, the old experiment
in modern form. Hughes received the emissaries cordially, but when
asked for a public statement, he simply responded with a request for
more information.

As these meetings were underway, a revolution in Guatemala toppled the unionist regime. A few die-hard federalists in El Salvador
and Honduras threatened intervention to restore their comrades, but
Hughes opposed any move to interfere in Guatemala's internal affairs. Failing to win over Guatemala's new rulers, the federalists
became disheartened and departed Tegucigalpa, their brief exercise in federalism the victim of nationalistic politics and American
indifference.[19]

The United States already possessed its own plan for dealing with
Central American disunity—a modification and restatement of the
1907 treaties. Happily, a suggestion for another conference arrived
from El Salvador, Honduras, and Nicaragua, following a war scare
and sporadic fighting. Presidents of the three republics had convened

on the U.S.S. *Tacoma* to thrash out their differences. In the spirit of amicability they had, once more, sent a peace proposal to Washington.

With Welles the virtual master of the proceedings, the conference began in December 1922. At the outset, the Central Americans agreed not to bring up the delicate subject of union. And to avoid embarrassment to the United States, they omitted discussions about the Central American Court of Justice. The result was a series of treaties containing prescriptions for ensuring the political harmony of the Isthmus. In the General Treaty of Peace and Amity the signatories solemnly promised to respect the territorial integrity of one another and pledged noninterference in any rebellion in neighboring states. They created a new court, with judges selected on merit rather than political favoritism. They agreed to hold inquiries to establish blame if treaties were violated. (Here the unstated presumption held that none of the governments really possessed the "facts" about border incidents or interference in the political troubles of their neighbors, but merely hurled accusations.) They revived the Tobar Doctrine, which stipulated nonrecognition of coup d'état governments unless legitimized by a free election. To this, the Central Americans, with Welles's reluctant blessing, attached an inflexible provision: if elections sanctioned a revolutionary regime, no revolutionary leader nor close relative nor high-ranking military or civilian official having been in power six months before or after the event could become president. This, presumably, would take care of agitators. When Welles broached a plan for limiting armaments, the Central Americans hailed him as a man of peace and then promptly drew up proposals for expanding their armies.[20]

In retrospect, the stipulations of the 1923 treaties appear unnecessarily severe. As imperfect as the 1907 arrangement had been, it had not served to exclude political aspirants tainted with a revolutionary background. The 1923 accord, it could be argued, placed such severe restrictions on the political participation of former revolutionaries (and their kin) as to perpetuate regimes in power and to virtually eliminate a truly popular political figure denied power because the incumbent ran a fradulent election. When the system came apart, as astute observers of the Central American scene knew it would, the

United States became more willing to accept authoritarian, personal rule which provided continuity and political stability as the alternative to political disarray.

In the somber aftermath of these sessions the great Honduran revolution of 1923–24 occurred. It fitted perfectly the scenario for Central American political violence. Since the beginning of the century United States policy had been geared to "neutralizing" the republic, as plotters from neighboring countries regularly exploited Honduran territory as a staging area. Honduras's political leaders called themselves Liberals or Conservatives. They debated mostly about patronage and the influence of the fruit companies—United, Cuyamel (later merged with United), and Standard—which ran the north coast as fiefdoms. The companies possessed private rail lines stretching from the ports of Tela, Trujillo, Puerto Cortés, and Ceiba to their plantations in the interior. Along these lines they operated company stores, stifling local business. What they used in the course of their operations was imported duty-free. They paid, ordinarily, no taxes, and they had power because they held notes on existing governments for debts contracted in earlier days.

When elections were held in 1923, the Liberals split into three factions. The strongest candidate among the Conservatives was Tiburcio Carías Andino, whose zealous adherents organized along the Nicaraguan frontier, threatening to install their hero by force of arms if he were denied the presidency. Typically, the Department of State manifested its concern for democracy and a "free" election. The American minister, Franklin S. Morales, had once served as bartender in the Hotel Pratt in Tegucigalpa, then returned to New Jersey, where he ingratiated himself with the political machine. His reward was the ministerial post in Honduras. During the crisis he was instructed to convey to President Rafael López Gutiérrez American devotion to the principle of fair elections. To achieve this end he appended his personal conviction that López Gutiérrez must rule firmly, even dictatorially, to insure an impartial contest!

López obliged by pressing some of the Liberals to withdraw from the presidential race, but they stoutly refused. At a critical moment, the Guatemalan government proposed mediation of the Honduran situation by the other republics, but Hughes refused. Guatemala, he believed quite rightly, had interfered too much in Honduran affairs. In any event the promised elections were finally held in October 1923 and, as feared, were marred by sporadic violence, mostly directed at Carías's followers. Carías claimed a majority, but the announced returns indicated only a plurality, which meant the national assembly had to choose the next president. But the assembly could not act because it lacked a quorum. The president declared martial law and ordered the arrest of two hundred Cariista leaders.

In Tegucigalpa Morales had immersed himself so deeply in Honduran internal affairs that he had become something of an embarrassment. American recognition of López's government was withdrawn. Carías, whose forces controlled the banana regions of the north coast and, allegedly, had United Fruit Company support, declared himself president. The State Department believed López had behaved unwisely but could hardly defy the 1923 treaties by suddenly recognizing Carías as the new Honduran president. In the contest for control, rival factions subjected the capital to shelling, extortion, and looting. When Morales objected to harassment of foreigners for forced loans, he incurred the wrath of the Liberals. As Carías's soldiers infested the hills surrounding Tegucigalpa, marines from the *Milwaukee* occupied the city and seized the radio station.[21]

It appeared to be a hopeless situation. In mid-April 1924 Welles arrived after a hectic journey from Santo Domingo. Hughes had given him virtually complete power over American policy in Honduras. He began by calling the various representatives of political factions to a conference aboard the *Milwaukee*. He cleverly prevented Carías's agents from using the ship's radio to communicate with their forces, who were winning the struggle for the capital, and obtained an agreement for a provisional president. Later, the Cariistas blamed their negotiators for conceding to Welles, for they had taken the capital during the negotiations.

The revolt had had its bizarre moments. American troops had landed to protect foreign lives and property, which had been threatened by the involvement of the fruit companies in the rebel cause. Cuyamel candidly admitted its decision to dispatch arms to one faction, in defiance of an American embargo, on the grounds it made for good business to do so. United, which backed Carías, appeared to have been motivated by loftier goals. Evidence indicated some of the arms brought into town by marines were spirited to Carías's followers and later used in the taking of the city.

Technically, Carías could not become president, but the provisional president moved ahead to cram his cabinet with Cariistas in preparation for Carías's anticipated triumph. Intent on preventing Carías's accession, Liberal opponents took to the country, raised an army, and resumed fighting. On the north coast foreign residents, alarmed by the sudden renewal of violence, demanded American protection. This time the government crushed the revolt. Carías emerged stronger and more popular than before, but he was again denied the presidency. Morales was recalled, and his successor, Stokeley Morgan, managed to mobilize opposition and even persuaded other Central American ministers to back "neutral" candidates. He requested the fruit companies, which Welles blamed for much of the trouble, to halt their loans to Carías. Embittered, Carías withdrew from the presidential race. Instead, a former associate, Miguel Paz Barahona, more compliant and no violator of the 1923 treaties, became president of the republic.[22]

Cuba: The Search for Order, 1919–1925

World War I brought an unprecedented prosperity to Cuba. In 1918 the entire sugar harvest was purchased by the Americans and their European allies. President Mario Menocal, his political safety ensured against Liberal assault by American intervention in 1917, blossomed as Cuban leader and *primus inter pares* among spoilsmen. As his predecessors had, he exploited the Department of Public Works as a source of profit. Assemblymen were suborned. Few cared, since all were getting rich from the bountiful harvest. The 1902 reciprocity treaty, which permitted Cuban sugar to enter American ports at reduced rates, enabled Cuban producers to dominate the American market and compete effectively in the world market. As the price escalated, sugar growers ambitiously expanded operations, setting fire to timberland to open new fields and subscribing fortunes to build more mills. American candy and soft drink companies moved in and bought mills to control their source of sugar. Cuban and American entrepreneurs maneuvered so feverishly in production that it became almost impossible to tell how much Cuban sugar was actually owned by foreigners. A liberal estimate in 1918 placed American investment at 50 percent.[23]

In May 1920 the price of sugar reached the dizzying height of twenty-two cents per pound. The world market, however, was already glutted, and during the summer sugar piled up on Havana docks, the prospective purchasers having cancelled their orders. By year's end the price dropped to less than four cents. Banks, which had loaned millions to finance wartime production, appraised the grim situation and looked to J. P. Morgan and Company for bail-out funds.

The financial crisis was aggravated by political tensions surrounding the presidential election. Menocal, the outgoing executive, wanted his protégé Alfredo Zayas in the presidential palace. In the fraudulent balloting on 1 November Zayas apparently won a narrow victory over ex-president José Miguel Gómez. As in the past, Liberals refused to acquiesce in such shenanigans and, a week after the voting, called for American supervision of new elections.

In Washington the Wilson administration, reeling from the shock of the League of Nations' defeat in the Senate, watched the deteriorating Cuban scene and, in early 1921, decided to act in order to "maintain a government that would protect life and property." Menocal warned that military intervention would precipitate destruction of American property, but the architects of American policy in the administration—Boaz Long, American minister to Havana, and Norman Davis, undersecretary of the treasury (who held financial interests in Cuba)—were not dissuaded. On 6 January the U.S.S. *Minnesota*, bearing General Enoch Crowder, creator of Cuba's electoral law, steamed into Havana harbor.

Crowder conducted his business from aboard ship. He issued suggestions, which were tantamount to decrees, to President Menocal, instructing the Cuban president about government debts, counting votes, and holding new elections. Menocal, Gómez, and Zayas were summoned to Crowder's cabin to listen to Sumner Welles's criteria for the Cuban president. He must be familiar with American wishes and amenable to advice from the American minister. With these admonitions, Cuba's politicians held another election, amid renewed fighting and perpetual bickering. Once more, the Liberals charged fraud and boycotted the proceedings; once more, Zayas was declared victorious.

The new president inherited a virtually bankrupt government unable to pay its civil servants and school teachers. Crowder, who had written a portion of Zayas's inaugural address, observed the president's despair impassively from his lair on the *Minnesota*. Desperately Zayas appealed for loans and found J. P. Morgan and Company willing to extend $50 million, with 10 percent of that amount available immediately to meet emergencies. The conditions for the loan were a pledge of "moralización," which meant political and economic reform, and reduction of government expenditures, permitting repayment of $20 million in three years.[24]

So the Cuban president ruled with the American soldier-lawyer looking over his shoulder, periodically contributing his thoughts. The American emissary's overriding goal was reform, particularly in Cuba's inept handling of public monies. In the first six months of 1922 he delivered a detailed commentary on Cuban elections, the national lottery, and budgetary reform. When the Cuban demurred, he threatened intervention. American banking houses intruded further into the economy as Crowder pressed his financial reorganization schemes. Anti-Americanism crept into Cuban press editorials. When scandals tainted the national lottery, Crowder ordered reforms; when the corruption led to Zayas's own ministers, the American demanded their removal from office. Under his severe regimen the national budget was sliced by 50 percent, civil servants were fired, and public works contracts were cancelled.

When Crowder spoke, Zayas and his cabinet listened and followed orders. In the end Cuba finally got its $50 million loan from J. P. Morgan. With such riches at his disposal the president embarked on a free-wheeling spending program. He fired the so-called honest cabinet demanded by Crowder, who had since become ambassador and now found it difficult to discipline his Cuban pupil. Payoffs and lucrative contracts reappeared in government dealings.[25]

But by 1925 American observers thought the Cuban political process had at last produced a truly notable leader capable of preserving

order in a disorderly society, for in that year Gerardo Machado, reformed cattle thief from Santa Clara, became president. In the early
years of the republic he had steadily risen in Liberal circles and in
1909 had assumed a post in Gómez's cabinet. Later he managed
Cuban Electric, which by 1925 thoroughly dominated Cuban utilities.
Like Gómez, Machado could be amiable, spirited, and casual. His
private moments were often spent in whorehouses or watching por-
nographic movies. When Machado assumed the presidency, most
Cubans anticipated another raid on the treasury, but that was characteristic of Cuban executives. What made Machado different was his
unequalled con-artistry in dealing with Americans. On a tour of the
United States he unabashedly glorified Calvin Coolidge and told an
audience of bankers their investments were absolutely safe in Cuba.
When among employers, he condemned strikes; when talking to
workers, he lauded the right to strike. He could be stridently nationalistic in his speeches in the Cuban countryside and obsequiously
deferential when discussing political matters with Americans. He in-
undated American critics with promises of reforms—in the lottery, in
education, and in the judicial system. He spoke of a new, mature
relationship with the United States, advocated a revised commercial
treaty, and talked soothingly about abrogating the Platt Amendment,
hated symbol of the island's dependence. His programs vaguely reflected Mussolini's fascist experiment in Italy but with a strong Cuban
flavor. Above all, he promised order.[26]

When Charles Evans Hughes left the State Department in 1925, the
Caribbean policy inherited from the Wilsonians had undergone subtle
alteration. The protectorate system, greatly expanded under Wilson,
had not been dismantled, but it had been noticeably modified. The
American military departed the Dominican Republic in 1922, returning power to Dominican politicians; and in 1925 the relationship of
the republic to the United States resembled more closely that created
in 1905 by Theodore Roosevelt. The Haitian occupation continued,
but it, too, had been changed considerably in the reorganization of
1922. In Central America, the United States still upheld the principle
of nonrecognition of revolutionary seizures of power, but Hughes
indicated that the Roosevelt Corollary, the policy sustaining the pro-

tectorate system, might not be justification for routine interference in the internal affairs of Latin American states.

In 1923, in a series of speeches commemorating the centenary of the Monroe Doctrine, Hughes reaffirmed the doctrine's original meaning —no interference in the Western Hemisphere by non-American powers. The republics were equal, he declared; the United States did not want to control their internal affairs but wanted to assist them in achieving "self-control." How "self-control" could be attained without the Roosevelt Corollary remained a problem for Hughes's successors.

5 • The Empire Embattled, 1925–1933

A characteristic of American policy in the Caribbean between 1925 and 1933 was Washington's reiteration of threadbare truths about political order amidst a rising condemnation of American power and a surge of hemispheric nationalism. In the late 1920s and early 1930s South American cultural nationalism, shaped by a generation of influential writers, swept the continent. The movement, which had been inspired by Latin American neutralism during the war, subjected the United States and its Caribbean policies to scathing abuse in both literary and political criticism. In the Pan American system, since 1889 dominated by the United States, Argentina openly challenged Washington's leadership; one of its most powerful writers, Manuel Ugarte, wrote glowingly of Hispanic traditions, averring that these were irreconcilable with the crass, "cold" values of North Americans. His Uruguayan contemporary, José Enrique Rodó, who died in 1917 at the apogee of American empire, had published his classic book, *Ariel*, in 1900. He sensed even then the divergence of beliefs between North American and Latin American cultures. Brilliantly exploiting themes in Shakespeare's *Tempest*, Rodó argued that Ariel, representing beauty and nonmaterialism, must serve as the Latin American ideal; Caliban, the other spirit, signifying materialism and crass Yankee virtues, must be rejected. The hemisphere must strive for democracy, he wrote, but it must rise above the material democracy of the North Americans. American-style politics, far from offering Latin Americans a lofty standard to emulate, symbolized political grubbiness and degeneracy. While no single Latin American nation could create the higher ideal, the Spanish-speaking societies together might attain the nobler goals of life. Spain, deprived of the remnants of Caribbean empire by the war of 1898, no longer threatened; the menace now was American power and American culture. Intellectuals traced the sources of the Latin American past to Spain, to the Indian, to the Negro, and even to the land itself. In such romanticizing about Latin American heritage, there was no accommodating the stern preachments about politics and social morality emanating from the United States.[1]

And within the United States a small but spirited group of anti-interventionists criticized American policy, focusing especially on the protectorate system as an outmoded structure in a modern world. One of them, Oswald Garrison Villard of the *Nation*, in the early twenties a spokesman for the Union Patriotique of Haiti, discovered new causes in the Nicaraguan debacle of 1927. By 1930 Cuban dictator Gerardo Machado's brutal regime stimulated atrocity stories in still another liberal journal, the *New Republic*. In the Senate the most outspoken critic of American hemispheric policy was perhaps William King of Utah; but William E. Borah, the lion of Idaho, a staunch isolationist, also persistently condemned American policy in the Caribbean. In 1928 a future president, Franklin D. Roosevelt, in a seminal article, "Our Foreign Policy: A Democratic View," argued persuasively that while American efforts might have accomplished much in tropical societies, they had simultaneously provoked condemnation. Where America erred, Roosevelt contended, was in its methods of empire-building, principally in its decision to intervene unilaterally in the internal affairs of smaller Caribbean states. In the future, he speculated, intervention to preserve order must have the collective approval of the Latin American republics.[2]

Nicaragua Again

In Honduras by 1924 American policy had apparently triumphed only by the brief introduction of marines and by the adroit bargaining of Sumner Welles. In neighboring Nicaragua, a protectorate since 1912, the grip of American rule appeared to have weakened.

Within the State Department those troubled about the continuation of the protectorate and the existence of a one-hundred-man legation "guard" derived some hope for change from the approaching Nicaraguan elections. Spurred on by its patron, the Nicaraguan government had retained a young American political scientist, Dr. Harold Dodds, to draft an electoral code. The Conservatives, perceiving any reform as a menace to their stake in the government, grumbled but went along with most of Dodds's proposals; the Liberals, out of office, viewed his handiwork as a godsend for getting into power. Suspicious of fraud, a quadrennial occurrence in Nicaraguan politics, the department pressed for American enforcement of Dodds's law. It also wanted a constabulary on the Dominican model to serve as a non-political national police force. Following an election held under these arrangements, Secretary of State Hughes believed, the marines could be withdrawn, and the republic at last might achieve political tranquillity.[3]

Such a plan might have had some success had it not been for the understandable reluctance of Nicaragua's interim executive, Bartolomé Martínez, who had succeeded to the presidency following Don Diego Chamorro's death in 1923, to permit Dodds and his associates sufficient authority to supervise the upcoming election. Martínez wanted to continue as president; and though constitutionally prohibited from succeeding himself, he had concocted a scheme for doing so. General Emiliano Chamorro, heir to his family's political fortunes, also coveted the presidency. Threatened by intemperate warnings from Washington, Martínez finally pulled out of the race but plotted against Chamorro. Anti-Chamorristas and some Liberals joined forces, promoting the Conservative Carlos Solórzano for president and the Liberal Juan Sacasa for vice-president. With Martínez appointees counting the ballots, Solórzano and Sacasa triumphed. In the aftermath of victory, and eager for American recognition, Solórzano promised full compliance with Dodds's code in the next election (1928) and in the meantime creation of a constabulary. He contracted with Major Calvin Carter of Texas to supervise the training of Nicaraguan recruits. In early August 1925 the legation guard, for thirteen years the symbol of American authority in the republic, left Managua.

As Solórzano tried to govern, Don Emiliano withdrew to his plantation, to grow corn and to plot. In late August, shortly after the departure of the legation marines, a small band of Conservatives invaded Managua's International Club, seized several prominent guests, and spoiled an otherwise perfect evening for the American minister. Chamorro was not directly responsible, but the fracas worked to his advantage. Harassed and intimidated, Solórzano solicited advice from Carter and even requested an American warship. When Chamorro surfaced in Managua, Carter delivered a stern warning about political agitation. But Chamorro's followers took La Loma, the fortress guarding Managua, and the general demanded a coalition cabinet.

Solórzano acquiesced. In the dickering the president named Chamorro general of the army.[4]

While the State Department assessed the political implications of the Nicaraguan conundrum and, especially, looked for violations of the 1923 treaties, Chamorro strengthened his hand. In mid-March 1926 he forced out the ill and besieged Solórzano and then summarily removed Vice-President Sacasa. The process vaguely conformed to Nicaragua's constitutional processes, but the American minister warned Chamorro that his government would not receive American recognition. Chamorro, who obtained contradictory advice from his private American sources, believed Washington was bluffing. He lauded the treaties of 1923, then promptly declared their inapplicability in the present political situation. Privately, he courted influential Americans with inducements for investment; publicly, he promised an era of political stability.

In June the regular American minister departed Managua on a leave of absence, turning affairs over to Lawrence Dennis, who in later years would emerge as America's leading intellectual mouthpiece for fascism. Among prominent Nicaraguans, grown weary in this war of nerves, he served as political advisor. Dennis told Chamorro to resign. The Conservatives called for national unity; the disenchanted Liberals, stimulated by Dennis's blandishments, rallied behind Sacasa's claim to the presidency. A makeshift Liberal force assaulted Bluefields and seized $160,000 from the national bank. Chamorro declared a state of war. In early May the marines returned to Bluefields, in order to protect the customshouse and "American lives and property."[5]

In Washington the befuddled Latin American Division of the State Department, genuinely reluctant to call for more marines, resorted to an oft-exploited device to settle what one writer dubbed the "Kentucky Feud" in Nicaragua—a conference. The warring leaders were invited to Corinto, the neutrality of which had been guaranteed by the American Navy. From the outset the two major factions quarreled over the presidency. The Liberals acknowledged receiving Mexican aid and vowed to fight if Sacasa were denied office. Little was achieved at Corinto; the American mediators emerged convinced that the Conservatives were willing to compromise but that the Liberals were unyielding. Sacasa, interviewed in Guatemala, disavowed the revolution waged in his behalf and professed his loyalty to constitutional government.

The Corinto conference was not a complete failure, however. Deprived of American recognition and confronting a growing rebellion, Chamorro abruptly resigned. The Nicaraguan assembly, dominated by Chamorristas, chose his successor, a man for many years in good standing with the United States, Adolfo Díaz.

The republic's new president delivered a somber inaugural and then publicly stated his expectation of American guarantees for Nicaraguan political stability. Liberals were invited to join the regime, but most refused in favor of continuing the war. The elevation of Díaz brought Sacasa into open defiance. Morally and materially sustained by an anti-American government in Mexico, Sacasa issued blunt pronouncements of his claim to power.[6] In American eyes he was now not only a rebel but an intransigent *político*. His cause, as Secretary of State Frank Kellogg believed, was part of the Bolshevist conspiracy. Mexican newspapers condemned American imperialism in Nicaragua, excoriated Díaz, and recognized Sacasa's makeshift government. In the Senate, Borah questioned the most recent landings of marines at Puerto Cabezas on Christmas Eve 1926; and in January 1927 Burton K. Wheeler of Montana, declaring Sacasa the lawful president of Nicaragua, sponsored a resolution calling for American withdrawal.

Despite professions of neutrality in the Nicaraguan civil conflict, the United States had virtually declared its sympathies with Díaz by recognizing his government and by landing marines in Liberal territory. By decreeing arms embargoes in neutral zones the marines stopped the flow of arms to Sacasa's troops from the outside. Securing the east coast by the end of January 1927, the American command turned its attention to the Pacific side. The *Galveston* docked at Corinto and dispatched 160 marines to Managua. Díaz reassured the Americans with promises of reforms and even extended a peace overture to Sacasa, but the State Department declared the Liberal leader unacceptable because he had resorted to force to obtain power.

When the Liberals shifted their attention to the Pacific coast, their forces inevitably confronted American troops. In early February, following a terrific struggle between government and rebel soldiers for

Chinandega, the American commander in Nicaragua, Admiral Julian Latimer, announced a neutral zone along the Granada-Managua-Corinto railroad. Díaz, in imminent danger, proposed a treaty, the provisions of which paralleled the Platt Amendment for Cuba. Coolidge and Kellogg realized it stood little chance of acceptance in the Senate. They had, seemingly, two choices: stand by and allow Díaz to be crushed; or send marines to quash the Liberal revolt, something guaranteed to incur Congressional wrath. A third possibility was a mediation of the conflict, and to this end Coolidge dispatched, in April 1927, a special emissary to the troubled land of lakes and volcanoes.[7]

Colonel Henry Stimson, a graduate of Yale and Harvard, secretary of war in the Taft administration, and field artillery officer in the war, knew little of Nicaraguan politics when he stepped from the U.S.S. *Trenton* at Corinto. An imposing man of sixty, he impressed both Conservatives and Liberals as sincere, dedicated, and devoted to bringing peace to this troubled Central American country that he persistently called "Nicaragewa." Stimson informed Díaz that he might continue as president only until a suitable replacement was named in the elections of 1928. Until then, he must placate the rebels by issuing an amnesty and permitting American troops to disarm both forces.

Liberals demurred on the point of Díaz's retention of power until the election and referred Stimson to Sacasa's minister of war and commander, General José María Moncada. Stimson and Moncada conferred at Tipitapa in what proved to be successful negotiation between two diverse personalities—the somber, well-educated, courtly American and the Nicaraguan ex-politician known for his military shrewdness, his ebullient and sometimes caustic manner, and his unmatched ability to consume liquor. Moncada wrote and fought with bravura and struggled for idealistic goals, but his career as a journalist and politician in the service of both Liberal and Conservative patrons had taught him the critical distinction between what was desirable and what was possible.

Mostly Stimson and Moncada discussed matters underneath a blackthorn tree by the Tipitapa River. The general castigated American support of Díaz; Stimson spoke of necessary political reforms and the willingness of his government to use force, if necessary, to pacify the country. The critical negotiations, Stimson later wrote, lasted only thirty minutes. Moncada left to discuss the peace plan with associates, and Stimson went back to Managua convinced that he had persuaded the Nicaraguan rebel. The day following the conference, Díaz announced an amnesty and invited prominent Liberals to join his cabinet.[8]

For the first time in many months the fighting stopped, and both sides, in accordance with Stimson's plan, began stacking their arms in the presence of American marines and burying the corpses of peasants killed and left to rot. The American minister, since 1912 a pivotal figure in the republic, emerged as the supreme counselor of the president. Marine officers began organizing a Nicaraguan constabulary and prepared to supervise the 1928 elections. Moncada's rebels drifted in from the mountains to surrender their arms. There were random clashes between marines and Nicaraguans in the Liberal city of León, and a recalcitrant rebel general who reputedly abused local citizens in Chinandega was stalked to his house by marines and shot dead by an American officer. (The general's mistress grabbed a machete, and she, too, was instantly killed.) But elsewhere in the lake towns the marines reported calm, and when Stimson left the country in mid-May, he spoke with satisfaction of accomplishment. Only in the north, in the mountains, were there rumors of more trouble. The marines would soon learn about one rebel who had not surrendered, a man named Sandino.

Augusto César Sandino's ties were with the Liberals, but his role as Nicaraguan rebel cannot be explained solely by the republic's family feuding. In 1926, when the commotion over General Chamorro's accession to the presidency plunged the country into civil strife, Sandino was working for the Huasteca Petroleum Company in Mexico. Urged by his father to return, he departed Mexico with $500 and a Smith and Wesson revolver. In Nicaragua he hired out to an American mining company but grew disenchanted over the country's political condition and the miserable lot of the miners. His years in postrevolutionary Mexico, with its social and educational experimentation and its sensitivity to Indian culture, had provided Sandino with a social conscience. Even so, Sacasa and Moncada remained somewhat suspicious of Sandino's offer of help. He built his army and acquired his weaponry with little assistance from the Liberal leaders, whom he considered inept. The Moncada-Stimson accord he labeled a sellout. When Moncada's troops began surrendering their rifles for $10 per weapon, Sandino and his followers retreated into the mountains, vowing to continue the battle.[9]

At first the American marine commander, General Logan Feland, assigned the task of tracking Sandino and dispersing his band to the Nicaraguan constabulary. But Sandino defied the Americans by seizing the San Albino Mining Company and from its headquarters denounced the intervention and proclaimed the unity of Latin Americans. One marine officer called Sandino a "mule thief," but the Nicaraguan's ringing declaration sounded a revolutionary nationalist note. In mid-July 1927 Sandino received a final demand to surrender. He responded by assaulting a combined marine and Nicaraguan constabulary unit in the village of Ocotal. After a fierce fight the rebels were finally dispersed by five deHaviland biplanes that strafed and bombed their positions. Though the Americans and their Nicaraguan allies won the battle of Ocotal, they had not won the war; Sandino's name was whispered about the republic, and his cause was soon publicized throughout the hemisphere.

Sandino and his army next took refuge near the Honduran border in a region historically neglected by Managua's governments and, because of its isolation, a traditional hideaway for bandits and rebels. It was January 1928. There were now more than 1,500 marines in Nicaragua, all of them, it was humorously commented, hunting one man. The main rebel encampment at El Chipote, a mountain surrounded by jungle, was strafed and bombed systematically. When it was finally taken by a marine ground attack, however, the conquerors found only straw dummies and hastily discarded supplies.[10]

Interviewed in his Nicaraguan lair by the writer Carleton Beals, Sandino gained still more publicity among the American public. The marines went ahead with their plans for supervising the election, unmindful of Sandino's stinging challenge that their presence in Nicaragua could not guarantee a free election. The prevalent American belief held that an honest ballot would solve Nicaragua's problems. Not trusting the republic's electoral bureaucracy, the Department of State appointed a special commission to draft a code and enforce it at the polling place.

The political aspirants, well aware of Washington's critical role, soon descended on the American capital to present their credentials. The most troublesome was Chamorro. In a conversation with the general on Long Island, Stimson politely informed him that he was ineligible; but other Americans, notably Chandler Anderson, former State Department counselor and Chamorro's advisor, encouraged his candidacy. When he pressed the issue, the department publicly announced his ineligibility. Moncada followed. He received a more favorable reception and a special endorsement from his old adversary, Stimson.

But back in Managua a defiant national assembly, dominated by Chamorristas, vetoed the proposed electoral plan. So Díaz merely decreed it as law. When two splinter parties, one of them adamantly against the intervention, organized and tried to enter the presidential race, the electoral commission denied them a place on the ballot. The election itself, probably the fairest in the republic's history with regard to curbing fraud and repeat voting, was finally held in November. Voters were dutifully registered by American supervisors and subsequently cast ballots at 432 polling places. To prevent repeat balloting election supervisors required each voter to dip two fingers in indelible mercurochrome. When the ballots were counted, Moncada, who had been promised an honest election by Henry Stimson, became president of Nicaragua.[11]

The election of a disenchanted Liberal, however, did not bring peace to the country. President-elect Herbert Hoover, on a goodwill tour of the hemisphere, stopped at Corinto and spoke of the limitations of intervention, knowing that Sandino continued to defy and embarrass the United States. Stalemated, the marines began gradually reducing their force in Nicaragua, at a rate corresponding to recruitment in the constabulary. American military and civilian representatives in the republic fell to quarreling over policy and particularly over the role of the guard. General Feland and the American commander of the constabulary vied for influence with Moncada, and their contentiousness sharply eroded American prestige. In early 1929 each received a new assignment.

At the beginning of 1929, there were 5,000 marines patrolling Nicaragua, but in July their number fell to 2,500, and in December to 1,800. Sandino, now a hemispheric celebrity, surfaced in Mexico, conversed with President Emilio Portes Gil and former president Plutarco Elías Calles. It was presumed he wanted political asylum, but in early May 1930 Sandino slipped back into Nicaragua. By now the Nicaraguan constabulary carried the burden of operations against Sandino's force. In March 1930 it had fought seven battles with the rebels with no fatalities. But in mid-June Sandino commanded some 400 to a mountain near Jinotega and there held off a combined air and ground attack until his men exhausted their supply of ammunition. Sandino himself was wounded in the battle, but before the guard could spring a final assault, the rebels stole away to the north.

Once more American marines took up the chase of the elusive bandit. They never captured him. He maintained his rebel force, eluded patrols, and in the spring of 1931 struck in the east, causing considerable damage to the radio station, camps, railroad, and commissaries of Standard Fruit. Stimson, on hearing about the rebel thrust, observed morosely that further marine landings would be unwise. The United States, he announced, could no longer guarantee American lives and property in Nicaragua. In the space of a few hours a traditional policy, forcefully enunciated by Roosevelt, nurtured by Taft, and righteously executed by Wilson, was quietly deemed inexpedient.[12]

True, the marines stayed in the republic to supervise the election of 1932. The American government, preoccupied with its own economic distress, evinced little concern for either candidate or his political profession. It simply wanted a government in Managua that would respect American interests and preserve, at least in form, constitutional precepts. Sandinista bands were active throughout the country during the spring, as Moncada and Chamorro reconciled their differences and agreed privately to deal with Sandino.

One paradox in the Nicaraguan debacle of 1926–33 was the 1932 electoral triumph of Dr. Juan Sacasa, the alienated and abused vice-president in whose name the flag of revolt had been hoisted in 1926. When the last marines left, Sandino came to Managua, drove gloriously through the city, and embraced Sacasa at the presidential place. He had arrived, he declared, to proclaim peace; his crusade to rid the republic of the Yankee invaders had ended. All the rebels were granted amnesty, and Sandino was even permitted a modest personal army of 100 men. In the ensuing weeks he busied himself organizing a self-sufficient agricultural colony, but he soon tired and reentered politics. His main fear seemed to be the overthrow of Sacasa's government by Anastasio Somoza, commander of the national guard. In February 1934 Sandino entered the capital to discuss with Sacasa and Somoza the disarmament of the last remnants of his old rebel band. Somoza feigned cordiality, but he and his most trusted officers were already plotting to assassinate Sandino.

From private discussions with Arthur Bliss Lane, the American minister, Somoza emerged confident of American moral support, if not outright collusion, in Sandino's elimination. The conspirators signed a death pact to seize and execute leading Sandinistas. Sandino himself was arrested as he left a dinner party for Sacasa and other prominent Nicaraguan politicians. He was taken immediately to a Managua airstrip and gunned down under the glare of headlights. Other Sandinistas were also executed, and by the end of the month Somoza, with the efficient support of the American-created national guard, eradicated the last remnants of Sandinista influence.

Sandino was eliminated, but his ghost still haunts the continent, and to this day many Latin Americans are unshaken in their conviction that the United States, acting through Somoza, ordered his death.[13]

Havana, 1928

On a beautiful Sunday morning in January of 1928, the American delegation to the Sixth Pan American Conference, headed by President Coolidge, with Secretary of State Kellogg, and former secretary of state Hughes, stepped ashore at Havana.[14] They were greeted by President Machado, entered automobiles, and proceeded triumphantly down Malecón Drive to the executive palace. Two hundred thousand Habaneros cheered the motorcade.

Coolidge and Machado delivered uninspiring addresses to the delegates. But the outward cordiality belied the deeper tensions in Havana, for it had long been felt within the State Department that the Nicaraguan intervention and, indeed, the protectorate policy would precipitate formal condemnations against United States policy in the hemisphere. For this reason Hughes had been singled out as the ablest defender of a policy under siege. In 1923, in a centennial commemoration of the Monroe Doctrine, he had delivered an uncompromising speech in its defense but, in a curious departure for Washington officialdom, had subtly divorced the doctrine and the Roosevelt Corollary.[15] At Havana he was expected to head off formal debate on controversial topics.

To his credit and with courage, Hughes adopted the reverse strategy. Invited to speak before the American Chamber of Commerce of Cuba, he boldly affirmed the principle of territorial integrity. When the Mexican delegation, in an obvious reference to Washington's domination of the Pan American Union, the administrative unit of the inter-American system, suggested a rotation for the governing board, Hughes graciously acknowledged the merits of the proposal, then deftly defeated it as impractical. The Latin Americans expected the Americans to defend intervention with platitudes about political order and hemispheric security; instead, they reached the end of the session visibly impressed by Hughes's deportment and increasingly annoyed at the persistent Argentines, his principal adversaries. The Mexicans promoted a resolution denouncing hemispheric wars; Hughes enthusiastically endorsed it.

Then came the argument over intervention. The hardliners wanted an absolute ban on intervention by one state in the internal affairs of another. In the Committee on International Law, the Argentine representative pressed for its adoption, failed, and stalked out. In the final plenary session, the issue surfaced again, and the otherwise somber meeting was suddenly transformed into an electrifying debate involving anti-American spokesmen from Haiti, the Dominican Republic, and Colombia. The tone of the speeches soon became abusive.

By the time Hughes finally rose to respond, the delegates preceding him had exhausted their repertory of anti-American slogans. Slowly he analyzed American policy and, in a brilliantly disarming manner, replied to the critics with a recitation on American independence, the protective benefits of the Monroe doctrine for Latin Americans, and the mandate of every civilized society to protect its citizens in a foreign land when governments in those countries were unable to protect them, a principle recognized in international law. Everybody knew he was talking about Nicaragua. Intervening for such nobler goals, he concluded, was not really intervention but "interposition."

He sat down amidst thunderous applause. The listeners may not have accepted his logic, but they admired his forcefulness in presenting it. Hughes's oratorical *tour de force* at Havana did not salvage the protectorate system. The Roosevelt Corollary was doomed, but at least he had momentarily saved his country from embarrassment.[16]

Herbert Hoover and the Caribbean

Tracing the origins of the "good neighbor" policy, a phrase still closely associated with Franklin D. Roosevelt, is a frustrating task of limited historiographical value. Of more importance is a probing of the subtle alterations in policy in these years preceding Roosevelt's vague reference to the good neighbor in his first inaugural address.

Hoover came to the presidency with a well-developed view about Latin America's place in the American economic scheme. After becoming secretary of commerce in 1921, Hoover, with his close advisor, Dr. Julius Klein, director of the Bureau of Foreign and Domestic Commerce, energetically pursued expansion of American trade and investment in the hemisphere. In the classical mold of industrial statesman, he looked to the monocultures to the south as suppliers of raw material for American industry. In the Commerce Department he assembled an impressive group of economic experts who provided technical advice to American companies doing business in Latin America and who scrutinized the periodic financial reviews emanating from hemispheric governments that were trying to borrow money from American bankers or promote bond sales among American investors.

Yet, despite Hoover's manifest concern for American economic interests in Latin America, he was no economic imperialist. He opposed forceful measures or even the threat of nonrecognition—the two most convenient weapons in dealing with recalcitrant Caribbean governments—to protect American investments. Critics such as Samuel Guy Inman and James Weldon Johnson, who decried Hoover's alleged commercialization of the diplomatic service, misinterpreted Hoover's motives. He constantly warred with the State Department over its loan policy: State viewed loans as political matters that had become controversial. Hoover, by contrast, distinguished between good loans (those for beneficial social services) and bad loans (those for purchasing armaments). Where loans went to productive purposes, Hoover believed, the Commerce Department should give its blessing.

The Hoover administration's direction of Caribbean policy was deeply affected by two traumatic events: first, the embarrassment to the United States in the Nicaraguan intervention and, second, the impact of the Depression on a Caribbean generation increasingly frustrated by the squabbling and ineffectiveness of democratic government and impressed by the political experiment in Mussolini's Italy and, later, in Hitler's Germany. The Nicaraguan adventure not only spawned widespread hemispheric condemnation but severely tested American prestige in the Pan American system.[17] Both Republican and Democratic leaders began to reevaluate Caribbean policy in the aftermath of the Havana conference. The onset of the Depression signalled the rise of a new generation of Caribbean politicians less committed to democratic values and more inclined to accept authoritarian methods in confronting economic calamity.

Most of the Latin American republics were export economies and suffered severely in the general decline in world trade after 1929. From 1929 until 1933, the volume of world commerce dropped by 25 percent; its total value, by 50 percent. Since Latin American economies were underdeveloped and integrated into the American-European economic orbit, the precipitous decline in the industrial nations had catastrophic consequences throughout the hemisphere.

The republics were also producers of one or two basic commodities and highly susceptible to fluctuation in trade. As prices for exports went down, their internal economies suffered noticeably. The majority of Latin American governments were heavily indebted to foreign creditors, and as prices for their products declined, they were hard pressed to meet installments on the foreign debt. In 1930 they began defaulting on their external obligations. It was estimated that as late as 1939, when economic prospects had improved, the American investor in Latin America could liquidate his portfolio for 14 cents on the dollar in South American bonds, 36 cents in Central American bonds, and 46 cents in West Indian holdings.

The economic calamity spawned powerful new political movements that were suddenly thrust into power by the loss of faith in the old order. In Argentina, ruled since 1916 by the middle-class Radicals, who had wrested power from the social oligarchy, an alliance of conservatives and generals took over in 1930. In Brazil, the first republic (created in 1889) also expired in 1930 in a conspiracy of political and military forces that gave power to Getulio Vargas, architect of Brazil's *Novo Estado*. In the Caribbean these years witnessed the rise of the nationalist strongman—Carías in Honduras, Ubico in Guatemala, Hernández in El Salvador, Somoza in Nicaragua, Trujillo in the Dominican Republic, and Batista in Cuba. Though each was a product of sometimes diverse political circumstance, each shared with his contemporaries a distaste for democratic methods, a fascination with totalitarian philosophy, and, especially, an awareness of the special relationship of the Caribbean republics with the United States.

In Central America, these changes meant, for one thing, a confrontation with the United States. The Tobar Doctrine, which forbade diplomatic recognition of coup d'état governments, had been the keystone of Central American policy since 1907. It had been reaffirmed in the 1923 treaties. In the twenty-year history of the application and misapplication of the doctrine, the United States had, on occasion, violated the principle in the interest of expediency, then righteously reasserted it. In any event, Hoover faced a disturbing succession of isthmian political crises which culminated in Central America's repudiation of the Tobar rule.

In December 1930 the president of Guatemala, Lázaro Chacón, resigned, and a council appointed his successor. Antigovernment politicians charged fraud, and during the ensuing brouhaha a military junta led by General Manuel Orellana seized power. Hoover and Secretary of State Stimson, concluding that Orellana's dramatic stroke violated the 1923 treaties, withheld American recognition. In early 1931 Orellana resigned; his successor, chosen by a compliant congress, was quickly recognized by the United States and the other Central American republics.[18]

This time the United States had its way, but its determination to uphold the Tobar Doctrine soon came under attack again, in tiny El Salvador. In December 1931, a year after Orellana's coup in Guatemala City, a small group of aggressive young officers, imbued with a sense of mission and modern political theory, took over in San Salvador. The president fled. His vice-president, Maximiliano Hernández, who enjoyed considerable popular support, claimed the office. In appealing for diplomatic recognition he argued that there had been no violation of the 1923 treaties; but following a hasty investigation of the circumstances of his accession by Jefferson Caffery, former minister to El Salvador, Stimson declared Hernández, like Orellana, unacceptable. Unlike his Guatemalan counterpart, Hernández held on; and under his austere but popular regime El Salvador's political reputation rose steadily among her isthmian neighbors. The other four republics dealt informally with Hernández but hesitated to extend formal recognition. The stalemate was finally broken in late 1932 by the British in a formal communication to San Salvador; France, Italy, Spain, and Germany soon followed. Shortly before the 1923 treaties were due to expire in 1933, two isthmian republics, Costa Rica and El Salvador, denounced them. The Tobar Doctrine, for years a political weapon in the struggle to enforce constitutional transfer of power in the Caribbean, now stood repudiated by the Central American republics. Hernández's government received the official acknowledgment of the other republics and, in January 1934, was finally recognized by the United States.[19]

El Salvador had not only defied the Tobar Doctrine and the treaties of 1923; it had defied the United States and American policy. Hernández had succeeded because his regime offered stability and a modicum of enlightened rule, and required no bank loans from New York for its survival. More than that, El Salvador had triumphed because the Hoover administration had quietly admitted to itself, if not to the American public, that the Roosevelt Corollary no longer served American interests. In his 1923 address on the Monroe Doctrine Hughes had denied that the doctrine justified American domination of the hemisphere. He stressed the doctrine's original goal of preventing European encroachments in the New World. In subsequent years the Department of State evaluated the hallowed policy and particularly its twentieth-century amendment, the Roosevelt Corollary. Before leaving office Kellogg authorized a study of the role of the corollary and its impact on the Monroe Doctrine. When finally published in 1930, the study became known as the Clark *Memorandum on the Monroe Doctrine*, after J. Reuben Clark, undersecretary of state, who compiled official statements into a compendium on the doctrine and Roosevelt's famous corollary. It was not Clark's intention to repudiate American policy. But in a revealing covering letter he expressed his own view that, first, the Monroe Doctrine governed United States–European relations concerning Latin America (or, as Clark expressed it, "U.S. versus Europe," not "U.S. versus Latin America"), and, second, the Roosevelt Corollary, rather than reinforcing the Monroe Doctrine, actually violated it. In his analysis the United States already possessed the right to intervene in the Caribbean by the principle of self-preservation.[20]

When the *Memorandum* finally appeared in print in March 1930, it was immediately hailed as a repudiation of the Roosevelt Corollary. Somewhat embarrassed by the fanfare and pressed by inquiries, the State Department merely pointed out that Clark's forwarding letter represented his own views and that, contrary to first impressions, American policy in the Caribbean had not been repudiated. Years later the diplomatic historian Robert Ferrell would call this a "repudiation of a repudiation."[21] This was not really the case. Clark had merely stated that the country had the right to protect its interests in the Caribbean on the grounds of self-preservation, not the Roosevelt Corollary. A small difference, perhaps, but the publication of the *Memorandum*, despite the Hoover administration's public qualifications, signalled the demise of the Roosevelt Corollary.

The Dominican Republic and Haiti

In 1922, following almost two years of intermittent negotiation with Dominican leaders, the United States announced the termination of the military government that had ruled the republic since late November 1916. The last troops departed in 1924, and a new era in Dominican-American relations began.

In the years after American departure Dominican politics settled into what cynical observers called a familiar routine: the aged president, Horacio Vásquez, got along well with Washington but proved ineffectual in dealing with the republic's volatile political factions. True, the country's finances were in better shape than at any other time since the days of Ramón Cáceres, and public safety, often disrupted in the civil commotions before 1916, was now presumably guaranteed by the constabulary, which, with the improved road system, constituted the best contributions of the American occupation. But the political hatreds, though less intense than in the old days, still exacerbated public tranquillity and opened new wounds.

Things went well for Vásquez until he had a falling-out with his vice-president, Federico Velásquez, over the president's decision to continue in office until 1930. Velásquez soon resigned. During the crisis Vásquez prevailed on the Department of State for guidance, but the response was vague, and from the president's point of view, unhelpful. A decade before, such a plea for political tutoring would have inspired the entire Latin American division to produce reams of memoranda. In 1929 Charles G. Dawes, the outgoing vice-president of the United States, arrived in Santo Domingo with a team of experts to assess Dominican finances. After three weeks of study, the commission announced that the customs collectorship, which was still in American hands, was well managed, but it went on to list numerous problems of mismanagement virtually everywhere else in the government's administration.

What precipitated the political turmoil of the next year, however, was not so much the deplorable condition of Dominican finances as Vásquez's decision to run for the presidency again in the 1930 elections. The constituent assembly of the preceding year had removed the remaining legal obstacles to his candidacy. As the political opposition reconciled itself to the inevitability of his participation in the forthcoming campaign, Vásquez, requiring specialized medical treatment, suddenly departed for the United States. To rule in his absence the president left José Alfonseca, a protégé.

Alfonseca was a bitter personal enemy of the former private and now head of the national guard, Rafael Leonidas Trujillo, Jr. The animosity between the two was so intense and so publicized that everybody in Santo Domingo, including the American minister, knew there would be trouble. Few, however, anticipated an alliance between Trujillo and former vice-president Velásquez. In February 1930 Velásquez declared against Vásquez. Trujillo allowed arms to be captured by Velásquez's followers and ordered his troops not to resist their movements. For a short time the American minister tried to mediate and even went so far as to request an American warship, but the Department of State, noting that American lives were not endangered, demurred.

The first casualty was the harassed Vásquez, who signed his resignation in the American legation and in the same act named Rafael Estrella Ureña as provisional president. The intent was to deny the presidency to the one person—Trujillo—who now held the real power in the republic because he controlled the national guard. Men who hated and feared Trujillo looked to Washington to prevent his accession.[22]

But 1930 was not 1916. Trujillo's old brigade commander, now serving in Haiti, personally appealed to his former subordinate to withdraw his candidacy, but Trujillo refused. When the elections were held, the national guard supervised the balloting, and Trujillo won handily. He was inaugurated in August, and almost immediately began to reconcile or intimidate his enemies. Even nature abetted his cause when, in early September, a hurricane smashed into Hispaniola and devastated a part of the republic. Trujillo rose to the emergency and noticeably enhanced his power in the country and, just as important, his image in the United States. In the aftermath an economic crisis threatened Trujillo's control of the republic, but the problem eased when he signed new agreements with American bankers.[23]

In later years, critics surveying the rise of Trujillo often argued that his triumph lay, not in his abilities, but in the willingness of the United States, having created the Dominican constabulary and trained Trujillo, to tolerate his accession to power. Trujillo's use of the constabulary as a political instrument has often been cited as circumstantial evidence of American collusion in what eventually became a brutal dictatorship. In truth, the United States may have been more than a passive observer of Dominican events, but it did not create Trujillo's dictatorship, and it created only one of the tools, the constabulary, with which Trujillo secured his grip on the country after 1930. Trujillo exploited traditional Dominican rivalries and the military at his command. In the initial years of his rule he offered an orderly regimen to a historically disorderly society. Even Henry Stimson, ordinarily an astute observer, thought Trujillo a worthy leader.

In neighboring Haiti the political transformation of the late twenties and early thirties took a decidedly different course. The political scene in Haiti in 1928 was still characterized by the presence of American troops and a subservient Haitian government headed by Louis Borno. President Borno ruled at the behest of the American high commissioner, John Russell. Both were universally despised by the average Haitian; Borno had been publicly booed in 1926 as he left on a visit to New York (and was, incidentally, booed in New York when he arrived).

   After almost a decade and a half the occupation had settled into dreary routine. Russell did not rule harshly, but he evinced little interest in winning adherents. In 1928 he permitted a national plebiscite to alter the 1918 constitution so as to allow, among other things, Borno to continue in office. In the Latin American Division, responsible for charting Haitian policy, the consensus was that Haitians were still not fit for democracy.[24]

   What abruptly changed things was a series of public disturbances in the fall of 1929. From the early 1920s the occupation had ruled virtually free of internal criticism, save for that of a few newspapers, whose editors had been periodically threatened, fined, or jailed. Most Haitians appeared stoically indifferent, but there were latent hatreds. The spark igniting those hatreds was provided by a student strike at the agricultural college of the Service Technique in October protesting changes in the rules for awarding scholarships. The strikers were soon joined by students throughout the country. For five weeks they refused to attend classes. They stormed the home of the Service Technique director. Russell quickly promised more scholarships, but by this time the agitation had captured public attention and, on 3 December, in a dolorous assessment of the situation, the high commissioner anticipated a student alliance with Haitian politicians and called for 500 marines.

The following morning the customshouse workers in Port-au-Prince struck. By afternoon the city's streets were thronged with Haitians hurling rocks at marines. The national guard, according to an American observer, did little to quiet the crowds. Sensing that the worst was yet to come, Russell proclaimed martial law, a move which Hoover and Stimson considered harsh but which was seemingly justified by subsequent events. On 6 December a marine contingent fired into a group of angry Haitians at Cayes, killing twelve and wounding twenty-three.[25]

The riots of 1929 underscored the real weaknesses of the occupation and demonstrated its widespread unpopularity. In such a volatile atmosphere Borno's candidacy for reelection in 1930 appeared laughable. The United States followed up the riots with another investigation, headed by Cameron Forbes, former governor of the Philippines. The commissioners arrived in Port-au-Prince and were greeted by 6,000 demonstrators. Defying Russell's code of social segregation, the commissioners fraternized with Haitians and ultimately won the confidence of the Haitian public. Russell tried to guide their work and shape their final report. He wanted official approval of the occupation, but Forbes knew his real mission was to prepare Haiti for the end of American rule. When Borno informed Forbes he intended to run for reelection, he was bluntly informed this would be contrary to American wishes. Borno then tried to undermine the commission's labors.

The last marine did not leave until 1934, but the decision to terminate the Haitian occupation was arrived at shortly after the Forbes Commission delivered its final report. The commission praised the material accomplishment in Haiti but noted sadly that the original goals of 1915 had not been achieved. Russell was removed in late

1930; with him went the post of high commissioner. In the next few years his successor, the American minister Dana Gardner Munro, concentrated on Haitianization, a program of gradual transfer of the treaty services to Haitians. The transition did not go smoothly because the Haitians quite naturally wanted a more rapidly paced turnover of responsibilities than the State Department believed prudent. Confronted with a resurgent Haitian nationalism, the department expressed its misgivings about Haitian capabilities and then quietly acquiesced. American business interests in Haiti, for twenty years protected by American supervision of the political and economic system, suddenly felt isolated and threatened. In 1933 National City Bank proposed selling the Banque Nationale to the Haitian government; two years later the transaction was completed. The American collector of customs, symbol of fiscal paternalism in the Wilson era, retained his position but with considerably less authority over internal finances. The financial protectorate lived on until the last bonds of indebtedness were retired after World War II.[26]

6 • Franklin D. Roosevelt & the Meaning of the Good Neighbor Policy

Sometime in the 1920s—the specific date cannot be fixed—Franklin D. Roosevelt, fifth cousin of a president who left his indelible imprint in the Caribbean, rejected Wilsonian concepts of Caribbean empire. To the 1924 Democratic party platform, to cite one example of his changing attitude, Roosevelt contributed a plank opposing intervention and promoting inter-American goodwill. To no one's surprise, he observed in 1927 that the Nicaraguan intrusion had damaged America's reputation. In the following year there appeared his article in *Foreign Affairs*, probably ghosted by Louis Howe but bearing Roosevelt's name, which criticized unilateral intervention and vaguely defined what later came to be called "collective responsibility."[1]

The key to understanding the Good Neighbor policy lies not in Roosevelt's intentions, which were, like his predecessors', to safeguard American interests, nor even in his silken phrases of friendship and understanding, but in the *several* ways he dealt with Caribbean problems. To legal-minded critics of the protectorate system, the reverse of intervention was, naturally, nonintervention, but to Roosevelt and his generation of Latin American advisers, choices often narrowed to style and means by which the United States achieved its historic goals of Caribbean security, political guidance, and subordination to the American economy. In this regard Roosevelt drew heavily on the advice of several political associates who had warned about the limitations of direct intervention in a time of economic depression and rising Caribbean nationalism. One of them, Sumner Welles, for a decade the servant of Republican presidents, became Roosevelt's agent in the Cuban crisis of 1933, his negotiator in the delicate Panamanian treaty talks of 1934–36, and, ultimately, the most important architect of the Good Neighbor policy.[2]

The Cuban Crisis of 1933

The origins of the Cuban upheaval of 1933 lay in explosive forces in the republic's history. Paramount among these was the emergence of a truly Cuban nationalism, which drew its strength mostly from bitterness generated by the Cuban-American relationship. The Platt Amendment, which had created the protectorate, was galling to a generation of young Cubans who matured in the 1920s. Just as hated was the island's economic dependence on the United States. In the sugar industry, American capital grew by geometric proportions after the war of independence. By 1925, when Gerardo Machado became president, fulfilling American wishes for a Cuban executive with a good business sense, Americans had approximately a $1.5 billion investment in the island, representing a 3,000 percent increase from Secretary of State Richard Olney's 1895 calculations of American holdings in Cuba.

Machado's Cuba was also a country devastated economically by the onset of a sugar depression. After the "dance of the millions" in 1920, when sugar prices reached the unprecedented height of twenty-two cents per pound, American investment poured into the island. The price of sugar soon dropped, but American companies moved further into controlling the industry. Cuba's old sugar elite, displaced by the new American owners, shifted into professional roles that serviced the industry and accommodated themselves to American domination. Machado's election symbolized the union.

But by 1925, the sugar economy had already entered a long period of decline that would last until World War II. The middle-class professionals who were the intermediaries between American investors and Cuban purchasers began losing strength; they were, increasingly, superfluous in an economy that produced too much sugar. After 1929, as Cuba's economy deteriorated and Machado's power diminished, the opposition that had sprung up against the dictator looked not only to Machado's removal but, in a vague manner, to the building of a new economic order in Cuba—an order of social justice and independence from American domination.

The immediate cause of the Cuban revolt of 1933 was Machado's corruption and especially the brutality of his regime. Americans had looked upon his accession to power as a sign of political maturity in the republic. Out of deference to prevailing attitudes in the United States, Machado had posed as a staunch advocate of sound business principles. In the early years of his administration he even tried to build a new political coalition in the spirit of "cooperationism." All the old animosities would be swept aside in the glorification of the new Cuba. Soon, opposition to cooperationism meant opposition to Machado. In the course of consolidating his power Machado tried to circumscribe his opponents by legal means, and when that proved ineffective, he began silencing them by illegal means. When he could not suborn his opponents, he dispatched his goon squads to beat them. Political exiles descended on the United States with gruesome stories of police terrorism and ghoulish tortures.[3]

When Harry Frank Guggenheim, with family ties in Anaconda Copper and Chilean nitrates, arrived in Havana as the new American ambassador in 1929, Machado's reputation had already withstood a considerable assault from the United States Senate, where Henrik Shipstead of Minnesota had denounced the Cuban president as a dictator. Officially, the American government still looked on Machado as a stern executive with unshakable convictions about American property rights. This view was reinforced by Guggenheim's glowing memoranda lauding Cuba's material accomplishments: from a ravaged condition in 1898 the country had achieved in three decades an impressive highway system, utilities, and public works. Only the national lottery and the periodic amnesty decrees, Guggenheim observed, tainted the government's accomplishments.[4]

Despite his record in public works, as Guggenheim soon discovered, Machado began to lose control of Cuban politics. When students demonstrated, he closed the national university. When professional groups protested the illegality of arbitrary rule, he broke up their meetings. Anti-Machado elements organized clandestinely in cells, known as A, B, C, etc., thus acquiring the name the ABC movement, and drew up manifestoes for Cuban social and economic rehabilitation. Occasionally ABC conspirators bombed public buildings or ambushed hated Machadista lieutenants. Genuinely concerned, Guggenheim advocated reforms as Machado's salvation, but the dictator correctly sensed that his opponents really wanted a new government. In 1932, following Machado's abrupt declaration of intent to rule until 1935, the country fell into disarray.[5]

Cuba thus became Roosevelt's first foreign policy crisis. Machado's adversaries recognized fully the impact their agitation was having on the United States, yet Machado, too, quickly perceived in early 1933 that he might exploit Roosevelt's promises about good neighborliness to his advantage. To be sure, the United States had the right to intervene under the Platt Amendment, but if it chose not to use force to restore order to the island, then would not Machado's hand be strengthened? Prominent American investors, some of whom possessed excellent contacts in the new administration, were apprehensive about their Cuban holdings. Others, like Secretary of State Cordell Hull, were concerned about the deleterious effects the Cuban crisis might have on the forthcoming Seventh Pan American Conference, scheduled to commence in Montevideo in December.[6]

Twenty-six years before, in another Cuban political crisis, Theodore Roosevelt had intervened, a prospect which Roosevelt and Hull seriously considered. Certainly they had no intention of doing nothing, that is, of allowing Cubans to settle their own affairs without any American involvement. Cubans on both sides of the civil struggle anticipated some kind of American action. It came in the person of a new ambassador extraordinary and plenipotentiary, Sumner Welles, who arrived in Havana in early May 1933 with a remarkably concise set of instructions. They were as follows: First, though the situation was doubtless grave, it did not warrant American military intervention under the third article of the Platt Amendment. Second, Welles might mediate the political controversy between Machado and his enemies. Finally, the United States wished to aid Cuba in developing measures to improve the island's economy.[7]

Had Welles followed these instructions, Machado might have survived and the course of Cuban history been different. But within a month the American ambassador was sounding out opposition leaders and suggesting to Roosevelt and Hull that if Machado proved unreceptive to his suggestions or his strategy of economic pressure, then the Cuban executive should resign. Welles's maneuvering among anti-Machado leaders left the unmistakable impression that he was secretly working against Machado. It also convinced some in the opposition, especially the Student Directory, that his expanded role symbolized a new kind of American domination. Despite these doubts, most of the anti-Machado elements approved Welles as mediator, and on 2 June he formally offered his services. The next day, a wary Machado accepted.

Welles's assumption of the role of mediator in no sense signalled Machado's triumph or the acquiescence of Machado's enemies. It merely bought time for both sides to reappraise their respective positions. Machado still believed he would survive, and his youthful opponents still nourished the dream of obtaining power and implanting their vague, idealistic, revolutionary goals in a reborn Cuba. What neither side fully appreciated was the immense power that accrued to the American ambassador as mediator. If the talks proved unsuccessful, Welles could blame matters on the political recalcitrants on both sides and demand stronger measures from his own government. In mid-July two of the revolutionary groups, demanding more concessions from Machado, withdrew from the discussions. As anti-Machado forces gave up hope, the ambassador increased pressure on the Cuban president. Machado, irritated, told his associates that Welles had little influence with Roosevelt and Hull, and at this time the secretary of state mildly criticized Welles for his exaggerated role in the Cuba quarrel.[8]

What salvaged Welles and ultimately ruined Machado was the strike that gripped Havana in early August. The Cuban executive quickly sensed the political implications of the strike and moved to smash it, but when police fired into a Havana mob, the entire city was angered, and the dispute spread to the rest of the country. At this point Welles, whose power escalated noticeably during these days, demanded Machado's resignation, in a manner indicating the Cuban president's voluntary surrender of office. In a desperate move Machado solicited support from his own generals, but they too called for his resignation. At Welles's suggestion Carlos Manuel de Céspedes was to take over as provisional president. Machado departed Havana for an extended "vacation" in the Bahamas. On the evening of the day these decisions were made, Welles received a congratulatory telegram from Washington.[9]

For the next twenty-four days Cuba had a government which, under different circumstance, might have united the revolutionary factions into a powerful constituency for social change. But Céspedes was virtually unknown to most Cubans and lacked the qualities for inspirational leadership. The ABC, which might have exploited the opportunity Machado's ouster created, obtained only two positions in the new government (in Treasury and Justice), and from this point declined in prestige. Elsewhere, Céspedes retained much of the inherited bureaucracy and thus did little to placate alienated Cubans who believed the old order needed to be shunted aside to make way for a new generation. In late August the Student Directory, which in the ensuing months would play a critical role in shaping public opinion, denounced Céspedes and demanded elimination of lingering Machadista influence, a new provisional government, and sweeping social and educational reforms. Haltingly Céspedes tried to respond, but he was already being undermined, as Machado had been, by his own military. This time the rebels were sergeants of the Columbia Military Union, acting, they said, on behalf of the forgotten common soldier. Machado's demoralized officers lost control, and the revolt spread to other military units throughout the nation. When the Student Directory committed itself to the revolt, Céspedes hurriedly vacated the presidential chair. The "authentic revolution" was now proclaimed throughout Cuba.[10]

The sergeants' revolt inaugurated a revolutionary regime, and with it, one of the most controversial chapters in Cuban history. From the Student Directory there came propaganda and proposals for broad changes in Cuban society. The revolutionary junta—it was called The Pentarchy—denounced the old order and proclaimed economic and social rehabilitation within the framework of the democratic process. A significant number of the revolutionaries were students, loosely organized but loudly proclaiming a new order; they were youngsters with idealistic, vague concepts of economic justice, bound by a passionate nationalism and exhibiting a sense of purpose and urgency. By contrast, the sergeants who had brought down Céspedes were largely apolitical. They had experienced poverty and social inferiority; now they suddenly possessed power and status and were determined to maintain their position. By virtually unanimous agreement their leader and acknowledged intellectual superior was a former clerk-stenographer named Fulgencio Batista y Zaldívar.

For four perilous months the new government, like some small craft lost at sea, rode the stormy waves, plunging forward into a dark unknown. The Pentarchy's leader, Dr. Ramón Grau San Martín, was a National University physician who had opposed Machado as early as 1926. For his courage he had suffered imprisonment and then exile. It was presumed Grau would be truly nonpolitical and unite the various revolutionary factions into a common quest for a reformed society. Simply stated, the government's mission was the fulfillment of the dream of 1898: a democratic Cuba based on political liberty and promoting social justice. Grau believed Cuba had at last arrived at a critical turning point in its tormented history. For him the revolution was socialistic, anti-imperialistic, and, above all, nationalistic.

Even as rumors told of an approaching American battleship with a marine contingent, the revolutionary government began dismantling the old order and building a new one. On 10 September it unilaterally annulled the Platt Amendment, symbol of the island's dependence on the United States. Ten days later the eight-hour day for laborers became law. In October there followed the prohibition of importation of cheap labor from Haiti and Jamaica; and in November, a decree requiring that 50 percent of the employees in all industry and commerce be Cuban. For the *colonos*, the sugar harvesters, Grau proclaimed land distribution and reduced interest on loans. Women received the vote, the Machado parties were abolished, and the rates of Cuban Electric were reduced by 40 percent. As Grau himself described the revolutionary process, the colonial economic structure was systematically demolished. Some of the older economic associations, of course, became alarmed at the torrent of reform legislation. Other economic interests, such as labor, which was already influenced by Communists, wanted more sweeping and fundamental change.[11]

Inevitably such significant economic changes antagonized those foreign, and especially American, interests with a considerable investment in the island. Grau suspended loan payments to the Chase National Bank and during a labor disagreement seized two sugar mills belonging to the Cuban-American Sugar Company. The government peremptorily halted the ploy of companies who sold out at low prices to other concerns in order to avoid taxes. In its final weeks of rule, when a strike closed Cuban Electric, the despised American subsidiary, the revolutionary regime assumed temporary supervision of the utility. Each time Grau encroached on the interests of a foreign firm, the revolution made new enemies and brought forth more denunciations, but in the charged political atmosphere such condemnations served only to move it toward more radical measures.

Grau's program provoked opposition from the left as well. Some of the more alienated students felt the revolution had been betrayed. The Communists believed Grau was just another bourgeois Cuban politician; in isolated districts they seized sugar mills and hoisted the red flag. The ABC, archenemy of Machado, soon became openly antagonistic. And there were the inevitable splinter factions of varying political persuasion whose members, for one reason or another, perceived in Grau's movement a threat to their own interests or plans for Cuba.

In time almost all these anti-Grau forces looked to Welles for guidance, support, and, if possible, decisive action. The ambassador's critical assessment of the revolutionary government had not only appeared in his official reports to Hull and Roosevelt but had been widely disseminated. Grau and his associates, Welles said, were naïve social visionaries incapable of giving Cuba the one thing it most desperately needed—order. And, as his instructions from Hull made explicit, the United States would not recognize a government unable to secure order and protect property. Had Grau been able to unite the competing factions into a cohesive force, he might have survived, but unable to consolidate civilian support, he could not deal with the rising power of the military and its commander, Batista. In the ritual of seemingly endless crises in November and December 1933, the government clung desperately to its authority, with Welles confidently predicting its imminent fall.[12]

Had Welles possessed unquestioned authority, he would have ordered 1,000 marines into Cuba, on the pretext of protecting the embassy, on the day after the sergeants' revolt. But Hull and Roosevelt had decided to wait. For one thing, they did not want to establish a government by force. Not only would such a move violate American neutrality; it would also redound to American disfavor throughout the hemisphere and jeopardize the administration's noninterventionist stance at the December Pan American conference. Hull had received disquieting reports of Communist influence in the Cuban government, but these had been discounted by Josephus Daniels, Roosevelt's old boss in the Navy Department, who was now serving the president as ambassador to Mexico.

Lacking official support for military intervention, Welles accomplished his goal by discrediting Grau's government and expediting its downfall. Weekly he catalogued Grau's defects and openly predicted his political demise. Little wonder, then, that the shrewdest politician in Cuba, Fulgencio Batista, sensed what opportunities awaited the leader who could guarantee order and thus win the favor of the American ambassador. When press reports about Hull's inclination to recognize Grau surfaced, Welles wired a pessimistic appraisal of the regime, and the secretary of state backed down. With Welles's blessing, Batista began negotiations with dissident elements; when these overtures failed to evoke much response, he closeted himself in Camp Columbia and tightened his grip on the military.[13]

In December Welles departed the island, convinced that his mission of discrediting Grau was justified. At Montevideo, where the Seventh Pan American Conference was underway, Cuban delegates fought a losing battle for hemispheric approval of Grau's government. A few days before Christmas a huge throng gathered at the presidential palace to praise the revolutionary leader. But it was too late. Grau had proved unable to organize a political party to bolster his government. The economy had not revived. The military stood aloof, its loyalty committed not to the president of the republic but to Batista.

When Welles's replacement, Jefferson Caffery, arrived in Havana in mid-December, he quickly dispelled any hopes for change in American policy. Unlike Welles, Caffery personally disliked Batista, but, as had his predecessor, he sensed Batista's centrality, his importance as an agent of stability. Batista would not move until he had Caffery's blessing and a prior commitment to recognize a new government. The Department of State demurred on this point, but Caffery's approval was taken for granted. On 14 January 1934, Batista called a meeting of Cuban political leaders at Camp Columbia to plan the republic's future. It was an unmistakable signal to the physician in the presidential palace. Grau resigned the following day, vowing to return. A week later he boarded a ship bound for Mexico. Batista wanted Carlos Mendieta as provisional president, but the other plotters insisted on Carlos Hevia, Grau's secretary of agriculture. Batista acquiesced, but when Hevia suddenly confronted new public disturbances, the junta reassembled at Camp Columbia, deposed him, and on 17 January named Mendieta as provisional president. Five days later the United States extended diplomatic recognition.[14]

The Economic Balance Sheet

Roosevelt often spoke of "giving Latin Americans a share," which presumably meant an opportunity to expand markets and to diversify monoculture economies. Defined in economic terms, then, the Good Neighbor policy embodied more than a philosophy of liberal trade, that hallowed doctrine embraced by Cordell Hull and implanted in the Reciprocal Trade Agreements Act of 1934. By that act, which was in fact an amendment to the Hawley-Smoot Tariff of 1930, the United States declared its intention to remove restrictive trade clauses in favor of reciprocal tariff reductions. Hull argued that the worldwide depression had been aggravated by economic nationalism; the remedy, he believed, lay in a thorough restructuring of international trade. Hull was particularly aggressive in promoting reciprocal trade agreements among Latin American countries, most of which, infused with a spirit of economic nationalism, had erected numerous trade barriers to safeguard their battered economies. These obstacles Hull sought to tear down, and in the process he intended to advance American economic interests.[15]

Where the Caribbean was concerned, Hull's program of economic liberalism aimed at achieving trade advantages for the United States so as to preserve American political and economic domination. Central American negotiations showed how New Deal economic internationalism actually worked against isthmian nationalism and the efforts of Central American republics to avoid incorporation into an American economic sphere. The United States agreed to admit Guatemalan products at greatly reduced duties if, in turn, the republic responded by lowering or abolishing its import restrictions on a wide variety of American products. At first the Guatemalan government resisted what it considered a threat to its economic survival, for it believed the large losses from reductions on import duties would necessitate an overhaul of the internal tax structure to compensate for declining import revenues. Later, when Jorge Ubico launched what would become a political dictatorship and needed American support, Guatemala acquiesced in American economic pressure, demonstrating its fidelity by abrogating its unconditional most-favored-nation arrangement with Great Britain. In Honduras, too, an authoritarian government adjusted to American economic overtures by accommodating American private business. Honduras enjoyed a highly favorable trade balance with Germany, yet under American prodding the republic repudiated its most-favored-nation agreement with that nation, as the Amerians wanted. In return the United States began purchasing some 90 percent of Honduras's banana crop.[16]

The most obvious contradiction of Good Neighbor economic liberalism occurred in Cuba. In adjusting to the new Cuba after 1933, the United States readily relinquished the Platt Amendment, for Batista guaranteed internal political stability and international cooperation. But Cuba was drawn closer to the American economic orbit, for Hull's economic liberalism, as Dick Steward has ably shown in his study of the economic aspects of the Good Neighbor policy, never extended to that republic. For example, American policy increased Cuba's dependence on sugar. The precipitous decline in Cuban sugar exports after 1929 lowered the republic's sugar income in 1933 to approximately 30 percent of its sugar earnings four years earlier. In part, this calamity had been brought about by the Depression, in part by overstimulation of Cuban sugar production by the American government during World War I and by American investors in the 1920s. Attempts to diversify the economy and thus reduce dependence on

sugar had been hampered by charges of graft and by American opposition. In 1931 Cuba agreed to limit production by entering into quota
agreements with other sugar producers, but the plan proved a failure
and severely damaged Cuba's share in the American market, for
sugar growers in American territories, not bound by quota restrictions, gained in proportion to Cuba's reductions.[17]

While it was willing to end the political protectorate, the Roosevelt
administration never intended to jeopardize American economic
interests in Cuba. In 1933, American investments in the republic
totalled almost $1.5 billion, a tremendous sum, the security of which
was threatened by Machado's inability to quell internal disorder and
by the revolutionary program of Grau's new order. The removal of
Grau, accomplished by the Welles-Batista collaboration, constituted
the first step in safeguarding this investment. The second and equally
important measure was a remodeled Cuban-American trade agreement. In May 1934 Cuban sugar came under a quota set by the United
States: 1,902,000 short tons at a duty of 1½–2¢ a pound. A new commercial treaty, replacing the Cuban-American treaty of 1902, offered
reductions on specified Cuban products imported into the United
States, but reciprocally Cuba had to reduce import duties on a variety
of American products. The treaty was virtually forced upon the republic, and its impact on the Cuban economy was considerable.
Among other things, the creation of a sugar quota, a seemingly beneficial gesture, helped to perpetuate a monoculture economy, for sugar
offered perhaps the only means by which the republic could earn
dollars in order to pay for the manufactured products it purchased
from the United States. Cuban intentions to diversify the economy
suffered. By defining its own interests in narrow terms, the United
States demanded such preferences for its products in the Cuban economy as to create, in effect, a marketplace.[18]

These were years when Batista, irritated by American economic
prescriptions, flirted with the left and pursued a Cuban variant of
economic nationalism by periodically threatening American investments. He delivered unsubtle critiques of the unfairness of the reciprocal trade program. There was speculation that Cuba might follow
the example of Lázaro Cárdenas's Mexico, which, in a labor dispute

between Mexican workers and American petroleum interests in 1938, suddenly nationalized the companies. But Cuba needed its sugar quota and could not so confront the United States. Batista modified his economic nationalism and became more cautious about promoting leftist experiments. Needing a secure Cuba, the United States responded with a supplemental trade agreement in December 1939, negotiated during Batista's highly publicized 1938 visit to Washington. He returned to Havana a hero, but in his dealings with the Americans he had sold out whatever reformist philosophy he had. Despite the promulgation of mild revolutionary promises in the Cuban constitution of 1940, American investments in the island were safe—as long as Batista remained.[19]

The Good Neighbor and Caribbean Dictatorship

Among the several charges leveled at American foreign policy after World War II was condemnation of the cozy relationship between the United States and Caribbean strongmen, notably Batista in Cuba, Trujillo in the Dominican Republic, and Somoza in Nicaragua. While professing democratic principles, this criticism held, American officialdom not only dealt with but actually sustained antidemocratic regimes in a part of the world where American political influence was strongest. The origins of such collusion with Caribbean dictatorship lay, presumably, in the Roosevelt administration's adjustment to and acceptance of the Caribbean dictator as the best alternative to direct intervention to guarantee stability and safeguard American economic interests.

Nicaragua after 1932 is a good example of such accommodation to dictatorship. In 1934 Anastasio Somoza, head of the American-created national guard, eliminated a popular anti-American, Augusto Sandino, and began consolidating his hold on the country. Somoza ruled from behind the scenes until 1936, when he deposed President Sacasa, in a manner blatantly in violation of the old Central American treaty system. By this time, however, the United States had pledged itself to nonintervention; and the treaties of 1923, by which it might otherwise have interfered, were defunct. In any event Somoza provided political order and fitful economic progress. Later, when the State Department grew apprehensive about Nazi infiltration in the hemisphere, Somoza, alert to Washington's priorities, struck an anti-German posture and won new converts in the United States.[20]

In other Caribbean nations, too, the 1930s witnessed maturation of the strongman as the pro-American bastion against internal disorder and European fascism. In Cuba, the acceptance of a firm and faithful ally came about because of the subtle and ingenious maneuverings of Batista in the uncertain days of 1933 and, later, because of his acute perceptions of American wishes. At the beginning of his meteoric rise, Batista expressed few political convictions, and certainly he projected no recognizable political philosophy or even a practical solution to Cuba's chronic troubles. Rather, his survival and triumph depended on his unmatched ability to discern American desires in Cuba. When Welles and Hull spoke of a government capable of guaranteeing order, Batista provided one.[21]

For Batista, 1933 was only the beginning. After his chosen candidate became president in 1934 and won speedy recognition from the United States, Batista promoted himself as a Cuban nationalist-reformer, as a model of leadership to inspire the frustrated revolutionaries of 1933, and as a guarantor of stability to reassure the Americans. In June 1934 ecstatic Cubans learned of the abrogation of the hated Platt Amendment; they were perhaps less conscious of the continued presence of American war vessels in Cuban waters and American military personnel at Guantánamo. Among Cubans, Batista stood as the provider of order—even Mendieta came to Camp Columbia to pay homage to the former clerk-stenographer. As a gesture of commitment to Batista, the president doubled the armed forces. By 1936 the military siphoned more than a fifth of the national budget, a proportion unheard of even at the height of Machado's dictatorship. In the old days the government exploited the military; with Batista in charge of the army, the military manipulated the government.[22]

In these years the American ambassador, Jefferson Caffery, wrote either dolorous reports about terrorist groups or depressing economic news. Mendieta lived from crisis to crisis, but Batista broadened his interests and won more praise. In a curious manner his prestige rose despite adverse publicity in American liberal publications, which sometimes portrayed him as the new Machado. An unofficial investigating commission, headed by the playwright Clifford Odets, arrived in Havana to assess political conditions. After detention and interrogation by Cuban police, it was denied permission to remain. Mounting criticism and political unrest finally brought down Mendieta, but Batista survived.

After Mendieta came Miguel Mariano Gómez y Arias, son of the second Cuban president. Presumably he had Batista's blessing. Gómez, however, dared to reassert civilian control over the military, and the two became enemies. Batista had his own dreams for a rejuvenated Cuba, but to enact his reforms he needed even broader authority for the Cuban military. In this sense, it could be argued, Batista was the true revolutionary fighting the unimaginative bureaucracy. Using an obscure 1936 decree he established 705 rural schools, each under a Cuban military officer. Within a few months some 35,000 children and 20,000 adults were participating in what was probably the most exciting and innovative program in Cuban rural education until Castro's revolution. To finance this ambitious venture Batista sought a nine-cent tax on every bag of sugar. Gómez challenged him, and Batista brought about Gómez's impeachment by the simple expedient of informing congress that failure to do so would lead to its dissolution by the military.[23]

After Gómez's impeachment, most Cubans thought Batista would simply take over as president, but he again looked for a puppet and found his man in Federico Laredo Brú, who promptly made a ringing endorsement of the military. In the next few years Laredo Brú stood by unobtrusively as Batista pushed his latest schemes, which included economic and social reform for the small sugar growers and the caneworkers, the *colonos*. In a candid moment Batista told one American observer his goal was the preemption of the Cuban left, but his overriding ambition was power. Within a few years, as economic conditions worsened, Batista quietly abandoned his flirtation with the left.

Thus, as in 1933, revolution was thwarted, this time by a leader who, until Castro, was the only one who had the personality, ability, and power to galvanize public support and build a modern, just social order in Cuba. In 1940, after a triumphant visit to the United States two years earlier, Batista, president-maker since 1934, took the oath as Cuba's seventh constitutionally elected chief executive. Whatever Cuba stood for in 1940 was doubtless embodied in this enigmatic figure who had, with the connivance and blessing of the United States, risen to command.[24]

As Batista legitimized his rule and enhanced his stature in American officialdom, another Caribbean dictator whose fortunes also depended on American goodwill busily consolidated his position. In 1933 Rafael Trujillo of the Dominican Republic had not yet become *El Benefactor*, nor did the banners proclaiming "Trujillo and God" adorn buildings in the capital. But he was already suborning opponents and eradicating enemies in his relentless determination to build a personal government that in time would rival the most authoritarian in the hemisphere.[25]

In his relations with the American government, Trujillo, well aware of adverse criticism among liberal United States journals, persistently but inoffensively sought to end the financial protectorate. In the calamitous aftermath of the 1930 hurricane, Trujillo ordered new financial measures to meet the emergency. In 1931 he signed into law a measure that violated the 1924 debt refunding arrangement, but his action precipitated no confrontation with the United States, for Trujillo contended that the law was designed to deal only with the current emergency. Three years later, as the Dominican economy improved, the 1924 plan was reinstated. Its restoration prompted favorable assessment in the State Department of Trujillo's financial responsibility. Trujillo now began to argue for a more fundamental change in the 1924 treaty in order to relieve the Dominican Republic of a burden that infringed upon its sovereignty and retarded its economic growth. When the department countered that the republic had not only an obligation to the 1924 convention but also to the holders of Dominican bonds, Trujillo responded that American investments would be safeguarded. The continuation of the financial protectorate, Trujillo observed, vitiated the meaning of the Good Neighbor policy. In 1940, following a heavily publicized visit to the United States, Trujillo had his way when the two countries agreed to a new treaty ending the customs receivership, years before its hitherto anticipated demise. Subsequently the Dominican government purchased the First National City Bank branch in Santo Domingo and created out of it a national bank. An obsequious Dominican legislature hailed Trujillo as the "Restorer of the Financial Independence of the Republic."[26]

Trujillo's ability to deal with adverse publicity was probably unmatched in the record of Caribbean dictators, as his handling of the 1937 Haitian massacre illustrated. Dominicans have always been sensitive about Haiti, an awareness heightened by stories from the era of Haitian domination in the early nineteenth century and by the mingling of Caucasian and Negro in Dominican society. Trujillo's experience with American military officers, who often denigrated Dominicans as "mongrels," perhaps made him more conscious of Dominican racial makeup and explained his immigration policies, which were designed to "whiten" the republic. In the fall of 1937 the Haitian legation accused Trujillo of ordering the deaths of 12,000 Haitians living in a remote region along the border. Some estimates placed the number as high as 25,000. Trujillo survived the controversy and even foiled the plots of Dominican exiles in Puerto Rico who were convinced that adverse publicity about such an enormous crime would topple him. To other hemispheric nations he sent word that Haiti and the Dominican Republic had arrived at an amicable settlement of all their differences. For a few weeks the Haitians were content, but in mid-November they suddenly requested an investigation and mediation by Cuba, Mexico, and the United States, invoking two of the eight inter-American treaties providing for peaceful settlement of disputes. Faced with the prospect of collective intervention, Trujillo now declared the issue a domestic problem.

Trujillo's publicity network in the United States had not yet reached that level of sophistication that it would later attain. Congressman Hamilton Fish, Jr., in a bitter speech, called the Haitian massacre an "atrocity." Some of his colleagues inadvertently came to Trujillo's rescue by pointing out that any interference in the republic's internal affairs violated the Montevideo and Buenos Aires nonintervention pledges and jeopardized the Good Neighbor policy.

Trujillo compromised, offering to pay Haiti an indemnity but insisting on a Dominican investigation of the Haitian incident. In agreeing to a settlement, Trujillo pledged his government to the principles of inter-American goodwill. In 1939, in order to commemorate its leader's contribution to hemispheric peace, the republic announced a "Trujillo Prize" of $50,000, and enthusiastically compared it to the Nobel Peace Prize![27]

The Good Neighbor in Panama

More than any other Caribbean protectorate, Panama was a stepchild of the United States. Its creation as an independent republic in 1903 had resulted as much from Theodore Roosevelt's anger over Colombian rejection of a canal treaty as it had from Panamanian conspiracy. Its survival, both political and economic, depended almost entirely on American policy and the canal; and as in Cuba, the long years of a close, dependent relationship with the United States had by 1933 led to deep resentment.[28]

By the 1920s Panamanian governments had learned to live with an American colony bisecting their country, and their efforts in Washington were directed generally at increasing Panama's economic benefits from the canal and the commerce generated by transisthmian traffic. In 1926 a new treaty modifying the Hay-Bunau-Varilla accord was negotiated, but it fell victim to nationalistic opposition in the republic. The onset of the Depression three years later in the United States severely curtailed American expenditures in the Canal Zone, and Panama's fragile economy was dramatically affected. In Panama City and Colón, at the Pacific and Caribbean canal entrances, respectively, the canal company's discharged West Indian laborers, imported years earlier, took up residence and became public charges.

In 1926 a number of antigovernment political leaders, intent on removing President Florencio Harmodio Arosemena, founded Acción Comunal and in the following years transformed it into a reformist political organization. On 2 January 1931 it overthrew the president in an opéra-bouffe coup. The ousted Panamanian executive, who had counted on American marines in the Zone to preserve order as authorized by the 1903 treaty, discovered to his dismay that the United

States had no intention of reversing Acción Comunal's revolt. The old political hierarchy, which had survived for nearly three decades by periodic threats of American intervention, suddenly found itself discredited. In the ensuing campaign for the Panamanian presidency, no candidate solicited American endorsement.[29]

In October 1933, during the most trying days of the Cuban crisis, the new Panamanian president, Harmodio Arias, Jr., arrived in Washington seeking enlarged Panamanian benefits from the canal. For Arias, the canal was an obsession, as it had been for so many Panamanians. In his student days at the London School of Economics he had approached the subject with an intellectually detached view. In 1911, three years before the canal was completed, he had published a slim but persuasive volume, *The Panama Canal: A Study in International Law and Diplomacy*, in which he had argued for its internationalization, a concept once espoused by such American secretaries of state as Henry Clay but thoroughly alien to American canal policy in the twentieth century. In his conversations with Roosevelt, Arias eschewed legalities and concentrated on practicalities. The canal, he wrote in a working memorandum for Roosevelt and Hull, must be operated efficiently, but Panama should be permitted to exploit commercial advantages created by canal traffic. Conflicts of an economic nature that could not be solved by direct negotiation should be submitted to arbitration.[30]

Arias's memorandum, modified by Hull, became the Roosevelt-Arias Accord. With its appearance in the fall of 1933 the mood in Panama about the republic's future brightened considerably, for Arias also gained a commitment to discuss the provisions of the Hay-Bunau-Varilla Treaty—despite the vigorous opposition of Canal Zone officials. They maintained that the canal had not yet been "completed," and that future construction would require ample legal authority to annex adjacent land for the protection and maintenance of the canal, a stipulation thoughtfully granted by Bunau-Varilla in 1903.

For 110 sessions Welles and his Panamanian counterparts, Ricardo Alfaro and Narciso Garay, ranged over the panoply of the American-Panamanian relationship. Alfaro was a kind of controlled fury, incensed at the humiliation of his country in its required obeisance to the Yankee giant, who revealed his animosity not in prolonged outbursts but in subtle barbs. At one point, during an exasperating session over radio stations in the republic, he blurted: "It is a moral sacrifice which in the position that Panama finds itself at present means a great deal." Canal technicians argued that Panamanian radio transmission might interfere with ship-to-shore communications. Welles pled for cooperation, but Alfaro continued: "Your cooperation is not at the expense of your sovereignty and ours is." Irritated, Welles broke in, saying that Panama had reversed the Biblical beatitude to read: "It is more blessed to receive than to give." But Alfaro had the last word: "We gave all we could in 1903."[31]

From two such titans a modified treaty constituted a diplomatic milestone. The despised article I of the 1903 convention, which legalized the protectorate, was excised; in its place there appeared another, obligating Panama to defend the canal, a cleverly worded stipulation that would later be used in the defense sites negotiations. The United States relinquished the right to acquire additional lands and waters to maintain or safeguard the canal, though once more Panama promised cooperation if such acquisitions were necessary. In the realm of commerce, the disputants compromised on the nagging problem of zone commissaries, which Panamanian merchants condemned as unfair competition. By the new treaty, zone businesses would be limited to those activities necessary for the protection, maintenance, sanitation, and defense of the canal. (Subsequently this provision would be liberally interpreted by canal officials.) To mollify Panamanian business interests, the treaty provided equal privileges to sell to transiting vessels. Finally, to compensate Panama for the reduced valuation of the American dollar in 1934, the canal annuity was "increased" from $250,000 to $436,000, though in this concession the republic gained no real increase in the annuity, for the dollar had been devalued by almost 50 percent.[32]

In later years Panama would once more become an embittered nation determined to undo the evil of 1903, but when Welles and Alfaro completed their discussions in early 1935 there existed, at least momentarily, a feeling of mutual respect, inspired by an American government which recognized an earlier injustice and made partial atonement for it. The treaty did not supplant but modified the Hay-Bunau-Varilla Treaty, yet its provisions were considered so magnanimous that canal officials and the military fought its ratification for three years. The United States retained control of the Canal and the Zone but gave up the Panamanian protectorate and managed to extend practical benefits and concessions to a small Caribbean country swept by nationalism. In Cuba, the Good Neighbor had not proved to be a very good neighbor, but in Panama the Roosevelt administration was more accommodating.

Puerto Rico at Midpassage

Following the American conquest of Puerto Rico during the Spanish American War, Puerto Ricans anticipated a relationship with the United States somewhat analogous to that enjoyed by the Florida and Louisiana territories. But Congress refused to endow Puerto Ricans with the political blessings extended to earlier territorial residents.[33] On the eve of the war, Puerto Rico had won an autonomous position within the Spanish empire; the conflict, of course, destroyed this structure and left instead political dependence on the conquering American army. The military ruled until 12 April 1900, when McKinley signed into law the Foraker Act (named after Senator Joseph Foraker but actually written by Elihu Root) providing civil government for "Porto Rico," as the Bureau of Insular Affairs spelled the name of the island for thirty years.

Unfortunately the Foraker Act failed to clarify the island's legal status. It did not grant American citizenship to Puerto Ricans but extended American protection to the island's residents. Until World War I Puerto Rico's legal position was defined chiefly in a series of 1901 Supreme Court decisions known as the Insular Cases, in which the justices declared the island to be neither American nor foreign territory. A governor and eleven-member council administered it with little regard for Puerto Rican sensibilities. The Jones Act of 1917 conferred American citizenship on Puerto Ricans and provided for a legislative assembly.[34]

Perhaps unintentionally, the Jones Act also encouraged political activity. In the first two decades after annexation Puerto Rican political activists were obsessed with the varying problems posed by Anglo-Saxon rule in a Hispanic society. The gaucheries of American governors determined to Americanize the island provoked denunciations in some quarters, notably in the Unionist Party, created in 1904, which called for Puerto Rican independence. The Nationalist Party, organized after passage of the Jones Act, assailed any accommodation with Washington as treachery. Ultimately, as reality overpowered ideology and compelled Puerto Rican political leaders to accept the American presence, more of them looked to autonomy as the only realistic goal. Luís Muñoz Rivera, father of the later governor Luís Muñoz Marín, made such an adjustment, which explained in part the son's labors for the commonwealth status conferred in 1952.

The political parties' fascination with the island's legal relationship to the United States diverted attention from the abysmal economic conditions and the disappointing material progress of Puerto Ricans from 1900 until the 1930s. In some instances local politicians actually collaborated with American governors in stifling a nascent trade union movement. There emerged a powerful element, called the *incondicionales*, who wanted to Americanize everything, to the point of substituting English for Spanish in the public schools.

These obsequious attitudes pleased such governors as E. Montgomery Reilly, a Harding appointee, who brought his skills as a Kansas City mortgage banker to the Puerto Rican governorship in 1921. With patriotic cocksureness he called Puerto Ricans who wanted independence "foreigners." Reilly lasted a year and a half, spending almost a third of this time in the States. What time he was in San Juan he expended in fighting with the island's political parties. Other governors, like Horace Mann Towner and the effervescent Theodore Roosevelt, Jr., possessed more engaging personalities and were more successful, though the latter committed an unforgivable *faux pas* by telling Puerto Ricans they should practice laughing at themselves. In most cases, the governorship was nothing more than a political plum delivered to a faithful crony.[35]

In the 1930s the United States paid more attention to Puerto Rican problems, not out of any commitment to improve the island's economic status, but simply because Puerto Rican observers saw in the New Deal some hope for relieving economic distress and abolishing social inequities. For them, the Puerto Rican dilemma was a problem that could never be resolved by unending constitutional wrangling or preoccupation with the structure of government.

Just as the Depression brought forth a new political order in the United States, the accumulated economic and social miseries in the American colony encouraged a new Puerto Rican political model, dedicated to social change and determined to begin by importing the New Deal to the Island. Initial efforts were sporadic, resulting in 1935 in the creation of the Puerto Rican Reconstruction Administration (PRRA), headed by the sensitive and knowledgeable Ernest Gruening. The PRRA advanced the ambitious goal of revamping a monoculture economy. Gruening promoted agricultural resettlement, diversification, cooperative farming, and a plan for industrialization. Named the Chardón Plan, after the University of Puerto Rico chancellor, it called for an economic revolution in a stagnant outpost of empire. Some of its endeavors proved chimerical; others died in the bureaucracy; but a few, such as the construction of low-cost housing, survived the decade and were integrated into postwar planning. Special investigations undertaken by Secretary of the Interior Harold Ickes and Eleanor Roosevelt raised Puerto Rican aspirations and convinced some islanders that Washington's historical preoccupation with constitutional questions was now supplanted by new priorities.[36]

The new mood inspired such rising leaders as Luis Muñoz Marín, who had spent enough time in New York to understand American ways and to comprehend American bureaucracy. Muñoz was fluent in both English and Spanish and adapted equally well to the rising young intellectuals in Puerto Rico and to Ickes, Henry Wallace, Harry Hopkins, and Rexford Guy Tugwell. Middle-class Puerto Ricans, impressed and moved by innovative thinking, began educating their children in American rather than Spanish schools. Though the New Dealers trained no special corps of civil servants to dispatch to the tropics, the New Deal years saw the arrival of impressive and dedicated public servants on the island.

As Gordon Lewis has shown in his monumental study of Puerto

Rico, New Deal performance rarely matched its professions.[37] The PRRA spent some $57 million in five years, approximately half of which went for salaries. Its relief measures reached 220,000 persons, yet, except for the hydroelectric program, the New Deal failed to industrialize the country. Certainly the rigid social structure was left virtually intact. Efforts to make sugar production more efficient, to resettle agricultural laborers, and to extend electric service into the countryside were often experimental and by 1940 were being curtailed to meet budgetary demands for other programs in the United States. Puerto Rico in 1940 had experienced seven years of hectic planning and erratic administration but still had so little to show for the effort that Tugwell, who became governor in 1941, entitled the account of his sojourn *The Stricken Land*.

Despite their concern and innovative thinking, the New Dealers shared with their Republican predecessors a basic distrust of Puerto Rican abilities, and they were disinclined to undertake the task of Puerto Rican development. In 1931 the American record had been aptly characterized as a "broken pledge"; in 1945, after more than a decade of frenetic planning and unequalled attention from Washington, the Puerto Rican experiment was termed an "unsolved problem." Sensitive administrators liked Gruening discovered that they had to compete for funds with rival agencies. The old hierarchy fought changes in the sugar industry, sabotaged the labors of New Deal agencies, and frustrated new proposals by lobbying in Washington. The sugar producers were so bold as to offer a public relations sinecure to Tugwell, apparently to remove him from the Agriculture Department and halt his efforts on behalf of Puerto Rican agricultural reform.

These were violent years in Puerto Rico. On Palm Sunday 1937 the police, angered by the murder of Chief of Police Francis Riggs, fired on unarmed Nationalist Party demonstrators in Ponce. Neofascism, virulently anti-American, flourished; and during the war some political leaders saw in a Japanese victory Puerto Rico's salvation. Even before Riggs's murder, sympathetic New Dealers became resentful over what they perceived as Puerto Rican ingratitude. In 1936 Maryland Senator Millard Tydings, a friend of the martyred Riggs, sponsored a resolution calling for a plebiscite to decide on the question of independence. The suggestions for this measure came from Ickes, presumably a friend of Puerto Rico in Roosevelt's cabinet, who had grown irritated with Puerto Rican grumbling and impatience. Whatever its merits, the Tydings bill, if approved, would have meant economic devastation, for it would have subjected Puerto Rican exports to American tariff. Its real purpose was to quiet the cries for independence.[38]

7 • The Impact of War

Through kind words and restraint Franklin D. Roosevelt changed the image of the United States in Latin America from predator to collaborator. In 1936, after his trouncing of Alfred Landon in the presidential election, his victory was interpreted throughout the hemisphere as a vindication of democracy. En route to the December Buenos Aires conference, he stopped briefly in Rio de Janeiro, where a throng of children waving banners cheered and sang the American national anthem. After a polite address to the Brazilian congress he was lauded as "the man." Arriving in Argentina, historically America's antagonist in inter-American politics, Roosevelt was acclaimed as a personable leader who understood the Latin character, a characterization rarely applied to American political leaders. His remarks about democracy at the opening session of the conference, wrote an El Salvadorean editor, inspired every hemispheric nation to collaborate with the United States in the search for peace.[1]

Though its head of state had been gloriously received in Buenos Aires, the United States in 1936 had no commitment from Latin America to the collective defense of the hemisphere. Roosevelt always stressed the fact that the Good Neighbor policy could never exist solely on American pledges of nonintervention and noninterference, but must also encompass Latin American reciprocity. By this, he meant a hemispheric contribution to the defense of the Americas, perhaps not by military participation against an enemy of the United States but certainly to the extent of providing defense sites or collaborating with American officials in eradicating Axis influence in the hemisphere. At Buenos Aires Roosevelt recommitted the United States to nonintervention; in return he expected the other republics to underwrite strong measures for collective action if hemispheric tranquillity were menaced. Instead, the other delegations, with Argentina leading the way, adopted a vague resolution agreeing to consult one another in the event the hemisphere was endangered by a foreign conflict. At the eighth inter-American conference at Lima two years later, when the dangers of European war were more appar-

ent, the United States emerged with a pledge of continental solidarity and, as at Buenos Aires, a promise of consultation if peace were
threatened, but it was understood that each nation would act unilaterally in dealing with foreign threats.[2]

The United States and the Axis Menace

In the years before World War I, as the protectorate policy evolved,
the United States had shown an inordinate concern over German
activity in the Caribbean. This fear had surfaced during the Venezuelan crisis of 1902–3, when German participation in the blockade of
a hemispheric republic lying on one of the sea approaches to the future isthmian canal had aroused suspicion of German intentions to
acquire naval sites in the New World. The crisis subsided under Theodore Roosevelt's diplomatic pressure, but American suspicions about
German designs remained.

Adolf Hitler's new order posed, by comparison with pre–World
War I Germany, a more ominous threat to American security in the
Caribbean. In the years after Versailles a sizable German community
matured in several Latin American nations, and in Berlin it was presumed that immigrants of German ancestry, though naturalized citizens of another land, maintained allegiance to the fatherland. For one
thing, German residents in Latin American countries tended to live
apart from the local population, educated their children in separate
schools where German was the language of instruction, and maintained contacts with the old country. After the Nazis took over, Hitler
used those agencies that already had information on Germans living
in foreign lands to propagandize the glories of the Third Reich.
When Joseph Goebbels became propaganda minister, these activities
accelerated. German communities throughout the Americas received
government reports and political news stressing German cultural
ties, the peaceful nature of German foreign policy, and the importance of loyalty to the fatherland.[3]

And, given the tremendous advances in German military technology in the thirties, the Caribbean on the eve of World War II appeared

vulnerable. Defense planners in Washington, for years accustomed to pittances in military appropriations, in 1939 found themselves facing the unsettling prospect of defending not only the continental United States but also a goodly portion of the Western Hemisphere with inadequate resources.[4] In such an atmosphere, it is easy to understand how a sensitive observer like Secretary of State Cordell Hull portrayed the new generation of Latin American nationalistic political leaders as protofascists. To Hull, even more than to Roosevelt, the smaller Caribbean nations appeared casually indifferent to the external military threat and the internal danger of subversion by fascist elements. Yet any unusual diplomatic pressure by Washington to compel Caribbean governments to undertake stronger measures against Axis activity was bound to have unfortunate repercussions and disturb the tenuous commitment made at the Lima conference.

American officials and especially American newspapers rarely distinguished between the variants of European totalitarianism in their analyses of the Axis threat to the hemisphere, but Latin American observers did make a critical distinction, as the case of Guatemala illustrated. In 1931 Jorge Ubico, one of the republic's most powerful rulers in all its turbulent political history, assumed the presidency. His regime sought cordial relations with the United States, but Ubico, sensitive to Guatemala's precarious trade balances, also sought the goodwill of Hitler's Germany, second only to the United States as a purchaser of Guatemalan exports. A significant German community had grown up in Guatemala since World War I and had entrenched itself by intermarriage with the republic's social elite. German residents acquired Guatemalan citizenship but retained strong ties with the old country. They operated some of the finest coffee fincas in the republic, managed retail stores in Guatemala City, and founded one of Guatemala's most prestigious banks, the Nottebohn Hermanos.

What aroused numerous American press declarations against Ubico's government was his reaction to Spanish fascism. To Ubico and his countrymen, General Francisco Franco was less the fascist than the Hispanic champion of *personalismo*. When Franco's Falange created a government, Ubico recognized it, principally because of its strong military character. (El Salvador and Nicaragua also recognized Franco's government shortly after Guatemala acted.) In a similar identification with Hispanic tradition, Ubico hailed Mussolini's fascist experiment in Italy. Hitler he considered inferior. At no time in the 1930s, even as Germany marched from one diplomatic triumph to another, did Guatemala deviate from Ubico's staunchly pro-American stance in world affairs. Yet the dictator's fascination with Franco, his respect for Mussolini, and his obvious disdain for Hitler were curiously inverted in American eyes as evidence of Axis penetration in Guatemalan affairs. In 1936, following Italy's abrupt withdrawal from the League of Nations, Guatemala also resigned from the League, prompting a fresh round of charges of fascist pressure, though Ubico's government stated that its decision was based on economic factors. Honduras and El Salvador left the League within the year, reinforcing American suspicions of Axis pressure in Central America.

After the Lima conference, which cleared Ubico's doubts about American resolve, the Guatemalan president undertook closer supervision of German activity in the republic. He invoked special restrictions prohibiting political activity by foreigners, including assembly, propaganda, and the wearing of uniforms. Germany championed Guatemala's long-standing claim to Belize, but when the European war erupted in September 1939 Ubico called in the British ambassador to inform him that, as a moral obligation, Guatemala would resume payment on its British debt, suspended as protest in the Belize dispute. Unfortunately these gestures did not dispel American suspicion of Ubico's fascist sympathies.[5]

In the American view, then, the Caribbean republics, rewarded by American disavowal of unilateral intervention, now stood obligated to integrate their collective energies in the common defense. This meant, generally, acquiescence in Washington's policies to secure the vital Caribbean area by strengthening American military installations, by acquiring new defense sites, and by forceful measures by Caribbean governments to rid their countries of subversive elements.

If threatened with economic retaliation from Europe, Roosevelt stated in his April 1939 Pan American Day address, the United States would extend economic support to Caribbean nations. Impressed by American resolve, a number of the Caribbean nations proposed the creation of an inter-American bank to expedite trade within the hemisphere and to facilitate exchange. But this suggestion incurred disfavor among some in the Roosevelt administration who felt that the Export-Import Bank, which sanctioned bilateral loans, already performed this task. At the Panama conference, which met in hectic session for eight days in late September and early October to consider hemispheric response to the outbreak of war, Latin American delegates renewed their efforts for the bank. In subsequent months the administration, using questionnaires submitted to each of the republics by the Inter-American Financial and Advisory Committee, at last produced a charter. Several respondents sounded an extremely negative note about the bank's operations. Nicaragua, for example, offered moral support but expressed doubts about its ability to help finance the bank. Other governments were skeptical about American commitments to purchase Latin American goods in sufficient quantity to permit repayment of bank loans. By May 1940 eight countries had committed themselves, but when the administration approached Congress for funding, the bank proposal encountered especially strong resistance from conservatives, who viewed it as a threat to American free enterprise in Latin America. Roosevelt's advisors, sensing further opposition, lost hope, and the bank bill died in committee.[6]

Economic considerations dominated the Panama conference, but its most publicized act was the Declaration of Panama, which forbade belligerent activity within a hemispheric "safety belt," a line drawn around the continent, excluding Canada and European territories, at an average distance of 300 miles from the coast. This proclamation was denounced by the belligerents, declared illegal by several eminent international jurists, and rudely violated in the dramatic battle between several British warships and the German pocket battleship *Graf Spee* off the Brazilian coast in late 1939. In the Caribbean the Declaration of Panama accentuated fears about defense and brought more pressure on the republics to increase their surveillance of German shipping in Caribbean ports in order to prevent these vessels from servicing German submarines. A related matter involved air and sea patrol by the American Navy along the Caribbean coast of the Central American isthmus, the northern coast of South America, and the chain of Antillean islands. Sumner Welles had raised this question at Panama and had found most of the delegates responsive to suggestions about collective patrols, though Mexico, where German propaganda efforts had met with some success, was initially skeptical. Despite Mexican hesitation, by the end of 1939 satisfactory agreements on this problem had been worked out with Caribbean governments.[7]

At the same time the State Department became concerned over the employment of German and Italian personnel in Latin American airlines. It was particularly alarmed about the German nationals who piloted aircraft for SCADTA (Colombian-German Air Transport Company), which operated in Colombia within flying distance of the canal. The department brought intense pressure on Bogotá to replace the German pilots and to take over SCADTA, which, incidentally, Colombia was eager to do. As matters developed, the Colombians could not move without substantial support from Panair, a Pan American World Airways subsidiary which, it was discovered, already owned 80 percent of SCADTA stock. Despite much wrangling Washington continued its efforts, and by March 1940 most of the German pilots had been removed.[8]

By the spring of 1940, when Hitler unleashed the German blitzkrieg against Western Europe, both the American government and the public recognized the vulnerability of the Caribbean. Before the fall of France, opinion polls revealed that two-thirds of the public supported direct military intervention in Latin America to forestall any German threat. To safeguard the Caribbean approaches to the Panama Canal, the United States possessed bases in Cuba and Puerto Rico, but lying south was a long string of islands, belonging to Great Britain, France, and the Netherlands, which collectively formed a shield guarding the Caribbean's eastern perimeter.

How to protect the Caribbean had long concerned the Joint Planning Committee of the Army and Navy. As envisaged by the committee in its series of Rainbow Plans, Caribbean defense must be given priority in securing the hemisphere against possible assault by Germany and Italy. To accomplish that goal, military planners concluded that the United States must strengthen its forces in the Canal Zone and, in addition, must obtain rights to use or develop defense facilities in Colombia, in Venezuela, and at Samaná Bay on the northeastern coast of the Dominican Republic. Acquiring additional bases in European possessions or in the Caribbean republics posed a political problem. Among the public there existed some sentiment for pressing European powers in default on war debts to cede their hemispheric possessions to the United States. Before joining the cabinet as secretary of the navy, Frank Knox had called for seizure of Caribbean bases to protect the canal. Though favored by such military analysts as Hanson Baldwin of the *New York Times*, acquisition of Caribbean sites by political intimidation, even if justified by military emergency, would have jeopardized American policy in the hemisphere and antagonized Western European governments.

Aside from discussions with the Dutch over leasing facilities in the Netherlands West Indies, the administration did little more about European territories in the Caribbean until the fall of France in June 1940. The prospect that Hitler might compel the defeated Western European nations to cede their Caribbean possessions to Germany now seemed frighteningly imminent. Two years before, in ruminating over this possibility, Roosevelt had suggested that the hemispheric governments should announce their opposition to any transfer of sovereignty over New World territories to a nonhemispheric power and, if necessary, should proclaim a kind of Pan American condominium over such possessions.

The suddenness of Hitler's attack and the rapidity of German triumph made this approach risky, for the creation of a condominium or trusteeship over endangered European territories would have involved lengthy and doubtless quarrelsome negotiations. In mid-April 1940 the Dutch government had expressed concern about a potential German assault on Venezuelan oil facilities at Curaçao and Aruba. The companies employed German workers and were doubtful of their loyalty. In anticipation of trouble the Navy sent more destroyers to San Juan, Puerto Rico, and Welles conferred with Venezuela's ambassador. The British, fearful of immediate danger to their oil supplies, landed marines in Aruba, reassuring the Dutch that they would withdraw when Dutch reinforcements arrived.[9]

The drive to prevent cession of European territories to Germany culminated in the summer of 1940. One hundred and twenty-nine years before, the House of Representatives, alarmed about the possible cession of Spanish Florida to a more formidable European power, had passed the No-Transfer Resolution forbidding the cession of Florida to a nonhemispheric nation. In the course of the nineteenth century, the resolution served as a parallel statement to the Monroe Doctrine; in the 1870s it became a corollary to the doctrine. In the spring of 1940, Congress again expressed its determination not to recognize transfer of New World territory from one non-American power to another. Going further, and manifesting a commitment to collective measures unknown to the generation of 1811, it resolved, if such transfers occurred, to consult with other hemispheric republics to determine appropriate action.

The resolution went out to Rome and Berlin on the day France fell, and to London, Paris, and The Hague a short time later. Already the State Department had made preparations to introduce the measure at the Havana conference in July, but in terms of immediate military threat, Congress had granted the President sweeping authority to defend the No-Transfer Resolution in the most expeditious manner. When, in response, Hitler's foreign minister Joachim von Ribbentrop denigrated the Monroe Doctrine and implied that the United States was arrogantly asserting its hegemony over Latin America, Hull labeled the doctrine a statement of self-defense, in no sense comparable to the imperial pretensions of Hitler's new order.

At Havana the no-transfer principle was even expanded to include such questions as the political relationship between European and Western Hemisphere nations as appropriate topics for collective concern. The Act of Havana pan-Americanized the No-Transfer Resolution but not without strenuous bargaining. Brazil, Mexico, and Cuba, nations of varying size and influence in the Pan American system, enthusiastically concurred; but others with territorial claims on European-held possessions—such as Guatemala, which coveted Belize, or Venezuela, which wanted a plebiscite to ascertain if the residents of Aruba, Curaçao, or Bonaire wished annexation to the "geographically closest hemispheric nation" (as Caracas so cleverly phrased it)—offered other solutions. Argentina, irritated by American sponsorship of the resolution, wanted to omit the Falkland Islands from inclusion, for they had been a subject of dispute between Buenos Aires and London since the 1830s. Hitler brought diplomatic and economic pressure to bear on the smaller and more vulnerable countries, some of which relied heavily on European markets and could therefore be severely damaged by retaliatory policies. The State Department launched a vigorous anti-German propaganda drive, and to compensate for Latin American losses in the European market, Congress increased the lending authority of the Export-Import Bank to $500 million. In the conference Argentina proved to be the most obstreperous, supporting the No-Transfer Resolution but opposing any plan for collective trusteeship. In search of unanimity, Hull delivered a dramatic personal appeal to Argentina's president. New instructions arrived from Buenos Aires, and the Argentine delegation capitulated.

Before the Havana conference adjourned, the hemispheric republics were suddenly confronted with an immediate problem relating to the French West Indies. Up to now, the main fear had centered on a forced cession of European territory to Germany. With the creation of a collaborationist French regime at Vichy, another danger materialized: Vichy's captive bureaucrats might willingly extend to Berlin considerable authority in French Guiana and the French Antilles—such as the use of ports or military bases—without actually transferring sovereignty over these possessions to Germany. As in the crises over Aruba and Curaçao, the British, fearful of some imminent German move, resolved to act with military measures. London was particularly alarmed over the presence in Martinique of a French cruiser and an aircraft carrier, the latter carrying 106 planes purchased from the United States and $250 million in French bullion hastily transferred from Canada. Trinidad's British governor had already urged his French counterpart for Guiana and the Antilles to declare in favor of Charles de Gaulle's Free French movement or, at least, to allow British surveillance of French territory. On 4 July Britain declared a blockade of Martinique.

Though Britain failed to consult the Americans before announcing the blockade, its action was not unanticipated in Washington, for on 1 July Welles had expressed to the British ambassador American opposition to any British preemptive authority over the French West Indies. Subsequently Roosevelt dispatched seven warships to Martinique to accompany the patrolling British ships. But having demonstrated its determination to police the Caribbean, the United States now found it difficult to thrash out a suitable arrangement between local British and French officials. The latter refused to resell the planes to the manufacturers or to permit internment of their ships in American ports.

In early fall 1940, alarmed over Vichy's intentions toward a beleaguered Britain, the United States informed the collaborationist French regime that a declaration of war against Britain would bring about an inter-American trusteeship over French colonies in the Western Hemisphere. Learning of French plans for military construction on Martinique, Roosevelt expressed his displeasure in forceful terms and demanded neutralization of France's hemispheric territories. Following another alarm over German-French intentions concerning Martinique, during which Secretary of the Navy Knox recommended the dispatch of 5,000 American troops to the island, an American admiral successfully negotiated an agreement with the French commissioner to neutralize the French West Indies. The United States did not invoke the Act of Havana during this crisis, but French anticipation of an inter-American trusteeship had prompted the Vichy government to mollify Washington by agreeing to neutralization.[10]

Negotiating for Bases in Panama

The destroyers-for-bases agreement was easily the most spectacular move in Roosevelt's defense strategy in 1940. Anxious to prevent German intrusion into the Caribbean, the United States suddenly had acquired ninety-nine-year leases at Newfoundland, Bermuda, the Bahamas, Jamaica, St. Lucia, Trinidad, Antigua, and British Guiana at a moment when the American military was unprepared to occupy them but when, unknown to the American public, it already enjoyed limited use of these facilities.

The negotiations with Britain overshadowed controversial negotiations with Panama for military leases in the republic. As late as 1935 canal authorities had concluded that the waterway, the "jugular vein" of hemispheric security, remained invulnerable to external attack. The Army, responsible for canal defense, had constructed what it considered a fortress in the Zone: four 16-inch and six 6-inch guns guarded the Pacific entrance; a 16-inch and a 14-inch guarded the Caribbean. To protect the flanks the military had its armed contingents and the presumably impenetrable jungle.

Rapid changes in military technology, especially in aircraft and aircraft carriers, made the canal strategy obsolete. Against an air attack the heavy artillery at canal entrances was relatively useless; the oceans, heretofore considered barriers protecting the Western Hemisphere, were now highways. These considerations prompted the War Department's hasty reassessment of canal fortifications, brought Hull to a worrisome analysis of fascist influence in countries lying within air striking distance of the canal, and precipitated intensive American efforts to remove German pilots and technicians from Colombian air lines.[11]

In Panama the new strategy called for an "outer defense line" far enough from the Zone to permit Army planes to intercept attackers before they reached the canal. Under the 1903 treaty, the procurement of additional land or waters for defense had posed no insurmountable difficulty, given the broad interpretations of treaty clauses. The United States held in perpetuity "the use, occupation and control of other lands and waters outside of the zone . . . which may be necessary and convenient for the . . . protection of the . . . canal." The 1936 modification, reflecting a heightened appreciation of Panamanian nationalism, established more rigid stipulations for territorial acquisition. The problem was now as much political as military.

The War Department had studied political and military problems relating to acquisition of land in Latin America in 1936 and had concluded, on a somewhat despondent note, that except for emergencies any military pressure for defense leases would arouse fear of American imperialism. Now, with the frightening implications of air power, there was no longer any prudent reason for hesitation: the prospect of a successful air assault on the canal locks outweighed any consideration for Panamanian sensitivities. To the Army the Hull-Alfaro Treaty of 1936 contained not only a pledge by the United States to stop interfering in Panamanian politics but also a promise by Panama to reciprocate in the vital area of canal defense. This could be done, as the War Department interpreted it, in a spirit of cooperation and in long-term leasing of Panamanian sites for defense installations.

For the Panamanian government such a proposal brought fears of the creation of "little canal zones" throughout the republic, fears that were not without justification. A week after the outbreak of the European conflict, the War Department submitted to the State Department a list of ten sites that were needed immediately for defense purposes. With the exception of Río Hato, which contained 19,000 acres, each of the sites was less than one acre. But the acreage was not the crucial issue. What the War Department wanted was leases for 999 (not 99) years and complete authority over the bases. When the State Department expressed its dismay at such terms and claimed that Panama would not settle for anything less than a lease time of, say, the duration of the military emergency and then would expect some control over Panamanian civilians on the bases, the only response from the military was a statement reaffirming Panamanian sovereignty and a pledge to channel civilian judicial problems to Panamanian courts. Any further concessions, General Daniel Van Voorhis, the Zone commander, told William Dawson, the American ambassador to Panama, would jeopardize military efficiency.[12]

The situation worsened when Arnulfo Arias, a physician educated at Harvard and at the University of Chicago, became Panamanian president in October 1940.[13] Fiery, xenophobic, and a power in the *panameño* political movement, Arias espoused such anti-American views that Hull lumped him into the protofascist camp. The Panamanian leader's policies were in fact a logical byproduct of decades of anti-American feelings. In a radio address shortly after taking office, he attacked Canal Zone military commanders for illegally trespassing on several proposed defense sites in the republic. Dawson feared a breakdown in negotiations when the War Department suddenly added another list of sixty sites to its original request.

When negotiations reopened in November, Arias appeared cooperative. He recognized Panama's obligations to canal security, but the Army's plan for base supervision was, in his opinion, a violation of Panama's sovereignty. No transfer of authority for the defense sites could be extended until the United States and Panama solved several broader problems: the impact of the installations on Panamanian security; smuggling between the bases and surrounding villages; the realty owned by the Panama Railroad Company, an American subsidiary, in Panama City and Colón; Zone commissaries, which, Arias said, still competed unfairly with Panamanian merchants; duration of the leases; and jurisdiction over each site.

Clearly, Arias wanted to negotiate issues going far beyond the immediate problem of defense sites. Army officials would be hesitant to spend time and money improving any site if the lease expired in four to six years, as Arias wished. There was much less time for bargaining with the Panamanian president, for canal defense was now receiving priority from the administration. More and more, Arias's far-reaching suggestions seemed to be political blackmail. What relationship, Hull asked, existed between Panama's military obligations and the commissary system? Still, as Hull and Dawson recognized, Panama would have to be mollified before the military could start construction at the new sites.[14]

Hull suggested reducing the 999-year requests to 99 in order to soothe Arias and mitigate his fears about Americanization of the Isthmus. In conveying the reworded proposals, Dawson emphasized Panama's obligation to canal defense, its monetary rewards for extending the leases, and, for the first time, the Army's willingness to permit Panamanian jurisdiction over civilian employees on the bases. Still, the advantage lay with Arias. He could delay transferring the sites until Panama got its assurances of economic assistance. If the American government refused, then occupation of the sites might be delayed interminably, prolonging danger to the canal. If the Army became irritated with these delays, it might occupy the sites without permission, enabling Arias to label the Good Neighbor policy as fraudulent and the United States, in a favorite term, as the "colossus of the north."

For the State Department, caught between an immovable Arias and an increasingly irritated Zone military, the only plausible solution was to show firmness and conviction yet provide Arias with some of the things he was demanding. On specific matters, such as jurisdiction over the sites or the amount of aid, no concrete agreement was reached as long as Arias remained in power. But with the hint of aid, Dawson discovered, Arias became more lenient, informing the American ambassador that if the American government declared that the canal was threatened, under the terms of the 1936 convention Pana-

ma was obligated to render assistance. In this manner the sites could
be occupied, with details to be negotiated later, and Arias could stand
before a suspicious national assembly, justifiably acquiescing in the
occupation.

In February 1941 Hull drew up the necessary statement, and the
occupation got underway the following month. But when State Department advisors arrived at what they considered a fair rental value
($19,000 annually for the sites plus consideration for Arias's public
projects), the Panamanian executive asked instead for completion of
twelve projects, at an estimated cost of $25 million, or advance pay-
ment on the canal annuity for fifty years. To complicate matters, the
military, the State Department, and Arias were still at odds over the
length of the leases; Arias felt a fair lease would be the duration of
the global crisis, meaning, presumably, until the end of the war. But,
the State Department wanted a commitment until the danger to the
canal had passed; and General Van Voorhis, a lease for at least ten
years. Van Voorhis, piqued over having to fly Panamanian officials
over proposed sites, now spoke darkly of dictating to Panama.

What followed in mid-1941 was Army occupation of the defense
sites without formal agreement on the issues of jurisdiction or of
economic compensation to Panama. In June negotiations were transferred from Panama City to Washington, where Welles, now undersecretary of state, assumed responsibility for their completion. The
Panamanians continued to worry about "little canal zones" strewn
about the republic; Welles spoke of isthmian obligations under the
1936 pact. No substantive decision was reached until the sudden overthrow of Arias in October. The new Panamanian president, Ernesto
de la Guardia, proved more conciliatory: the stalled negotiations were
resumed, and in early 1942 a settlement was reached. Occupation
of defense sites would terminate one year after a treaty ending the
war. Arias's suggested rent of $4,000 per hectare, which had been
called outrageous, was scaled down to $50 per hectare, except for the
large site at Río Hato, which would be leased for $10,000 annually.
Panama would also receive economic aid for the completion of several
public works projects, but the amount was to be much less than Arias
had demanded.

One troublesome element in this confrontation was the charge of profascism leveled at Arias. Such comments reflected the understandable fear by Americans in 1941 that Western democratic institutions and values were losing out in the struggle for the hemisphere. A more judicious characterization of Arias would have been Panamanian nationalist; he styled his politics "Panama for the Panamanians." The national constitution of 1941, reflecting his views, discriminated against foreigners. The government forbade the use of English in business negotiations and discouraged the sale of English-language newspapers. But Arias also sponsored a Panamanian social security system and an agricultural bank, similar in intent to New Deal reforms. His querulous disposition and his skepticism of American military planning made him a likely target for those critics who, like Hull, saw in him a new breed of hemispheric fascist. The Panama negotiations revealed, among other things, that even the weakest Latin American republic, in assessing the Good Neighbor, wanted proof as well as promises.[15]

The Caribbean in Wartime

The United States entered the war expecting wholehearted cooperation from the Caribbean republics; and with the exception of Panama, the Roosevelt administration encountered no immediate difficulties. At the special conference at Rio de Janeiro in 1942, where Hull's determination to mobilize a solid front withered under Argentine defiance and Chilean skittishness, Welles accepted a compromise that did not require the severance of diplomatic relations with the Axis powers. By contrast, the Caribbean republics broke relations; and by the time the Rio meeting ended, Costa Rica, Panama, Cuba, Nicaragua, Honduras, Guatemala, and El Salvador had declared war.[16]

Having acquired Caribbean defense installations in the destroyer deal, the United States military moved rapidly to transform languid British colonies into vigorous outposts of Caribbean defense. The initial apprehension about constructing bases in sufficient time to meet the anticipated German threat was, in retrospect, an exaggerated fear. Once plans were drawn up and material brought in, work on the sites advanced rapidly. By December 1941 the airfields were ready for battle.

American commanders soon discovered that their main problems stemmed mostly from poor social relations between troops and the local population. American soldiers arrived in an unknown environment, ill-informed about the history, culture, or social peculiarities of the Caribbean. Usually, rifts occurred because of charges of price-gouging by local merchants, but other clashes had racial overtones. On Trinidad, for example, racial animosity flared between white soldiers and black Trinidadians. Until mid-1942 the State Department deliberately avoided dispatching blacks to West Indian sites for fear local whites might be disturbed over the presence of black soldiers. In most situations, the personality of American commanders was of critical importance: if commanders were capable and sensitive to local attitudes, problems were dealt with and unpleasantness avoided.

The United States, not the Caribbean nations, intended to defend the Caribbean. Five days after Pearl Harbor, Secretary of War Henry Stimson discovered the Army and Navy had not yet resolved the command problem for the Caribbean theater, but a week later the Navy assumed primary responsibility for sea defenses, in accordance with Roosevelt's designation of the Caribbean as a coastal frontier. The Army retained responsibility for the defense of Panama and the canal. The War Plans Division Rainbow 5 plan went into effect, and reinforcements were speedily dispatched to Caribbean bases. The number of air and ground personnel sent in December was more than twice what had been assigned to the area in the previous eleven months. Because the canal was considered vulnerable to Japanese assault, Army garrisons in Panama initially received the largest quota of men and materiel. One year after the Pearl Harbor attack, the Caribbean Defense Command reached a total of 119,000 men, half of them stationed in Panama.[17]

Rainbow 5 anticipated war with Germany and Italy with Europe as the battleground; the Caribbean, Army and Navy strategists had surmised, was relatively safe from attack. The assignment of a majority of the troops and equipment to Panama reflected military thinking that a greater danger lay in a carrier strike against the canal from the Pacific. In the course of things, the canal was never seriously threatened, and the only Axis attack against Caribbean territory occurred in February 1942, when German submarines sank five tankers, four British and one Venezuelan, at Aruba. Two of the ships were anchored in San Nicolas harbor. After they were hit, the German U-boat surfaced and fired on the oil refinery, causing a fire. Later, as planes flew over the area searching for German submarines, a U-boat severely damaged an American tanker anchored only four miles from the airfield. In the next month submarines sank 21 ships; in May the losses reached 35 ships. The total by the end of the year climbed to a staggering 336 ships, approximately 1.5 million tons. After that, however, the antisubmarine patrols and decline in U-boat activity sharply reduced shipping losses in the Caribbean theater, to 35 ships in 1943 and only 3 in 1944.[18]

The war's most lasting impact was not the naval assault of German submarines but the intrusion of American economic and political power. In an earlier era, the United States had ordinarily manifested its will in the Caribbean by issuing hortatory pronouncements or, in more serious situations, by sending a warship or by landing marines. In World War II the United States sent more than diplomats or marines. It dispatched military missions and economic advisors; it created bustling towns to service its military installations; and it became the purchaser of Caribbean products and the supplier of manufactures to Caribbean consumers.

Roosevelt spoke of the wartime relationship as the "policy of the good partner," which meant that the hemisphere had progressed beyond good neighborliness to participation in the common struggle for the common good. To promote the new order, the American government greatly expanded its cultural programs for the hemisphere, including a tour of Latin America by Yale's glee club. Committees on agricultural education, foreign students, and exchange fellowships and professorships promoted cultural togetherness. The Office of Coordinator of Inter-American Affairs, under the leadership of Nelson Rockefeller, beamed anti-Axis radio broadcasts, distributed free magazines (*En Guardia* was the best known), and hired Walt Disney to produce cartoons with Latin American themes.[19]

The loss of European markets and the uncertainties of imports seriously damaged the already fragile Caribbean economy. Cuba fared better than the other republics because its prewar government had undertaken a program of diversification, particularly in agriculture; in 1942 Batista announced that in order to meet wartime needs certain crops must be grown in designated areas. In Haiti and the Dominican Republic, more dependent on the outside world than Cuba, import problems were aggravated by the limited availability of gasoline and tires for the vehicles that distributed food. By mid-1942, it was estimated, Haitian imports had fallen to 49,000 metric tons annually, a considerable part of which were foodstuffs.[20]

In Puerto Rico and the smaller European dependencies of the Antilles the economic situation was even worse. Before 1941 Puerto Rico utilized only 20 percent of its crop land for subsistence products. The remainder of its food arrived by ship, yet the amount of imported food fell dangerously in 1942, to a point equal to 20 percent of annual prewar food imports. Shortages of raw materials and export equipment closed down Puerto Rican factories and precipitated widespread unemployment. Left to fend for themselves, the Antillean outposts of European empire hurriedly developed new agricultural sources. In Barbados, which had raised only 5 percent of its food before the war, the colonial government decreed that 25 percent of arable land on each plantation must be sown in food crops. Other islands adopted similar plans, but shortages persisted because of the limitation of arable land. In Puerto Rico, for example, the cultivation of all arable land with subsistence crops would not have satisfied domestic food requirements.[21]

Concerned for the well-being of the Caribbean and mindful of its own interests, the United States promoted public works to relieve unemployment and pressed responsible European governments to alter the political practices in their Caribbean colonies in anticipation of political unrest stemming from the economic situation. The United States favored policies that expanded the franchise, as in Jamaica, or modified the constitution, as in Barbados. For the future, Washington enthusiastically supported the Anglo-American Caribbean Commission, created to study a broad range of problems—education, health, social welfare, economics, labor, and agriculture. One of its earliest recommendations called for pooling and distributing food by small vessels sailing between the islands. In 1943, as the food problem became more critical, Cuba, Haiti, and the Dominican Republic signed a cooperative agreement by which food was stockpiled in Cuba and shipped at American expense to other islands.[22]

The war fostered a mutual dependence. It was official policy not to discriminate against Latin America in the allocation of materiel and facilities, and the American government established price levels on manufactures shipped southward, in years when American producers held a virtual monopoly on consumer products sold to Latin Americans. Equally apparent was the American wartime reliance on Latin America for a variety of materials, particularly rubber, sisal, and antimony, all theretofore procured from Asian sources; and other vital products such as asbestos, manganese, silver, vanadium, bauxite, zinc, copper, and henequen. In 1942 the United States contracted to purchase Haiti's entire cotton crop until the war ended; the next year it bought the entire sugar crop of the Dominican Republic, Cuba, and Haiti. American companies operating in Latin America received tax incentives by changes in the internal revenue code so as to encourage market expansion. By such means the American economic grip on the hemisphere expanded, though without the earlier opprobrious characterization of "dollar diplomacy."

Military missions flourished in the Dominican Republic and Panama; and air bases sprang up in Cuba, Haiti, Panama, and other South American sites, notably in Brazil. A land-sea route connected Florida, Cuba, Haiti, the Dominican Republic, and Puerto Rico, over which military and civilian supplies traveled. Of the almost $500 million in military equipment distributed to Latin America under Lend-Lease, Caribbean nations received only about $15 million. (Brazil alone got $375 million and Mexico, $39 million.)

In sum the war tied the Caribbean more closely than ever to the United States by every standard. European markets had been disrupted, if not permanently lost, and the smaller republics had only the United States as a source for manufactures and food. Increased American demand for Caribbean products offset the decline by European purchasing, but in a significant way it also retarded Caribbean economic diversification by preserving the area's monocultural character. The republics fared well in the balance of trade, but they could not exploit dollar reserves to buy more American goods. Latin America's portion of American exports actually declined, from roughly 17 percent of all American exports in the 1930s to about 12 percent during the war.[23] What this meant, among other things, was a dramatic wartime inflation. Building enormous dollar reserves by its exports of raw materials to the United States, the Caribbean republics, as well as the other larger states of South America, soon discovered they were spending more for fewer consumer goods. Despite wartime wage increases, real purchasing power did not increase, and at the end of the war virtually every Caribbean republic suffered from inflation. When American agencies attempted to mitigate these inflationary tendencies by imposing controls on export prices, they encountered resistance from Caribbean importers, who wielded more political power than did wage earners. The one country whose economy suffered least, as David Green has shown in his critical study of the Good Neighbor policy, was Argentina, which maintained its political defiance of Washington until the last year of the war. A perceptive economist and expert on price controls observed that in effect the United States granted these countries a paper credit. Their only salvation was the prospect that in the postwar era Latin America would receive its fair share for sacrifice in the struggle against totalitarianism.[24]

From Missionary Diplomacy to the Good Neighbor Policy: An Assessment

In 1961 Bryce Wood, in a scholarly account of New Deal hemispheric policy, observed that Franklin Roosevelt, mindful of the pitfalls encountered in the Nicaraguan and Cuban crises of 1927 and 1933, consciously pursued a Latin American policy predicated on nonintervention, noninterference, and reciprocity.[25] The United States pledged nonintervention at Montevideo and Buenos Aires in 1933 and 1936; its government, reversing earlier policies, practiced noninterference when several Latin American countries nationalized foreign property, and confined its protests to normal diplomatic channels. In return, as the global situation deteriorated and the country moved to bolster hemispheric defense, the United States expected reciprocal gestures in military and political cooperation.

In fact, the transition from Republican to Democratic administrations, from Harding, Coolidge, and Hoover to Roosevelt, brought differences in Caribbean policy less striking than has heretofore been presumed. In 1921, when Wilson left the White House, the image of the United States in the Caribbean was that of a puritanical nation enforcing political order and civic morality in the tropics. A dispirited corps of Navy and Marine officers ran Haitian and Dominican affairs; in Cuba, an American emissary, dictating from aboard a United States warship docked in Havana harbor, had virtually determined the Cuban presidential election and remained for several years to advise the republic's new executive. In Nicaragua, a financial protectorate and a legation guard presided over a demoralized political system. Panama existed as an independent republic in name only; it represented more closely a southern fiefdom of the United States, its destiny dictated by the course of American canal policy.

In the ensuing years all this began to change. Republican leaders in the 1920s were responsive, not so much to pleas for leniency for the protectorates created by their predecessors, as to rising criticism at home, particularly from the Senate. Harding and Hughes dismantled the Dominican military government by doing what Wilson and Lansing had refused to do in 1916: permitting a notorious gaggle of bickering Dominican politicians to reclaim authority, subject, of course, to their promise to repay American creditors. The Haitian occupation dragged on but with the manifest indifference of the Haitian people and noticeably declining enthusiasm in the United States. Panama could have gained a modification of the 1903 canal treaty in 1927 had its political leadership not surrendered to an embittered public protest against it. In 1925 Machado's inauguration portended a new era in Cuban politics, and at the same time the Nicaraguan situation seemed sufficiently promising to justify withdrawing the legation guard. In the meantime the United States, in the Central American treaties of 1923, reaffirmed its faith in constitutional processes and treaty law as the antidote for isthmian political violence.

The Nicaraguan intervention of 1926–27 was a departure from these trends in America's Caribbean policy, but it proved less a reversion to Big Stick diplomacy than an unsettling portent of a troubled future where a guerrilla force in a small country, inspired by a charismatic leader and aroused by nationalistic goals, could hold its own against American power. The lessons learned in Nicaragua—disarm the rebels and give the country a fair election—may not have been the right ones.

The Depression accelerated political and economic changes in the Caribbean and brought to power a new generation of Caribbean leaders, indifferent and even hostile to American professions of benevolent intervention and receptive to more radical political theories, such as European fascism, severely modified to adapt to the currents of Caribbean nationalism. In Panama, the change took the form of a middle-class political revolt aimed at getting a bigger share of canal benefits. In Cuba, it appeared first as a bitter and violent opposition to Machado and then as an experiment in socialism ultimately frustrated by the United States. In the Dominican Republic, Nicaragua, Guatemala, and, after Grau's departure, in Cuba, it was typified by the rise of the strongman who preached internal reforms to assuage the left and stabilized the political situation in order to impress the United States.

Franklin Roosevelt, as committed as his predecessors to preserving American interests in the Caribbean, responded to these political fluctuations in different ways. In Cuba, his emissary, Sumner Welles, undermined a revolutionary government by conspiring against it. In the ensuing decade, the United States suborned the inheritor of Cuban power, Fulgencio Batista. In the Dominican Republic, the American government accommodated and sometimes even praised what ultimately became a brutal dictatorship. In Nicaragua, it acquiesced in—and some critics say, supported—the creation of a political fiefdom. To Panama it offered material blessings from the canal in return for concessions to its demands for defense sites throughout the republic.

In the mid-1930s several of the Caribbean nations exhibited interest in diversifying their economies and assuming political stances which, though not expressly anti-American, were certainly less responsive to American wishes than previous Caribbean governments had ever dared be. What destroyed such aspirations was the outbreak of the European war, which disrupted Caribbean commercial ties to the Old World and sharply increased its dependence on the United States. The war brought new United States demands for political and economic conformity, this time in phrases extolling hemispheric unity as proof of democratic worthiness. Caribbean political leaders who sounded even remotely fascist stood condemned as betrayers of the faith. Aware of its vulnerability, the Caribbean once more, as it had been compelled to do so often, found its destiny bound up with that of its northern neighbor.

Part III
The United States and the Modern Caribbean

8 • The Cold War, 1945–1960

Latin America emerged from the war with high expectations for a more prosperous future. In the grand struggle against totalitarianism, the republics had dutifully subordinated their economies to the service of the United States and had accumulated goodwill and tremendous dollar reserves. In the euphoric afterglow of victory they expected to share in the postwar bounty. They exhibited an optimism about Latin America's economic prospects in a restructured world and, especially, about Latin America's role in the postwar global concerns of the United States.

But after 1945 the interests of the United States and the hemispheric republics diverged. For its part, as demonstrated in the conferences at Chapúltepec, Rio de Janeiro, and Bogotá, the United Sates wanted an orderly hemisphere, loyal to its cold war policies but undemanding of economic assistance. The republics, by contrast, were impressed by American military and economic might in 1945, but their expectation of high priority in Washington's global strategy soon turned to bitter disillusion. The southern half of the hemisphere, geographically remote from the European and Asian theaters of East-West conflict, was presumed safe from Communism. The United States, when it evinced any interest in hemispheric problems, ordinarily emphasized political fidelity. Latin America, beset by economic and social pressures and aptly characterized as the "revolution of rising expectations," was burdened by the profound task of adjustment to a modern world.[1]

The Caribbean republics dutifully ratified the Inter-American Treaty of Reciprocal Assistance of 1947, commonly known as the Río Pact, which pledged solidarity against external aggression. And at Bogotá in 1948 they endorsed the creation of the Organization of American States. In the course of the following years seven Caribbean governments also ratified the Treaty of Pacific Settlement, or Pact of Bogotá, which provided for settlement of disputes by peaceful means. The United States, which objected strenuously to one clause requiring foreign citizens to resort to domestic courts in the country where they were living rather than appealing to international tribunals or their own governments in the settling of disputes, refused to ratify the pact.

One test of Latin America's political loyalty in the postwar years was its opposition to the global Communist threat as defined by Washington. Internally, the republics cracked down on Communists, broke diplomatic relations with Moscow, and generally followed American leadership in the United Nations. But even in the most rigorously anti-Communist societies, the survival of old-line Communist organizations was remarkable. Batista's Cuba of the 1950s, for example, was religiously anti-Communist in style but surprisingly tolerant of Communists at home.

At both the Río and Bogotá conferences the American delegation sounded an anti-Communist alarm, but Latin Americans were reluctant to respond until the Bogotá riot of 9 April 1948. The riot, which erupted during the conference, was precipitated by the assassination of a popular public figure. The allegation of Communist instigation prompted the conference to pass a stern anti-Communist resolution. Two years later, when the Korean War broke out, the votes of Cuba and Ecuador proved critically important in the Security Council's resolution calling for North Korean withdrawal to the thirty-eighth parallel. And in the General Assembly debate on Korea, Latin America lined up behind the United States.

As the war progressed, fifteen of the republics offered supplies, services, or, in a few instances, troops to the United Nations forces. Costa Rica, Cuba, Panama, and El Salvador pledged "volunteers," but the number of troops offered was generally too small to meet American demands for 1,000-man contingents, with shipping and materiel for sixty days provided by the nation sending the troops. In Cuba, Batista's offer to dispatch a battalion to Korea was defeated by a Communist campaign which effectively used the slogan "No cannon fodder for Yanqui imperialists." Of the remaining republics, only Colombia, which sent a frigate to Korean waters, contributed militarily to the war.

Encouraged by the United States, Latin America had undertaken ambitious industrialization schemes in an effort to diversify its economy and in anticipation of rising demand for consumer goods. Wartime shortages stimulated these efforts. For the Caribbean, such plans would mean an end to the old denigrating remarks, so often repeated in Paris, London, and Washington, that the region produced only coffee and bananas. Industrialization even on a minor scale meant not only economic diversity and vitality, but the promise of a living standard closer to that of Western Europe or the United States. An extravagant forecast, perhaps, but with American economic assistance and its unsurpassed technical capabilities, the dream appeared not so preposterous after all.

But by the war's end the United States was more concerned with its own domestic economic needs and global politics, and with its ambitious plan to revitalize world capitalism. To be sure, it acquiesced in Latin America's insistence on a regional political entity, the Organization of American States, distinct from the United Nations, but in the economic sphere the republics soon realized they had slipped from a position of centrality to the periphery in American calculations. Since 1941 Latin America had accumulated some $4.4 billion in dollar reserves, but this vast sum was mostly a paper credit. American commodities now available to hemispheric consumers rose rapidly with the lifting of price controls, but prices for these heretofore scarce items escalated even faster. The International Monetary Fund estimated that durable goods exported to Latin America cost twice as much in 1948 as they had ten years previously. In the first three years after the Japanese surrender, Latin Americans spent some $2.7 billion for American products, depleting their dollar reserve by two-thirds.

To finance ambitious new projects the republics looked naturally to the United States, which in 1948 set out to rehabilitate the Western European economy with the Marshall Plan. In their expectation that the United States would be grateful for wartime collaboration and embark on a Marshall Plan for its own hemisphere, the republics were soon disappointed. At the Rio conference in 1947, when hemispheric delegates broached the matter of public aid, Secretary of State George C. Marshall coldly informed them that they must look to American private, not public, investment as the source of their capital needs.

Prospects for private capital from American sources were dim. In fact, American investments had declined from $3.5 billion in Latin America in 1929, to $2.8 billion in 1941. During the war Washington encouraged potential investors by attaching a clause to the 1942 In-

ternal Revenue Code granting companies receiving most of their income from Western Hemispheric investment exemption from excess
profits tax and a 14 percent reduction in corporate income taxes. But
such incentives did not dramatically reverse the downward trend.
Latin American bonds, widely promoted in an earlier day, proved no
longer popular, a declining fortune explained largely by memories of
poor bond performance in the thirties. In brief, investors believed
Latin America to be a bad risk. Direct American investment in the
republics in 1948 amounted to $3.7 billion, slightly higher than the
1929 level but hardly sufficient to finance the hemisphere's postwar
needs. To compound this financial misery, British investments, which
had amounted to £1.13 billion in 1940, fell by approximately one-
third from 1945 to 1951.[2]

The Insular Caribbean at Mid-Century

The war promised much in material and political benefits but delivered less than expected to Caribbean peoples. Among the European
dependencies, the conflict with totalitarianism had generated modest
reforms, but these political gestures fell far short of a democratic
revolution. Britain, for example, altered the internal political system
of her West Indian possessions only in the aftermath of severe labor
disputes (which broke out before the war), polite pressure from the
United States, and the publicity surrounding the Indian and Burmese
independence movements after 1945. By the end of the war the Caribbean had seen so many fact-finding commissions come and go that
the public was at best skeptical of British intentions. Less had been
expected of France during the years of German occupation; after
liberation, the French government simply incorporated its Caribbean
colonies into the larger French empire. The Dutch colonies, elevated
in law from the lowly colonial status into more prestigious and presumably more deserving "outposts of empire," were the most backward of the European possessions. The war generated few democratic
reforms in the Dutch empire.[3]

Among the independent republics the most depressed and depressing was Haiti. Idealized by poets, tutored by American marines, Haiti in 1950 was in general what it hád been in 1900: a pre-industrial society inhabited by ignorant, diseased peasants oblivious to the outside world. In other circumstances it might have become a symbol to oppressed peoples or perhaps a model for the emerging African nations of later years. After all, it was the first slave society to overthrow white rule. Yet it offered little inspiration to Caribbean slavery's black descendants. The years of American rule had left the republic virtually unchanged except for some limited advances in agriculture and public health. Otherwise the country still suffered from staggering social and economic maladies. In the cities, workers were only dimly aware of modern advances in labor organization and law. In the countryside, a rural peasantry tilled the eroded soil with primitive tools. Illiteracy ranged at 90 percent of the population; one in six school-age children actually attended school, and 80 percent of them never advanced beyond the second grade.[4]

During the war Haitian politics was dominated by Élie Lescot, a mulatto, who had succeeded the aging Sténio Vincent, another mulatto, in 1941. Lescot was secure as long as he possessed the friendship of Trujillo in the Dominican Republic and received aid from the United States. Trujillo had financed Lescot's bid for power in 1941, but two years later they became enemies, and Trujillo even offered fifteen Haitians $30,000 and arms (obtained from the Dominican Republic's Lend-Lease agreement with the United States) to kill Lescot. The conspiracy fell through, but in 1945, when Lescot cancelled elections, Trujillo published letters implying Lescot was a Dominican puppet.[5]

Lescot's relations with the United States also deteriorated. After Pearl Harbor, Americans began investing heavily in the Haitian-American Society for Agricultural Development (known by its French acronym, SHADA). Established as an autonomous organization, its board nonetheless reported directly to the Haitian government. Using the law of eminent domain, SHADA seized thousands of acres of land, much of it tilled by illiterate peasants, cut down mango and breadfruit trees, and in their place planted crypotosegia shrubs, which would, it was believed, yield rubber. The program proved a failure and caused Lescot considerable embarrassment. Haitian businesses profited in the vigorous black market during the war, but in 1945 the American retrenchment seriously damaged this prosperity. When Lescot asked for a loan in 1945, he was turned down.

The next year Lescot suddenly closed down a hostile newspaper, an act that precipitated a strike among high school and university students, who looked upon the paper as an outlet for their protests. Sensing Lescot's weakness, the United States legation informally counselled American businesses in Haiti to drop their support for the Haitian president. The Haitian military, alert to subtle shifts in American opinion, correctly inferred that the United States wanted Lescot removed. A short time later the Haitian military command announced the president's resignation.[6]

In succeeding years Haiti experienced a political and social diversity in its leadership unknown in previous eras of its turbulent history. Socialist and even a Communist political organization appeared. But the real contest for power lay in the confrontation between the mulatto elite and a rising generation of blacks. A charismatic young mathematics teacher, Daniel Fignolé, led a workers' movement and campaigned energetically among Haiti's black masses. (One drawn into his entourage was a thoughtful, clever physician, trained by American medical personnel during the war, and a disciple of voodoo —François Duvalier.) As these political rivalries unfolded, the blacks looked to Fignolé, still too young for the presidency, and President Dumarsais Estimé, a black of peasant origin. Estimé had been chosen president by a national assembly frightened by a black throng in the streets of Port-au-Prince. In office Estimé had to live with the sobering realization that Fignolé was the real hero of the Haitian masses. Estimé permitted freedom of the press, tolerated criticism, and gave the workers an increase in their daily wage. He began a social security program, promoted tourism, and paid off the odious 1922 American loan, thus releasing the Banque Nationale from the grip of Wall Street. But the blacks suddenly thrust into power sometimes behaved arrogantly, antagonizing the mulattos, who in turn found their champion in a stern military officer, Paul Magloire. As mulatto anger increased, Magloire decided to act. In May 1951 he seized power, sending Estimé, his wife, and four children into exile in New York.

To American observers Magloire seemed the ideal leader for Haiti. He guaranteed order, and he promoted the arts. The church blessed him, and the American embassy (the status of the American mission having been raised) praised him. For Haitians everywhere he committed his government to ending corruption and uplifting the common man. For the American government he promised to fight Communism. He even met with Trujillo, rightly feared by most Haitian leaders, at a small border village and signed a friendship treaty in which the two vowed, among other things, to fight a holy war against the Communists.

Four years after the reconciliation with Trujillo, in 1955, Magloire descended on Washington. He spent an evening in the White House and then addressed Congress with appropriate comments on a new era in Haitian-American relations. There followed, a few days later, a triumphant ticker-tape parade in New York City and still another press conference, in which he assured his listeners that Haiti would never turn Communist because its material blessings were already equitably distributed.

In the following spring Vice-President and Mrs. Richard M. Nixon reciprocated by stopping in Port-au-Prince on their return from a goodwill visit to the Dominican Republic. Haiti had already signed its military assistance agreement, as provided by the Mutual Security Act of 1951, which protected the republic from the international Red menace. In 1953 Haiti became the first Caribbean republic to sign a treaty with the United States encouraging private American investment by voiding such problems as currency inconvertibility and losses by expropriation.[7]

In the fifties Haiti was one of the few Latin American recipients of American public aid, but Washington's largesse was insufficient to save Magloire. By the time of Nixon's visit the Haitian economy was on the verge of collapse. Frustrated, Magloire began harassing his enemies and, like Lescot a decade before, provoked the students. On 21 May 1956, the national assembly declared a state of siege. In the commotion Duvalier plots were hatched throughout Port-au-Prince. Duvalier waited until September to announce his presidential ambitions, which he concealed until he visited the English-language newspaper, *Haiti Sun*, to inquire about the American opinion of him. When Magloire staged a comeback by making a hasty visit to the United States, thus giving Haitians the impression of continuing support from Washington, Duvalier's minions circulated rumors that the Americans really wanted Duvalier as president. In December Magloire called in Ambasssador Roy Davis to inform him that because of unsettled conditions the upcoming elections should be postponed. But Davis recommended instead that Magloire resign. When Magloire could get no support from his own military, he acquiesced in the American ambassador's recommendation.

In the ensuing political campaign Haitians uninhibitedly celebrated the prospect of a democratic era. Of the four presidential contenders, one, Duvalier, promised to restore the dream of Estimé. Duvalier portrayed himself as a mere country doctor, beloved by the peasants and praised by the Americans. The campaign was characterized by bombings, plottings, and countless rumors, but Duvalier emerged victorious. In his first presidential press conference he professed his love for the people and his intention to transform Haiti into the "spoiled child" of the United States.[8]

Under Duvalier Haiti avidly pursued American aid; his neighbor in Ciudad Trujillo had already learned the art of self-promotion as Caribbean anti-Communist.

During the Second World War Rafael Trujillo had steadfastly posed as an anti-Nazi, struggling "in defense of democracy and civilization," as he told Roosevelt. In 1944 the Dominican-American relationship cooled somewhat when Ambassador Ellis Briggs began avoiding public meetings with Trujillo and described him, accurately, as a dictator opposed to fundamental democratic principles. The contretemps ended when Briggs left for another post in 1945; his successors in the American embassy inclined toward lavish praise for Trujillo's sense of public mission and his staunch anti-Communism.

The Dominican government, notorious for its suppression of fundamental political rights, survived external assaults in these years. The Caribbean Legion, organized by political exiles and leftists and sustained by liberal regimes in Costa Rica, tried several times to topple both Trujillo and Anastasio Somoza of Nicaragua. In 1947 the legion organized an expedition at Cayo Confites, Cuba; but the Cuban government, sensitive to hemispheric criticism about the use of its territory for revolutionary activity, withdrew its support and arrested the conspirators. Trujillo, alert to his momentary advantage, struck back, accusing the plotters of being agents of the international Communist conspiracy. Two years later Trujillo was embroiled in a dispute with the Haitians, during which the Council of the Organization of American States investigated Haitian charges that Trujillo had hired assassins to kill Haitian leader Dumarsais Estimé. Relations improved when the two countries signed a declaration of friendship, and Trujillo turned to other plots against him. In June 1949 his troops intercepted and easily crushed an invasion at Luperón Bay, which Trujillo said had been sponsored by Cuba and Guatemala. When, in 1950, Haiti renewed charges of Dominican meddling, the OAS, invoking the Rió treaty, investigated the problem. Its report severely criticized the Dominican Republic, Cuba, and Guatemala but found Haiti blameless of any plotting against other governments. The OAS conclusion, wrote the eminent inter-Americanist Arthur Whitaker, was legally proper but meant, in effect, that Trujillo's despicable dictatorship, under assault from the outside, had been certified by the supreme body of the inter-American system.

How Trujillo dealt with the United States offered still another illustration of his ability to survive and even prosper despite the unsavory character of his regime. In 1945 the State Department denied Trujillo an export license for munitions he had purchased in the United States. He was initially angered at American ingratitude for his loyal wartime support. The denial, based mostly on Assistant Secretary of State Spruille Braden's accurate description of the Dominican Republic as a totalitarian state, merely prompted Trujillo to build his own arms and munitions industry. Later, he drew closer to the United States and began receiving military equipment from Washington. In 1949 Trujillo paid off the remainder of the Dominican Lend-Lease debt of almost $93,000, and in consideration of the republic's security requirements, he also got $500,000 in small arms and other military hardware, sold under the Surplus Property Act, for the cut-rate price of $23,000. After passage of the 1951 Mutual Security Act, Trujillo was able to purchase sophisticated military weaponry. From 1952 until his death in May 1961, Trujillo received more than $6 million in military equipment from the Americans.[9]

El Benefactor, as Trujillo was obsequiously called by his minions, carefully crafted his friendship with both the American government and the American public by the use of lobbyists and, occasionally, ghost writers, who turned out adulatory pieces for popular magazines. Sometimes, however, his prestige was momentarily damaged by spectacular revelations of some atrocity committed on his orders. In March 1956 Dominican agents allegedly kidnapped a former Dominican citizen, Jesús de Galíndez, then lecturing at Columbia University and writing a study called the "Era of Trujillo," from a New York subway station. In December a Eugene, Oregon, aviator, Gerald Murphy, who flew for Dominican Airlines, disappeared in Ciudad Trujillo. Congressman Charles Porter, who represented the home district of the aviator, charged that Murphy had flown Galíndez to the Dominican Republic and subsequently had been killed. As magazines and newspapers picked up the story, Trujillo launched a counterattack, denouncing Porter and other critics as Communists and Communist sympathizers. He retained a prominent New York civil libertarian, Morris Ernst, to review the case. After looking into the matter, Ernst declared Trujillo innocent of any wrongdoing.[10]

Whenever criticized, however slightly, in Congress or in the American press, Trujillo generally countered with a barrage of favorable publicity. On Capitol Hill he was touted as one of the most munificent employers of lobbyists and public relations specialists, hired to look after the Dominican sugar quota and Trujillo's image. After the Galíndez affair his reputation never quite recovered. Porter's accusations precipitated a prolonged debate in both houses of Congress, during the course of which one senator remarked that the Dominican Republic could not possibly be a dictatorship because elections were regularly held. Others, more thoughtful in their analysis, argued that, however odious Trujillo's regime, the United States should not interfere in the Dominican Republic's internal affairs.[11]

For Cubans, the years after 1945 symbolized less the high drama of Soviet-American confrontation than the destruction of a dream: the failure of Ramón Grau San Martín (elected in 1944) and the Authentic revolution to fulfill the promise of 1933. The former physician, whose idealism and radicalism had frightened Sumner Welles eleven years before, took the oath of office in one of the most enthusiastic public celebrations in Cuban history. The people, he proudly proclaimed, had taken over. Some old faces from the 1933 experiment reappeared. The more conservative and foreign elements were at first apprehensive of sweeping changes, but Grau and his supporters soon confirmed by practice what thoughtful observers had already deduced. Ensconced in power, the revolutionaries of 1933 looked more and more like the grafters of the Zayas era. Batista had gotten rich in office, but Grau and his cronies stole more than he. The stench of corruption in the Cuban government during these years was mitigated only slightly by the sweetness of sugar profits. Graft pervaded every level and was so deeply entrenched, one historian of Cuba has written, that only a thorough revolutionary cleansing could have eradicated it.[12]

Grau's successor, Carlos Prío Socarrás, took over in 1948, in an era when Americans associated Cuba with rum, the rumba, and vacations at plush Havana hotels. Prío, like Grau, was an old revolutionary gone to seed. He gave aid and comfort to the Caribbean legionnaires plotting against Trujillo, then suddenly withdrew his commitment after public disclosure.

Prío really preferred long casual afternoons at his farm sipping daiquiris and gazing at a nearby waterfall. Gangsterism flourished in Cuba during these years, and Prío made a show of cracking down on thugs while forming friendships with others in the underworld. He diverted attention by ostentatiously promoting public works projects, but such critics as Eduardo Chibás began asking publicly how Prío could buy so much property for himself yet always claim that the national treasury was bankrupt.[13]

In the atmosphere of prosperity, however, there existed a political malaise. In March 1952, a few months before scheduled elections, Batista, a candidate for the presidency, suddenly seized power in a bloodless coup. His excuse was that he wished to save the country from Prío, who was, allegedly, plotting to annul the elections and rule by decree. Circumstantial evidence, especially some revealing confidential remarks made by Prío, seemed to validate the story. But in fact, the plotters of 1952 were all military men eager for advancement and only tangentially concerned about the corrupt civilian regime.

The coup was quickly and professionally carried out. Business hardly interrupted operations on the day Batista made his move. In seizing power he of course violated the 1940 constitution, a document he had always praised but now repudiated in favor of a higher law. In April Batista's reassuring face appeared on the cover of *Time* magazine. His government won quick recognition from Washington and public praise from American businessmen with connections in the republic.[14]

Batista fitted perfectly the cold war image of the valiant Caribbean strongman maintaining public order, promoting American-style progress, and displaying ritual anti-Communism. He promised everything but miracles: protection of life and property, completion of Prío's public works schemes, and enticement of foreign capital. Some older Cubans, remembering Batista's leftist ways in the 1930s, were reassured by his political tolerance, despite his defiance of the constitution in taking power. For example, the Communists, who had held two posts in Batista's 1942 cabinet, had little influence in the new regime, but they did enjoy freedom of expression and the right to organize. Communism was an external, not an internal, menace. There were, of course, the inevitable political disturbances, some precipitated by university students who refused to accept Batista's claims to legitimacy, with others traceable to plotting by ex-president Prío. But to the outside world Cuba seemed the fulfillment, at long last, of the Wilsonian dream of an economically progressive society. Batista hired a publicist, Edmund Chester, who wrote an adulatory biography, *A Sergeant Named Batista*, about a poor soldier who loved his country and rose to save it. President Eisenhower's ambassador, Arthur Gardner, lauded Batista with such effusive praise that he became at times an embarrassment to the dictator. Havana dazzled American tourists with glittering night life. Cuban magazines and newspapers advertised a rich variety of American goods, and American autos clogged Havana streets. Batista's Cuba fulfilled an old American dream: the island had become a marketplace.[15]

The Isthmus and the Problems of Modernization

In Panama and in Central America, as in the insular Caribbean, the postwar era witnessed an accelerating demand for change. For the first time in isthmian history, elitist governments confronted what has been aptly called a "revolution of rising expectations." In each of the six republics, the pressure for modernization took different forms. In Panama, predictably, postwar politics centered on increased benefits from the canal and the volatile issue of "sovereignty" over the Canal Zone. Costa Rica, more homogeneous and historically more stable than its neighbors, in 1948 was swept by political turbulence which ended triumphantly for liberal forces. In Nicaragua, a rightist dictatorship created in an era of American intervention matured, promoting public order and promising material benefits. In Guatemala a leftist government plunged into social and economic reforms, incurred the wrath of the United States, and was toppled.

Panama emerged from the war unreconciled to professions of American benevolence and goodwill. For one thing, the wartime defense sites agreement was not satisfactorily worked out. As envisioned by Panama, the pact of 1942 was only a temporary lease of national domain to the United States in the interest of hemispheric defense. Panama wanted abrogation of the agreement at the end of hostilities; the United States insisted on occupation of the sites until the passing of the global emergency. Throughout the war Panamanian negotiators had pressed for fulfillment of Arias's public works projects, which could be completed only with American aid, but their American counterparts appeared more concerned with canal defense than with isthmian economic development.

Eventually the commitments were honored but never to Panama's satisfaction. When the Japanese surrendered, the Panamanian government plunged almost immediately into a campaign to end the defense sites agreement. In the national assembly there were angry demands for evacuation of the bases within a year. An official request for evacuation arrived in Washington shortly; instead of drafting an immediate reply, however, the United States waited eleven months to respond and then audaciously presented Panama with a new defense sites convention. The Panamanian government restated its demand for immediate evacuation of the bases, and in September 1946 the American forces actually began withdrawing. But at the same time the United States went ahead with negotiations for a new defense sites treaty. A storm of public wrath and press hostility surrounded the debates on the proposed agreement, and in December the treaty was decisively defeated in the national assembly.[16]

In 1949 Arnulfo Arias, a *bête noire* of the United States, returned to power in a skillful coup orchestrated with the aid of Police Chief José Antonio ("Chichi") Remón. Arias resurrected the old economic demands of 1941, but his attitude toward the United States had obviously mellowed considerably. He swore to defend the canal in the cold war and pledged his support of American policy in Korea. In May 1951, however, following a losing constitutional battle in which Arias tried to reinstitute his own fundamental law of 1941, he suddenly resigned. Chichi Remón had withdrawn his support at a critical moment in the contest. In 1952, after a succession of interim executives, Remón won the Panamanian presidency.

Remón was determined to obtain a new treaty with the United States. In October 1953 he arrived in Washington and presented to President Eisenhower a dignified, lucid plea for greater Panamanian benefits from the canal. The Zone's rigidly segregated social structure was still intact; its pay scales, divided into the detested "gold" and "silver" standards, which permitted payment of West Indians and Panamanians at tropical rates, persisted despite the economic concessions of the 1936 treaty. Eisenhower pledged a renewed commitment to the spirit of the Roosevelt-Arias Accord of 1933, specifically to apply the "principle of equality of opportunity and treatment" to Americans and Panamanians in the Zone. The new treaty, ratified in 1955, increased Panama's canal annuity to almost $2 million, extended its tax jurisdiction over Panamanians working in the Zone, abolished the monopoly on transisthmian communication held by the Panama Railroad, and ended the practice, humiliating to Panamanians, of dispatching Zone trucks into Panama City and Colón to collect the garbage.[17]

Having made what it considered to be major economic concessions to Panama, the Eisenhower administration pled the treaty's cause before a suspicious Senate alert to apparent diminution of American authority in the Zone. The lobbying against the treaty of 1955 was intense, and after it was finally passed and ratified, Zone officials simply neglected to carry out its stipulations. Nothing in any of the canal treaties prohibited American authorities in the Canal Zone from conducting operations considered necessary to the maintenance and protection of the canal. In the broadest meaning of the term, maintenance of the canal might include such diverse businesses as an ice cream parlor or a dairy farm. Panamanians employed in the Zone continued to labor on the "silver" roll.[18]

In November 1959 serious rioting erupted along the Panamanian–Canal Zone boundary. Paradoxically, the immediate cause of the disturbance was not so much the question of employment as the symbolic issue of Panama's insistence on the right to fly its flag in the Zone as a gesture of "titular sovereignty." In the 1955 treaty discussions Panamanian negotiators had tried, unsuccessfully, to obtain American approval to fly the Panamanian flag on ships transiting the canal (warships excepted) and in specified places in the Zone, and acceptance of both Spanish and English as official Zone languages. The Department of State, fearing that it would be opening a Pandora's box of related questions, refused.

On 3 November, Panamanian Independence Day, Augustino Boyd, former foreign minister and the descendant of a prominent isthmian family, and Professor Ernesto Castillero Reyes, author of a well-known history of the republic, led a march into the Zone in order to hoist the Panamanian flag. Zonians immediately criticized the move as a gambit for attention, and they pointed out that the Panamanian colors had always flown in the Zone on Independence Day. Once the demonstrators arrived at the entrance, the march deteriorated into a brawl. Panamanians later charged that a Zone policeman had trampled on their flag. In retaliation, a crowd thronged the American embassy, pulled down the flag, and tore it to shreds. Convinced that Boyd and Castillero could not control their followers, the Zone governor ordered the entrances closed. When police tried to repel the Panamanians with riot sticks, tear gas, and water, the crowd began throwing rocks and burning cars. It soon became obvious that the regular police could not quell the rioters, and the governor requested regular army troops to guard Zone entrances. That night Panama was declared off-limits to servicemen, and civilians were warned not to enter the republic. The count of wounded at day's end was 120.

Dismayed at this violent turn of events, Eisenhower stated in a press conference the following day that United States–Panamanian relations had been a "model" of cordiality. His Panamanian counterpart blamed the event on American failure to provide Panama with a larger share of canal revenues. The isthmian press, analyzing the riot, drew extreme conclusions: the English-language *Star and Herald* blamed the trouble on Communist conspirators; the Panamanian papers anticipated Eisenhower's suppression of the republic in a "Hungary-style" operation. Late in the month, the violence flared anew when a second flag mission was stopped at the Zone gates, this time by Panamanian national guardsmen. Frustrated, the crowd retreated into Panama City and began looting stores and destroying foreign-owned businesses.[19]

These incidents occurred when Eisenhower was on the verge of making what was, in retrospect, a courageous decision. Labeled a satanic fiend by several Panamanian editorialists, Eisenhower had already decided on yielding to Panamanian demands to fly the republic's flag in the Zone as a symbol of Panama's titular sovereignty. The importance of such a gesture had been stressed by his brother, Dr. Milton S. Eisenhower, who in 1958 had undertaken a fact-finding mission in the hemisphere. The concession was considered an important one. Through the years, the State Department had argued that, whatever goodwill might be generated by the act, the flying of Panama's flag in the Zone would raise legal questions about American operations there. Congress, heavily influenced by its own canal specialists, notably the intractable Pennsylvania Democrat Daniel Flood, looked suspiciously on any act, however generous, which diminished or qualified American domination of the canal.

To reconcile Panamanian demands with Congressional skepticism, Eisenhower announced in September 1960 that both flags would be flown in Shaler Triangle, a small plot of ground along the Zone boundary.[20] Annoyed and determined to block the president's move,

Congress attached an amendment to the annual appropriation bill denying federal funds to pay for the flagpoles, but Eisenhower used his emergency fund to defray the costs. His decision pleased neither side. Panama began asserting even stronger claims, and Congress looked upon the gesture as a concession to violence. The House Committee on Foreign Affairs issued a strongly worded statement reaffirming the primacy of American control of the canal. Noting Panamanian claims that the republic received inadequate compensation from canal revenue, the committee cited the $40 million technical aid, sanitary appropriations, voluntary relief, and road construction contributed to the republic's welfare by the United States from 1945 to 1960. Though admitting that the flying of the Panamanian flag in the Zone mollified anti-American critics, the committee nonetheless disapproved of making a concession that was a departure from established policy.[21]

Of the six isthmian republics Nicaragua exhibited the most slavish devotion to American cold war imperatives. Its obeisance to the United States in international politics had become commonplace after the rise of Anastasio Somoza in the early 1930s. Effectively and sometimes brutally using the American-created national guard, Somoza smashed virtually every leftist element in the country. By the end of the war his power stood unchallenged. His internal policies seemed at first glance bewildering. He promoted public development and disestablished the Catholic church, which pleased the moderates; he stifled the press and broke up labor unions, which of course delighted the right. Though nominally a member of the Liberals, the anti-American party of the protectorate era, Somoza unapologetically kowtowed to the United States. Fittingly, the American embassy in Managua stood next door to the presidential palace.

As Somoza's political power expanded, so did the family's wealth. An estimate in 1970 placed his holdings at 50 percent of Nicaragua's agricultural output, with extensive investments in mining, trade, and manufacture both inside and outside the republic. Under his aegis Managua, devastated by an earthquake in 1931, emerged as an impressive, vigorous metropolis. Somoza's enormous wealth aroused envy and political opposition after 1945, but he effectively overcame such challenges by a shrewd combination of repression and moderate social legislation.[22]

Like Zelaya, another Liberal, Somoza meddled in the affairs of his neighbors, but unlike his controversial predecessor he never incurred Washington's wrath. In 1948, when dissident Costa Ricans led by José Figueres instigated a revolt on behalf of a Liberal politician who had been denied the presidency, Somoza sent aid to the harassed Costa Rican executive. As Somoza later explained, he dispatched troops in support of a legitimate government but withdrew Nicaraguan forces at the special request of Secretary of State George C. Marshall, then attending the Bogotá conference. The rebels won in the struggle, and the ousted president sought refuge and more aid in Managua. Costa Rica, sensing trouble from Somoza, requested an investigation by the Organization of American States, which sent a special board of inquiry to San José and Managua. In February 1949, following OAS criticism of both parties, Somoza signed a friendship pact with Costa Rica.

For a few years relations between the two countries were relatively quiet, but in April 1954 the Nicaraguan government publicized what it termed irrefutable evidence of a Costa Rican plot against Somoza's life. Somoza indicted the Caribbean Legion and by implication Figueres, the most illustrious figure in the legion and now president of Costa Rica, for the conspiracy. Figueres's enemies organized a border attack from Nicaraguan soil, with their advance covered by several of Somoza's planes. When Costa Rican forces crushed the invasion and damaged the planes, Somoza rushed tanks and troops to the border. At the height of the crisis, the United States Air Force flew six C-47s to San José, an unmistakable signal to both sides to stop the fighting. Several months later, however, Somoza bought twenty-five P-51 Mustangs from a Swedish arms supplier and once more threatened his neighbor. This time Washington sent six jet fighters to the Canal Zone to discourage Somoza from providing support for an anti-Figueres invasion with the Mustangs. Figueres appealed to the OAS. In a daring but somewhat comical reaction Somoza demanded a personal showdown at the border. Reinforced by Nicaraguan guardsmen, the invaders actually crossed the border. On this occasion the OAS investigating unit undertook its aerial surveys in American Navy planes.

In these conflicts with Costa Rica Somoza did not enjoy the unquestioned support of the United States, yet in the United Nations and in other cold war disputes Nicaragua always voted with the United States. Somoza privately complained that the Americans did not reciprocate. True, Nicaragua had its security treaty with Washington, but Somoza often had trouble acquiring munitions from American sources. American economic assistance was limited to funds for inter-American and Atlantic-Pacific highway construction.[23]

In the end Somoza finally received American consideration. In September 1956, while attending a reception in the old Liberal citadel of León, Somoza was shot four times by an assassin. Gravely wounded, he was flown back to Managua by an American helicopter. American surgeons from the Canal Zone hurried to the Nicaraguan capital and, at Eisenhower's suggestion, transported Somoza to the superior medical facilities in the Zone. For four hours the finest American neurosurgeons labored to save the life of a Caribbean dictator hated by his neighbors, but after a momentary improvement, Somoza lapsed into unconsciousness and died. The Latin American left wing was immediately heartened. Figueres, traveling in Europe when he heard the news, found renewed faith in democracy. In El Salvador, where the assassin had lived, a joyous celebration erupted. Uruguay's national assembly praised Somoza's murderer. But in Nicaragua Somoza's sons, holding total power over the national guard, retained control and continued the dynasty.

The Guatemalan Affair, 1954

Somoza's meddling in Costa Rican politics angered Central American liberals and occasionally annoyed the United States, but at no time did Washington consider Nicaragua a menace to American hemispheric interests. Guatemala, by contrast, offered what Eisenhower and Secretary of State John Foster Dulles interpreted as irrefutable evidence of Communist intrusion in the Americas. The leftist government of

Jacobo Arbenz, they believed, contaminated hemispheric democracy; like dedicated surgeons removing a tumor, they were determined to excise the malignancy.

The origins of the 1954 American-Guatemalan confrontation presumably lay in the social revolution begun with Ubico's overthrow a decade before, and with the subsequent rise to the presidency of an exiled university teacher, Juan José Arévalo. The opposition, intimidated and factionalized under Ubico, contained reformist elements that agreed that Guatemala desperately needed political democracy, economic planning, and national integration of Indian, rural peasant, and urban laborer. To achieve these lofty goals, Arévalo preached a vague philosophy that he called "spiritual socialism," in which materialism was subordinated to human dignity. In Guatemala spiritual socialism challenged the old entrenched interests—the oligarchy and the church.

As exiles returned after the revolution they joined in a vigorous national reorganization. The Left, more disciplined than other political factions, dominated the unions. The Communists infiltrated the major labor organizations and enjoyed some success in shaping Arévalo's labor policies. By 1950, when Arévalo stepped down, the Communists were entrenched in the Central Labor Federation, known by its Spanish acronym, CTG, and had, despite Arévalo's energetic efforts to stop the practice, operated schools that trained labor organizers in Marxist doctrine. In retrospect, the Communist gains among Guatemalan labor were not surprising, given the virtual nonexistence of realistic alternatives and the ability of the Communists to provide Guatemalan workers, historically abused and exploited, with material improvement and a sense of solidarity. Industrial wages, to cite one example, rose 80 percent in the six years after Ubico's overthrow. Under CTG influence Arévalo established an Institute of Social Security and aggressively promoted public works and other social programs benefitting Guatemalan workers.[24]

The military, a bastion of conservative thought, was alarmed by Arévalo's political and social reforms and tried on twenty occasions to overthrow his government, but Arévalo survived, several times by the expediency of arming urban workers. Despised by the oligarchy, Arévalo had by 1950 also incurred, paradoxically, opposition from a tiny but vocal radical faction for moving too slowly with Guatemala's social revolution. In that year, as political tension mounted in anticipation of a presidential election, Arévalo cracked down on the more unruly Communist elements. In the ensuing campaign, however, the major Communist organizations supported Arévalo's choice for president, Jacobo Arbenz, defense minister and candidate of the National Renovation Party.

Arbenz began his presidency amidst high expectations of continuing and even expanding the social revolution of the Arévalo years. He turned his attention more and more to the plight of Guatemala's rural peasant. Since the early days of the republic these country laborers, mostly Indian, had lived outside the monied economy, kept down by a medieval land tenure system and suppressed by the oligarchy. Arbenz struck directly at the largest landowners. In June 1952 the government announced agrarian reform, which provided for expropriation of untilled land above a certain acreage. Landowners would receive compensation in bonds, while the landless would get title to or at least use of the land in return for a part of the crop. By comparison with other agrarian reform programs, Guatemala's law was not punitive, but Arbenz did expropriate some 1.5 million acres, compensated by $8.4 million in bonds.[25]

The law's application against the United Fruit Company, which lost almost half its 470,000 acres to Guatemala's agrarian experiment, further crippled the republic's relations with the United States. Liberal Guatemalans despised United Fruit for its economic power and monopoly of railway traffic from the capital to the Caribbean coast. Dulles, whose old law firm of Sullivan and Cromwell represented United Fruit, had already become convinced of Guatemalan perfidy. In the United Nations, Guatemala brazenly followed a pro-Soviet line; in 1953, when Joseph Stalin died, he was eulogized by Guatemala's national assembly and its major newspapers. To an America obsessed with the notion of a global, monolithic Communist conspiracy, Guatemala's peculiar political makeup of reformers, idealists, and Communists easily lent the impression of a Soviet satellite blossoming in the heart of the Americas. In the Organization of Central American States, El Salvador's foreign minister called for an anti-Communist front to meet the Guatemalan challenge.

Guatemala's conservatives, until then ineffective in their opposition to the regime, found new hope in the increasingly strident American criticism of Arbenz's leftist policies. One of the president's enemies, Colonel Carlos Castillo Armas, who had been imprisoned after an unsuccessful coup in November 1950, had escaped and begun plotting a revolution with General Miguel Ydígoras Fuentes. The two received aid from Trujillo, who hated Arévalo and Arbenz and wanted revenge for a 1949 abortive invasion of the Dominican Republic originating in Guatemala; from Somoza, who resented Arbenz's support of his enemy Figueres in Costa Rica; and from El Salvadorean officials alarmed over Guatemala's flirtation with the Soviet Union. The Central Intelligence Agency became involved in fall 1953. Equipped and trained by CIA operatives in Nicaragua, Castillo's band of 168 men slipped into Honduras, in preparation for the assault on Arbenz's government.[26]

From this point the Guatemalan affair is the unfolding drama of two related conspiracies against Arbenz. The first was a calculated movement by Dulles to expose Guatemala as a hemispheric pariah in the inter-American system and, with the assistance of Henry Cabot Lodge, Jr., to prevent Guatemala from presenting its case in the United Nations. At the Tenth Inter-American Conference in Caracas, which convened on 1 March 1954, Dulles and Guillermo Toriello, Guatemala's fiery foreign minister, exchanged angry words about Communist intrusion in Arbenz's regime. In the end Dulles obtained a sweeping resolution, wrung from Latin American delegates naively anticipating economic assistance for their fidelity to American policy, which, though not naming Guatemala, declared Communism to be incompatible with the inter-American system. The resolution passed with Guatemala casting the sole negative vote; Mexico and Argentina, suspicious of American motives, abstained. Dulles now believed the United States possessed a hemispheric mandate for its anti-Arbenz campaign.

Alarmed by these threats, Arbenz bought arms from Communist sources. The United States had refused to sell Guatemala arms after 1948 and had, by applying diplomatic pressure on other countries, prevented Arbenz from procuring weapons elsewhere in the West. But in 1954, as the political crisis worsened, Guatemala finally obtained 2,000 tons of Czech arms and munitions, transported on a British freighter chartered by a Swedish company that had taken delivery at a Polish port. When news of the purchase leaked out, Arbenz's status as a fellow traveler was presumed, though informed sources claimed that Arbenz had first approached armaments manufacturers in Western countries, where he was rebuffed, and only in desperation had turned to the Eastern Europeans.[27]

In May the internal situation in Guatemala rapidly deteriorated. Arbenz imposed restrictions on assembly, authorized widespread arrests and interrogation of political enemies, and, according to later revelations, permitted torture. On 18 June, the day Toriello requested the Security Council of the United Nations to investigate the Guatemalan situation, Castillo began his revolution. The ensuing U.N. debate coincided with Castillo's advance on Guatemala City. In the Security Council only the Soviet delegate supported Guatemala. Lodge argued disingenuously that the struggle involved only Guatemalans pitted against Guatemalans. Other members of the council looked to the O A S as the proper agency to conduct an inquiry. On 20 June the council called for a ceasefire. Two days later, Castillo lost two of his three support planes; to replace them, Eisenhower ordered the transfer of two P-51s to a third country, which in turn would send them to the Guatemalan rebels. In the United Nations Guatemala revived its complaint, arguing that the resolution of the twentieth had been violated. Once more the United States exercised diplomatic pressure, this time on Britain and France, to stop the Security Council from pursuing the Guatemalan complaint on the specious reasoning that the matter was hemisphere, or "family," business. When Britain and France abstained in the crucial voting, Guatemala's case in the United Nations was doomed.[28]

The second conspiracy against Arbenz originated in the American embassy in Guatemala City. Castillo's main force consisted of only about 150 men. The other rebel elements had either scattered, been arrested, or were killed in the initial fighting. Castillo's puny air force bombed the capital and demoralized the city, but his main ground force was stalled far from the capital when Arbenz finally gave up. In the critical weeks of June Guatemala's senior military officers, disturbed over the antagonism between the republic and the United

States, decided not to support the president of the republic. On 25 June they sent Arbenz an ultimatum asking for his resignation; if he refused, they threatened to ally with Castillo. In desperation the president ordered distribution of arms to public organizations, but his order was never carried out.

Through these tumultuous days American ambassador John Peurifoy had not been an idle spectator. The anti-Arbenz sentiment of the embassy was widely publicized. After a courier had delivered the military's ultimatum to the president's office, the officers gathered with Peurifoy at the embassy to plan their next move. After the session, they decided to deliver a second ultimatum to Arbenz demanding that he fire the judicial and civil police chiefs, transfer authority to a military junta, and vacate the presidential palace immediately. Under siege, betrayed by his senior military officers, Arbenz addressed the nation by radio and announced his resignation, which he blamed on mercenaries hired by the United States. He recommended Colonel Carlos Enrique Díaz as provisional president, but conservative officers and Peurifoy refused to accept anyone closely identified with the regime. Wearing a pistol in a shoulder holster, Peurifoy confronted Díaz at Díaz's house. The American ambassador renewed his case for Castillo, and after further backstage maneuvering, the generals announced on 1 July in favor of the rebel commander.[29]

The battle for Guatemala was over, and the republic's destiny now lay, as Dulles phrased it in a national television and radio address, "with the people." Castillo moved quickly to demolish the Communist labor unions and to stifle the pro-Arbenz political organizations. He ordered new voting requirements which, in effect, disfranchised most of the population, and returned expropriated lands to United Fruit.

Shortly after his triumph, Castillo proudly announced an American economic grant of $6 million.

9 • The Cuban Revolution

The Cuban revolution easily qualifies as the most dramatic event of twentieth-century Caribbean history. It brought to power an intensely anti-American political leader of indisputable charisma, Fidel Castro Ruz, whose personality shaped the course of Cuban revolution.[1] In time the revolution transformed Cuba into a modern Soviet-style society, in which the credos of American progressive thought and Anglo-Saxon democratic virtue were spurned in favor of Marxist guidelines, modified by Cuban predilection. At the height of Cuban-American antagonism in 1961–62, the United States and the Soviet Union, Castro's newfound benefactor, almost plunged the globe into a nuclear holocaust in a confrontation over Cuba. By its nature the missile crisis focused almost exclusively on the rivalry of two super-powers, distracting attention from the political and cultural impact Castro's revolution would have on the Caribbean world. For the first time, a small Caribbean nation, reared in the shadow of American power, successfully challenged American hegemony in the American Mediterranean.

The Origins of Castro's Revolution

Though the United States exercised considerable political and economic influence in Fulgencio Batista's Cuba, the struggle begun in 1953 by Fidel Castro was not a revolution against American power. Castro's intent, which he stated eloquently in "History Will Absolve Me," his peroration delivered during the trial for the assault on the Moncada barracks in July 1953, was the restoration of constitutional government. But interspersed in the rambling speech was frequent condemnation of social and economic injustices, which, presumably, a triumphant revolution would eradicate. In a prophetic passage Castro condemned foreign intrusion into Cuban life, particularly foreign ownership of Cuban utilities and roughly half the island's arable lands. Imprisoned on the Isle of Pines, Castro honed "History

Will Absolve Me" into a powerful tract which became, after the victory of 1959, the fundamental statement of the revolution.[2]

In 1955 Castro won his freedom in a general amnesty proclaimed by Batista. He was now something of a celebrity and, shortly after his release from prison, made a whirlwind entry into Havana. An Ortodoxo by political profession, he might have rejoined that element and, like its most prominent members, spent the next few years engaged in discreet opposition to Batista's regime. Instead he left for Mexico, where, despite some harassment from a suspicious government, he organized a Cuban invasion. When the plotters came on hard times, they were aided by external sources, notably Lázaro Cárdenas, leftist president of the thirties, and former Cuban executive Carlos Prío Socarrás, who apparently contributed handsome sums for training and equipping the invasion force. In December 1956, after a difficult voyage from Mexican waters, the invaders landed in eastern Cuba. Castro lost most of his party in the landing, but a handful (twelve has been chosen as the symbolic number) survived, to make their own way into the Sierra Maestra and begin the struggle.

The guerrilla war which ensued and which, on 1 January 1959, brought down the Batista regime was at first not widely publicized to the outside world. Americans vacationing in Havana read censored news reports of bandits in Oriente province, but they knew next to nothing of Castro, his cause, or his political philosophy. What acquainted Americans with Castro and his war was a famous interview he had in February 1957 with Herbert Matthews of the *New York Times*. Batista had disseminated reports that Castro was dead and his movement virtually crushed, but Matthews returned from the Sierra with contrary, startling information. Prodded by the reporter as to his views on socialism, imperialism, and the United States, Castro described his cause as nationalistic, anti-imperialistic, and anticolonial, but he quickly reassured his interrogator that he held no hatred for the American people.[3]

From the Matthews interview Castro won widespread attention and considerable sympathy for his cause, though his utterances about the United States were more self-serving than candid. No sincere Cuban nationalist, mindful of the pervasive American influence on the island since independence, could have honestly proclaimed faith in American benevolence and values as a prescription for Cuba's needs. As Castro demonstrated convincingly from his first days in power, anti-Americanism, which permeated his orations, had proved more useful than Marxist thought in galvanizing the Cuban masses. Anti-Americanism ran deep in Cuban history and was doubtless the most potent force in Cuban nationalism. Socialism, too, had a long history among Cuban intellectuals. Castro ingeniously wedded the two in his revolutionary message.[4]

In the aftermath of his victory and especially after the revolution turned violently to the left, some American observers became convinced that, in a perverse way, the United States had elevated Castro to power. The most extreme views came from former ambassador Arthur Gardner, who admired Batista and wanted the CIA to assassinate Castro; his successor, Earl E. T. Smith, who adopted a more neutral position while in Havana but after leaving bitterly expressed the opinion that Castro's success was explained by decisions made by liberal sympathizers on the fourth floor of the State Department; and from Batista himself, who in exile wrote of a prosperous anti-Communist Cuba undermined by internal treachery and American indifference, as manifested by the arms embargo of 1958 which gave Castro, Batista argued, an unfair advantage. Over the years these and other interpretations of Cuba's "loss" appeared, each story begetting a different tale about the revolution and its origins.[5]

In fact Castro's victory owed very little to American actions in the late fifties, though Castro cleverly exploited the anti-Americanism ingrained in Cuban thought. Doubtless he profited by the Matthews interview. But the cause was successful because Castro's rebel force fought a truly epic struggle and capitalized on inherent weaknesses in Cuban society, causing Batista's regime to crumble from within. As Ramón Ruíz has observed in his brilliant essay on the origins of revolutionary Cuba, the island in 1958 was better off economically than most other Latin American countries, but it had a fragile social structure which made it vulnerable to Castro's assault. At the top was an Americanized elite whose political and economic power rested mostly on American capital. (Castro vilified this element as the betrayers of Cuban nationalism.) On the bottom were the Cuban masses, not so poor as their Latin American brethren but exploited by a mismanaged economy dependent on foreign capital and the vagaries of the sugar market. Between were the middle sectors, many of whom had opposed Machado and, in the 1950s, silently suffered Batista's corruption. In the final years of his regime, however, these mostly urban middle-class Cubans became disillusioned with Batista and ceased to support him. Some saw Castro as the restorer of democracy but, later, opposed his shift to national economic planning and adoption of Marxism. Like the elite, the middle sectors of Cuban life were fractured; unlike the ruling elements, they were deeply disillusioned by the course of Cuban politics but were so splintered they could fashion no effective alternative. The Castroites, a determined minority, capitalized on these inherent weaknesses in Cuban society and offered in 1959 what appeared to be a viable alternative: a revolutionary program, complete with symbols, slogans, and plans, to revitalize Cuba and fulfill a historic promise. It was the enactment of this program that precipitated the confrontation with the United States.[6]

The Bay of Pigs

In early January 1959, in the first days of victory, Castro was a popular figure throughout the Western Hemisphere. He symbolized the valiant warrior of Cuban democracy, the champion of the Cuban masses, the restorer of honest rule. But already the revolution was making decisions which in Castro's mind would undo the wrongs perpetrated on Cuba and settle old scores with Batistianos. In the beginning came demands for revenge against Batista henchmen who had not escaped with the dictator and stood charged with political crimes. The trials were public, with Castro himself often serving as prosecutor, in a setting unlike the somber courts of justice which, Anglo-Saxon societies argue, guarantee objectivity and impartiality. By the strictest rules of procedure, the presentation of evidence, and the availability of friendly witness, the trials Castro staged for the Cuban masses were not fair. Most of the condemned were, in point of fact, guilty of brutality, torture, and other excesses; they deserved the punishment meted out to them. But rebroadcast in the United States, the trials of Batistianos were viewed as a political circus, complete with the crowd screaming for its next victim. When criticism reached Castro, he reacted angrily in a prolonged oration to some one million Habaneros gathered in front of the presidential palace. In a theme that would soon be familiar, he accused his detractors of defaming the revolution.[7]

When he traveled, Castro boasted that the revolution would become the model for Latin American protest. In Caracas, where he was lionized by enthusiastic Venezuelans, he told his listeners, some of whom a year before had helped to overthrow a hated military dictatorship, that the Cuban revolutionary experience proved a guerrilla force could defeat a modern army. Venezuela had just installed a reformist government headed by Rómulo Betancourt of Acción Democrática. By most standards Castro and Betancourt should have been kindred spirits, but here and in subsequent addresses Castro made clear that Venezuela's leftist experiment hardly compared with Cuba's thorough revolution. From the first days of rule, then, Castro advocated and in several instances actually tried to export his revolution, a policy that terminated ignominiously with the fateful venture of Ernesto ("Che") Guevara in Bolivia eight years later.[8]

In mid-April 1959 Castro arrived in the United States for ten days of speechmaking, public appearances, and discussions with American officials. Cubans closely followed his itinerary and remarks. Far too often they had witnessed the return of a new president from Washington, mouthing nationalist homilies but abetting American influence in the Cuban government. It is still unclear whether Castro came to seek aid for his ambitious programs or merely to enjoy the spotlight. He told one associate, who subsequently became disillusioned and went into exile, that he intended to refuse any proffered aid but only as a ruse to strengthen his bargaining position with the Americans. After meeting with Nixon (Eisenhower was away on a golfing trip) and other American officials, Castro proudly announced he was seeking no handout. Cuba really wanted a new trade treaty with the United States, one that did not perpetuate Cuban dependence on the American economy. There were inevitable questions about his political philosophy, to which he responded, in characteristically flamboyant fashion, with condemnation of dictators, denial of Communist influence in the revolution, and commitment to nonintervention.

Nor, apparently, was Castro cultivating Soviet friendship—at least not yet. During a reception at the Cuban embassy he ignored the Russian representative and even made a point of mentioning that Cuba had no diplomatic relations with the Soviet Union.[9]

What Castro most likely wanted in 1959, Maurice Halperin has speculated, was peace with honor—that is, an accommodation with the United States but an arrangement that paid proper deference to Cuban nationalism. By accepting American aid he would doubtless have left many Cubans with the suspicion that he had violated national honor, an ignominy common to most of his predecessors. Already the revolution had aroused American ire by Castro's decision to send armed expeditions, composed mainly of exiles, on abortive invasions of Haiti, Nicaragua, the Dominican Republic, and Panama.[10]

Philip Bonsal, the last American ambassador in Havana before the diplomatic rupture of January 1961, called these early months in Castro's relations with Washington a time of "benevolent, if nervous, watchfulness." After meeting with the Cuban leader, Nixon wrote a trenchant critique of Castro as a Communist or, at least, a man naive about Communism. The vice-president sent this memorandum to the Central Intelligence Agency, the State Department, and the president. With it he also sent a recommendation calling for the organizing of Cuban exiles to overthrow Castro. Uppermost in the minds of American officials was the unsettling prospect of another Guatemala, a leftist regime shifting even further leftward as it came to be dominated by Communists. Remembering the events of 1954, these officials argued that the best time to remove such a government was before its Communist elements were in control. In Guatemala the Arbenz regime had posed a threat to American interests, and it had been easily, and cheaply, overturned. Not surprisingly, what had happened to Arbenz figured heavily in Castro's calculations, too.[11]

Within three months of Castro's takeover, Che Guevara's economic program was already transforming Cuba's economy and its relationship to the United States. In March the government "intervened" in Cuban Telephone, owned by Americans, but neither Bonsal nor his Washington superiors chose to make the issue a test of American resolve. The agrarian reform law, promulgated in mid-May, also affected American holdings, and Bonsal responded with a declaration that the United States accepted agrarian reform laws, if fair compensation was granted to the owners. After conversing with Castro, he emerged apparently reassured that the American holders of Cuban property would be fairly treated. When actual seizures began the following month, some of the first affected were American owners of large ranches. As the program accelerated, owners contended the seizures were being carried out arbitrarily without adequate recourse to the courts. In late October the American ambassador formally protested to the Cuban government, but also restated his belief that conflicts arising from the application of the law could be negotiated.[12]

Though both governments issued conciliatory statements, neither proved willing nor could really afford to meet the other halfway. Castro dared not acquiesce in American pressure, lest he lose face among his countrymen; Washington could not bring itself to deal with a small country as an equal. From the American government, there came reassurances about Cuba's right to shape its internal economic affairs without outside interference, but these expressions were always coupled with forceful assertions about the rights of American property owners in Cuba. From the Cuban government came stern assessments of the republic's economic position together with promises of fair treatment of foreign holdings. When, in late January 1960, Washington indicated a willingness to negotiate differences while upholding its legitimate interests in Cuba, Havana reaffirmed its respect for Cuban-American friendship. A month later Castro proposed sending a special Cuban commission to the United States to discuss differences, but he wanted prior assurance that Congress would not reduce Cuba's sugar quota. The American government, considering the request inimical to its interests, refused.[13]

From the early weeks of 1960, then, both Castro and Washington sensed there was little prospect for reconciliation. The Eisenhower administration already had other ideas for dealing with Castro.

The date for the planning of the Cuban invasion of April 1961 cannot be fixed precisely. Eisenhower stated publicly after leaving office that he issued orders to form and train a brigade of Cuban exiles on 17 March 1960, but the idea had been recommended by Nixon in his memorandum prepared during Castro's visit almost a year earlier. Certainly the plan was broached before Castro's revolutionary decrees inflamed American feeling, or the visit to Havana of Soviet First Deputy Premier Anastas Mikoyan in mid-February 1960 to sign a trade treaty with Cuba, or the resumption of Cuban-Soviet diplomatic relations on 7 May.[14]

As the invasion plan was being shaped, the diplomatic situation deteriorated. In June 1960 Castro ordered American and British refineries in Cuba to process Soviet crude oil. They were apparently ready to acquiesce in the demand but, after severe pressure from the American government, resisted the order. In retaliation, Castro seized the refineries. A month later Eisenhower announced suspension of Cuba's sugar quota, amounting to 900,000 tons, for the remainder of the year, a costly blow to Castro's shaky economy. The suspension set off a new round of confiscations and seizures of American property. As these events unfolded, a concert of American officials and businessmen operating in Cuba tried to damage the island's technical capacity by shifting key personnel back to the United States. Castro struck back by importing foreign technicians. On 7 August, reacting to Nikita Khrushchev's July boast about "protecting" Cuba with Soviet rockets, the State Department declared to the OAS that Cuba had in effect allied with the Soviet Union and Red China.[15]

When John Fitzgerald Kennedy and Richard Nixon squared off in the presidential race in the fall, the Cuban problem was already a major issue. In the campaign it was Kennedy, the young challenger to the old order, not Nixon, the cold warrior of the fifties, who successfully exploited the theme of the "loss" of Cuba to Communism. The vice-president, of course, knew what preparations were being undertaken to remove Castro, but as he noted in his apologia, *Six Crises*, to inject details of the plan into the campaign might easily have led to public disclosure of the operation. In view of the disaster that ensued, such revelations, even for political purposes, might well have saved Kennedy and the nation from the ignominy of the Bay of Pigs.

Even before the Kennedy-Nixon debates, Castro had further antagonized the United States. From Moscow, Khrushchev, savoring the Cuban-American imbroglio, declared the Monroe Doctrine dead. In the OAS foreign ministers' meeting in San José, Costa Rica, the American delegation sought censure for Castro's government. The proposal failed, and the Americans fumed as the Cuban premier nationalized some $900 million in American property in August. The following month, reinforced by Soviet support, Castro returned to the United States. On his second visit he took the United Nations by storm, his flamboyant style equalled only by Khrushchev's famous shoe-banging antics in the General Assembly. Castro spoke to the Assembly for four and a half hours, at times demonstrating great oratorical eloquence, but irritating the chair with his philippics against both Kennedy and Nixon. In a highly publicized encounter, he embraced Khrushchev, his new ally. Later, when his plane was detained at the airport because the Cuban delegation had not paid its hotel bill, Castro flew home aboard a Russian jet.

On 14 October Castro ordered nationalization of the sugar industry. With this act the last American property in Cuba fell victim to the revolution. In the United Nations Cuba made repeated charges of an American plot to invade the island, accusations which the American delegate called "monstrous distortions and downright falsehoods." The Cuban representative restated the charge at a Security Council Meeting on New Year's Day 1961. On the following day Castro, accusing the American embassy in Havana of spying against the Cuban government, banished all but 11 of the embassy's 300 employees from the island. On 4 January the United States severed diplomatic relations. The last strand of official contact between the two adversaries was now broken.[16]

When Kennedy took office, the plans for removing Castro had been altered considerably since Nixon's recommendation of 1959. As earlier envisioned, the assault brigade would be composed of Batistianos who had fled Cuba in the aftermath of Castro's victory. The CIA had anticipated landing exile groups in Cuba and then keeping them supplied to carry out guerrilla war, as Castro had done. Now, in 1961, the situation was more complicated. The new recruits were not Batistianos but civilians of varied professions and political philosophies. Some wanted to restore the gambling and vacation paradise of pre-Castro Havana; others wanted a truly democratic nation. In a special category were former Castroites who had grown disenchanted with Castro's leftist philosophy and were now ready to fight.

One of the most virulent of the anti-Castroites among the new arrivals from Cuba was Manuel Ray, who had organized a resistance movement against the Cuban leader in several Cuban cities. The CIA had evidenced little apparent interest in Ray's movement and in another guerrilla operation in the Escambray Mountains, eight miles from the site eventually chosen for the invasion. (The CIA claimed that it had difficulty contacting either group.) A small amount of aid had been dropped by planes flying out of Guatemalan fields for the Escambray rebels, but in their final weeks of operations they had begged for more assistance. In November 1960 Castro's forces finally isolated the Escambray guerrillas and destroyed their operation. In the same month Ray secretly left Cuba for Miami to plead for American support for his urban guerrilla force. But the CIA planners had already concluded that the best course lay in a conventional landing by exiles, supplied by American ships and protected by American planes, at some remote spot along Cuba's long coastline.[17]

Most of the Cuban exiles lived in Miami, where they survived on the handouts of friends or on money from their CIA contacts. The agency's most important functionary in Miami was Frank Bender, a former German refugee. Bender was insensitive, spoke no Spanish, and knew little about Latin America. He intimidated exile leaders with his power and bankroll. But the newer recruits, like Ray, refused to go along with Bender and the CIA's theory of invasion. Ray and his followers insisted that any assault had to be coordinated with a revolt against Castro from within. Believing the exile front to be too much under American domination, Ray maintained a special Cuban organization, the MRP (Revolutionary Movement of the People, in its English translation). Ray's slogan was "Castroism without Castro." The CIA distrusted Ray and his MRP followers because it could not control them, and in time Ray and Bender became bitter enemies. Some of the older Cuban exiles also distrusted Ray and openly called him a Communist. Only reluctantly did Ray refrain from publicly criticizing the CIA plan.

After the invasion failed, Ray was eased out of his post by other MRP members who believed the CIA's dislike for him would damage the movement's relationship with the American government. Thus,

the American strategists who had conspired to oust Batista undermined an anti-Castro rebel dedicated to the creation of a democratic,
progressive, non-Communist Cuba.

At the training camps in Guatemala the Cuban exiles, many of
whom were seasoned guerrillas, soon discovered that their American
instructors were preparing for a conventional military operation. A
force of 1,500 could not defeat Castro's military and peasant brigade
in traditional battle. Nor did the Cubans see much advantage in training on volcanic terrain dissimilar to the Cuban landscape where they
would be fighting. But the CIA operatives tolerated little criticism
and even shipped several of the more outspoken Cubans back to
Miami.

Most Americans may have doubted the invasion rumors sprinkled
in the press and noised about Havana, but Castro did not. In fall 1960
he undertook a counteroffensive. In the United Nations the Cuban
delegate charged that the United States was plotting the overthrow of
a legitimate government. In Miami Castro's agents gathered information from their contacts among the exile community. In Cuba the
premier mobilized the population for an invasion. So energetic were
Castro's preparatory measures that the Cuban economy actually
suffered from the diversion of men and materiel, and on the day Kennedy took office Castro called a halt to the mobilization. He had expected the invasion to take place the previous November, in the final
months of Eisenhower's administration. Kennedy, Castro hoped,
might seek an accommodation.[18]

What occurred in the following months, however, was Kennedy's
acquiescence in invasion plans inherited from his predecessor. In
Miami and at the camps in Guatemala, the domination of the CIA
over the exiles was complete. Under CIA pressure only the most
trusted and subservient Cubans were left in command of the brigade's
units. The others, suspect because of their prior association with
Castro or their political philosophies, were either demoted or shipped
back to Miami. Ray and the MRP were the most severely treated. A
week before the invasion, after considerable White House pressure,
the MRP was assigned a role in the invasion, and 100 MRP fighters
were ordered to Guatemala. But the CIA effectively undermined

the order by taking them to a farm outside Miami and holding them incommunicado. About 200 other dissidents in Guatemala were arrested when they refused to serve under former Batista officers. Most of them were soon released, but the more defiant ones were kept in Guatemala until after the invasion.

The CIA, embarrassed by the May 1960 loss of a U-2 spy plane over Russia, was on the spot, and did not want outspoken anti-Castro dissidents spoiling the operation. American prestige was also at stake. Kennedy assumed office after an intense campaign in which he spoke often of the decline of American power and especially of Latin American alienation from the United States. His hemispheric experts— Adolf Berle, Arthur Schlesinger, Jr., and Richard Goodwin—were perceptive, talented observers of Latin America, whose talents might have been exploited in arguments against the CIA plan. Instead, they actually reinforced it. Berle had served in Brazil and as assistant secretary of state for inter-American affairs. He was devoted to hemispheric democracy. Using the example of American pressure on Argentina during World War II to compel that nation to choose the democratic side, he argued that the United States confronted a similar situation with Castro's Cuba. There was, moreover, the parallel between the Marshall Plan, which had restored Western European prosperity after the war, and the Alliance for Progress, which aimed at rehabilitating Latin America. In the former case, the United States had backed the Marshall Plan with the Truman Doctrine, i.e., with military assistance to nations fighting Communism. Now, Berle contended, it must undertake forceful measures to advance the cause of the alliance.

The CIA had created a plan for invading Cuba which, by its estimates, was foolproof. Impressed by the agency's blueprints, the Joint Chiefs of Staff enthusiastically endorsed it. Unable or unwilling to deny the plan's feasibility, Kennedy's Latin American experts used their expertise to justify it. And Kennedy himself, afraid to cancel the plan and suffer the consequences, plunged ahead, stipulating only that no Americans could be involved in the actual landing.

In the weeks before D-day the American planners arranged a reconciliation between the dissident Cuban political organizations. The

MRP discovered, to its surprise, that its demands—Cuban supervision of operations, emphasis on aid to the Cuban underground, and removal of Batistianos in the Guatemalan camps—would be met. But all this was designed to mollify Ray and his fractious followers. When the time came for choosing a provisional government, it was not Ray but Dr. José Miró Cardona, Castro's first premier, who was selected. Ray became his lieutenant. On 22 March 1961, Miró proclaimed the Revolutionary Council as the provisional government, which was to assume authority once the invaders were established on Cuban soil. Its program was moderate: reaffirmation of the 1940 constitution, moderate land reform, and assurances to Americans whose property had been seized that they would be compensated. The MRP, in a supplementary statement, promised to retain state control of utilities and banks.

In the final week before the invasion, as Kennedy still grappled with whether to go ahead or not, the press nearly broke the story. Rumors about a Cuban invasion were rampant in Miami. Earlier, in the fall of 1960, Ronald Hilton, a respected Latin American scholar from the Institute of Hispanic American Studies at Stanford University, published a story about the Guatemalan camps. In December a *St. Louis Post-Dispatch* journalist actually flew to Guatemala and found the training sites. A long story followed in the *New York Times* in January.[19]

Yet despite this publicity the president did not call off the attack. The first strike was delivered on 15 April by two B-26 bombers, each painted with Castro's revolutionary air force insignia, against the airfields at Camp Libertad and San Antonio de los Baños. Another plane bombed the fields at Santiago. The purpose of the Havana raid was to knock out Castro's air force of fifteen B-26s and three T-33 jet trainers and thus protect the landing from air assault. But the raid proved a costly blunder: Castro's puny air force was not destroyed, and those planes surviving the attack were devastatingly effective in the following days.

Already American cargo planes had picked up the exiles in their training camps in Guatemala and flown them to Puerto Cabezas, Nicaragua, where President Luís Somoza bade them farewell. The

Cubans were convinced the United States would not let the invasion fail. As their ships plowed through the Caribbean to their homeland, they did not know about Kennedy's decision not to follow the 15 April strike with a second sortie to finish off Castro's air force.

In the early morning of 17 April the ships of Brigade 2506 hovered off the southern Cuban coast near Playa Girón and Playa Larga, the latter located at the end of the Bay of Pigs. Within a few hours the first group landed, encountered slight resistance, and brought ashore almost 900 tons of supplies and 4,000 weapons, to be distributed to Cubans joining the attack. By daybreak, however, Castro was already in full counterattack. His six planes took off with instructions to concentrate on the supply ships. One sank the *Houston*, which carried the communications supplies and the brigade's fifth battalion; the others knocked out the *Marsopa*, from which the invasion was being coordinated, and eight smaller vessels. Cut off from their ships, the invaders were now confined to the beaches and surrounding swamps. In the following hours the brigade's B-26s came in, but Castro's T-33 jets easily shot down five of the twelve rebel planes. The assault force moved farther inland and along the coast but, isolated from the support vessels and unable to inspire a popular uprising, was doomed. Taking personal command of the counterattack, Castro moved in the militia, slowly wearing down the attackers and forcing them back towards the beach.

In Havana, Cubans listened to music on the government radio station. In New York, the Cuban Revolutionary Council boasted of the grand invasion to liberate Cuba. But at the battle site the invaders were already retreating into the swamps around the bay, perhaps realizing for the first time that they would not be reinforced. Across the island Castro's police swept down on politically suspect Cubans. On the evening of the second day, 18 April, Richard Bissell, mastermind of the operation, called the president at a state dinner to report the bad news and persuade him to authorize an air strike. But Kennedy had already stated publicly that no Americans would be involved, and he denied Bissell's request. After the first day the invaders, deprived of their supply and communications vessels, had little chance. A second air strike on the following day, a much debated issue in the aftermath, would probably not have changed the outcome.

As Kennedy adviser Roger Hilsman cogently expressed it, the real battle was for the loyalty of the Cuban people. This battle Castro won. Through the long months of preparation, the American planners and their Cuban exiles had accepted unquestioningly the assumption that Castro ruled by force and fear. Given a clear alternative, they believed, the Cuban masses would unite behind a revolutionary movement aimed at overthrowing Castro. In the tense days of mid-April 1961 Castro proved he had the loyalty of the Cuban people.

In the following weeks Castro exulted in victory. Throughout the island there took place wild celebrations of David's triumph over Goliath. Throughout the hemisphere and among nonaligned nations of Asia and Africa the United States was vilified. It had attempted, as Hans Morgenthau wisely observed, to intervene in Cuba but at the same time to refrain from violating the cherished principle of nonintervention. It sought removal of Castro but did not want to antagonize the nonaligned countries. In the end it lost on both counts.

In victory Castro could afford magnanimity, and he showed it—not to the United States, whose actions, he said, proved American conspiracy, but to the exiles of Brigade 2506. On 26 April Castro himself interrogated some one thousand Bay of Pigs prisoners in a marathon televised "trial." He reasoned, joked, persuaded, and within a brief time had his subjects commenting on various aspects of the revolution and Castro's political philosophy. At no time did Castro become angry, though he was taken aback by pointed references to Communist intrusion in the revolution. To one captive he declared: "You are the first prisoner in history who has the privilege of arguing in front of the whole population of Cuba, and the entire world, with the head of a government you came to overthrow."[20]

Most of the Batistianos among the prisoners were executed, but Castro viewed the others as misguided. After the televised trials he made it known there would be no mass executions. Within a few months negotiations began between Castro and private American interests for ransoming the Bay of Pigs prisoners. After some $53 million in medicine and food was paid, Castro released them in late 1962. They returned in time for Christmas, but before they departed Cuba, Castro told them that next time there would be no prisoners.

The Missile Crisis

The Bay of Pigs not only enhanced Castro's prestige, but the confrontation with the United States also distracted those who were critical of the serious shortcomings of the Cuban economy. When the American government shortly stepped up its efforts to isolate Cuba economically, as Castro prophesied, the revolution had already formed a new ally, the Soviet Union. Anyway, the worldwide condemnation of the Cuban invasion indicated that it might be the United States, not Cuba, that would be isolated.

In August 1961 Cuba and America collided again, this time in the inter-American economic conference at Punta del Este, Uruguay. The occasion was a discussion of the Alliance for Progress, the massive program which, as Kennedy pointed out, would prevent violent change by making peaceful change possible. Though the American delegation busied itself drumming up support, the celebrity of the conference and the folk hero of Montevideo was Che Guevara, Castro's emissary. Addressing the delegates Guevara proved uncharacteristically accommodating, as he predicted that Cuba's revolution would achieve the goals of the alliance and promised that the revolution would not be exported. By implication he may have been extending a peace offer to Washington; most certainly the Cubans had not yet bound themselves inextricably to the Russians. There still existed some hope for a Cuban-American dialogue if the Americans would promise to respect the revolution and extend trade and the Cubans would pledge not to export the revolution.[21]

Whatever Guevara meant, a Cuban-American reconciliation was not in the offing. Washington kept pressing for another conference to expel Castro's government from the OAS. The presidents of Argentina and Brazil defied both the military and conservatives in their countries by receiving Guevara. Subsequently they were both forced out. One by one, Latin American governments broke relations with Cuba; in November 1961, Venezuela, ruled by a reformist regime, became the seventh hemispheric nation to close its Havana embassy. In retaliation Castro screamed his defiance and, in December, proudly proclaimed what his detractors had always suspected: "I am a

Marxist-Leninist." The next month, when the O A S reconvened to
deal with the Cuban issue, the United States won its anti-Cuban resolution by browbeating and bribing its neighbors. In the end Cuba was
expelled from the O A S, but Osvaldo Dorticós, the Cuban delegate,
had the last word when he declared that Cuba might be barred from
the O A S but not expelled from the hemisphere.[22]

After the expulsion Castro delivered a ringing speech urging Latin
Americans to join the struggle against imperialism by emulating the
Cuban example. The Chinese, already champions of guerrilla war,
praised him, but the Russians, who were busily promoting coexistence
with a number of Latin American governments, gave his speech only
perfunctory approval. Internally, Castro moved against dissidents
and toward revolutionary solidarity. The old Communists were eased
out, but Castro made sure their replacements realized he was the
Líder Máximo of the revolution.

Impressed with Castro's steadfastness and Cuba's march toward
socialism, the Russians were also apprehensive about Cuba's relations
with the Chinese. Moscow moved rapidly to secure Cuban loyalty. On
May Day 1962, the Russians declared Cuba an ally, not as highly regarded as the Eastern European bloc but more important than devia-
tionist Yugoslavia. Soon the two countries signed another commercial
treaty, committing the Soviet Union to purchase between two and
three million tons of Cuban sugar in 1962. In the months following,
the relationship was momentarily marred by minor incidents, such as
vocal Russian technicians bemoaning the laziness of Cuban workers,
or Cubans grumbling about the arrogant Russians. But Castro set
things straight by praising the Soviet people, the Communist party,
and Nikita Khrushchev. The generosity of his remarks was explained
less by his conviction than by his realization that Cuba, its economy
faltering, desperately needed Soviet aid.

Cuba's worsening economic situation also made Castro more aware
of the potentially devastating consequences of another invasion. In
the United States the Cuban Revolutionary Council still functioned.
With renewed American support and the lesson of the Bay of Pigs
uppermost in mind, the second wave of invaders would not repeat
previous mistakes. In spring 1962 invasion rumors spread throughout the exile community. If another invasion came, Castro reasoned,

his own troops, loyal at the Bay of Pigs, might not remain so, given the depressing economic picture and persistent grumbling about food and other shortages. This time Kennedy would not allow the invasion to fail.[23]

Knowing this, Castro sent his brother Raúl to Moscow on 1 July to secure Russian protection for Cuba. The Russians promised to increase their military aid and to send SAM (surface-to-air) and medium- and intermediate-range missiles equipped with nuclear warheads. The origins of this agreement are obscure. There is considerable speculation that Krushchev had such a plan in mind even before Raúl Castro arrived. Russian motives also remained unclear. Missiles fired from Cuba would do no greater damage than those fired from Soviet soil, though they would avoid early radar detection. Khrushchev's probable motive was psychological: by installing Russian missiles only a hundred miles from the United States—in its backyard —he could, in one brilliant ploy, overcome Russia's nuclear disadvantage, intimidate his American adversary, and impress the Chinese with Russian resolve.[24] Cuba could not be defended by conventional means, as could the eastern European satellites. Thus, the missiles afforded Khrushchev the most prudent method of satisfying Russian interests. To the United States his decision posed the most frightening possibilities.

Whatever Khrushchev's or Castro's motives, Cuba became, with the introduction of nuclear missiles, more than a "thorn in the side," the phrase Senator J. William Fulbright had employed during the Bay of Pigs crisis. Before the Russians sent the missiles, Castro already possessed the best-equipped army of any Latin American nation. With the new agreement Cuba would receive bombers and missiles capable of devastating American cities if the United States launched another invasion.

Kennedy was not plotting another invasion, but he was daily reminded of the Cuban situation. On 31 August, Senator Kenneth Keating, Republican of New York, stated on the Senate floor that some 1,200 Russian troops were stationed in Cuba. He went on to warn of metal structures designed, apparently, as the foundations for missile launchers. Reports from exiles of Soviet activity in remote portions of the island added to Keating's charges, though the senator himself adamantly refused to reveal his sources. Already the CIA had photographs taken by a U-2 plane which revealed work on a SAM site, but Kennedy and his advisors looked upon the construction as part of Castro's defense efforts rather than as a structure for offensive weapons. Kennedy was visibly concerned about the impact of the Cuban situation on the approaching congressional election in November. In early September, during a discussion with Soviet ambassador Anatoly F. Dobrynin, Kennedy was assured that the Soviet Union would undertake no dramatic action that might affect the elections. When asked about Soviet aid to Cuba, Dobrynin reaffirmed his government's position that Castro was receiving only defensive weapons.[25]

But as Dobrynin spoke, the initial shipments of missiles were en route to Cuba. On 8 and 15 September Russian lumber freighters bearing medium-range missiles docked in Havana and were secretly unloaded. Kennedy delivered a public warning, aimed as much at Keating and the American public as at Russia and Cuba, in which he declared that offensive weapons in Cuba would bring about American action. As the weeks wore on, news magazines and the American press continued to raise questions about Soviet aid to Castro, speculating that Russian assistance included nuclear weapons.

But not until mid-October did the CIA, which had been conducting reconnaissance over eastern Cuba, confirm the existence of missile sites in the western portions of the island. On 16 October McGeorge Bundy informed Kennedy of the most recent photographs. Additional flights in the next few days photographed three IRBM and six MRBM installations in various stages of completion. On that day, too, there occurred the first of many meetings of the Executive Committee of the National Security Agency, which debated and defined American policy during the next two harrowing weeks.[26]

To many, the missile crisis marked the high point of the Kennedy presidency. During those frightening days of late October, when the world seemed close to nuclear destruction, the young president appeared never to lose his mastery over unfolding events. The 22 October speech to the American public in which Kennedy announced a "quarantine" of Cuba and threatened the Russians with nuclear retaliation conveyed both a sense of resolve and righteousness. And in the postcrisis analyses Kennedy's decision to use a quarantine rather than an air strike or invasion was interpreted as the height of strategic brilliance, a plan faultlessly executed.[27]

In this dramatic confrontation the two superpowers negotiated with one another, leaving Castro and the Cubans as objects to be bartered. Kennedy demanded that Russia remove the missiles; Khrushchev agreed, provided Kennedy pledge not to invade Cuba. Subsequently the two countries supported a U.N. inspection to verify that the missiles had, in fact, been dismantled and shipped back to Russia.

But what of Castro's role in the crisis? Throughout the critical weeks of October the Cubans prepared for an invasion. Youngsters ambled about Havana carrying small arms and knives, waiting for the Yankees. The missiles, of course, still belonged to the Russians and could be fired only on Russian command. But Castro lashed out against those who condemned Cuba as a client state that had traded masters. When Castro learned of the Kennedy-Khrushchev deal, about which he had not been consulted, he sent a trenchant message to the United Nations, stating that Kennedy's promise was meaningless unless the United States agreed to cease the economic blockade, stop subversive activities, respect Cuban air space, and get out of Guantánamo.[28]

This time the world paid attention to the Cuban leader. For those who doubted Cuban resolve, Castro belatedly declared his opposition to a U.N. inspection that would, he said, "humiliate the Cuban people." U Thant, secretary-general of the United Nations, personally conveyed the proposal for inspection to Castro. During the secretary-general's visit to Havana, Castro demonstrated unsurpassed courtesy, for U Thant had often championed the cause of small states and had insisted on respect for Cuban sovereignty. In the course of their discussions the secretary-general also revealed an American promise to lift the blockade and a pledge not to undertake aggressive actions against Cuba. In retrospect, some observers have interpreted U Thant's message as Kennedy's efforts at reconciliation.[29] But Castro did not pursue the matter. If the Russians took back their missiles, that was their business. (But Cubans were chanting, "Nikita, Nikita, what you give, you can't take away.") Otherwise, Castro rejected any accommodation with his American enemy.

The Isolation of Cuba

In his defense of Cuban sovereignty Castro had defied both super-powers, but he quickly realized that Cuba could ill afford to antago-nize the Soviet Union. Following the Soviet-American understanding and the removal of the missiles, the Chinese tried to woo Castro from his Soviet ally. When China congratulated Cuba on its bravery during the missile crisis, Castro proclaimed a new era of unrelenting struggle against imperialism in Latin America. But within weeks the Soviet Union initiated a diplomatic offensive to lure Castro back into the fold. In February 1963 the Russians promised to defend Cuba against aggression. In Soviet eyes Cuba had proved itself worthy of alliance with the Soviet Union and would be permitted to develop its socialist revolution along distinctly Cuban lines. From the United States came more rumors of invasion. In a celebrated incident, a mysterious launch attacked a Russian freighter loaded with Cuban sugar. But on 10 April 1963, in a surprising move that stunned the exile commu-nity, Kennedy withdrew American support from the Cuban Revolu-tionary Council, the main exile organization.

But Castro was not reconciled by Kennedy's move, and he shortly left Havana for a visit to the Soviet Union. In Russia the Cuban leader signalled his commitment to the Soviets in their ideological struggle with the Chinese. He dutifully praised the Russians for their steadfast loyalty to the Cuban revolution, even though in October 1962 the Russians had negotiated with Kennedy without consulting Castro. To the Russians, Fidel was the great anti-imperialist hero; he received the Order of Lenin, pinned on his jacket by the chairman of the Presid-ium of the Supreme Soviet. Cuban socialism was welcomed into the fold, though not until Castro acknowledged his error in pushing in-dustrialization at the expense of agriculture and admitted that the future of Cuban socialism depended on sugar.[30]

Castro returned to Havana with promises of Russian aid. Cubans who recalled the bonanza era of American consumer products on dis-play in Havana stores would soon discover in their stead Russian goods, which were ordinarily both more expensive and shoddy. To avoid inevitable comparisons, Castro lauded Russian achievements and pointed out the virtues of Russian life, commenting, for example, on the modern subways in Kiev and their filthy and deteriorating counterparts in New York City. The Russians were now the purchasers of Cuban sugar, Castro pointed out, and they paid better prices than Cubans received under the old "preferential" agreements with the United States. The consummate goal of Cuba was now the ten-million-ton harvest, never achieved in the sixties, but a revolutionary effort to which Castro referred again and again.

Just as Cuba was being absorbed into the Soviet bloc, Castro received the startling information, conveyed by the French correspondent Jean Daniel, that a Cuban-American dialogue was possible. In the fall of 1963 William Attwood, an American official at the United Nations, responding to presumably official Cuban overtures, recommended opening talks with Castro. Before any meeting could be set up, Kennedy left on his fatal Texas trip. But a few weeks before Dallas, Kennedy spoke to Daniel and expressed his view that Cuba had suffered politically and economically during the era of American domination and that the United States was responsible for the character of the Batista regime. The problem now, as Daniel related Kennedy's conversation to an enthralled Castro, was the threat of the Soviet presence in Cuba to American security.[31] Castro, who had apparently wanted some kind of accommodation with the United States, reacted enthusiastically to Daniel's words. On 20 November he told the journalist to return to Washington and express his desire for peace. When news of the terrible event in Dallas reached him, he exclaimed: "Everything is changed."[32]

In the aftermath of Kennedy's death the United States, convinced that economic coercion would ruin Cuba and destroy Castro, expanded its anti-Cuban measures. The economic blockade became hemispheric policy, and in July 1964, at an OAS foreign ministers' meeting in Washington, the delegates voted 15 to 4 to condemn Cuba for aiding guerrillas in Venezuela. Invoking the Río treaty, the OAS resolved to sever diplomatic and commercial relations with Cuba, cease trade except in food and medicine, and impose restrictions on travel to Cuba. Three years later, at another OAS session, it was recommended that the shipping of government-owned goods on vessels entering Cuban ports be prohibited. A stipulation was attached that strongly urged Western European nations to reduce their trade and financial dealings with the Cubans.[33]

In time the blockade proved a bitter disappointment. Western European and Japanese businessmen engaged in a thriving trade with Castro in defiance of their American ally. The British sold Leyland buses to Castro on credit, and the Canadians supplied wheat, which was shipped to Havana on Soviet vessels. Even the world's staunchest anti-Communist, Francisco Franco of Spain, bought Cuban sugar and arranged to build Castro a fishing fleet.

10 • The Turbulent Sixties

Following the election of 1960 Latin America figured heavily in American foreign policy. The challenge of Cuba and Castroism prompted the United States to retaliate against what it considered a menace to its strategic interests. And the Kennedy administration felt compelled to offer a non-Marxist alternative to the Latin American demand for change.

America's answer to Castroism was the Alliance for Progress, a bold and innovative program aimed at modernizing a region that had been historically and stubbornly resistant to change. In nearly every Latin American republic there were powerful, if disorganized, demands for change. In the 1950s, as the United States settled into a cold war deadlock with the Soviet Union, several Latin American leaders had proposed ambitious programs for hemispheric development. At the time most American aid was concentrated in technical assistance, sale of agricultural commodities, and support for American exports to Latin America. Toward the end of the Eisenhower era, however, political unrest drove out dictators and brought into power a new generation of Latin American leaders—such as Castro in Cuba, Rómulo Betancourt in Venezuela, and Alberto Lleras Camargo in Colombia—who were dedicated to restructuring national economies and modernizing political systems. When Batista fell and Latin America pressed for aid, Eisenhower responded with $350 million as the initial capital for an Inter-American Development Bank. There soon followed another $500 million to finance Latin American public housing, agricultural credits, and education. Shortly after taking office, Kennedy greatly enlarged the pledge to a multibillion dollar program, financed by both Latin American and United States public and private aid. The goal was nothing less than Latin American rehabilitation. As expressed in the Charter of Punta del Este, the alliance called for 2.5 percent annual economic growth rate, a more equitable distribution of national wealth, trade diversification, emphasis on industrialization, greater agricultural productivity, an end to illiteracy, agrarian reform, increased life expectancy, public housing for the poor, stable price levels, tax reform, and economic development. All these were to be achieved within the processes of political democracy.[1]

Kennedy and the Caribbean

As much as anyone, John F. Kennedy sensed the vital importance of the Alliance for Progress as an alternative to Castroism, yet the record of Kennedy and the alliance in the Caribbean proved a disappointment. For one thing, alliance funds were unevenly distributed in the region. Cuba received no aid from the alliance. At the first conference at Punta del Este, Che Guevara had boasted that Cuba would attain the charter's goals long before the rest of Latin America. Elsewhere, the United States chose to shower its funds on "showcase" governments, such as that of Juan Bosch in the Dominican Republic. When Bosch fell in a military coup in 1963, aid was halted, though it was later resumed on a smaller scale. In Haiti the United States stopped aid entirely in the wake of publicity over political excesses under Duvalier. At Punta del Este II, when the United States orchestrated Castro's expulsion from the OAS, Haiti held a critical vote, for which it extracted a pledge for funds to improve Port-au-Prince's airport. (After the Cuban vote, however, other problems developed, and the United States refused funds for the airport. It did support a modest medical research program.)[2]

In Panama and Central America the alliance had a more dramatic, though less publicized, impact. The Inter-American Development Bank made loans for regional programs. In a much smaller but significant way alliance funds helped to build a water system in a Honduran village and to construct public housing in Los Pocitos, Panama.

But Kennedy seemed less interested in Caribbean economic development than in achieving political stability. Critical of the old order and of Eisenhower's support of the dictators, Kennedy was, like his predecessor, hostile toward leftist movements espousing Marxist solutions to economic ills and challenging American interests. He looked suspiciously at the political trend in British Guiana and the rise of the popular but mercurial Marxist leader Cheddi Jagan. With his wife,

Janet, Jagan had created the People's Progressive Party, a powerful force representing mostly the 300,000 East Indians who comprised half of British Guiana's population. In 1961 Jagan won election as premier. The British, who had jailed Jagan several times for political activities, were now apparently prepared to work with him and accept Guianese independence. Jagan desperately needed aid for his country but made it known that if the United States or Britain refused economic support, he would turn to the Soviet Union.

When Jagan visited Washington in October 1961, he laid out his grandiose plan for Guianese development to Kennedy. He wanted, he told Kennedy, an independent socialist society. They spoke at length about political theory—both had studied in London under the eminent Harold Laski—and though finding common ground on numerous issues, Kennedy refrained from committing the United States to the $40 million in aid Jagan requested. Later, the president agreed to review requests for special projects but expressed serious reservations about Jagan's ability to preserve parliamentary democracy. When Jagan departed, he pledged himself to a democratic Guiana. A special mission left for Georgetown to ascertain Guianese economic requirements and recommend assistance.

But in the following months Kennedy became even more skeptical about working with Jagan. The American Institute for Free Labor Development (the Latin American agency for the American Federation of Labor) and its chief functionary, Serafino Romualdi, had long opposed Jagan for his allegedly Communist sympathies. When Jagan pushed for a new labor law which the AIFLD opposed, an intense debate ensued, punctuated by violence and public disorder. In the commotion the British dispatched a warship to Guiana. Though Kennedy had objected to Jagan's Marxist leanings, he had earlier stated that Jagan's victory in an honest election could not be disregarded. In fact, Kennedy was sufficiently alarmed about the possibility of Jagan's ruling an independent Guiana that he urged the British to delay granting independence until a more acceptable leader emerged.

In 1963 the colony suffered a prolonged strike of sugar workers, who engaged in sporadic violence. British troops began patrolling Georgetown. The conflict had racial overtones stemming from the historic black–East Indian hostility and the enmity of the strikers, who were almost all black, toward Jagan's government. The columnist Drew Pearson charged that the strike had in fact been incited by the CIA, using the union as a front, as a means of delaying Guianese independence and destroying Jagan's credibility. In the aftermath, the British, with American approval, concocted a plan for proportional representation which, in effect, undermined Jagan's political strength and enabled the more tractable black leader Forbes Burnham to gain power. In 1966 British Guiana, saved from Jagan, became the independent state of Guyana.[3]

Similarly, the United States demonstrated that its tolerance of leftist regimes elsewhere in the Caribbean had limits. In March 1963 President Manuel Ydígoras Fuentes, anti-Communist leader of Guatemala, was forced out of office by a military takeover. Ydígoras had provided training sites for the CIA before the Bay of Pigs invasion. The year before the scheduled presidential election, Ydígoras, in an apparent effort to influence the selection of the next president, suddenly shifted his politics leftward by advocating tax and agrarian reform. Public violence erupted, and terrorists planted bombs in Guatemala City. Because of his inability to check the unrest, Ydígoras, a former general, became an embarrassment to the Guatemalan military. A deeper motive behind the coup, however, was the military's fear of the presidential candidacy of Juan José Arévalo, Guatemala's leftist chief executive from 1944 to 1950 and a leading candidate in the 1963 elections. Since leaving office in 1950, Arévalo had become a powerful influence among Latin American critics of the United States. His widely read tract, *The Shark and the Sardines*, was a scathing assessment of American policy in the hemisphere. When it appeared that Arévalo might be elected, the American government expressed concern about another Castro in the Caribbean. Within the Kennedy entourage the arguments for and against Arévalo turned on the question of taking a chance on the Guatemalan leader in the hope that he might be another Betancourt, then considered a staunch friend of the United States. But Kennedy had sacrificed too much prestige at the Bay of Pigs and dared not face charges of losing Guatemala to the Communists. Sensing the American predicament, the Guatemalan generals moved quickly by deposing Ydígoras, installing a military regime, and suspending the presidential election. Kennedy had little trouble accommodating the new order in Guatemala City, for the military's sudden seizure of power really served American interests.[4]

Kennedy's reaction to the October 1963 military coup in neighboring Honduras was somewhat different. For six years the republic had been ruled by Ramón Villeda Morales, whose term had only eighty days left when he was toppled. Villeda was, by Central American standards, a progressive, but he was also a determined foe of Communism and had publicly condemned Castro. And like Bosch in the Dominican Republic, Villeda conducted his anti-Communist crusade through legal means.

Villeda's politics constituted a major departure in Honduran political history. In 1954 he had emerged as the choice of frustrated Honduran reformers and intellectuals and, though clearly the popular selection for president, had been denied office by clever maneuvering among conservative elements. Two years later, however, a cabal of alienated young officers who identified with Villeda's antitraditionalist politics seized power and then turned the presidency over to him. Realizing his dependence on these young officers, Villeda moved cautiously with his social programs and dutifully allotted a fourth of the national budget to the military.

The misalliance came apart when Villeda created a civil guard as a counterbalance to the army. His political adversaries, the Nationalists, drew more and more officers into the fold by charging that the civil guard preempted the military's traditional role of defender of national order. Villeda's personal choice as his successor, Vice-President Modesto Rodas Alvarado, built an effective labor and peasant following by promising even more reforms than Villeda. When the Liberals convened, they chose Rodas over Colonel Oswaldo Lopez, who had expected Villeda's support. The Nationalists, believing power should rightfully return to them after six years of Liberal rule, openly encouraged the military to prevent Rodas's election.

On 3 October the officers, declaring the Villeda regime had disgraced the nation, sent the president and Rodas into exile in Costa Rica and named Lopez president. Ensconced in power, the generals nonetheless reassured the public that a civilian regime would be instituted after an electoral census, new electoral laws, a constituent assembly, and a new election. Criticizing Honduran events as a setback to democracy, the Kennedy administration suspended diplomatic relations and halted military assistance. American disapproval did not deter Lopez in his determination to impose a strict political regimen upon Honduras, and the United States capitulated and recognized his government within a year.[5]

The Dominican Republic offered Kennedy an opportunity to act decisively in support of progressive democracy. On 31 May 1961, a carload of conspirators ambushed and killed Rafael Trujillo and ended thirty-one years of totalitarian rule in the republic. But Trujillo's death did not destroy the power structure he had created, nor did it remove the Trujillo family from national politics. Through direct and indirect means the Trujillos owned virtually the entire Dominican economy: they possessed, for example, 1.5 million acres of the nation's finest sugar estates and operated more than 100 factories and commercial enterprises employing upwards of 60,000 workers. The national guard, the most heralded accomplishment of the American occupation, remained; and though the death squad which eliminated Trujillo was made up of disenchanted Dominican officers, the guard was, presumably, still loyal to the family.

Outside the family others hoped to inherit Trujillo's position. One, Joaquín Balaguer, was a Trujillo protégé, but he was regarded as a man of decent if politically conservative views. The professional and propertied interests, whose ancestors had ruled the republic before Trujillo came to power, wanted to reassert their power. With Balaguer they created a political coalition, the National Civic Union. When two of the Trujillos, returning from a short exile, attempted a coup, the Union, morally sustained by the presence of American warships lying off Santo Domingo, prevented it. It was a rare instance where gunboat diplomacy served the democratic process.

In the following months a party system of sorts emerged, and political figures driven out by Trujillo returned. One was a chain-smoking, charismatic poet named Juan Bosch, who built a political party, the Dominican Revolutionary Party, from the ranks of the peasantry, labor, and the lower middle class. On 20 December 1962, Bosch won an overwhelming victory in the election. Two months later he took the oath of office, the republic's first democratically elected chief executive in more than thirty years.

For the next seven months Bosch conducted an exciting, if somewhat unorthodox, political experiment. He proposed that the old Trujillo estates, which comprised the best land in the republic, be carved up and redistributed to poor farmers. Urban wages rose, and the government extended its controls over private businesses. The new constitution of April 1963 reflected Bosch's secularism with its provisions for divorce, civil marriage, and government supervision of parochial schools. A chaotic administrator, Bosch tirelessly roamed the country, promising agrarian reform, more controls over business, and closer scrutiny of foreign investment. In one decree he ordered the confiscation of excess profits of a foreign-owned sugar company.

His major error was his advocacy of a controversial constitutional amendment declaring the military to be an apolitical institution and providing for use of the armed forces to foster social and economic development. His tolerance of the Communist party angered the more conservative officers, especially a virulently anti-Communist and devout Catholic named Elías Wessin y Wessin. On 12 July 1963 Wessin y Wessin and his fellow officers demanded that Bosch adopt an anti-Communist stance. After receiving this ultimatum, the president rushed to San Isidro Air Base, from which the officers had issued their demand, to explain his strategy of dealing with the Communists by allowing the party to organize and participate in politics. Outright persecution, Bosch contended, would mean dictatorship. In his anger he ordered Wessin y Wessin and the other supporters of the ultimatum reprimanded.

But they were not punished. Wessin y Wessin and his cohorts launched a counteroffensive. On 25 September, at three in the morning, troops stormed the presidential palace. Bosch was arrested, the national assembly dissolved, and the 1963 constitution abrogated—all, the military said, in the best interests of the nation. A civilian council took over, pending scheduled elections for 1965, but it was clear that the real authority lay with the military.[6]

Reflecting on these disappointing events in the Dominican Republic, Kennedy seemed only mildly disturbed and, in fact, unsurprised. His personal view was that the United States had accomplished all it could in the republic through its aid program and the display of force that discouraged a return by the Trujillo family. Bosch had tried to govern a nation lacking a democratic tradition, infested with Trujillo sympathizers, and beset with severe economic problems.[7]

Bosch again went into exile, but in less than two years, the hatreds and frustrations surrounding Bosch's overthrow would resurface in one of the most controversial and explosive incidents in Caribbean history.

Panama and the Canal

Lyndon Baines Johnson often spoke of the war in Southeast Asia as a legacy from John Kennedy. Another legacy was a long-standing dispute with the republic of Panama over the question of Panamanian sovereignty in the Canal Zone, an imbroglio commonly known as the "flag controversy."

In 1960 Panama held its presidential election. The government candidate, Ricardo Arias, was defeated by Roberto Chiari, leader of a coalition of four of the eight opposition factions. To a large degree, isthmian politics had always represented family feuding more than political principles or programs. The election of Harmodio Arias in 1932 was an exception, and the nomination of Chiari was supposed also to constitute a change, for the president-elect had followed a tough line in American-Panamanian relations. Students believed that Chiari would lead the rising tide of nationalism by demanding greater concessions from the United States and, if necessary, by asserting Panamanian sovereignty in the Canal Zone. The older families, usually eager to exploit anti-Americanism, feared that renewed violence might precipitate socioeconomic upheaval in Panama, and thus they looked to Chiari to maintain the status quo.

Thus, Chiari found himself between two formidable forces—the aristocracy, which possessed the republic's wealth, and the students, who wielded political power in far larger proportion than their counterparts in neighboring Central American nations. The demands of the students that the Yankees get out of the Zone altogether were not lost on political leaders. In 1961 three parties—the National Liberal (then in power), the Patriotic Coalition, and the Civil Resistance—signed the famous Carta de San José, which asserted that the United

States must relinquish its commercial monopoly in the Zone and share political jurisdiction with the republic. Panamanians complained bitterly that the "dual" salary scale remained and that workers were still segregated in labor assignments.

But in 1964, the Panamanian government, reporting on economic trends, claimed that conditions were improving. From 1950 to 1962, the number of Panamanians employed by the Zone had increased from 11,000 to 13,000 and the wages paid them, from $15 million to $31 million. The result was a gradual rise in the per capita monthly salary of these same employees, from $98 in 1950 to $212 in 1962. This improvement was due, the government report stated, to changes in the types of jobs and to revisions in the salary or wage rate, as the treaty of 1955 had forecast.[8]

Under pressure from the more strident nationalists, Chiari asked President John F. Kennedy in late 1961 to consider another revision of the canal treaty. But Kennedy refused because of possible adverse political reactions in the United States and in the Canal Zone and, more important, because the likelihood of a sea-level waterway would necessitate a new canal treaty. Given this prospect, renegotiation of the 1903 treaty would become moot. The discussions would revive animosities over the "sovereignty" issue and perhaps impair plans for the new canal. In June 1962 Kennedy agreed to appoint negotiators to discuss United States–Panamanian private business in the Canal Zone market. The president was also willing to help solve the persistent wage disputes and to improve employment opportunities for Panamanians. Finally, Kennedy and Chiari arranged for the display of the Panamanian flag in the Zone.

The Eisenhower solution of 1960—the flying of Panama's colors in Shaler Triangle, a small plot overlooking downtown Panama City—had since proved unacceptable to Panamanians. Following the Kennedy-Chiari communiqué, both flags were to be raised over the Bridge of the Americas (called Thatcher Ferry Bridge by American residents), completed in 1962, and at the canal administration buildings in Balboa Heights and Cristóbal. The terms of the agreement stipulated that wherever civilian officials raised the U.S. flag in the zone, they should also fly the Panamanian flag. But American authorities in the Zone sought to appeal the "dual flag" question to the courts in order to test its constitutionality. Legal action brought inevitable delay, and the Kennedy-Chiari statement, which might have mitigated much of the rising hostility, was not immediately put into effect.

Instead, in early 1963, the governor of the Canal Zone began flying both flags in seventeen different places in the Zone. By his order of 30 December, the American flag was removed from other spots where it had previously been displayed. It was the removal of the American flag that precipitated antagonism. Many of the Zone's residents considered the hauling down of the Stars and Stripes an unwarranted retreat, and they were as determined as the Panamanians to fly their flag in conspicuous places. One of these places was on the flagpole of Balboa High School.[9] When the students returned from their vacations, they found that the flags were not to be raised again in front of the schools. More than 400 of Balboa High's students sent a letter of protest to President Johnson.

On 7 January 1964, five Canal Zone Junior College students hoisted the United States flag in front of the high school in violation of the governor's orders. Despite the angry protests from bystanders, school officials lowered the flag and confiscated it an hour later. After the first period, the students returned, raised the flag once more, and this time left guards to prevent school authorities from removing it again. Through the night about twenty-five students guarded the flagpole while sympathetic residents and parents supplied them with food and blankets. Although officials did not intervene, the governor issued a statement calling on the citizenry to obey the flag decrees. But the flag-raising was defiantly repeated at eight different locations, and a motorcade picketed the governor's residence. After issuing still another appeal, the governor departed for the United States on the afternoon of 9 January.

Meanwhile, news of the flag incident at Balboa High School became known to students at the Panamanian National Institute. They, in turn, decided to carry their own flag into the Zone, and on 8 January institute leaders met with the principal of Balboa High and the Panama Canal information officer, Frank Baldwin. The Panamanian students gave no indication that they planned a march the next day, but at 4:45 P.M. on the next day approximately 200 institute students paraded into the Zone carrying the Panamanian flag, placards, and banners. The intention of the students was to raise the flag in front of the high school, but the policeman in charge refused them. Apparently, from later accounts, he agreed to allow the students to place the flag at the foot of the pole and sing the national anthem. Unfortunately, the policeman spoke through a translator, and the Panamanians may have thought that he had indeed granted their original request. As the students debated what to do, the crowd of Zonians surrounding the flagpole grew to about 450. When protests and exchanges became more intense, the officer in charge ordered the demonstration cancelled. The Zonians began pushing forward, and in the ensuing scuffle the police employed their riot sticks. At this crucial moment, the Panamanian flag was torn. In their retreat from the Zone, the institute students smashed windows and street lights and overturned garbage cans. By 7 P.M. the majority had departed. The fleeing students found larger crowds of Panamanians already gathered at the border, demanding entrance into the Zone. A call to the Guardia Nacional of Panama got no response, and the Canal Zone police, undermanned, now readied tear gas and drew their revolvers in a show of force, but the size of the crowd had so increased that officials requested army troops.

The Panamanian government seemed to be making little effort to deal with the threatening situation, and the local radio and television stations made matters worse with highly inflammatory broadcasts. Some Panamanians ransacked the besieged Panama Railroad station. Zone police began firing, at first over the heads of the people, then, allegedly, point-blank into the shouting Panamanian crowd. The mob, repulsed at the boundary, proceeded to destroy foreign symbols within their reach: cars were overturned and set ablaze, the Pan American Airways building was encircled and attacked with stones and bricks and then gutted by fire.

On the Canal Zone side, looters rushed into the area through a gap in the fence and stormed the Hotel Tivoli, an impressive old Victorian structure where Theodore Roosevelt had once slept. Troops sent to the Tivoli were sniped at from the Panamanian side. General O'Meara, in command of the regular soldiers, ordered his men to return the fire and, after failing to obtain Panamanian government cooperation to stop the sniping, brought in marksmen. Throughout the tenth the snipers and marksmen fired at one another. The firing and destruction diminished over the next two days, but the scene obviously remained tense and critical. On the morning of January 13, the Guardia Nacional finally appeared.

When news of the Panama City riots reached Colón on the opposite side of the Isthmus, Panamanian demonstrators gathered and proceeded into the Zone town of Cristóbal, where they were allowed to raise their flag and sing their national anthem. Zone officials proved cooperative and understanding, but as the crowd moved back to the Panamanian side several cars were damaged. Joined by a larger group, the Panamanians broke windows in the Masonic Temple and the YMCA; and at 10:30 P.M., 9 January, U.S. troops arrived to restore order. Members of the mob grabbed at bayonets as the soldiers formed a barrier along the boundary, and desultory firing continued throughout the night and for the next three days. By the time Panamanian guardsmen appeared on 13 January, three American soldiers had been killed by sniper fire.[10]

The bitterness and hostility of the streets were not erased by diplomatic appeals. When President Johnson received news of the fighting, he ordered General O'Meara to guard the Zone boundary and sent Thomas Mann, assistant secretary of state, to the Isthmus to investigate. On 10 January the Inter-American Peace Commission of the Organization of American States heard Panama's contentions of United States aggression and agreed to study the case and make recommendations.[11] While U.N. ambassador Adlai Stevenson deplored the eruption in Panama and castigated the mobs for destroying American property, President Chiari prepared to break diplomatic relations with the United States. Simultaneously the Panamanian government denounced all treaties with the United States and announced that the charge of aggression would be presented to the United Nations. Chiari's conditions for negotiations were (a) an indemnity for damages caused during the rioting, (b) the flying of the Panamanian as well as the American flag in the Canal Zone, (c) removal of barricades between Panama City and the Zone, and (d) withdrawal of American troops.

The favorable response of both governments to pleas from the OAS and from other Latin American states to discuss their differences proved premature. Much of the difficulty was a matter of semantics, especially varying interpretations of the Spanish verbs *negociar* and *discutir*. Chiari's government swore that the Johnson administration had agreed to negotiate and not merely discuss a new treaty. This interpretation was denied by Washington. At last, Ellsworth Bunker and Miguel Moreno, representatives to the OAS from the United States and Panama, respectively, were able to overcome the problem of semantics; and thus, it was the OAS rather than the United Nations that provided the forum for discussion. Subsequently, Johnson became more flexible to Panamanian demands for settlement and agreed to review all matters relating to the riots, the canal, and canal treaties. Had the president not taken this step, the situation might have deteriorated, for Panama threatened to carry the republic's case to the General Assembly of the United Nations.

The tense atmosphere lasted through February and into March. Bunker accused both the Chiari administration and Communist agitators of fomenting discord. Proprietors of downtown Panama City cafés nailed up signs warning Americans to keep out. On walls, light poles, and even billboards there appeared placards denouncing the Zonistas in slanderous terms. The ill feeling afforded ample opportunity for the publication of leftist tracts excoriating Yankee imperialism and demanding neutralization of the canal, nationalization of the Canal Zone, and formal judicial appeals to the United Nations and the International Court of Justice.

One international legal body, the International Commission of Jurists, investigated the riots after a formal request by the National Bar Association of Panama. Specifically, the latter charged the Zone police and military with violations of articles 3, 5, and 20 of the Universal Declarations of Human Rights of the United Nations. These articles dealt with personal security; protection against cruel, inhumane, or degrading punishment; and the right of peaceful assembly and association. The commission dispatched a three-man team, composed of a Swedish judge, an Indian arbiter, and a Dutch professor, which left Geneva for Panama on 1 March.

The conclusions of the investigating team rejected the harsher accusations of the Panamanian Bar Association and condemned both governments for their actions during the riots. In the judgment of the investigators, the discord of January 1964 had constituted a "real threat to life and security, which could only be met with strong measures." The investigating trio, however, indicted the American police and military for the degree of force employed to restrain the rioters. In particular, the group cited instances where Zone police fired into the crowd rather than employing water jets to accomplish the task, or where army marksmen used high velocity rifles to return snipers' fire. The final report of the commission blamed the Panamanian government for its three-day delay in sending national guardsmen to the riot areas and for its failure to curtail the inflammatory radio and television broadcasts. Finally, the investigators regretted that Zone police had not given sufficient protection to the National Institute students on the afternoon of 9 January.[12]

Throughout the hectic months of February and March 1964 Panamanian spokesmen insisted that diplomatic relations would be restored only if the United States agreed to discuss the entire spectrum of canal issues. It was 3 April before relations were resumed by a joint declaration in which the two governments announced that they would appoint special representatives to seek a solution. On this basis, President Johnson appointed former secretary of the treasury Robert Anderson and Panamanian president Chiari named Jorge Illueca as delegates to the special conferences.

Everything went wrong with the talks from the outset. Principally this was due to the fact that the two governments had not yet settled the question of *discutir* and *negociar*: the Panamanian spokesman contended that the United States had promised to negotiate a new treaty in the 3 April agreement restoring diplomatic relations. Moreover, President Chiari and his successor, Marco Robles, continued to search for third-party assistance, primarily from other Latin American republics, to build another canal. For more than six months the United States delayed before finally accepting in December the Panamanian argument that there must be a new canal treaty and a new canal.

Whatever its faults, the old treaty of 1903, modified in 1936 and 1955, contained numerous provisions that protected American security interests; and to replace it completely with a new instrument was a formidable task. Debate on this issue centered on the following points:

1. Jurisdiction of the United States in the Canal Area (a euphemistic term more palatable than Canal Zone)
2. Definition of *sovereignty*
3. Statement on criminal and civil jurisdiction
4. Determination of the annuity, tolls, taxing authority, and costs of the canal
5. Powers of the canal authority
6. Life of the new treaty

An added burden was the separate but related problem of military bases in Panama. The present military establishment had been erected at a cost of $760 million and included several air fields and army bases, training grounds, a jungle warfare school, facilities for instruction in guerrilla subversion, and a hemispheric command center.

The military question proved to be less crucial to Panamanian negotiators than the more fundamental issues of politics and economics. Illueca sought a settlement that would erase forever the colonial image of the Canal Zone, restrict American jurisdiction to the basic necessities of operation and maintenance of the canal, provide greater economic opportunities for Panama in canal trade, and allow Panamanian participation in the new canal authority. This would mean termination of several Zone auxiliary services, such as the sale of commercial products to residents, thus creating a larger market for Panamanian merchants. Under the new arrangement, Panama believed, the Zone would become an integral part of the republic: Panamanian stamps would be used; Americans would be taxed by Panama; Spanish would be the official language; and the Panamanian flag would replace the Stars and Stripes in the canal area. As for the canal itself, Illueca stated that his government wanted joint administration of the waterway and payment of a portion of the transit fee collected from each ship.[13]

The formal acceptance of Panama's plan came in a statement by President Johnson in December 1964 in a national television address. Briefly, the president said that the United States intended to construct a new sea-level canal, presumably in Panama but possibly in Colombia or Costa Rica–Nicaragua, and to negotiate a new canal treaty. Stressing that the American government was not yielding to threats of violence, Johnson added that the new canal treaty would effectively recognize Panamanian sovereignty in the Canal Zone. The United States would retain the necessary authority to operate and defend the canal.

At the time of the announcement (issued simultaneously in Panama by Robles) the details apparently had not yet been worked out. During the ensuing months the public learned that the negotiators were working on three treaties: a replacement for the 1903 treaty, a second treaty for the defense of the canal, and a third for a sea-level waterway. The Treaty of 1903 would be abrogated and replaced by another canal treaty that would terminate either on a specified date or upon the opening of a new sea-level canal, whichever occurred first. The new canal treaty would enlarge Panamanian jurisdiction over the Zone establishment, but the economic interests of the Americans already living and working there would be protected.

News of the discussions, the details of which were reported in the press, immediately provoked a storm of criticism from several members of Congress, notably Representatives Daniel Flood of Pennsylvania and Leonor Sullivan of Missouri. For years Flood had made the canal his favorite specialty, and he was quick to point out that any deviation from full control of the canal or Zone was tantamount to appeasement. He traced the Panamanian campaign to achieve full sovereignty over the Zone directly "to the Bolshevik Revolution of 1917 . . . and the international Communist conspiracy."[14] Sullivan's arguments rested on more credible grounds, namely that canal concessions would mostly benefit Panama's elite.

The negotiation and completion of the three new treaties in mid-1967, however, brought favorable public response. A few newspaper editorials concurred with Representatives Flood and Sullivan that the prospective treaties were in fact a sell-out to Panamanian demands. But a greater number believed that the concessions of the United States were a prerequisite for American-Panamanian harmony—in the "spirit of the Good Neighbor"—and served the interests of the United States. In one stroke, these newspapers said, the Johnson administration had helped to eradicate a long-standing economic and political injustice and had promoted American prestige throughout the hemisphere. In Panama the United States had an old canal and an old treaty; now was the time for a new treaty and a new canal.[15]

As predicted, the new treaties granted extensive powers to Panama. For the operation of the canal area, the two countries named a Joint Administration of five Americans and four Panamanians. The administration would follow employment policies based on the principle that the canal was a primary source of Panamanian employment and that equality of treatment, regardless of nationality, should be the rule in employment. The Joint Administration would issue permits to live in the canal area, supervise the servicing of ships, operate the Panama Railroad as a public carrier, and continue to provide public services, such as education and health; but within five years it would discontinue the various department and grocery stores, cafeterias, hotels, laundries, gasoline stations, and related services. Wherever possible, however, the Joint Administration would promote business activities in the canal area. In the critical area of education and public order, the new canal treaty allowed the continued operation of the one school system (except that Panamanians living in the canal area might be transferred to Panamanian schools), and by a special grant of authority from the republic, it permitted the maintenance of law and order by the Joint Administration.

The Panamanian negotiators also won out in their struggle to receive compensation based on the tonnage passing through the canal. Under treaty provisions the Joint Administration would pay to the republic an annual payment of $0.22 per long ton of commercial cargo of yearly transits. (The amount was to be $0.17 at first, then would be increased in five years to $0.22.) The United States would retain $0.10 per long ton, with the remainder being used for canal expenses. In accordance with the principles of 1914, the canal would remain neutral, with both Panama and the United States responsible for its protection. The new canal treaty was to remain in force until 31 December 1999, or until one year following the opening of the new sea-level canal, whichever occurred first. At that time, the old canal would become the property of the Republic of Panama.

Similarly, Panamanian aspirations found fulfillment of long-standing goals in another proposed treaty providing for canal defense. The defense pact stipulated that both countries must aid in the security of the canal, with Panama obligated to provide defense sites to the American military. Such commitments would be applied to any new sea-level waterway in Panama.[16] Unlike previous arrangements, the future defense area would be under the Panamanian flag and Panamanian law, although American authorities might have concurred jurisdiction over those cases involving violation of the laws of both nations. In these situations, Panama would enjoy primary jurisdiction, unless the act involved treason, sabotage, or espionage. The United States would not exercise jurisdiction over any Panamanian unless he was a member of the American armed forces. The defense treaty was designed to lapse five years after the expiration of the new canal treaty or when the United States was no longer responsible for defense of the canal, whichever occurred later.

The 1967 treaties were never ratified. In Congress they were opposed by a phalanx of representatives and senators who viewed any relaxation of American control in the Zone as detrimental to American security. In Panama the treaties came under attack from outspoken nationalists who wanted to end American influence on the Isthmus. In 1968 Arnulfo Arias, the bête noire of the Roosevelt administration, became president of Panama for the third time. Arias was determined to control the national guard. A few days after his inauguration, a group of guard officers led by Colonel Omar Torrijos ousted Arias. Torrijos espoused a reform program somewhat akin to that voiced by the Peruvian generals who also took power in 1968 and were moving against foreign companies. Nationalism gripped the country, and Torrijos spoke defiantly about Panamanian aspirations for the control of the Zone. In the furor the three treaties of 1967, Lyndon Johnson's legacy to Panamanian-American reconciliation, perished.

The Dominican Intervention

Under Kennedy, American policy toward the Dominican Republic had been opportunistic. Kennedy had disapproved of the Trujillo regime and, after Trujillo was killed, had demonstrated American opposition to a takeover by the dictator's family, thus ensuring United States identification with Juan Bosch. But when Bosch fell after seven frustrating months, Kennedy became more cynical about the prospects for democracy in the republic. Johnson, like Kennedy, wanted to prevent another Cuba in the hemisphere. In the uncertain aftermath of Bosch's government, any leftist movement that appeared even remotely susceptible to Communist influence was looked upon in Washington as a potential threat to American interests. This fear, reinforced by Johnson's obsession with Communism, would precipitate the intervention of 1965.[17]

American scrutiny of potentially troublesome Communist elements in the republic antedated Bosch's inauguration and continued into his presidency. His tolerance of Communist organizations prompted American observers to assess Bosch as weak and naive and to denigrate his "democratic experiment." In Bosch's last weeks, Ambassador John Bartlow Martin requested a visit by an aircraft carrier to restore the president's rapidly dwindling prestige. He was told that a military show of force would be made only if the Communists threatened to take over. Martin, initially sympathetic to Bosch, became disenchanted with the unpredictable Dominican and, after the military ousted him, made it known that the United States, though displeased with the military takeover, was also opposed to Bosch's return to power. Such negative assessment of Bosch's ability would play an important part in the decision, made more than a year later, to intervene.

In fall 1963 Bosch went into exile, and a triumvirate ruled the republic for several months. It then gave executive power to Donald Reid Cabral, a handsome, politically conservative Dominican with socially prominent family ties. Believing the Dominican military now had dissident leftist groups under control, the United States shifted its attention to other Caribbean issues. Reid promoted political order and economic austerity, a policy that Johnson's Latin American advisors believed sensible in a small country with a turbulent past and an uncertain future.

But the hatreds and passions engendered by Bosch's overthrow did not abate. Dominicans who had not been avidly pro-Bosch but who disapproved of his ouster, and even some Dominican military officers, began planning to reinstate the former president. In a country whose politics has often been chaotic and given to isolated violence, these groups vowed to restore constitutional government by methods which, in American eyes, seemed unnecessarily disruptive. They demonstrated, disseminated leaflets, negotiated, cajoled, instigated strikes, and engaged in a series of comical coups, all abortive. Reid, harassed from the left by pro-Boschites, had to endure attack from the right by business and professional elements who chafed under the government's economic austerity program. His political challengers were Bosch and another exiled former president, Joaquín Balaguer. Bosch's followers wanted to put him back in power without an election, on the grounds that he had not been permitted to finish his term.[18]

Increasingly isolated in his own country, Reid ostentatiously identified with American interests and continually sought support from the new American ambassador, William Tapley Bennett. Just as Martin had reflected Kennedy's concern with Bosch's democratic experiment, Bennett aggressively promoted Reid's brand of political conservatism and economic planning. Indeed, Bennett's support of Reid became so open that it proved an embarrassment to both. Nationalistic Dominicans decried Reid's dependence on Bennett's goodwill, and in Washington, the criticism of Reid's government cast doubt on the wisdom of Bennett's unqualified support of Reid. Bennett's most glaring error was a public statement in February 1965 denigrating both Bosch and Balaguer. In early April, a few weeks before the revolt toppled Reid's government, a secret CIA assessment revealed that only 5 percent of Dominican voters supported Reid. This survey was presented to the State Department as evidence for dissuading Reid from running in the forthcoming election. Following a special meeting on the Dominican issue called by Assistant Secretary Jack Hood Vaughn, the department ordered Bennett to Washington. As he was leaving the country, pro-Bosch organizers were already planning to restore constitutional government in the republic.[19]

The revolt began on Saturday, 24 April, when the conspirators seized Radio Comercial and announced the arrest of General Marcos A. Rivero Cuesta, whom Reid had ordered to deal with dissident officers. Soon, enthusiastic pro-Bosch and pro-Balaguer crowds gathered in Dominican towns. Reid moved quickly to stamp out the revolt by sending reinforcements to Ozama Fortress in Santo Domingo and to the police barracks at the national palace. In other locations government police dispersed demonstrators. By evening the capital appeared normal, and the initial reports reaching Washington predicted that Reid would retain control.

But Reid had not dealt with the main source of trouble: the dissident officers within the Dominican military who were responsible for the coup. They reiterated their demand for a return of constitutional government and restoration of the presidency to Bosch. When Reid refused, rebel troops seized the fire station in the early hours of Sunday, 25 April. By daylight, reports of a deteriorating situation in Santo Domingo had already reached the Operations Center of the State Department. In the Dominican capital Reid, lacking control over his own military, now made a desperate appeal to the United States embassy for American intervention.

In its initial assessment of these events the embassy severely miscalculated the strength of Bosch's following. Embassy reports claimed that military support for Bosch was limited to a tiny group of officers. The embassy's main concerns were the safety of American residents and the degree of Communist participation in the revolt. It presumed that real power lay with a cadre of military officers—the most important of whom was General Elías Wessin y Wessin—who would, presumably, install a junta and hold new elections in the fall. But these officers were uncertain about their strategy and responded cautiously to Reid's overtures for assistance. The Bosch officers moved decisively. A deputation led by Colonel Francisco Caamaño Deñó, who would later emerge as the most important rebel leader, arrested Reid and shortly afterwards announced Bosch's imminent return, a pledge broadcast the following day (Monday) by Dominican radio and newspapers. In Puerto Rico the exiled former president prepared to return to the Dominican Republic.

Of critical importance in the first two days of the revolt was the attitude of the American embassy toward Bosch, the anti-Bosch officers clustered around Wessin y Wessin, and the Communists in the rebel camp. Generally the embassy regarded Bosch as a failure and opposed his return to power. It looked to Wessin y Wessin and his cadre to form an interim government. If the anti-Bosch generals proved unable to quash the revolt, the embassy speculated, then civil war would ensue, enabling the Communists to take advantage of the confusion and create another Cuba. When the Wessin y Wessin force got word Bosch was returning, it ordered the strafing of the presidential palace, an action that brought even larger numbers of Bosch supporters into the streets. Until the strafing occurred, the embassy's course had been to avoid interference, believing Wessin y Wessin and his comrades operating from San Isidro Air Base would bring order. When they failed to quell the public disturbances, the embassy requested American troops to protect American lives and safeguard the embassy.

Pressed by Washington to monitor the activities of Dominican leftists who had infiltrated the rebel movement, the embassy began sending detailed reports of potentially troublesome Dominican Communists. Often these reports were inaccurate and misleading about the number of Communists participating in the pro-Bosch uprising. The rebel commanders, desiring to avoid any confrontation with the United States, guaranteed the safety of American lives and property. As word spread of an imminent attack on the city by the anti-Bosch officers at San Isidro, the rebels tried to persuade the embassy to negotiate a truce. Though American officials were able to obtain postponement of an anticipated assault on rebel positions by Wessin y Wessin's forces, they were mainly concerned with the problem of evacuating American residents and the return of Ambassador Bennett.[20]

On Tuesday, the fourth day of the crisis, the San Isidro officers launched their offensive, crossing the Ozama River, pushing several blocks beyond the bridge, and killing hundreds of soldiers and civilians. Rebel leaders, shaken by the ferocity of the attack, seemed ready to negotiate and appealed to Bennett, who had just returned from Washington, to intercede. But the American ambassador was unwilling to act as mediator, probably because he believed Wessin y Wessin would prevail and the revolt would be crushed. In Washington the crisis atmosphere dissipated by Tuesday evening. But early Wednesday morning new reports from Santo Domingo indicated the anti-Bosch drive had been stopped by inspired rebel resistance.

At this juncture came another appeal for American intervention, this time from a member of the anti-Bosch faction, Colonel Pedro

Benoit, who reinforced his argument with accusations of Communist participation in the revolt. The San Isidro officers knew well the powerful impulses that would register in the American mind at mention of Communist intrusion in the rebel cause. Already the rebels had run afoul of Bennett and the American residents in incidents at the Hotel Embajador, where large numbers of Americans were staying, and at the embassy itself, which had come under fire.[21]

The first contingent of American troops, approximately 500 marines from the U.S.S. *Boxer*, landed on Wednesday, 28 April. That night Johnson explained in a nationwide address that the marines had landed to protect American lives, but it was clear he had something much larger in mind when he spoke of not tolerating another Cuba in the Western Hemisphere.[22] In less than a week a factional dispute between Dominican politicians and military officers had escalated to a point where, in the president's mind, American prestige and security were at stake. In recounting these days Johnson would explain that the initial landings had been justified to protect American lives and the embassy, but, in fact, the exaggerated reports of Communist infiltration of the rebel movement had convinced the president of the need for a massive show of force. The final decision was reached at a special meeting on Thursday, 29 April, in an agreement between McNamara, Rusk, General Wheeler, Admiral Raborn, and American officials in Santo Domingo. Paradoxically, the authorization for a large American force included a disclaimer in which the conferees expressed their faith in the principle of nonintervention, while they accepted intervention only as a last resort.

Throughout the evening an air armada flew toward the Dominican capital. From after midnight until noon on Friday, 33 C-130s and 111 support planes landed at San Isidro Air Base. During the following seven days American aircraft would average almost 250 flights daily at the Dominican air field, bringing 23,000 American troops.[23]

Ashore, American forces established an international security zone (ISZ) for safeguarding the embassy and providing sanctuary for foreign nationals. It was soon apparent that the regular Dominican military, whose strength and determination American officials had overestimated from the beginning, could not contain the rebels. This meant American troops from San Isidro would have to cross the Ozama and move west into the city to join forces with the marines patrolling the ISZ. If that were done, as former ambassador John Bartlow Martin pointed out, then United States troops might encounter Dominican resistance. Johnson seemed hesitant about such a confrontation, but he was so concerned about a potential Communist takeover that he did not rule out the possibility.

The United States had already presented its justification for the intervention to the Organization of American States. The OAS Council had, on Friday morning, called for a security zone and cease-fire, but beyond this limited measure it registered sharp disagreement about going further. Johnson's commitment to an OAS solution and support from Latin American governments inspired few in the hemisphere and, in several instances, prompted severe criticism from Latin Americans who charged the president with practicing a modern version of gunboat diplomacy. Derogatory remarks about the OAS attributed to Johnson circulated among the Latin American embassies. The "Johnson doctrine," which permitted unilateral American intervention in a Latin American country threatened by an internal Communist menace, took its place in the hemispheric lexicon with "Roosevelt Corollary."[24]

Following the OAS ceasefire, proclaimed on 30 April, Martin, who knew most of the Dominican officers from his earlier sojourn in the country, arrived as special negotiator. He went first to San Isidro, where he found Bennett with Wessin y Wessin. The ambassador was now committed to supporting the American military's plea for even more troops, basing his argument on the continuing—and, as later shown, largely spurious—reports of rebel atrocities and Communist participation in Caamaño's force. In Washington, Bennett's superiors speculated that the ambassador's publicized remarks might have damaged American overtures to the OAS. After talking to Wessin y Wessin and Bennett, Martin met with Caamaño on the following day. The rebel leader was especially concerned that both sides obey the cease-fire and that American troops remain within the international security zone. Martin, describing the encounter later in a magazine article, characterized Caamaño as a "potential Castro."[25]

To American commanders, however, it was by now clear that the United States could not stabilize affairs in the capital unless the two components of its forces—the 500 marines in the ISZ and the much larger body of troops flown into San Isidro—were united. Joining these two bodies meant a cordon from the river that cut through or at least skirted rebel-held areas. By Sunday, 2 May, the White House granted the request, and the State Department drew up a detailed justification for repositioning American troops and, in the same document, restated its case for the entire intervention. The proposal was then submitted to the OAS, whose approval the United States wanted. By early Monday airborne units from San Isidro had established a military corridor connecting the force at the base with the marines in the ISZ. At the same time, they had also isolated the rebel force within the city.

Its military forces in Santo Domingo united, the American government spent the next days justifying the intervention to an increasingly skeptical world. In this undertaking, considered as important as the actual intervention, Martin played a crucial role. He interviewed the rebel leader, Caamaño, and, later, the hero of the rebels, Bosch, still in exile in Puerto Rico. Until his encounter with Martin, Bosch apparently held to the belief that the United States might support his return. But Martin arrived for the sole purpose of convincing the exiled Dominican president to accept the American position in the crisis, a plea reinforced by a special telephone call from Abe Fortas, a Johnson advisor, asking Bosch to condemn the Communist elements in the revolution. (The number of Communists in the rebel camp identified by American estimates jumped dramatically from three to fifty-eight, then down to fifty-four, and back to seventy-seven. Ultimately, when the press revealed the unreliability of official reports, the administration settled on a much smaller number, contending, nevertheless, that even a few dozen were extremely dangerous.)

American forces, augmented by Brazilian and Honduran troops to give the impression the intervention had hemispheric support, remained in Santo Domingo for a year. Following the revolt, the United States irritated the various Dominican factions by its capricious support and its equally capricious dropping of one Dominican leader

after another. Reid, who had originally requested American intervention, was swept aside. His successor, provisional president Jose Rafael
Molina Ureña, failed to win American approval. The new heroes were
Wessin y Wessin and Colonel Benoit, leader of the junta created by
the San Isidro generals. Bosch stood no chance of winning American
approval. Martin pushed Antonio Imbert, one of the assassins of Trujillo, but Imbert too fell from grace, and Johnson's advisors reopened
negotiations with Bosch to learn his recommendations. In mid-May a
special team, composed of McGeorge Bundy, Thomas Mann, Jack
Hood Vaughn, and Cyrus Vance, arrived in San Juan to discuss the
problem of succession with Bosch. From this exchange came the name
of Silvestre Antonio Guzmán, Bosch's secretary of agriculture. Guzmán left for Washington to be interviewed. In Santo Domingo the
Bundy team tried to persuade the various functions to accept Guzmán, but Wessin y Wessin and his followers preferred to live with the
junta that had been hastily formed by Imbert. In the course of these
negotiations Imbert suddenly launched an assault against the rebels,
his operation sustained in large part by American funds. Just as dramatically, Guzmán fell from grace in Washington, and American officials began talking about a new coalition. As the proposals were
sounded, Imbert, with Americans acquiescence, struck once more at
the rebels, reducing their influence.

But Imbert fell again in American estimation. In early September
the United States threw its support behind a provisional government
headed by Hector García Godoy, Bosch's foreign minister. García
Godoy gave the country nine months of effective government. The
San Isidro officers were systematically bribed or exiled. Under intense American pressure Wessin y Wessin sold his $25,000 house for
$50,000 and was asked to leave Santo Domingo in the "interests of
peace." In a rage he ordered his tanks to move against the city, but
they were stopped by American patrol units. Wessin y Wessin received a visit from a senior American officer. He was given the post
of Dominican consul in Miami and hurriedly flown out of the Dominican Republic to take up his new duties.[26]

Puerto Rico: America's Ireland?

In the course of the 1960s America's role in the Caribbean would ultimately be judged by the confrontation over Cuba and the Dominican intervention. Not so apparent to observers of American policy was the failure of the American colonial experiment in Puerto Rico. As attention focused on the Cuban challenge, American leaders could cite Puerto Rico as a showcase of democratic capitalism. Yet the popular image of a vigorous, progressive Caribbean society belied the reality of internal tensions and uncertainties brought about by rapid modernization, the clash of Anglo-Saxon and Hispanic cultures, and differing perceptions of progress.

In large part, the story of postwar Puerto Rico is the history of the commonwealth—the Estado Libre Asociado, as Puerto Ricans know it —and an extraordinarily talented Puerto Rican politician, Luis Muñoz Marín, who can justifiably be called its creator. In the 1930s, as Puerto Ricans suffered from American neglect and inept New Deal polities, Muñoz was an outspoken nationalist who admired Pedro Albizu Campos, champion of insular independence. But when Muñoz's party, the Popular Democrats, emerged victorious in 1940, he began turning his attention to immediate economic problems, such as the island's high unemployment rate. During the war Muñoz urged a vigorous program of state capitalism, but by 1945 he had abandoned it because Puerto Rico, unable to set its own tariffs or control its own shipping, was even more dependent on the American economy. A second effort at indigenous economic planning after the war also proved a dismal failure. In 1948, Puerto Ricans paid almost 30 percent more than American consumers for food; insular unemployment continued at high levels. The surplus population emigrated to the United States, which absorbed some 250,000 Puerto Ricans in the decade beginning in 1942.

In 1945 Senator Tydings, who had proposed a bill for granting Puerto Rico its independence in 1936, sponsored a similar measure in the Congress, a proposal which received the approval of thirty-one Puerto Rican legislators and forty-two mayors. But Muñoz opposed the plan, arguing, with considerable forcefulness, that Puerto Rican independence, however appealing to nationalist sentiment, would mean economic disaster. Separated politically from the United States, the island would be unable to obtain the economic and commercial benefits that it enjoyed in its "special relationship" with Washington. When President Truman asserted in 1946 that Puerto Rico had three choices—independence, statehood, or dominion—Muñoz rejected the first two and, modifying the third, suggested the "commonwealth of the associated people of Puerto Rico." Such a solution, he argued, would protect the island's economy and preserve its cultural identity.

In 1948, fifty years after the American conquest, Muñoz became Puerto Rico's first elected governor. On the surface Muñoz's cherished commonwealth idea seemed a sensible solution to the Puerto Rican and the American dilemma. Puerto Ricans' hearts yearned for independence, but their heads told them that independence meant economic disaster. Their American overlords, conscious of the breakup of colonial empires in Asia and Africa and the growing restiveness among the European dependencies in the West Indies, found in the commonwealth proposal a mechanism for preserving a colony by calling it by another name. On 4 July 1950, the president signed Public Law 600, which gave Puerto Rico a republican government and a constitution with a bill of rights. The law was then submitted to a Puerto Rican plebiscite.

Already, the plan had precipitated intense discussion among Puerto Ricans. In October the island was convulsed in the Nationalist Insurrection. The Nationalist party had championed independence for years, mostly by pamphleteering and occasional protest. In the 1950 affair some of its members were charged for illegal transportation of arms. A group of Nationalists attacked the governor's residence, La Fortaleza, and others seized the police station in Arecibo. Muñoz declared a state of emergency and mobilized the national guard, which shortly occupied the University of Puerto Rico, considered a haven for Nationalist agitators. In four other cities the guard and Nationalists shot it out. When the insurrection was over, there were twenty-four deaths, several hundred wounded, and many more arrests. The climax came on 30 October, when the police surrounded the house of Albizu Campos, the fiery old Nationalist who had spent ten years in a federal penitentiary in Georgia for political agitation. Someone opened fire, and a shootout ensued. When it was over, Albizu Campos and his comrades, suffocated by a tear-gas barrage, were taken away unconscious. The next day, in Washington, two Nationalists attempted to assassinate President Truman.[27]

In March 1952 the new constitution easily won approval in a plebiscite, but the Nationalists persuaded many voters to abstain. Those who participated had been told by Muñoz that the commonwealth ended every manifestation of colonialism in Puerto Rico. In fact, this was not the case. When the constitution came back to the Congress, two amendments (which Puerto Ricans never got a chance to approve) were attached limiting the authority of the Puerto Rican government. Any amendment to the Puerto Rican constitution had to be compatible with Law 600, the Puerto Rican Law of Federal Relations, and the American Constitution.

The new arrangement, Nationalists charged, was merely a cosmetic alteration of the Jones Act of 1917, which had blatantly declared that American laws—internal revenue codes excepted—had the same force in Puerto Rico as in the United States. Despite these criticisms, the United States, with Muñoz's energetic support, now appeared before the United Nations to argue that Puerto Rico was no longer a colony and that therefore the U.N.'s Committee on Information from Non-Self-Governing Territories could no longer require periodic reports on the island. By a narrow margin the American position was sustained.[28]

Dedicated Nationalists continued their agitation for independence, however. On 2 March 1954, four of them fired randomly in the U.S. House of Representatives, wounding five congressmen. Their leader, a woman, was wrestled to the floor and disarmed, screaming in Spanish and English, "I love freedom. I love my country."[29]

Muñoz had already begun an enthusiastic campaign for economic development, calling the program by a wartime slogan, "Operation Bootstrap." American investors were promised tax exemptions, cheap labor, and a stable political environment, things the other Caribbean republics could not offer. In Puerto Rico the sugar industry, which for centuries had been the dynamic economic and social force in Caribbean societies, was already in a sharp decline. Muñoz's ambitions for a prosperous Puerto Rico looked to light industry and manufacturing, to a Puerto Rico of urban dwellers and not illiterate and underfed agricultural laborers. Operation Bootstrap revolutionized the economy: by 1953, the program could boast of 300 new plants and 25,000 new jobs. Per capita net income had risen from $122 in 1940 to $426. Before the end of the decade industry had replaced agriculture as the island's chief income producer. In 1959, with the building of two oil refineries, came the beginnings of a petrochemical operation aimed at diversifying the economy and lessening Puerto Rico's reliance on light industry.[30]

As Puerto Rico entered the 1960s, then, it exhibited the characteristics of a model colonial enterprise: a vigorous economy safely insulated from the Communist peril. Muñoz himself loomed even larger as Kennedy identified American goals in Latin America and the Alliance for Progress with the Puerto Rican "miracle." Another Puerto Rican, Teodoro Moscoso, who had been head of the Puerto Rican Development Agency, joined the Latin American task force authorized by Kennedy and was later named coordinator of the Alliance for Progress. Muñoz and Moscoso had personal contacts with the Latin American non-Communist civilian leaders who represented, in American eyes, the alternative to Castro.

Yet, for all the laudatory comments about Puerto Rican progress, the island continued to be a troubled society. True, the Cubans were dependent on the Russians, but Puerto Ricans were dependent on the United States to a greater degree. Puerto Ricans still produced things they did not consume, and still consumed products they did not produce. And the status question remained a divisive issue.

In 1964 Muñoz ended an era by stepping down, naming Roberto Sanchez Villela as his successor. The Puerto Rico Sanchez Villela inherited was now a society plagued by economic and social troubles—a persistently high unemployment rate and urban problems similar to those of large American cities. Though emigration to the mainland eased the unemployment burden, many who had taken residence stateside had confronted a hostile environment in New York slums and were trickling back to San Juan. With industrial change came the inevitable crowding into Puerto Rican cities, followed by hurried, and usually inadequate, public housing and the mushrooming of slums. A rising middle class, which consciously emulated American tastes, enjoyed a better life than any Puerto Rican ever dreamed of in the old days. But the new paradise also had its social flotsam, the rising numbers of welfare and food stamp recipients, who constituted an embarrassingly high proportion of Puerto Ricans on the federal dole.

In 1968, for the first time in Puerto Rican history, a pro-statehood candidate, Luís Ferré, a wealthy businessman and organizer of the New Progressive Party, won the election by capitalizing on a feud among the Popular Democrats. Ferré and the New Progressives argued that only by joining the union as the fifty-first state could Puerto Rico guarantee its continued enjoyment of the full economic benefits of American society. The philosophy of the party was aptly summed up in its motto: statehood, security, progress. The commonwealth, Ferré contended, rested on a Congressional act, Public Law 600, which could be repealed, but Congress could never expel a state from the union.

The drive for statehood precipitated still another debate over status. For a time, the commonwealth adherents found a kindred spirit among the *independistas*, the Puerto Rican Independence Party. Sanchez Villela spoke angrily against the conscription of Puerto Rican youth into the United States Army. Violence directed against American property, especially the large chain businesses and hotels, escalated sharply. *Ramparts* magazine, in a special report, estimated $25–75 million in fire damage to American property from 1967 to 1970.[31]

In most analyses Puerto Rico is depicted as a "third world" society striving for modernization but determined to resist Americanization. A more apt comparison, as Albizu Campos sensed and Gordon K. Lewis has suggested, is that of Puerto Rico and Ireland. The similarities between Irish and Puerto Rican nationalist thought are striking. Both islands were conquered, Ireland by the Tudors and Puerto Rico by the Americans; both have experienced a history of agitation and the occurrence of "massacres"—Oliver Cromwell's bloody suppression of the Irish at Drogheda and the 1937 Ponce confrontation in which the police shot unarmed protestors—which play a powerful role in nationalist mythology; both have been ruthlessly subjected to alien culture and religion. Both the Irish and the Puerto Ricans have performed menial labor for their conquerors. Both had their compromisers—Parnell and Muñoz Marín—who tried to mediate between mother country and colony. In both there matured a generation of embittered and sullen people who sensed deeply, even as their economic lot improved, that they were oppressed. Britain divided Ireland between north and south, between Catholic and Protestant; American rule has divided Puerto Ricans who have emigrated to the mainland from those who have remained on the island.[32]

But Puerto Rico has not yet arrived at the place in history at which Ireland found itself at the end of World War I. The *independistas* have declined in their appeal at the polls, but they have always argued that voting in the commonwealth is another exercise in colonial authority. The statehooders, many of whom are American transplants and Cuban exiles, want to guarantee their economic future by making the island a state. In the 1976 American presidential election, both candidates declared in favor of Puerto Rican statehood if Puerto Ricans voted for it. But Congress would have to approve the incorporation of another state, a new state with an alien culture and sufficient population to warrant congressional representation larger than that of twenty existing states. Puerto Rico is an island apart, but it is not another Hawaii waiting for its mainland benefactors to confer statehood, nor is it another Philippines, too remote and too alien to warrant inclusion as an equal in the Union. Puerto Rico is unique in the American empire, and what happens to it may well determine the final judgment on America's role in the Caribbean.

The United States and the Caribbean in the Cold War

The Dominican intervention scarred that republic and disillusioned a generation of Dominican leaders. Juan Bosch felt especially aggrieved, as he lost all faith in the ballot box and "Anglo-Saxon democracy." In the years after the 1965 revolt he turned once more to writing and produced a bitter tract called *Pentagonism: A Substitute for Imperialism*. Pentagonism, he wrote, is imperialism at its most advanced stage. The military conquers its own country, not by making war on the people, but by sending expeditions to foreign places—to Vietnam and Latin America—not to conquer territory but to exercise influence and obtain economic resources to bolster the war machine at home.[33]

What occurred in the Dominican Republic in 1965 revealed, as Theodore Draper wrote in his bitter account of the intervention, the "abuses of anti-communism." By exaggerating and grossly distorting Communist participation in the rebellion, the United States embarked on a massive intervention to prevent another Cuba. But the ill result of what was committed in the name of combatting Communism was the destruction of a democratic experiment in a Caribbean republic striving to survive after thirty-one years of brutal dictatorship. True, the democratic experiment had not been successful. Bosch's flaws were obvious even to sympathetic Dominicans, but what he represented was probably the best the republic could produce at that moment in its history. His overthrow in 1963 was not due to American conspiracy, but his return to power two years later was prevented by an unspoken alliance between rightist Dominican military officers and an American president obsessed with Communism.[34]

The Dominican intervention also revealed a deeper failure of American policy in the modern Caribbean. After 1945 virtually every Caribbean nation witnessed, to some degree, internal pressures for modernization, pressures that have been described as the "revolution of rising expectations." Caribbean participation in World War II introduced monocultural societies with strong traditions of authoritarian rule to the powerful presence of a wartime American economy. The experience left a profound impression, generating demands for economic modernization and destruction of the old political order. Where authoritarian governments held on, as in Nicaragua and the Dominican Republic, the leaders provided a surface modernization, usually in the form of new highways or modern office buildings, while they left the social structure intact. In other countries, such as Guatemala or Cuba, the old order itself was directly challenged; in the latter it was ultimately expunged by Castro's revolution, but in the former, with the connivance of the United States, the entrenched elements reasserted their power and reversed the programs of a reformist government.

One of the sadder results of World War II was American inattention to the pressing postwar needs of a region that had dutifully subordinated its politics and economies to the American will. All the hemispheric republics emerged from the war with high expectations of a better future, but the Caribbean nations, lying closer to the United States and better acquainted with American political and economic values, anticipated even more strongly the benefits of the American triumph over fascism. Within a short time the dream was shattered, and the Caribbean nations realized that, if anything, the war had distorted their economies by disrupting European trade patterns and advancing American economic influence.

In several countries—Cuba, Nicaragua, and the Dominican Republic—authoritarian governments, reconciled to the anti-Communist mood of Eisenhower America, brought their countries into the American sphere by providing a congenial atmosphere for American investment and by acquiescing in America's global anti-Communist mission. Cuba became in the 1950s a slavish imitation of cold war America and, perhaps because of Cuban devotion to American ways, consciously repudiated American values of order and progress under Castro. The Cuban revolution not only transformed Cuba but dictated the course of America's Caribbean policy. Whatever urgency lay behind the Alliance for Progress and Kennedy's advocacy of a democratic Caribbean, American fears of "another Cuba" explained the direction of American policy. Preventing another Castro became the overriding American goal in the modern Caribbean. Even Kennedy, philosophically indisposed to dictatorship and military government, nonetheless accepted both in preference to leftist movements like Castro's.

11 • The End of Empire

By 1970 the Caribbean empire of the United States, fashioned in the age of Theodore Roosevelt and Woodrow Wilson and refashioned in the age of Franklin D. Roosevelt, was already disintegrating, but the American people were scarcely aware of its demise.

In the first third of the twentieth century, American leaders had been willing to dispatch gunboats and land marines to chastise factious Caribbean politicians and maintain order in the tropics. In some instances American proconsuls (usually naval or marine officers untutored in colonial rule) had actually staffed the bureaucracies of Caribbean governments. But in the late 1920s this seemingly acceptable alternative to outright annexation caused some unanticipated problems. The second Nicaraguan intervention showed that a disciplined guerrilla movement, exploiting latent anti-American feelings, could fend off the hemisphere's strongest military. Sandino's movement brought to an embarrassing close the initial phase of American empire in the Caribbean. Its goals had been stable political systems ruled by "good men" exercising "sensible" judgments and willing to defer to American tutelage—in other words, a collection of client states nurtured on the values not of Wall Street but Main Street.

Sandino's war not only ended the first American empire; it revived the anti-imperialist movement in the United States. And the depression that followed further damaged the cause of those who urged a continuing military presence in the Caribbean on the reasoning that interventions of the Nicaraguan variety were costly to the country's prestige and to its pocketbook. The situation that confronted Franklin Roosevelt in 1933—a Cuban revolution that displayed both anti-American and socialist impulses—called for his most artful political manipulation to maintain American suzerainty in Cuba (and symbolically in the rest of the Caribbean). It is doubtful that Congress would have sustained a military intervention in Cuba, given the grim economic conditions in the United States. Roosevelt surrounded the island with warships, turned his back on the generation of Cuban revolutionaries who had overturned a brutal dictatorship, and found a surrogate to run the country.

In the early years of the century Theodore Roosevelt asked only for Caribbean leaders who did not exhibit the "revolutionary frame of mind," respected American power, and never expected much from a people he considered inferior; Wilson demanded "decent" governments ruled by "good men"; FDR publicly stated that "they [Latin Americans] think they're just as good as we are, and some of them are" and "should be given a share." When queried about America's unsavory dictatorial Caribbean allies, he privately declared, "They may be SOBs, but they're *our* SOBs." John F. Kennedy offered them an alternative to Fidel Castro.

The New Caribbean

Kennedy's name still evoked a warm response among Latin Americans in 1969 when Richard Nixon, whose 1958 visit to Latin America had provoked their wrath, began talking about a "new partnership" with hemispheric nations and dispatched Nelson Rockefeller on a special mission to assess hemispheric conditions. The Alliance for Progress was already in disarray, and Nixon had declared it a failure anyway. Latin Americans, apprehensive about Nixon's foreign policy priorities, were heartened by the Rockefeller mission and its straightforward, if occasionally pessimistic, judgment about the hemisphere at the end of the 1960s.

The Rockefeller Report offered the predictable opinion that the United States had a special relationship with Latin America and the unexpected recommendation that the quality of life for Latin Americans, despite the billions spent in Alliance programs, was far short of expectations and had to be improved. But the United States, Rockefeller said, could no longer tell Latin American governments how to improve the lot of their people. Implicitly the Rockefeller Report expressed a sentiment that Latin American leaders, following their meeting at Viña del Mar, Chile, explicitly told Nixon: the United States must treat Latin American nations as equals.[1]

The consensus of Viña del Mar declared the Alliance for Progress a noble effort whose programs lamentably had not been carried out, expressed a preference for trade over aid, specifically calling for a removal of the economic barriers against Latin American products in American markets, and demanded the right to shape Latin American foreign policies according to each nation's self-interest rather than America's priorities. In a less strident fashion the Rockefeller Report called for many of the same things, adding a recommendation for a Secretary of Western Hemisphere Affairs in the American government and, in order to "strengthen internal security," a Western Hemisphere Security Council (with its center lying outside the United States) that could direct the training of Latin American military and police in antiterrorist tactics. Neither the secretary nor the council became a reality, though in the following decade Latin American militaries and police—many trained in the counterinsurgency school in the Canal Zone—enhanced their counterterrorist techniques in a sometimes frighteningly gruesome manner. Similarly the political exile in Latin America, who historically had been able to flee his own country and find refuge in another, discovered that many Latin American governments were sharing information on political dissidents.

In the area of trade the image of the United States in the Caribbean fell not so much because of Nixon's indifference but because of congressional laxity in passing new legislation and, afterward, anger over the 1973 oil embargo. Like other third-world nations, Caribbean countries resented import duties on their manufactured goods shipped to the United States, arguing that such levies obligated them to export only raw materials and kept their economies dependent on the industrial giants. Out of the meeting at Viña del Mar in 1969 came the unmistakable message that Latin America wanted the United States to lower its tariff barriers. Latin American leaders called for a General System of Preferences (GSP), and the Nixon administration began working to implement it, but Congress tarried until 1974, when the Trade Act was passed just before adjournment of the legislative session in December. The act offered GSP, which the smaller Caribbean nations desperately needed, but Congress, infuriated over the oil embargo, which was really an embargo by the *Arab* oil exporters, denied GSP benefits to members of the Organization of Petroleum Exporting Countries (OPEC) and to producers of raw materials who joined a cartel. Venezuela, the creator of OPEC, had not subscribed to the 1973 embargo, but stood condemned and suffered Congress's wrath, as did Jamaica, which was moving to form the International Bauxite Association, essentially a cartel of bauxite producers.[2]

When Nixon talked about the "new partnership" and "new dialogue" with Latin Americans, he had in mind the larger states of the hemisphere, whose size, population, and economic potential made them worthy in American estimation. The Caribbean countries are small, and consequently less worthy of American esteem. But through the Caribbean, with its microstates, factional politics, stagnant economies, and polyglot societies, swept powerful changes that in the 1970s ended America's Caribbean empire.

Perhaps nowhere in the Caribbean were changes more dramatic than in the Commonwealth Caribbean, the string of islands from Puerto Rico reaching almost to the Venezuelan coast. After World War II the French decided to transform their West Indian possessions into departments of metropolitan France, but the British government, its resources for empire severely drained by the war, began the long process of granting its West Indian colonies autonomy and then independence. In 1958, at British urging but under West Indian direction, the Commonwealth Caribbean created the West Indian Federation, with headquarters in Trinidad. The intent was a loose federation aimed at fostering political and cultural solidarity and breaking down the economic barriers between the islands. From the first the federation ran into difficulties. For all their similarities—stagnant agricultures, heavy unemployment, and unfavorable trade balances with Europe and the United States—the individual member states behaved in a frustratingly provincial manner, and in 1961 the federation collapsed when Jamaicans voted to pull out and chose complete independence in 1962. Trinidad and Tobago followed in the next year, Barbados in 1966. British Guiana, scheduled for full independence in 1966, had, along with British Honduras, declined to participate in the federation.

In the early 1960s there was every indication that West Indians were exchanging one imperial master for another. Nowhere did the phrase "America in Britain's Place" seem more apt than in the English-speaking Caribbean. The process had begun during the war, when American soldiers, stationed at the bases leased to the United States, had delivered a cultural shock to isolated communities accustomed to mimicking English ways. Afterward, American cultural and economic influences remained: West Indians devoured the Hollywood tough-guy films (especially Humphrey Bogart flicks) of the forties and fifties, and American products replaced English manufactures as the most sought after goods in the islands. American multinationals, such as Texaco, Reynolds, Alcoa, and Kaiser moved into Trinidad and Tobago, which has oil, and into Guyana and Jamaica, which have bauxite. Consequently these corporations established economic empires that carried enormous political influence. Tourism, touted as the salvation of dependent economies, brought affluent Americans sporting their material wealth in island cultures of the dispossessed.

The political leadership was initially susceptible to American wishes. The Kennedy administration effectively delayed British Guiana's independence until it could be assured that one Marxist, Forbes Burnham, non-aligned, could be maneuvered into power over another Marxist, Cheddi Jagan. When Alexander Bustamante became the first president of an independent Jamaica in 1962, he proudly identified Jamaica's destiny with the West and declared that the United States could establish a military base in his country without a commitment of foreign aid. For them and Trinidad and Tobago's fiery scholar president, Eric Williams, Fidel Castro was anathema.[3]

But in the 1970s American power in the English-speaking Caribbean waned. One factor, clearly, was the heightened awareness of West Indians of their economic dependence on Europe and especially the United States and their determination to do something about it. In 1968 they formed the Caribbean Free Trade Association (CARIFTA); the following year, the Caribbean Development Bank; and in 1973, the Caribbean Community (CARICOM). None of these received any significant American opposition; indeed such trade organizations were heartily endorsed by the Rockefeller Report. But in the process the larger West Indies states became more aggressive in dealing with American multinationals and in defying American strictures on consorting with Castro's Cuba. In Guyana, Burnham proclaimed a "cooperativist republic" and nationalized Reynolds Aluminum. In Trinidad and Tobago, Eric Williams, who disdained Castro's economics, had invited foreign capital into the country in the 1960s in an effort to build "another Puerto Rico," and then discovered in the early 1970s that chronic unemployment and economic stagnation survived. After the Black Power riots of 1970 Williams declared that the government itself would pursue a more active role in the economy, a move to the left that was accelerated by the rapid rise in oil prices. In Jamaica, Michael Manley, unlike Bustamante, admired Fidel Castro and effectively brought the powerful aluminum companies to heel with government levies. In 1974 Manley declared Jamaica a "democratic socialist" state: private enterprise would remain but the old capitalist system with its attendant evils, he declared, would be wiped out.[4]

One measure of imperial dominion is the ability of the metropole to control the actions of its wards on sensitive issues, and one of the most inviolable rules of American empire in the 1960s had been the policy of isolating Cuba in the western hemisphere. In the following decade that rule came under increasingly vigorous assault and finally collapsed. The forces responsible for its demise were, ironically, increasing criticism of the policy *within* the United States, rising antagonism toward American domination of the OAS among its Latin American members, and, finally, Cuba's changing role in hemispheric affairs.

In 1964 Secretary of State Dean Rusk had declared that there were two "non-negotiable issues" with Cuba: its military alliance with the Soviet Union and its export of revolution. In 1975 the Cuban-Soviet military link was as strong as ever, but Castro no longer appeared to pose a military threat to his Caribbean neighbors, and Secretary of State Henry Kissinger announced that "we are prepared to move in a new direction if Cuba will." Actually, much had happened since Nixon became president to improve Cuban-American relations: the United States had withdrawn from Vietnam and Soviet-American tensions were easing, which had a beneficial effect on Cuban-American relations; and Castro had demonstrated a willingness to accept some kind of understanding on dealing with skyjackers. In the Senate William Fulbright and Frank Church, early critics of the Vietnam War, urged a review of American policy toward Cuba. After Nixon's China trip it was commonly noised on Capitol Hill that if the president could travel thousands of miles to Peking surely he could go to Havana. (Nixon considered China a major power; Cuba, in his estimation, was not, and he had no intention of bounding down the ramp of the presidential jet to grasp the hand of Fidel Castro with the élan he had displayed in greeting Zhou Enlai.)

The State Department moved at a glacial pace, but the Senate pressed its case for changing Cuban policy. In 1974 the special consultant to the Foreign Relations Committee finally got official clearance to visit Cuba, where the Cubans told him that the policy of isolation had been a failure. Cuba still suffered, however, particularly from the difficulties of obtaining spare parts and other manufactures which the Soviets could not supply. But Castro, because of his pride and his desire not to antagonize the Soviets, wanted the initiative for change in the relationship to come from Washington. Senators Jacob Javits, Claiborne Pell, and, later, George McGovern visited Cuba with much fanfare and returned with the impression that Castro wanted to normalize relations.

So, at the OAS foreign ministers' meeting in Quito, Ecuador in 1974, prospects appeared likely for ending Cuba's isolation, if not a formal resumption of diplomatic relations between Cuba and the United States. The United States declared it would abstain, and Venezuela and Costa Rica, the most aggressive among the Latin American governments wanting to lift the embargo, believed the other hemispheric representatives would follow. But in the vote on lifting the embargo (which required two-thirds for passage) six abstained—the United States, Haiti, Guatemala, Bolivia, Brazil, and Nicaragua. The proponents were furious, arguing that the United States secretly lined up the abstaining votes, and were doubly angered because Kissinger was away on one of his Middle Eastern jaunts.

American clout in the OAS declined in the 1970s. Since its founding in 1948 the OAS had always had the image of being an organization dominated by the United States, though in the 1960s the Latin American members played an increasingly important role in its most sensitive agency, the Inter-American Economic and Social Council. After the Dominican intervention in 1965 (during which Lyndon Johnson made a derogatory comment about the ability of the OAS to deal with crises), its prestige suffered. Though there was a major reorganization in 1967, aimed in part at enhancing Latin American influence, the OAS entered the decade of the 1970s with only a shadow of the prestige and power it had in the Kennedy years.

Latin American countries had already begun to move away from American direction, particularly in the economic sphere. In 1964 they organized the Latin American Special Coordinating Commission (CECLA) intended to represent Latin American nations in negotiating trade and tariff issues with the United States and the European common market. At OAS sessions the Latin American representatives began holding private sessions to agree on issues and would afterward summon the American delegate to listen. One student of the inter-American experience, William D. Rogers, who had served with the State Department's Latin American division in the Kennedy years and returned there a decade later, argued in 1973 that the United States should seriously consider pulling out of the OAS.[5]

Already, the disenchantment with the organization had prompted Latin American governments to create alternative hemispheric economic and political structures. In 1975, twenty-five Latin American governments, led by Venezuela, Mexico, and Cuba, met in Panama and founded the Latin American Economic System (SELA), which defiantly excluded the United States but included Cuba. SELA's membership incorporated not only the Caribbean's leftist governments but some of the American faithful such as Honduras, El Salvador, Nicaragua, Haiti, and the Dominican Republic. Their politics differed dramatically, but these disparate regimes were drawn together by their desire to gain some measure of control over prices for their raw materials, to create Latin American multinationals to supplant the powerful multinationals of industrial countries throughout Latin America, and to pool resources for their own development plans. In brief, in the 1970s the Caribbean joined the Third World.[6]

Cuba's role in Caribbean affairs improved dramatically in this decade. In 1970 most Caribbean nations, including those only recently emerged from British rule, had little contact with Cuba. For most Caribbean peoples, Castro was a pariah, a puppet of the Soviet Union. Privately even the Soviets had grown critical of Castro's "adventurism" in Latin America. After Che Guevara's crushing defeat in Bolivia, the Soviets became so disenchanted with Castro, it was rumored, that they were ready to turn to his presumably more reliable brother, Raúl, to direct the faltering Cuban economy. But, as he so often has been able to do, Castro showed he was extraordinarily capable in manipulating even his chief benefactor. When the Soviet Union invaded Czechoslovakia in 1968, there was an outpouring of criticism, but not from Fidel, who supported the Kremlin's decision to crush the defiant regime in Prague. Four years later, following a showdown conference in Moscow, Castro agreed to streamline the hopelessly confused Cuban bureaucracy in accordance with Soviet recommendations. Cuba became a member of the Council for Mutual Economic Assistance (COMECON), the basic economic agreement of the East European socialist states. Within the Cuban hierarchy, Fidel remained number one, Raúl number two.

In Washington all this reconfirmed the prevailing wisdom that Castro was still Moscow's lackey. But to other Caribbean leaders Castro began to appear less a revolutionary threat and more the responsible leader of a third-world society confronting the same economic problems as his Caribbean neighbors. The Cubans still trained their quotas of guerrillas, though here their skills began to slip, apparently, following a disastrous guerrilla foray into the Dominican Republic. Castro began courting Caribbean politicians, trying to break the economic blockade imposed by the United States. In 1971 Cuba had a consulate in Jamaica as its only official contact with any Caribbean nation; five years later, it had diplomatic ties with the Bahamas, Barbados, Colombia, Guyana, Jamaica, Panama, Trinidad and Tobago, and Venezuela. In 1977, despite American concerns over Castro's African policy, the United States and Cuba opened "interests sections" in Havana and Washington.

Castro's African policy, particularly the sending of troops to Angola in 1975 and Ethiopia two years later, viewed in Washington as little more than symbolic evidence of Cuba's subservience to the Soviet Union, also enhanced Cuban prestige in the Caribbean, especially among black West Indians. In 1970 black power riots rocked Trinidad and Tobago (then frantically trying to build its oil economy on the "Puerto Rican model") and the Dutch colony of Curaçao. Though the precipitating issues were largely economic—heavy unemployment and bleak prospects for those entering the job market—the rallying cry of black power aroused lingering hatreds from the West Indian slave past and long years of servitude to white societies and revived sentiments of ties with Africa. The Cubans, who were already forging links with African nations, capitalized on these feelings. Guevara had made a much-publicized African tour in 1964 and, the following year, joined the Lumumba guerrillas in the Congo before going off to the wilds of Bolivia where he died. After the revolutionary commitment to liberate Latin America waned, Castro declared that Africa was the next arena in the struggle against imperialism, and the Cubans stepped up their activities in Africa with technicians and military instructors.[7]

"It's Our Canal"

Throughout the century Panama had been a ward of American power—sometimes compliantly or sullenly acquiescing in American priorities for its strategic needs on the isthmus, or occasionally, as in 1959 and 1964, violently reacting to the overwhelming American presence in the strip of territory dividing the republic. When the United States altered the political relationship, it almost always looked upon the act as a noble gesture to Panamanian pretensions or sensibility. Panamanian leaders were generally cast in the role of unruly nationalists in their homeland, bitterly assailing the patent inequities of the 1903 canal treaty, or in the role of obsequious plea bargainers when dealing privately with American leaders who with a slight show of philanthropy—as Lyndon Johnson demonstrated after the 1964 riots—would appear to grant some major concession.

After 1968 the relationship between the two countries underwent substantive change.[8] In that year the Panamanian national guard, under the leadership of an obscure colonel, Omar Torrijos, overthrew the thrice-elected Arnulfo Arias and for the first time established a military government in Panama. After 1941, when Arias was first tossed out, the guard had begun to play a more important role in Panamanian politics, especially when "Chichi" Remón used it as a stepping-stone to power, but the Panamanian military had never ruled outright until Torrijos seized power.

Plainly Torrijos was something new in Panamanian politics. The national guard, which Remón had used fairly effectively against the oligarchy, now became the champion of economic and social reform. Torrijos barnstormed the country sporting military fatigues proclaiming his "different revolution," outlawed political parties, effectively suppressed the ordinarily unruly national assembly, stifled the press, and launched ambitious rural and urban development programs which alarmed private property holders. All of this brought condemnations that he was trying to be another Castro (whom Torrijos unabashedly admired). In fact, as Walter LaFeber has observed, Torrijos's leftist nationalism owed less to Castro than to the stern brand of anticommunist, reformist militance inculcated in Latin American militaries in the counterinsurgency courses at the School of the Americas in the Canal Zone. Torrijos's style was as emulative of John Wayne (later a supporter of the Panamanian leader) as of Castro. Torrijos radically changed the way Panamanian governments dealt with isthmian social and economic problems; he also altered the way Panama dealt with other countries, particularly the United States.

At first Torrijos did not make the canal the obsessive issue of his politics, as have so many Panamanian politicians. But in 1973 the Panamanian economy, reacting to downturns in the American economy and to the oil embargo, began to slip, and Torrijos shifted his priorities. Panama, historically important as a crossroads of international trade, became an international banking center. Huge amounts were channeled through Panamanian branches of international banks— very little, of course, remaining in Panama—but the hospitality Torrijos showed to international bankers gave him another source of aid and, more importantly, leverage with institutions that carried considerable weight in Washington. As his ambitious domestic programs faltered, Torrijos turned to the moribund canal issue. Declaring the 1967 treaties dead, he began rallying international support for a new canal treaty, even going so far as to embarrass the United States by hosting a meeting of the United Nations Security Council in Panama, at which the United States delegate had to exercise a rarely used American veto to kill a pro-Panamanian resolution.

Psychologically, Torrijos could not have chosen a better time to press the United States on the canal. America was reeling under the twin shocks of Watergate, which eroded public confidence in presidential authority, and Vietnam, which clouded America's international authority. Seizing on Nixon's and Kissinger's boast about a new dialogue with Latin America, the Panamanian leader plunged into what would turn out to be a prolonged debate waged through diplomatic channels and in the often volatile courts of Panamanian and American public opinion. Panama triumphed in the diplomatic arena, it appeared, when in February 1974 Kissinger and Panamanian foreign minister Juan Tack agreed on an eight-point understanding to negotiate a new canal treaty abolishing the 1903 pact, redefining United States security interests on the isthmus, abolishing the despised Canal Zone, and, at a fixed date, giving Panama complete control of the canal. Ellsworth Bunker, eighty years old and a skilled, tough bargainer, headed the American negotiating team.

The diplomatic talks broke down in 1975 when the American military, as it had done in the late 1930s, insisted on concessions—in this instance, fifty-year leases on military bases for canal defense—which Panamanians angrily refused to concede. Neither side could agree on a specific date for turning the canal over to Panama. In Congress news about the discussions invigorated the canal lobby, led by Congressman Daniel Flood, who gleefully mobilized a noisy campaign against new treaties with patriotic appeals glorifying America's imperial age and denunciations of any suggestion about "giving away our canal." (Among other points, Flood insisted that the ten-mile-wide strip traversing Panama was "the Canal Zone" and not "the *Panama* Canal Zone.") Revelations about graft and chicanery in Torrijos's camp did not help the Panamanian cause, though, ironically, Torrijos's severe methods in dealing with his leftist critics at home silenced charges that the Panamanian maximum chief, as he was called, could not provide a "stable" Panama through which a "safe" canal could be operated. Efforts to portray him as a disciple of Castro were defused by support for Panama's position from such diverse American conservatives as John Wayne and William F. Buckley, Jr.

By the end of 1975 the American presidential race was already underway, and the canal inevitably became a rallying cry in the stormy campaign. Soon, millions of Americans, most of them having only a vague awareness of the political history of the canal, were being told that the United States was on the verge of "giving it away." (In one political cartoon a tired businessman relaxing at a bar turns to a friend and says, "For years I never thought about the Panama Canal, now I can't live without it.") Anger and frustration over the Vietnam debacle suddenly poured forth in a ringing reaffirmation of American empire in the Caribbean, so irrationally powerful that even the normally un-flappable Kissinger was provoked by one chest-thumping canal pro-tector (in this case, George Wallace) to declare that the United States must preserve *unilaterally* the right to protect the canal *indefinitely*. The remark precipitated a riot in Panama.

In Congress the defenders of "our canal" were shrill in their at-tacks. Senator Strom Thurmond (citing every source, it seemed, but Scripture) contended that the United States had "bought" the canal and the Canal Zone not once but four times, overlooking the fact that the American government had thus been paying annual rent on some-thing it "owned" since 1903. And in the House, where sentiment for keeping the old treaty was even stronger, Congressman Gene Snyder of Kentucky announced that American sovereignty over the Canal Zone was as sanctified as American ownership of New York City. In the Republican primaries, Ronald Reagan revived a fading campaign against Gerald Ford with ringing declarations about "our canal—we bought it and paid for it." (Of course the canal is "ours," said Senator S. I. Hayakawa of California, "we stole it fair and square.") Ford, the inheritor of Nixon's Panama policy, had to adopt a hardline position for the rest of the campaign. Even Jimmy Carter was compelled to take a stand in the televised debates when he announced that as president he would "never give up complete control or practical control of the Panama Canal, but . . . would continue to negotiate with the Panama-nians." His stand essentially represented Ford's position.

Once in office, Carter continued to negotiate. In a somber cere-mony in September 1977 at the ornate Pan American Union building, the president met with Torrijos (who was neatly dressed in a business suit) to sign two canal treaties.

The canal treaties of 1977—a new canal treaty and a neutrality treaty—did not immediately end the American empire on the isth-mus, but they significantly altered the physical and legal symbols of imperial dominion. John Hay's and Philippe Bunau-Varilla's artfully constructed canal convention of 1903, which had served as the legal bedrock on which an American colony grew, passed into history. The new canal treaty erased the Canal Zone and Canal Zone Government as legal entities, substituting a Panama Canal Commission (made up of five Americans and four Panamanians), which would run the canal until December 31, 1999. The "ancillary enterprises" —commissaries, restaurants, bakeries, dairies, public entertainment, garages, health services, a printing plant—justified as "vital to canal operation" by earlier generations—were abolished; and, after a transition period of thirty months, so too were the schools, courts, and prisons that taught the English tongue and dispensed the Anglo-Saxon common law. In short, the new treaties dismantled an American-created socialist experiment in the tropics. American employees—some of them third-generation canal residents—were provided with employment safeguards, but the new arrangement clearly intended greater access for Panamanians to the coveted skilled positions, and many Americans, angry over being "sold out" by their own government, began leaving.[9]

The "Calzones" had carried on a fierce campaign against the treaties back in the states, but they had obviously failed to arouse much support from a jaded American public grown weary of tropical empire. Much more effective was the combination of military and civilian critics of the neutrality treaty. The Joint Chiefs of Staff, taking the position that the canal could be better protected by a "friendly Panama," argued that the waterway was less vital to American security in the nuclear age. But several prominent retired officers, aligned with hardline civilian supporters of a stronger defense, contended that eventual Panamanian control of the canal severely jeopardized American interests in what was still a crucial commercial and military link between the Atlantic and Pacific coasts.

This opposition, too, collapsed eventually under the powerful influence of international bankers, shipping lobbies, and key senatorial converts to the new treaties, notably Howard Baker of Tennessee, who pointed out that even after 1999, when the canal becomes Panama's property, both Panama and the United States would retain the right to defend it. This right included, according to a Senate reservation from Dennis DeConcini of Arizona, the use of military force in Panama. On this point, understandably, there were differing interpretations of the neutrality treaty in Panama. After December 31,

1999 only Panama may have bases in Panama (unless, as the amendment sponsored by Senator Sam Nunn of Georgia states, the Panamanian government decides to permit extending the American military leases). Even as it was approving the treaties, the Panamanian government reaffirmed its sovereignty over all its territory, though it agreed that in a crisis American ships could pass to the "head of the line" for canal transit.

The Fall of the Somoza Dynasty

At the beginning of the 1970s, Nicaragua was still firmly in the grasp of the family that had ruled it since 1936, when Anastasio Somoza García, head of the national guard, ousted the civilian president and became leader of his country. After Somoza's assassination by a fanatic in 1956, his two sons, Luís and Anastasio, ran Nicaragua, one as president, the other as head of the national guard. Neither Somoza was a fiend like Trujillo, but the family dominated Nicaraguan politics and economy to a degree rivaling that of the Dominican dictator. It owned the biggest businesses and the best agricultural land. Its economic domain encompassed so much it was virtually impossible to do business in Nicaragua without dealing with the Somoza family, and foreign investors, including Americans, generally bypassed Nicaragua. The Somozas managed to survive the noticeable American disenchantment with dictators in the late fifties and especially in the early sixties, when the Kennedy administration expressed disapproval of military governments.

Ever since Sandino's murder there had been opposition, usually in the form of old-line conservative politicians or defiant newspaper editors, whom Anastasio junior tolerated. Many Nicaraguans could not read, so the press often felt free to issue ringing indictments of the regime; but the people could see and hear, so television and radio were severely circumscribed. And there was a violent opposition, the Sandinista Liberation Front, which in 1970 was composed of isolated guerrilla bands that posed no direct threat to the regime.

After 1972, however, when Managua was devastated by an earthquake, Somoza's control over the country began slipping. Natural disasters in the Caribbean have had a way of making or breaking careers: Anastasio senior, for example, greatly enhanced his image among Nicaraguans (and the American military) by his take-charge manner during the 1931 earthquake, just as Trujillo rose in Dominican (and American) estimation by the leadership he displayed following the 1930 hurricane that leveled Santo Domingo. After the 1972 disaster, which destroyed downtown Managua, the government announced that the capital would be rebuilt—on land owned by the Somozas. Already the family and its cronies had been brazenly pocketing aid sent to earthquake victims. Then Somoza began moving into businesses politely reserved for other prominent Nicaraguan families, and the opposition to the regime from the small but influential Nicaraguan bourgeoisie mounted.

The leader of the moderate opposition, as it came to be known, was Pedro Joaquín Chamorro, scion of an old Nicaraguan family and editor of *La Prensa*, an anti-Somoza paper. Chamorro organized the scattered anti-Somoza political parties and a couple of labor unions into the Democratic Union of Liberation. It soon had a rival for public attention, the reinvigorated Sandinista Liberation Front (FSLN), which probably contained only about a hundred members, but which managed to make national (and international) headlines with its daredeviltry. In late December 1974 the FSLN brazenly kidnapped a dozen prominent Nicaraguans at a Christmas party in Managua and held them for the ransom of one million dollars, the release of fourteen comrades, and safe passage to Cuba.

Somoza was incensed and in 1975 began a long campaign to eradicate the Sandinistas. He got additional military aid from the United States, created a counterinsurgency force, and declared a state of siege. In the northern countryside, the guard conducted a brutally repressive campaign, driving the peasants into resettled areas. The outrages committed in the antiguerrilla drive aroused the animosity of the church, which condemned the regime as early as 1977, and eventually of the American government, which under Jimmy Carter was just launching its human rights campaign in American foreign policy.

In his posthumously published autobiography, Somoza argued that the "betrayal" of Nicaragua by the United States began at that time. As the Carter administration stepped up its human rights campaign, singling out Nicaragua for special condemnation, it was also decreasing its military aid to the Somoza regime. In Nicaragua the moderate opponents of the dictator (who had always managed to awe Nicaraguans by his crafty dealings with Americans) were emboldened to new attacks; and the Sandinistas launched a series of desperate raids. There were tentative links forged between factions of the Sandinistas and the moderate enemies of the regime.

Then, in January 1978, Pedro Chamorro was assassinated, and the country was convulsed by civil commotion. Prominent businessmen called a general strike and demanded Somoza's resignation. Somoza of course refused, and Nicaragua endured another six months of violence. All the while, the moderate opponents of the regime looked to the United States, which had put the Somozas in power, to kick them out. But that meant the United States would be intervening in the internal affairs of Nicaragua even though, as Somoza angrily observed, the Carter administration was already intervening in Nicaragua by laying down rules of proper conduct in the civil war.

And it was a civil war in which the Sandinistas, the flow of events moving inexorably with their cause, brilliantly capitalized on the disillusion of the moderates and the uncertainties of American policy. Realizing they could not get rid of Somoza by appealing to the United States, the moderates began shifting to the left with the Sandinistas, just as Carter was promoting a "dialogue" between Somoza and the moderates, which the American president followed up with a highly publicized letter in which he *praised* Somoza for significant improvements in human rights. In August 1978 the Sandinistas took fifteen hundred hostages in a raid on the National Palace, obtained the release of fifty-nine political prisoners, and, as crowds cheered wildly, gloriously flew off to Panama. Insurrections broke out in several cities, provoking retaliation by the national guard in a three-week military campaign against its own people in which three thousand died.[10]

An old fear, reminiscent of Kennedy's remark about American priorities following the assassination of Trujillo in 1961, now returned to haunt the American government. Disgusted with the right but fearing the left, the American government in late 1978 and early 1979 sought in Nicaragua a political solution of the middle. But the "middle" in Nicaragua had already become so disenchanted by the shifting courses of American policy and a growing awareness that the United States no longer controlled what was happening in Central America that it offered no viable alternative. Somoza shrewdly realized that if the United States had to choose between Somoza and the Sandinistas, it would choose Somoza, so he stalled, giving the Americans signals that he was negotiating with the opposition, even though the opposition demanded his resignation, which the American government would not force Somoza to give. With renewed aid Somoza improved the guard's firepower, then summarily rejected any suggestion of resignation.

When the Sandinistas launched their final campaign in June 1979, the world watched Nicaragua descend into a bloody civil war. The savagery of the conflict was revealed nightly to millions of Americans, who watched the callous shooting of a network television correspondent as he lay on the ground at a government checkpoint. Somoza himself took command of the antiguerrilla campaign, but as the days wore on it became obvious he was losing. The United States and the OAS launched a last-minute negotiating effort, this time including Somoza's resignation as a key element in the proposal. The American government, however, no longer had the clout to determine events in Nicaragua, and the Provisional Junta representing the Sandinista guerrillas and the opposition front sensed the weaknesses of American power. Failing to keep the Sandinistas out of the new government, the United States shifted its strategy, saying that it would "arrange" Somoza's resignation and provide economic aid for the new government.

Somoza and his closest associates and their families fled to Miami.[11] Behind them lay a devastated country, its economy shattered, its future uncertain. Nicaragua had experienced savage civil war before in the twentieth century, but the war against Somoza seemed the most savage of all. Anti-Americanism ran strong among the victors—in a sense, the Sandinistas had won the victory the marines had denied to Sandino fifty years before—but the revolution produced no Castro, no *líder máximo* to vilify the Yankee monster at mass rallies. Thrilled by their triumph, the inheritors of Nicaragua were stunned by the awesomeness of the task lying before them. Pulled by the opposing forces of ideological commitment to reconstruct Nicaraguan society and of practical realization that they must first rebuild what was destroyed, they struck a middle course. The Sandinistas welcomed the scores of Cuban and East European technicians, doctors, and teachers for their ambitious social programs yet maintained fragile ties with the United States and its pledges of economic assistance.

The Central American Crisis

The 1980 American presidential campaign, waged exactly twenty years after the volatile Kennedy-Nixon cold war debate over Cuba, produced no anguished cries over "who lost Nicaragua." But Reagan, like Kennedy in 1960, capitalized on American frustration over its tarnished image in the Third World, tragically symbolized by the Iranian hostage crisis. The new administration, led by such forceful ideologues as Secretary of State Alexander Haig and Ambassador to the United Nations Jeane Kirkpatrick (a Democrat who had excoriated the intellectual hypocrisy of Carter's human rights policies), believed the United States could successfully counter Soviet and Cuban influence in an explosive region. Their persuasive reasoning relied on two criteria that had been absent in Vietnam: Central America, lying much closer to our border, was strategically vital, and the six countries (excluding Panama), despite their variations in political traditions, had a republican heritage. The essential flaw with this presumably unambiguous approach was that it portrayed Central America as another battleground in the East-West conflict, which inevitably reminded Americans of the frustrations they had endured in Southeast Asia.

Reagan began with some tough rhetoric and a singleminded policy in Nicaragua. He condemned the Sandinistas for turning to Marxist doctrines as a solution to their economic crisis. Then he promptly cut off vital American economic aid, which for the Nicaraguan rulers made socialism more appealing and the quickly proffered aid from Cuba, Libya, Eastern Europe, and the Soviet Union more necessary. Thus, very soon after the ignominious collapse of Carter and the Democrats, Reagan and the Republicans seemed determined to replay history in the Caribbean basin. Just as Kennedy had chosen Cuba as an issue to confront the Soviets twenty years before, Reagan and his hawkish advisors decided that a hard line in the isthmus, farther away but presumably no less vital to American interests, posed some liabilities but offered bigger opportunities for American policy.

And, just as a hawkish administration in 1961 had justified its tough policies with a Cuba *White Paper*, the Reaganites, in office less than a month, threw down the gauntlet with a stridently anticommunist manifesto on the Salvadoran civil war.[12] Arguing that the Salvadoran guerrillas espoused Marxist doctrines (which was true), the Salvador *White Paper* then concluded that the inspiration for the rebellion and most of its arms came from the Nicaraguans, who acted largely as faithful purveyors for the Cubans. The report displayed errors of hasty composition and misleading argument, which critics ranging from the *Los Angeles Times* to the *Wall Street Journal* pounced on, and the administration shortly published a second edition but clung to its fundamental thesis that El Salvador's troubles stemmed mostly from Cuban and Soviet meddling. Despite its failure to mold a consensus for its tough policies among the public and on Capitol Hill, the administration plunged ahead. Using the CIA as a conduit, it launched a covert war against Managua's new rulers with subsidies to anti-Sandinista rebels operating out of Honduras, undertook some controversial initiatives for holding military exercises with the presumably compliant Hondurans, and sharply escalated its military aid to the Salvadorans.

By defining Central America as foremost a security issue, the Reagan administration, unlike its predecessor, left no doubt that American *strategic* interests in the region weighed more heavily in American calculations than concern for the well-being of Central Americans themselves. As Reagan declared before a joint session of Congress in April 1983: "The National security of all the Americas is at stake in Central America. . . . We have a vital interest, a moral duty and a solemn responsibility."[13] What this meant, in effect, was a dramatic increase in military and economic aid to El Salvador (because it was fighting a "Marxist guerrilla" insurrection abetted by the Nicaraguan Sandinistas) and Honduras (because its military, just as influential as the Salvadoran in national politics, transformed the country into a training base for United States troops and provided sanctuary for Nicaraguan rebels fighting the Sandinistas). The administration expressed doubts about negotiating a Central American truce (the best-known efforts came from the so-called Contadora group: Mexico, Panama, Venezuela, and Colombia), occasionally in stridently defiant tones. Such a militant approach to the Central American crisis obviously heartened the isthmian defenders of the status quo and, as so often happened in the past, revived Latin American charges of American imperialism. But Reagan and the more ideological cold warriors of the administration spoke ominously of "falling Central American dominoes" and "waves of refugees flooding our shores." Although the debate in 1984 over a controversial immigration-reform proposal (the Simpson-Mazzoli bill) was especially bitter, the American public, perhaps because of lingering unpleasant memories of Vietnam, was never fully persuaded by the administration's arguments over the "vital" stakes in Central America.

Perhaps, if Congress's persistent criticism of his Central American policies reflected an uncertainty in the national mood about *what to do* in Central America, the American people sensed that the real stakes there called for much more than the country *could do* there. In the Kissinger Commission Report on the isthmian crisis (delivered in early 1984) the distinguished members of the panel concluded, after repeating the warnings about the gravity of the threat to American interests, that "the conditions of Central America [poverty, illiteracy, infant mortality, chronic political violence, and so on] call to our conscience."[14] After providing millions of dollars to bolster the Salvadoran and Honduran regimes (and, in a less publicized isthmian crisis, to sustain the faltering economy of Costa Rica), the United States would have to expend billions later to rectify those Central American injustices that fueled revolution. To accomplish *American* goals in Central America—political stability, individual freedom, economic opportunity, and societies that nourish those values—we would have to annex the isthmian countries as states in the Union.

The frustrations the United States has experienced in trying to manipulate the Central American situation by political maneuvers and military threats have been evident. In El Salvador, for example, the Reagan administration, initially suspicious of the political candidacy of the Christian Democrat José Napoleón Duarte (because of Duarte's gestures toward negotiation with the Salvadoran rebels), moved noticeably toward support of Duarte (with charges of CIA financing of his 1984 presidential campaign) on the persuasive argument that Duarte and his kind represented the "last best hope" for political decency in Central America. This acceptance came about despite Duarte's acquiescence in a Salvadoran government program of "reform with repression" and continued military interference in civilian affairs, theretofore a violation of Christian Democratic credos. In neighboring Honduras, the heightened American military presence has done little to sustain Honduran sentiment for neutrality or, indeed, a sense of independence. The price of Honduran subservience is the noticeable shame among ordinary *hondureños* that their country is swiftly becoming an American military base. By such unequal partnerships, as evidenced by the legacy of anti-Americanism in Cuba and Nicaragua, suppressed enmities are nurtured.

Guatemala offers an even more embarrassing example of how a vigorous anticommunist program, begun with American intervention in 1954, has developed into an official policy of slaughter in the countryside, with such ferocity that since 1978 Guatemala has ranked consistently among the governments most notorious for state terrorism. The Carter administration condemned Guatemala's systematic violation of human rights, and Guatemala responded by severing its military alliance with the Americans. As one Guatemalan officer explained matters: "If we want to kill each other off, it's our business. The United States has no right to interfere."[15] Jimmy Carter and most Americans were doubtless incredulous at such bluntness; General Custer and his contemporaries of a century ago surely would have understood.

The Future of the Caribbean

In the past—certainly from the age of Theodore Roosevelt and the imperial grandeur Americans associate with his blustering rhetoric and forceful policies in the Caribbean—the United States has been concerned more with political power (who shall rule) than the fundamental issue of *how* Caribbean societies shall be ruled. Sandino's war ended the first epoch of American empire in the Caribbean. The fall of Somoza, America's last surrogate (the "last Marine," as the Sandinistas like to say), ended the second. The "little Caesars" of the Caribbean are gone, unless one counts Jean-Claude ("Baby Doc") Duvalier of Haiti, who does not wield much influence in Washington, and Fidel Castro, sometimes called the "last of the Caribbean caesars," who is in no sense an American surrogate.

The impact of America's declining influence in a region it once proudly referred to as the "American Mediterranean" has registered on the national psyche. Once an American president identified "decent democratic regimes" as our ultimate preference for the kinds of government we must strive for in the Caribbean; now, a generation later, the American ambassador to the United Nations argues that the choice must be authoritarian governments because the only alternative is a totalitarian regime. A generation ago an American president identified the Caribbean (and Latin America generally) as the one region in the world where the United States as example could make a noticeable difference in the future of millions. Nowadays his successor warns ominously of a Caribbean convulsed by revolution and of refugees "flooding our shores." The attorney-general, commenting on a controversial immigration bill before the American Congress, reinforced the president's warning with his own apocalyptic remark, "We can no longer control our borders." Little wonder, then, given the declining fortunes of American goals elsewhere, that Americans exulted at the country's triumph over six hundred or so Cubans in the Grenada invasion in 1983. Or saw in Reagan's Caribbean Basin initiative, with its frankly modest economic commitments, a fleeting opportunity to turn around the diminishing fortunes of American-style economies.

Americans of Theodore Roosevelt's day, readily accepting the geopolitical arguments that the American Mediterranean must be protected against interlopers, undertook the role of policing the tropics, all the while justifying their nation's frankly interventionist practices with self-serving platitudes about "uplifting backward peoples" by "teaching them to elect good men." Americans of our time still fear the outsider (in Theodore Roosevelt's day, Germany; nowadays, the Soviet Union) in the Caribbean. They frantically look for non-Marxists, men like Duarte in El Salvador, in an effort to avoid more "Castros," strident Caribbean nationalists constantly assailing the Yankee giant and cavorting with the Russians.

Yet, except possibly as a last resort, the prudent response to such modern dangers and provocations is not the sort of retaliation that Theodore Roosevelt and his generation would have approved—sending gunboats to chastise recalcitrant governments of small countries or dispatching soldiers to run their affairs is no longer appropriate, however appealing a military response might be to an America that has lost a war in faraway Asia and desperately wants a victory in the nearby Caribbean. The states of the Caribbean are as fractious and disunited as ever, but a revival of military intervention by a frustrated America would unite them in a collective protest. We would gain little of lasting value by such a crusade, and we would have to expend far greater sacrifices than Theodore Roosevelt's generation did in attaining the victory.

Three-quarters of a century ago Americans looked at the turbulence of the Caribbean and, perhaps remembering their own history, attributed its problems to political instability and economic backwardness. In the past generation the Caribbean has experienced remarkable economic advances, yet it remains plagued by political discontinuity. Central America, though racked by political commotion, enjoyed one of the fastest economic growth rates in the world from the early 1950s until the overthrow of Somoza and the outbreak of civil war in El Salvador in 1979. But the ruling elite in Central America (except in Costa Rica) refused to incorporate a new generation into the prevailing order, despite the proliferation of political parties, elections, debate, and the requisite ingredients for democratic societies. Preaching to Central Americans that elections and American-style politics are restoratives to their diminished faith in democracy is not likely to win many converts.

If American empire in the Caribbean is no longer practicable nor statehood possible, the role the United States can play in this vitally important region in the coming years will depend on how realistically we adjust to the "new Caribbean." We must now have a revolution in our own thinking about the Caribbean based on the following general precepts:

First, we must view the Caribbean as we did in Theodore Roosevelt's day: as the most important region in the world to us not only for *strategic* reasons but even more for *demographic* reasons. Since the mid-1960s most of our immigration has been from Latin America.

The principal source of immigrants is Mexico, but the Caribbean has figured heavily in this flow of human beings. Early in the twenty-first century, it is estimated, Hispanics will be the largest minority in this society.

Second, we must be willing, more than ever before, to treat with the states of the Caribbean as equals even though in size, economic output, and military strength they are not. In other words, we must forget Franklin Roosevelt's quip about "our SOBs" and remember his words about being a "good neighbor."

Third, we need to accept the notion that, given the economic liabilities most Caribbean states have inherited, neither American-style capitalism nor Soviet-style communism can provide future generations of Caribbean peoples with the kind of society they need or, more important, want. They are quite capable of seeing the flaws of Cuban socialism as well as its benefits without our having to draw them a picture. Besides, the most successful socialist experience of the modern Caribbean was an American import—the Panama Canal Zone.

Fourth, as long as Castro is in power, reconciliation with Cuba is not likely, but the Cubans (even Castro) have expressed a willingness for greater economic contact. We no longer believe the Russians or Chinese will renounce socialism; we should not expect the Cubans to do so. We cannot do very much about the Cuban-Soviet relationship (which now costs the Russians about four billion dollars a year) as long as we insist on instructing the Cubans how they must behave internationally or run their affairs. Nor should a more realistic policy toward Cuba suffer because of the electoral votes of the state of Florida.

Fifth, the United States can best dramatize its willingness to deal with the Caribbean as an equal rather than a superior by extending statehood now to Puerto Rico. The most harmful element in our historic relationship with the Caribbean (and, indeed, with all Latin America) has been our insistence that American-style democracy is necessary for Caribbean progress while at the same time believing that Caribbean peoples are culturally unsuited for it.

Finally, we must indicate now, by military restraint and a decided preference for "decent democratic regimes," that we will not, indeed cannot, dictate the course of the Caribbean and that we will not be responsible for the kind of societies and governments the Caribbean adopts. If statehood is objectionable and empire unworkable, then nationhood for the English-speaking states of the insular Caribbean and for the Central America isthmus offers an opportunity for Caribbean peoples that imperialism and outside interference have always denied them. We can demonstrate what kind of nations we hope Central America and the insular Caribbean will become. The choice is theirs and ours.

Bibliographical Essay

Caribbeana offers a rich and varied scholarship in history, political science, economics, anthropology, law, and other disciplines. This essay will be confined primarily to books, mostly historical in their approach, which deal with American policy toward the Caribbean.

General surveys of Caribbean history are numerous but uneven in scholarship and coverage. If one exempts the European dependencies, about which there exists a considerable scholarship, the best introduction to modern Caribbean history is Robert Crassweller, *The Caribbean Community: Changing Societies and U.S. Policy* (New York, 1972), which is less a historical summary than a current commentary about the problems and the future of a region with many variations but a common destiny. Germán Arciniegas, *Caribbean: Sea of the New World* (New York, 1946) deals mostly with the pre-1900 Caribbean but considers themes relevant to the twentieth century. Chester Lloyd Jones, *The Caribbean since 1900* (New York, 1935) is now outdated. The most recent one-volume survey is Eric Williams, *From Columbus to Castro: The History of the Caribbean, 1492–1969* (London, 1970), written from the perspective of a West Indian political leader. For an economic and social analysis, published shortly after World War II but with still fresh judgments, see Paul Blanshard, *Democracy and Empire in the Caribbean* (New York, 1947).

Historical surveys and analyses of United States–Latin American relations, which include much material on U.S. policy in the Caribbean, generally fall into one of three categories. J. Lloyd Mecham, *A Survey of United States–Latin American Relations* (Boston, 1965), and Graham Stuart and James L. Tigner, *Latin America and the United States*, 6th ed. (New York, 1975), are texts, though the latter contains much more on the Caribbean than normally found in surveys of this genre. A second variant is the interpretive account, the standard for which remains Samuel Flagg Bemis, *The Latin American Policy of the United States: An Historical Interpretation* (New York, 1943), geopolitical in approach, tendentious in judgment, and didactic in comment. The most recent efforts to supplant Bemis are Robert Burr, *Our Troubled Hemisphere: Perspectives on United States–Latin American Relations* (Washington, 1967), a Brookings Institution study; and Gordon Connell-Smith, *The United States and Latin America: An Historical Analysis of Inter-American Relations* (New York, 1976), which portrays the inter-American relationship as the effort of one great power to impose its will on a collection of weak countries. Finally, works by Latin Americans, such as Ramiro Guerra y Sánchez, *La expansión territorial de los Estados Unidos a expensas de España y de los países hispano-Americanos* (Havana, 1935), and Carlos Ibarguren, *De Monroe a la buena vecindad* (Buenos Aires, 1946), border on being polemics. Salvador de Madariaga, *Latin America between the Eagle and the Bear* (London, 1962), and Dexter Perkins, *The United States and Latin America* (Baton Rouge, 1961), are heavily interpretive. The best brief history is Edwin Lieuwen, *United States Policy in Latin America: A Short History* (New York, 1965), which emphasizes the years since 1945.

There are no satisfactory works tracing the United States–Caribbean relationship from the early nineteenth century, when a distinctive Caribbean policy emerged, until the present. Dexter Perkins, *The United States and the Caribbean*, rev. ed. (Cambridge, Mass., 1966), is essentially a commentary on the modern Caribbean since 1945. An older though still useful work is J. Fred Rippy, *The Caribbean Danger Zone* (New York, 1940), which covers the nineteenth century, the establishment of the protectorates, and concludes with the Good Neighbor policy.

For comparison of United States and European empires in the Caribbean see Harold Mitchell, *Europe in the Caribbean: The Policies of Great Britain, France, and the Netherlands towards Their West Indian Territories in the Twentieth Century* (Stanford, 1963); Mary M. Proudfoot, *Britain and the United States in the Caribbean: A Comparative Study in Methods of Development* (New York, 1954); and Annette B. Fox, *Freedom and Welfare in the Caribbean: A Colonial Dilemma* (New York, 1949). Lester D. Langley, *Struggle for the American Mediterranean: United States–European Rivalry in the Gulf-Caribbean, 1776–1904* (Athens, Ga., 1976), concludes with a discussion of the United States–European adjustment in the Caribbean following the war with Spain. Warren Kneer, *Great Britain and the Caribbean, 1901–1913* (East Lansing, Mich., 1975), argues that London continued to challenge American economic encroachment in the Caribbean and Central America after 1898.

The Protectorate Era

W. H. Callcott, *The Caribbean Policy of the United States, 1890–1920* (Baltimore, 1942), has been virtually superseded by Dana Gardner Munro, *Intervention and Dollar Diplomacy in the Caribbean, 1900–1921* (Princeton, 1964), which offers detailed analysis of the interventions and crises, largely from a State Department perspective. More informal, and occasionally more discerning, accounts of the interventions may be found in A. L. P. Dennis, *Adventures in American Diplomacy, 1896–1906* (New York, 1928), and W. F. Sands, *Our Jungle Diplomacy* (Chapel Hill, 1944). For a European perspective see Jacques Crokaert, *La méditerranée américaine: l'expansion des États-Unis dans la mer des Antilles* (Paris, 1927). Latin American writers have been extremely critical of the protectorate policy. I. Fabela, *Los Estados Unidos contra la libertad: Estudios de historia diplomática americana* (Barcelona, 1921), discusses American interferences in Cuba, the Dominican Republic, Panama, and Nicaragua. Scott Nearing, *The American Empire* (New York, 1921), should be read with the more favorable assessment by Stephen Bonsal, *The American Mediterranean* (New York, 1913). Julius Pratt, *America's Colonial Experiment: How the U.S. Gained, Governed, and in Part Gave Away a Colonial Empire* (Englewood Cliffs, N.J., 1950), analyzes United States colonial policy.

Theodore Roosevelt still occupies a formidable place in the historiography of United States–Caribbean relations. An older but still essential analysis of Roosevelt's Caribbean policy is Howard Hill, *Roosevelt and the Caribbean* (1927; reprint ed., New York, 1965); but Hill's treatment has been modified by Dana Munro, who argues that Root played a more important role in Caribbean policy than historians earlier recognized, and by Howard K. Beale, *Theodore Roosevelt and the Rise of America to World Power* (1956; reprint ed., New York, 1970), which contains a detailed account of the second Venezuelan crisis. The scholarship on the United States–European confrontation in the Caribbean is dominated by works on Anglo-American relations: R. G. Neale, *Great Britain and United States Expansion* (East Lansing, Mich., 1966); A. E. Campbell, *Great Britain and the United States, 1895–1903* (London, 1960); Charles Campbell, *Anglo-American Understand-*

ing, 1898–1903 (Baltimore, 1957); and Bradford Perkins, *The Great Rapprochement: England and the United States, 1898–1914* (New York, 1968). Alfred Vagts, *Deutschland und die Vereinigten Staaten in der Weltpolitik*, 2 vols. (New York, 1935), and Mariano Picón-Salas, *Los días de Cipriano Castro*, 2nd ed. (Barquisimeto, Ven., 1955), present differing perspectives on the Venezuelan crisis of 1902–3. J. Fred Rippy, "The Initiation of the Customs Receivership in the Dominican Republic," *Hispanic American Historical Review* 17 (November 1937): 419–57, is definitive.

The Panama affair is still rightfully remembered as the "blackest spot" in United States policy in the Caribbean and is ordinarily cited as representative of Roosevelt's intentions in the Caribbean. Dwight Miner, *The Fight for the Panama Route: The Story of the Spooner Act and the Hay-Herrán Treaty* (New York, 1940), presents a detailed account, largely from the American perspective, but with considerable coverage of Colombian problems in the canal negotiations. Antonio J. Uribe, *Colombia y los Estados Unidos de América: El canal interoceánico; la separación de Panamá; política internacional económica; la cooperación* (Bogota, 1931), is by one of Colombia's foremost diplomatic historians. The essential documents on the revolution are reprinted in U.S., Senate, *Diplomatic History of the Panama Canal: Documents*, 63rd Cong., 2nd sess. (Washington, 1914). Philippe Bunau-Varilla, *The Great Adventure of Panama* (New York, 1920), offers some insight into the thinking of a crafty man.

For the Cuban experience of 1899 to 1909, the following are essential: David Healy, *The United States in Cuba, 1898–1902: Generals, Politicians, and the Search for Policy* (Madison, Wis., 1963); Louis R. Pérez, Jr., *Cuba between Empires, 1878–1902* (Pittsburgh, 1983), thorough and definitive; and Allan R. Millett, *The Politics of Intervention: The Military Occupation of Cuba, 1906–1909* (Columbus, Ohio, 1968) based largely on military records. On Wood see the older biography by Herman Hagedorn, *Leonard Wood, 1860–1927: A Biography*, 2 vols. (New York, 1931). James Hitchman, *Leonard Wood and Cuban Independence, 1898–1902* (The Hague, 1971), supplements Hagedorn's account of Wood's mission in Cuba. Ramiro Guerra y Sánchez, *Cuba en la vida internacional* (Havana, 1923), emphasizes the impact of the Platt Amendment. Philip S. Foner, *The Spanish-American-Cuban*

War and the Birth of American Imperialism, 1895–1902, 2 vols. (New York, 1972), reflects modern Cuban nationalism. Russell H. Fitzgibbon, *Cuba and the United States, 1900–1935* (Menasha, Wis., 1935) has not been superseded but is modified somewhat by the account in Lester D. Langley, *The Cuban Policy of the United States: A Brief History* (New York, 1968). Herminio Portell Vilá, *Historia de Cuba en sus relaciones con los Estados Unidos y España*, 4 vols. (Havana, 1936–41), is a comprehensive assessment by a famous Cuban historian exiled in the United States after Castro's revolution came to power.

A. Martínez Moreno, *La conferencia de Washington de 1907 y la corte de justicia centroamericana* (San Salvador, 1957), assesses the Central American dilemma in 1907. There is no satisfactory biography of Zelaya in English. See J. D. Gómez, *General José Santos Zelaya, 1854–1919* (Managua, 1940). Zelaya wrote two defenses of his policies: *Refutation of the Statement of President Taft* (Paris, 1911), and *La revolución de Nicaragua y los Estados Unidos* (Madrid, 1910). R. R. Hill, appointed to the high commission in Nicaragua in the 1920s, assesses the 1911 treaties in *Fiscal Intervention in Nicaragua* (New York, 1933). Harold Denny, *Dollars for Bullets: The Story of American Rule in Nicaragua* (New York, 1929), is a journalistic account. The classic study of economic penetration, with considerable emphasis on Nicaragua, is Scott Nearing and Joseph Freeman, *Dollar Diplomacy: A Study in American Imperialism* (New York, 1925). The most recent assessment of Taft's foreign policy, which considers dollar diplomacy in detail, is Walter V. Scholes and Marie V. Scholes, *The Foreign Policies of the Taft Administration* (Columbia, Mo., 1970). A handy collection of documents, which contains, among other materials, the Dawson Agreements and the Knox-Castrillo convention, is U.S., Department of State, *The United States and Nicaragua: A Survey of Relations from 1909 to 1932* (Washington, 1932).

The relevant chapters in Arthur Link's *Wilson: Confusions and Crises, 1915–1916* (Princeton, 1964), and his *Wilson: Campaigns for Progressivism and Peace, 1916–1917*, delineate Wilson's reasons for the Haitian and Dominican interventions. Several chapters in G. W. Baker, Jr., "The Caribbean Policy of Woodrow Wilson, 1913–1917" (Ph.D. diss., Univ. of Colorado, 1961), have appeared as articles; see the notes to Chapter 3, below. Selig Adler, "Bryan and Wilsonian Caribbean Penetration," *Hispanic American Historical Review* 20 (1940): 198–226, is vital for explaining Bryan's version of "public" dollar diplomacy. The standard work on Latin America and World War I is Percy A. Martin, *Latin America and the War* (Baltimore, 1925).

The Haitian intervention has received more scholarly attention than its Dominican counterpart. The best known histories of Haiti are Dantes Bellegarde, *Haïti et son peuple* (Paris, 1953), and idem, *Histoire du peuple haïtienne* (Port-au-Prince, 1953). H. P. Davis, *Black Democracy: The Story of Haiti*, rev. ed. (New York, 1970), is heavily political. Robert D. Heinl and Nancy Gordon Heinl, *Written in Blood: The Story of the Haitian People, 1492–1971* (Boston, 1978), is comprehensive. Ludwell L. Montague, *Haiti and the United States, 1774–1938* (Durham, N.C., 1940), remains the standard diplomatic treatment, though it needs revising and updating. Carl Kelsey "The American Intervention in Haiti and the Dominican Republic," *Annals* of the American Academy of Political and Social Science 100 (March 1922): 109–202, is detailed but uncritical. The most recent studies are Hans Schmidt, *The United States Occupation of Haiti, 1915–1934* (New Brunswick, N.J., 1971), which is highly critical and stresses the cultural impact of American influence, and David Healy, *Gunboat Diplomacy in the Wilson Era: The U.S. Navy in Haiti, 1915–1916* (Madison, Wis., 1976), which relates the intervention largely through the perspective of Admiral William Banks Caperton, commander of the interventionist force. Arthur C. Millspaugh became a financial advisor in the occupation and wrote an even-handed account, *Haiti under American Control, 1915–1930* (Boston, 1931). Bellegarde published several studies on the occupation, among which is *L'occupation américaine d'Haïti: ses conséquences morales et économiques* (Port-au-Prince, 1929). Suzy Castor, *La ocupación norteamericana de Haiti y sus consecuencias, 1915–1934* (Mexico City, 1971), emphasizes economics.

Bruce Calder, *The Impact of Intervention: The Dominican Republic during the U.S. Occupation of 1916–1924* (Austin, Tex., 1984), supersedes Melvin Knight, *The Americans in Santo Domingo* (New York, 1928). Stephen Fuller and Graham Cosmas, *Marines in the Dominican Republic* (Washington, 1975), is essentially a report on the military government. The classic study by Sumner Welles, *Naboth's Vineyard: The Dominican Republic, 1844–1924*, 2 vols. (New York, 1928), reflects the author's involvement in dismantling the protectorate and his racial predilections. Otto Schoenrich, *Santo Domingo: A Country with a Future* (New York, 1918), captures the meaning of benign imperialism. The most thoughtful account of these years is Luís F. Mejía, *De Lílis á Trujillo: Historia contemporánea de la república dominicana* (Caracas, 1944); the most vitriolic, Max Henríquez Ureña, *Los yanquis en Santo Domingo* (Madrid, 1929). For Wilson and Nicaragua, see the studies cited above and those following on the Nicaraguan intervention of 1926–27. On the question of Wilson and the Tinoco brothers in Costa Rica see G. W. Baker, Jr., "Woodrow Wilson's Use of the Non-Recognition Policy in Costa Rica," *The Americas* 22 (July 1965): 3–21; and A. González Flores, *Manifiesto a mis compatriotas, noviembre de 1919* (San Jose, C.R., 1919).

Between Two Wars

The best introduction to the postwar period and the twenties is Dana G. Munro, *The United States and the Caribbean Republics, 1921–1933* (Princeton, 1974), written from the perspective of a State Department policymaker in the period. Joseph Tulchin, *The Aftermath of War: World War I and United States Policy toward Latin America* (New York, 1971), says a great deal about postwar economic problems. Kenneth Grieb, *The Latin American Policy of Warren G. Harding* (Fort Worth, 1976), is generally favorable to Harding and Hughes. R. Hernández-Usera, *Semillas a voleo* (Madrid, 1925), deals with American policy in the Caribbean. Charles Evans Hughes, *Our Relations to the Nations of the Western Hemisphere* (Princeton, 1928), offers something more than an official pronouncement of American policy.

On the Haitian and Dominican debate of the early 1920s the most thorough treatment, though defensive in tone, is U.S., Senate, Select Committee on Haiti and Santo Domingo, *Inquiry into Occupation and Administration of Haiti and Santo Domingo: Hearings*, 67th Cong., 1st and 2nd sess., 2 vols. (Washington, 1921–22). Most of the testimony relates to Haiti. Sumner Welles, who handled the Dominican negotiations, still awaits a biography. F. E. Mejía, *Alrededor y en contra del plan Hughes-Peynado* (Santo Domingo, 1922), is a pamphlet about the plan of 1922 to remove the marines. For Haiti in the 1920s see the work by Schmidt mentioned above, and the following: E. G. Balch, ed., *Occupied Haiti* (New York, 1927); J. H. Craige, *Black Bagdad* (New York, 1933), by a marine on assignment in Haiti in the 1920s; B. Danache, *Le Président Dartiguenave et les Américaines* (Port-au-Prince, 1950); and J. H. McCrocklin, *Garde d'Haïti: Twenty Years of Organization and Training by the United States Marine Corps, 1915–1934* (Annapolis, 1957), an unacknowledged reprint of a Marine Corps report.

The official reference on the 1923 conference is U.S., Department of State, *Conference on Central American Affairs, Dec. 4, 1922–Feb. 7, 1923* (Washington, 1923). H. Key, *Kaffee, Zucker und Bananen* (Munich, 1929), emphasizes economics; Vicente Sáenz, *Norteamericanización de Centro America* (San Jose, C.R., 1925) is by a lifetime critic of the United States. On the fruit companies see C. D. Kepner, Jr., *Social Aspects of the Banana Industry* (New York, 1936), and J. Soothill, *The Banana Empire* (New York, 1953). On Cuban policy in the 1920s the most analytical work is Robert Freeman Smith, *The United States and Cuba: Business and Diplomacy, 1917–1960* (New York, 1960), which deals primarily with economic matters. Cosme de la Torriente, *Cuba en la vida internacional: Discursos*, 2 vols. (Havana, 1922), represents the views of a long-lived survivor of the war of 1895–98.

The most recent scholarly studies in English on the Nicaraguan intervention of 1927 are William Kamman, *A Search for Stability: United States Diplomacy toward Nicaragua, 1925–1933* (Notre Dame, Ind., 1968), which is cautious and detailed; and Neill Macaulay, *The Sandino Affair* (Chicago, 1967), which makes superb use of military records to paint a flattering portrait of the Nicaraguan rebel and make an unflattering comment on American policy in Central America. Gustavo Alemán Bolaños, *Sandino, El libertador: la epopeya, la paz, el invasor, la muerte* (Mexico City, 1952), represents the work of an exiled Nicaraguan who was hostile to the United States. Stimson penned his thoughts in a short volume, *American Policy in Nicaragua* (Managua, 1927). The goals of the Nicaraguan liberals are delineated in H. Osomo Fonseca, *La revolución liberal constitucionalista de 1926* (Managua, 1958). Ramón Romero has analyzed the personalities of Sandino and Somoza in *Sandino y los yanquis* (Mexico City, 1961), and *Somoza, asesino de Sandino* (Mexico City, 1959). The latter is a rambling critique of the politics of the Somoza family. Marvin Goldwert, *The Constabulary in the Dominican Republic and Nicaragua: Progeny and Legacy of United States Intervention* (Gainesville, Fla., 1962) is the standard monograph on the creation of the national guard in both protectorates. Most of the contemporaneous material in English on the Havana conference is official in nature. There is a favorable account of Hughes's role in Merlo J. Pusey, *Charles Evans Hughes*, 2 vols. (New York, 1951).

Herbert Hoover's claim to authorship of the Good Neighbor policy is due to the persuasiveness of Alexander DeConde, *Herbert Hoover's Latin-American Policy* (Stanford, 1951). But Bernardo Jiménez Montellano, *Fundamentos jurídicos de la solidaridad americana* (Mexico City, 1948), argues that Coolidge deserves the honor. On Stimson see E. E. Morison, *Turmoil and Tradition: A Study of the Life and Times of Henry L. Stimson* (Boston, 1960); Stimson and McGeorge Bundy, *On Active Service in Peace and War* (New York, 1948); and Stimson, *The United States and the Other American Republics: A Discussion of Recent Events* (Washington, 1931). For the Clark memorandum and the dispute over recognition of Maximilian Hernández Martínez the most recent commentaries are articles: Robert Ferrell, "Repudiation of a Repudiation," *Journal of American History* 51 (March 1965): 669–73; Gene Sessions, "The Clark Memorandum Myth," *The Americas* 34 (July 1977): 40–58; and Kenneth Grieb, "The United States and the Rise of General Maximilano Hernández," *Journal of Latin American Studies* 3 (November 1971): 151–72.

G. Pope Atkins and Larman C. Wilson, *The United States and the Trujillo Regime* (New Brunswick, N.J., 1971), emphasizes the years after 1941. The best account in English of Trujillo's life is Robert Crassweller, *Trujillo: The Life and Times of a Caribbean Dictator* (New York, 1966), a work of considerable insight into the psychology of authoritarianism. On the Haitian withdrawal see the works by Munro and Schmidt. For the Forbes Commission consult U.S., Department of State, *Haitianization of the Garde, Withdrawal of Military Forces from Haiti, and Financial Agreement* (Washington, 1933); and idem, *Commission for Study and Review of Conditions in Haiti: Report* (Washington, 1930).

Edgar O. Guerrant's *Roosevelt's Good Neighbor Policy* (Albuquerque, 1950) has been completely superseded by Bryce Wood, *The Making of the Good Neighbor Policy* (New York, 1961), which argues that the United States, reacting to the Nicaraguan and Cuban crises of 1927 and 1933, respectively, altered American policy in accordance with the three principles of nonintervention, noninterference, and reciprocity. By contrast, David Green, *The Containment of Latin America* (Chicago, 1971), argues the Good Neighbor was only a guise for advancing United States economic domination. Francisco Cuevas Cancino, *Roosevelt y la buena vecindad* (Mexico City, 1954), is the best-known work on the subject in Spanish.

For Machado and the Cuban convulsion of 1933 there are several excellent works in English. Smith's *The United States and Cuba* devotes considerable attention to the American economic impact on Cuba. By far the most sensitive study of the rebellion and its background is Luis Aguilar, *Cuba, 1933: Prologue to Revolution* (Ithaca, N.Y., 1972). Carleton Beals, *The Crime of Cuba* (Philadelphia, 1933), and Leland Jenks, *Our Cuban Colony: A Study in Sugar* (New York, 1928), are both extremely condemnatory of American policy. Jules R. Benjamin, *The United States and Cuba: Hegemony and Dependent Development, 1880–1934* (Pittsburgh, 1977), emphasizes the years after 1925.

On United States–Panamanian relations see Walter LaFeber, *The Panama Canal* (New York, 1978). William D. McCain, *The United States and the Republic of Panama* (Durham, N.C., 1937), devotes one chapter to the Good Neighbor policy. Its Panamanian counterpart is Ernesto Castillero Pimental, *Panamá y los Estados Unidos*, new ed. (Panama City, 1964). Lawrence Ealy, *The Republic of Panama in World Affairs* (Philadelphia, 1951), assesses the republic's relations with other powers. There is a need for a social and political history of the Canal Zone. Wayne Bray, *The Common Law Zone in Panama* (San Juan, 1976), addresses itself to the question of sovereignty. Gerstle Mack, *The Land Divided: A History of the Panama Canal and Other Isthmian Projects* (New York, 1944), and David McCullough, *The Path between the Seas: The Creation of the Panama Canal, 1870–1914* (New York, 1977), have descriptive chapters on working and living in the Zone in the early days.

Thomas Mathews, *Puerto Rican Politics and the New Deal* (Gainesville, Fla., 1960), is an incisive, careful study. For a much broader treatment the classic study is Gordon K. Lewis, *Puerto Rico: Freedom and Power in the Caribbean* (New York, 1963). On the Puerto Rican "problem" before 1933 see Truman R. Clark, *Puerto Rico and the United States, 1917–1933* (Pittsburgh, 1976).

Despite the recent revisionist study by David Green, *The Containment of Latin America*, there is a need for further work on Roosevelt's relations to Caribbean dictators. Irwin Gellman, *Batista and Roosevelt: Good Neighbor Diplomacy in Cuba, 1933–1945* (Albuquerque, 1973), performs that task for Cuban-American relations, 1933–45, and could serve as a model for studies on F D R and Trujillo or Somoza. Dick Steward, *Trade and Hemisphere: The Good Neighbor Policy and Reciprocal Trade* (Columbia, Md., 1975), contains an excellent discussion about the special character of Cuban-American trade.

Of the numerous diplomatic histories surveying the United States and World War II, the most detailed in treatment of the Caribbean are William L. Langer and S. Everett Gleason, *The Challenge to Isolation, 1937–1940* (New York, 1952); and idem, *The Undeclared War, 1940–1941* (New York, 1953). Alton Frye, *Nazi Germany and the American Hemisphere, 1933–1941* (New Haven, 1961), is disappointing for the Caribbean, but John A. Logan, Jr., *No Transfer: An American Security Principle* (New Haven, 1961), is excellent for the Havana conference of 1940. On military action in the Caribbean see the two volumes in the series The United States Army in World War II, The Western Hemisphere: Stetson Conn and Byron Fairchild, *The Framework of Hemisphere Defense* (Washington, 1960), and Conn, Fairchild, and Rose Engelman, *Guarding the United States and Its Outposts* (Washington, 1964). On probable wartime economic issues consult Percy W. Bidwell, *Economic Defense of Latin America* (Boston, 1941). The following contemporaneous works relate to individual countries or regions: Ricardo J. Alfaro, *Los acuerdos entre Panamá y los Estados Unidos* (Panama City, 1943); Salvador Díaz Versón, *El nazismo en Cuba* (Havana, 1944); I. Lourié, *Haiti: The Ally of Democracy* (Port-au-Prince, 1942); Cosme de la Torriente, *Libertad y democracia* (Havana, 1941), who considers Cuban politics; and Salvador R. Merlos, *Centro-américa en el conflicto* (San Salvador, 1942). A wartime report on the European dependencies is U.S., Department of State, Anglo-American Caribbean Commission, *The Caribbean Islands and the War* (Washington, 1943).

The United States and the Modern Caribbean

On the evolution of the "new Caribbean" the best introductions are Franklin Knight, *The Caribbean: The Genesis of a Fragmented Nationalism* (New York, 1978), a brief history of the insular Caribbean from a Caribbean perspective; and Vicente Sáenz, *Centroamérica en pie* (Mexico City, 1944), a politically liberal view with qualified support for the Good Neighbor Policy. John D. Martz, *Central America: The Crisis and the Challenge* (Chapel Hill, 1959); Mario Rodríguez, *Central America* (Englewood Cliffs, N.J., 1965); and Franklin D. Parker, *The Central American Republics* (London, 1964) have been superseded by Ralph Lee Woodward, *Central America: A Nation Divided* (New York, 1976), which blends social, economic, and political history and concludes with a superb bibliographical essay. On the problems confronting the English-speaking Caribbean, Gordon K. Lewis, *The Growth of the Modern West Indies* (New York, 1968), is an exhaustive political and social commentary carrying the story from about 1918 to 1964. It should be supplemented with a later study, Gérard Pierre-Charles, *El Caribe Contemporáneo* (Mexico City, 1981), which takes the view that the United States remains an imperialist menace in the region. Juan Bosch, *De Cristóbal Colón a Fidel Castro: El Caribe, Frontera Imperial* (Madrid, 1970), is an indictment of imperialism.

On the postwar Caribbean see the works by Paul Blanshard, *Democracy and Empire in the Caribbean: A Contemporary Review* (New York, 1947), and Annette Baker Fox, *Freedom and Welfare in the Caribbean: A Colonial Dilemma* (New York, 1949). For a vigorous support of intervention against dictatorship see William Krehm, *Democracia y tiranías en el Caribe* (Mexico City, 1949). Colin Rickards, *Caribbean Power* (London, 1963), focuses on the Commonwealth Caribbean. On the Caribbean Legion, the older, romantic study by Alberto Bayo, *Tempestad en el Caribe* (Mexico City, 1950), has been supplanted by Charles Ameringer, *The Democratic Left in Exile: The Antidictatorial Struggle in the Caribbean, 1945–1959* (Coral Gables, 1974). The series on the Caribbean, edited by A. Curtis Wilgus, published from 1951 to 1966 at the University of Florida, examines topics from diplomatic relations to health problems.

Much more needs to be done on the United States and the Batista dictatorship of the 1950s. Edmund Chester, *A Sergeant Named Batista* (New York, 1954), is adulatory and unreliable. Ruby Hart Phillips, *Cuba, Island of Paradox* (New York, 1959), is a somewhat conservative comment by the *New York Times* correspondent in Havana. Batista's *Growth and Decline of the Cuban Republic* (New York, 1964) is an apologia. John Dorschner and Roberto Fabricio brilliantly recapture the decadence of Batista's Cuba on the eve of Castro's triumph in *The Winds of December* (New York, 1980). An analysis of Castro as a Cuban "Bonaparte" forms the central theme of Samuel Farber, *Revolution and Reaction in Cuba, 1933–1960: A Political Sociology from Machado to Castro* (Middletown, Conn., 1976).

For the Dominican Republic and Haiti from 1945 to 1961 the following proved most useful: G. Pope Atkins and Larman C. Wilson, *The United States and the Trujillo Regime* (New Brunswick, N.J., 1971); Jesús de Galíndez, *La era de Trujillo* (Ciudad Trujillo, 1955), the study by the martyred exile; and Germán Ornes, *Trujillo: Little Caesar of the Caribbean* (New York, 1958), also unflattering to *El Benefactor*. Virgilio Díaz Ordóñez, *La política exterior de Trujillo* (Ciudad Trujillo, 1955), is a court history. Howard Wiarda, *Dictatorship and Development: The Methods of Control in Trujillo's Dominican Republic* (Gainesville, Fla., 1968), demonstrates how Trujillo controlled the basic institutions of Dominican life; and Bernard Diederich, *Trujillo: The Death of the Goat* (Boston, 1978), tells how he died. For postwar Haiti, the United Nations published an incisive economic study in 1949 entitled *Report of the United Nations Mission of Technical Assistance to the Republic of Haiti*. On politics see Dantès Bellegarde, *Dessalines a parlé* (Port-au-Prince, 1948); Colbert Bonhomme, *Révolution et contre-révolution en Haiti de 1946 à 1957* (Port-au-Prince, 1957), which comments on Magloire; and Bernard Diederich and Al Burt, *Papa Doc: The Truth about Haiti Today* (New York, 1969), a savagely critical biography. Robert and Nancy Heinl, *Written in Blood: The History of the Haitian People* (New York, 1978), is a sweeping account of the black republic from earliest times to the 1970s.

The section on United States–Panamanian problems in the 1950s and 1960s is from Lester D. Langley, "U.S.–Panamanian Relations since 1941," *Journal of Inter-American Studies and World Affairs* 12 (July

1970): 339–66. It should be supplemented with Walter LaFeber, *The Panama Canal: The Crisis in Historical Perspective* (New York, 1978), which is somewhat pro-Panamanian; and Paul Ryan, *The Panama Canal Controversy: U.S. Diplomacy and Defense Interests* (Stanford, 1977), which is a critical assessment of the 1977 treaties by a former naval officer. For two of many Panamanian tracts on the canal see Victor F. Goytía, *La función geográfica del istmo* (Panama, 1947); and David Turner Morales, *Estructura económica de Panamá* (Mexico City, 1958).

On the Guatemalan affair, Richard Immerman, *The CIA in Guatemala* (Austin, Texas, 1982), is essential. Guillermo Toriello, Guatemala's foreign minister in 1954, wrote *La batalla de Guatemala* (Mexico City, 1955), an anti-American tract. Jaime Díaz Rossotti, *El carácter de la revolución guatemalteca* (Mexico City, 1958), is also critical of American policy. Daniel James, *Red Design for the Americas: Guatemalan Prelude* (New York, 1954), is an anticommunist manifesto. Cole Blasier devotes considerable attention to Guatemala as a test case of United States response to a revolutionary regime in *The Hovering Giant: U.S. Responses to Revolutionary Change in Latin America* (Pittsburgh, 1976). Though it is undeniably polemical, Juan Jose Arévalo's *The Shark and the Sardines* (New York, 1961), remains a powerfully persuasive work among Latin Americans. An exhaustive scholarly assessment of Guatemalan institutions from an anthropologist's perspective is Richard Adams, *Crucifixion by Power* (Austin, Texas, 1970).

The most critical study of the Alliance for Progress is Jerome Levinson and Juan de Onís, *The Alliance That Lost Its Way: A Critical Report on the Alliance for Progress* (New York, 1970). There is a detailed discussion about the troubles of British Guiana in the early sixties in Ronald Radosh, *American Labor and United States Foreign Policy* (New York, 1969). Kennedy's reaction to various military coups in 1962 and 1963 is analyzed in Edwin Lieuwen, *Generals vs. Presidents: Neo-militarism in Latin America* (New York, 1962).

The Cuban revolution has spawned an enormous literature, with no end in sight. At the center of this literature, of course, is Castro, who commands more interest than the revolution that bears his name. On Castro and the origins of the revolution, the following are essential: Herbert Matthews, *Revolution in Cuba* (New York, 1975), which is sympathetic; Hugh Thomas, *Cuba: The Pursuit of Freedom* (New York,

1971), a monumental work which traces Cuban history from 1762 to modern times; Theodore Draper, *Castro's Revolution: Myths and Realities* (New York, 1962) and *Castroism: Theory and Practice* (New York, 1965), which contend that Castro won because of an alienated middle-class disgusted with Batista's government; and Andrés Suárez, *Cuba: Castroism and Communism, 1959–1966* (Cambridge, Mass., 1966), which explores Castro's sometimes mystifying relations with the communists.

For the Bay of Pigs the most dramatic accounts are Haynes Johnson, *The Bay of Pigs: The Leaders' Story of Brigade 2506* (New York, 1964); Karl Meyer and Tad Szulc, *The Cuban Invasion: The Chronicle of a Disaster* (New York, 1962); and Peter Wyden, *Bay of Pigs: The Untold Story* (New York, 1979), based on interviews with former CIA agents involved in the operation. The meaning of the Missile Crisis has become a matter of considerable concern for political scientists who study the "making" of policy. In this genre the most imaginative work is Graham Allison, *Essence of Decision: Explaining the Missile Crisis* (Boston, 1971). The most exciting, albeit biased, accounts are in Thomas, *Cuba*, already noted; Arthur Schlesinger, Jr., *A Thousand Days: John F. Kennedy in the White House* (Boston, 1965); and Maurice Halperin, *The Rise and Decline of Fidel Castro: An Essay in Contemporary History* (Berkeley, 1972), a frank account of the glories and defects of Castro. Lynn D. Bender, *The Politics of Hostility: Castro's Revolution and United States Policy* (Hato Rey, Puerto Rico, 1975), assesses the Cuban-American relationship after the missile crisis.

The Dominican Intervention of 1965 continues to inspire both scholarly and polemical assessments. In the former category the most reliable accounts in English are Abraham Lowenthal, *The Dominican Intervention* (Cambridge, Mass., 1972) and Piero Gleijesis, *The Dominican Crisis: The 1965 Constitutionalist Revolt and American Intervention* (Baltimore, 1978). John Bartlow Martin wrote of his experiences in the republic in the early sixties in *Overtaken by Events: The Dominican Crisis from the Fall of Trujillo to the Civil War* (Garden City, N.Y., 1966). Two journalistic accounts of the civil war are Dan Kurzman, *Revolt of the Damned* (New York, 1965); and Tad Szulc, *Dominican Diary* (New York, 1965). Juan Bosch has recorded his frustration in *The Unfinished Experiment: Democracy in the Dominican Republic* (London, 1966). The

Fall 1977 issue of *Revista/Review Interamericana* focuses on Caribbean dictatorship and includes an essay comparing Balaguer and Trujillo.

The literature on modern Puerto Rico is enormous, with studies tending to fall into one of three categories. In the first are works of the "modern miracle" genre, such as Earl Parker Hanson, *Transformation: The Story of Modern Puerto Rico* (New York, 1955); or Harvey Perloff, *Puerto Rico's Economic Future: A Study in Planned Development* (Chicago, 1949), which glorify the island's economic growth and Americanization. In a second category are more scholarly studies, such as Henry Wells, *The Modernization of Puerto Rico: A Political Study of Changing Values and Institutions* (Cambridge, Mass., 1969), or Robert W. Anderson, *Party Politics in Puerto Rico* (Stanford, 1965), which strive for objectivity and analysis. Perhaps the best literature on modern Puerto Rico, however, lies in a third category, the "advocacy" school of Puerto Rico writers who deplore Americanization and the destruction of the island's Hispanic heritage. Foremost among them is Gordon K. Lewis's monumental study, *Puerto Rico*, already noted. This work should be supplemented with Lewis's *Notes on the Puerto Rican Revolution* (New York, 1974), a sweeping indictment of the American presence; Manuel Maldonado-Denis, *Puerto Rico: A Socio-Economic Interpretation*, trans. Elena Vialo (New York, 1972), which has a socialist flavor; and Louise Samoiloff, *Puerto Rico: The Case for Independence* (Boston, 1974), which does a cost estimate for Puerto Rico's independence. On the lot of the Puerto Rican poor there are numerous studies. Two classics are Sidney Mintz, *Worker in the Cane: A Puerto Rican Life History* (New Haven, 1960); and Oscar Lewis, *La Vida* (New York, 1966).

On the politics of the Caribbean community see Sydney Chernick, *The Commonwealth Caribbean: The Integration Experience* (Baltimore, 1978); and Anthony Payne, *The Politics of the Caribbean Community, 1961–1979* (Manchester, England, 1980). For the region's changing international position, see Richard Millett and W. Marvin Will, eds., *The Restless Caribbean: Changing Patterns of International Relations* (New York, 1979). The OAS and the inter-American system are assessed from varying perspectives in John Martz and Lars Schoultz, eds., *Latin America, the United States, and the Inter-American System* (New York, 1979); and Roger Fontaine and James D. Theberge, eds., *Latin Amer-*

ica's New Internationalism: The End of Hemispheric Isolation (New York, 1976). Theberge and other experts assess Soviet power in the Caribbean in Theberge, ed., *Soviet Seapower in the Caribbean* (New York, 1972).

The most exhaustive treatment of the "evolved" Cuban revolution is Jorge Domínguez, *Cuba: Order and Revolution* (Cambridge, Mass., 1976), which interprets the revolution in the perspective of twentieth-century Cuba and concludes there is much more continuity between the old and new Cubas than scholars have recognized. Maurice Halperin, *The Taming of Fidel Castro* (Berkeley, 1981), covers the years from 1964 to 1968. Edward González takes a critical look at Fidel and Fidelismo in *Cuba under Castro: The Limits of Charisma* (Boston, 1974). On Cuba's "new internationalism" in the 1970s see Cole Blasier and Carmelo Mesa-Lago, eds., *Cuba in the World* (Pittsburgh, 1979); and Jacques Lévesque, *The USSR and the Cuban Revolution* (New York, 1978).

On the Somoza dynasty see Alberto Toledo Ortíz, *Grandes reportajes históricos de Nicaragua* (Managua, 1972), and the acidly critical account in English, Richard Millett, *Guardians of the Dynasty* (Maryknoll, N.Y., 1977). Somoza's posthumously published autobiography, *Nicaragua Betrayed* (Boston, 1980), is sometimes revealingly candid about the relations between Somoza and the United States. Adolfo Gilly, *La nueva Nicaragua: anti-imperialismo y lucha de clases* (Mexico, 1980), is an interpretation of the Sandinista movement by a journalist from a leftist Mexican periodical. William LeoGrande, "The Revolution in Nicaragua: Another Cuba?" *Foreign Affairs* 58 (Fall 1979): 28–50; and LeoGrande and Carla Anna Robbins, "Oligarchs and Officers: The Crisis in El Salvador," *Foreign Affairs* 58 (Summer 1980): 1084–1103, offer cogent analyses of these two crises and can be supplemented by such diverse works as Richard Feinberg, ed., *Central America: International Dimensions of the Crisis* (New York, 1981); Don Etchison, *The United States and Militarism in Central America* (New York, 1975); William R. Cline and Enrique Delgado, eds., *Economic Integration in Central America* (Washington, 1978); and Royce Q. Shaw, ed., *Central America: Regional Integration and National Political Development* (Boulder, Colo., 1978).

The literature on the modern Central America crisis is expanding rapidly, offering considerable prospect for improving our understanding of what is going on there. Edelberto Torres-Rivas, *Interpretación del desarollo social centroamericano* (San José, 1977), reflects dependency theory, as does Walter LaFeber, *Inevitable Revolutions: The United States in Central America* (New York, 1983), who sees isthmian upheaval as a breakdown in the American economic system abroad. For a sometimes breezy, sometimes gruesome account see Thomas Buckley, *Violent Neighbors: El Salvador, Central America, and the United States* (New York, 1984). Richard Alan White skillfully implants the "another Vietnam" thesis into *The Morass: United States Intervention in Central America* (New York, 1984). Tom Barry et al., *Dollars and Dictators: A Guide to Central America* (New York, 1983) reflects the publishing philosophy of Grove Press but is rewardingly abundant in statistics. On the crisis in individual countries see Samuel Stone, *La dinastía de los conquistadores* (San José, 1975), a sociological dissection of the Costa Rican elite; John A. Booth, *The End and the Beginning* (Boulder, Colo., 1982), for the Sandinista triumph in Nicaragua; Tommie Sue Montgomery, *Revolution in El Salvador: Origins and Evolution* (Boulder, Colo., 1982), who blends detachment and sympathy in her account of the Salvadoran guerrillas; Enrique Baloyra, *El Salvador in Transition* (Chapel Hill, N.C., 1982), who is more analytical; and Thomas Bonner, *Weakness and Deceit: U.S. Policy and El Salvador* (New York, 1984), who is bitterly condemnatory of American policy.

The "readings" books on Central America tend to fall into three categories. Analytical essays include Howard Wiarda, ed., *Rift and Revolution: The Central American Imbroglio* (Washington, 1984); Steve Ropp and James Morris, eds., *Central America: Crisis and Adaptation* (Albuquerque, N.M., 1984); and Robert Leiken, ed., *Central America, Anatomy of Conflict* (New York, 1983). Examples of advocacy essays are Martin Dishkin, ed., *Trouble in Our Backyard: Central America and the United States in the Eighties* (New York, 1983); and the Stanford Central America Action Network, *Revolution in Central America* (Boulder, Colo., 1983). Finally, there are "pot-pourri" collections of essays, news columns, personal testimonies, and documents, such as Jonathan Fried et al., *Guatemala in Rebellion* (New York, 1983); and Marvin Gettleman et al., *El Salvador: Central America in the New Cold War* (New York, 1981).

All of these works tend to be critical of the U.S., occasionally savagely so. For a defense of American policy, see the El Salvador *White Paper* (both editions), which appeared in 1981; and the Kissinger Commission *Report*, an extensive summary of which appeared in the *New York Times*, 12 January 1984.

Notes

Prelude • A Vision of Empire

1. Margaret Leech, *In the Days of McKinley* (New York, 1959), pp. 288–91.

2. On the peace conference in Paris see H. Wayne Morgan, ed., *Making Peace with Spain: The Diary of Whitelaw Reid, September–December 1898* (Austin, Tex., 1965); Bingham Duncan, *Whitelaw Reid: Journalist, Politician, Diplomat* (Athens, Ga., 1975), pp. 185–95.

3. On the nature of American expansionism before the Civil War see Frederick Merk, *Manifest Destiny and Mission in American History* (New York, 1963); and David M. Pletcher, *The Diplomacy of Annexation: Texas, Oregon, and the Mexican War* (Columbia, Mo., 1973).

4. Richard Challener, *Admirals, Generals, and American Foreign Policy, 1898–1914* (Princeton, 1973), pp. 12–44.

5. David Healy, *U.S. Expansionism: The Imperialist Urge in the 1890s* (Madison, Wis., 1970), pp. 130–36; Benjamin Kidd, *The Control of the Tropics* (New York, 1898), pp. 49–58.

6. On the image of "enemy and ally" see Gerald Linderman, *The Mirror of War: American Society and the Spanish-American War* (Ann Arbor, 1974), pp. 114–47.

7. 182 U.S. 244 (1901).

8. Leland Jenks, *Our Cuban Colony: A Study in Sugar* (New York, 1928), pp. 21–39; on the economic foundations of the "new empire," see the classic work by Walter LaFeber, *The New Empire: An Interpretation of American Expansion, 1860–1898* (Ithaca, N.Y., 1963), esp. pp. 1–61, 150–96.

9. John A. S. Grenville and George Berkeley Young, *Politics, Strategy, and Diplomacy: Studies in Foreign Policy, 1873–1917* (New Haven, 1966), pp. 158–78.

1 • Theodore Roosevelt and the Big Stick

1. Lester D. Langley, *The Cuban Policy of the United States: A Brief History* (New York, 1968), pp. 115–17; David Healy, *The United States in Cuba, 1898–1902: Generals, Politicians, and the Search for Policy* (Madison, Wis., 1963), pp. 44–45, 55–56.

2. Hugh Thomas, *Cuba: The Pursuit of Freedom* (New York, 1971), pp. 421–23.

3. Elihu Root, *The Military and Colonial Policy of the United States*, ed. Robert Bacon and James B. Scott (Cambridge, Mass., 1916), pp. 189–90; J. J. Le

Riverend Brusone, "Historia Económica," in Ramiro Guerra y Sanchez, ed., *Historia de la nación cubana*, 10 vols. (Havana, 1952), 9:287, 299–300; Leland Jenks, *Our Cuban Colony: A Study in Sugar* (New York, 1928), pp. 44–45.

4. Herman Hagedorn, *Leonard Wood, 1860–1927: A Biography*, 2 vols. (New York, 1931), 1:190–91; Leonard Wood, "The Military Government of Cuba," *Annals* of the American Academy of Political and Social Science 21 (March 1903): 153.

5. R. L. Bullard, "Education in Cuba," *Educational Review* 23 (April 1910): 381.

6. Leonard Wood, *Report of the Military Governor of Cuba, 1901*, Serial Set 4269, pp. 36–37.

7. Dana G. Munro, *Intervention and Dollar Diplomacy in the Caribbean, 1900–1921* (Princeton, 1964), p. 26; Russell H. Fitzgibbon, *Cuba and the United States, 1900–1935* (Menasha, Wis., 1935), pp. 75–76; Healy, *U.S. in Cuba*, pp. 170–78.

8. Lester B. Shippee, "Germany and the Spanish-American War," *American Historical Review* 30 (July 1925): 758–59, 763; Andrew White, *Autobiography*, 2 vols. (New York, 1905), 2:168–69.

9. *Daily Chronicle* (London), 26 March 1898.

10. Denis Judd, *Balfour and the British Empire: A Study in Imperial Evolution, 1874–1932* (London, 1968), pp. 313–14; A. E. Campbell, *Great Britain and the United States, 1895–1903* (London, 1960), pp. 149–50.

11. J. A. S. Grenville, "Great Britain and the Isthmian Canal," *American Historical Review* 61 (October 1955): 51–52, 64–65, 66–67.

12. Mariano Picón-Salas, *Los días de Cipriano Castro*, 2d ed. (Barquisimeto, Ven., 1955), p. 9; Alfred Vagts, *Deutschland und die Vereinigten Staaten in der Weltpolitik*, 2 vols. (New York, 1935), 2:1525–30, 1537–41.

13. Dexter Perkins, *The Monroe Doctrine, 1867–1907* (Baltimore, 1937), pp. 332–37, 387–88; Seward W. Livermore, "Theodore Roosevelt, the American Navy, and the Venezuelan Crisis of 1902–1903," *American Historical Review* 51 (April 1946): 456–69; Howard K. Beale, *Theodore Roosevelt and the Rise of America to World Power*, Collier Books ed. (New York, 1970; orig. pub., 1956), pp. 135–45, 336–39.

14. Munro, *Intervention and Dollar Diplomacy*, pp. 78–101; J. Fred Rippy, "The Initiation of the Customs Receivership in the Dominican Republic," *Hispanic American Historical Review* 17 (November 1937): 419–57. See also the relevant chapters in Luís F. Mejía, *De Lilís á Trujillo: Historia contemporánea de la república dominicana* (Caracas, 1944); and Sumner Welles, *Naboth's Vineyard: The Dominican Republic, 1844–1924*, 2 vols. (New York, 1928).

15. In this section I have relied heavily on David McCullough, *The Path between the Seas: The Creation of the Panama Canal, 1870–1914* (New York, 1977).

16. Lawrence O. Ealy, *Yanqui Politics and the Isthmian Canal* (University

Park, Pa., 1971), pp. 52–55, argues that Democrats preferred the Nicaragua route.

17. On Bunau-Varilla and Cromwell see the article by Charles Ameringer, "The Panama Canal Lobby of Philippe Bunau-Varilla and William Nelson Cromwell," *American Historical Review* 68 (January 1963): 346–63.

18. Munro, *Intervention and Dollar Diplomacy*, pp. 40–41.

19. Dwight Miner, *The Fight for the Panama Route: The Story of the Spooner Act and the Hay-Herrán Treaty* (New York, 1940), discusses the Colombian negotiation in detail. For a Colombian view see Antonio J. Uribe, *Colombia y los Estados Unidos de América: el canal interoceánico; la separación de Panamá; política internacional económica; la cooperación* (Bogota, 1931), pp. 113–31. Frank Gatell surveys the historiography in "The Canal in Retrospect: Some Panamanian and Colombian Views," *The Americas* 15 (July 1958): 23–36.

20. Even Samuel Flagg Bemis, the most defensive exponent of American policy in the Caribbean, admitted the Panama affair constituted a "black mark" on the United States. See *The Latin American Policy of the United States: An Historical Interpretation* (New York, 1943), p. 151. E. Taylor Parks, *Colombia and the United States, 1765–1934* (Durham, N.C., 1935), pp. 395–426, describes American intervention as immoral.

21. Charles Ameringer, "Philippe Bunau-Varilla: New Light on the Panama Canal Treaty," *Hispanic American Historical Review* 46 (February 1966): 28–52, argues that Bunau-Varilla granted unnecessary treaty concessions, then compelled the Panamanians to accept.

22. *The Story of Panama: Hearings on the Rainey Resolution before the Committee on Foreign Affairs of the House of Representatives* (Washington, 1913).

23. Enrique Gay-Calbó, "Insurrección de 1906," in Guerra y Sanchez, *Historia de nación cubana*, 8:17–29.

24. Roosevelt to Joseph Foraker, 28 September 1906, quoted in Foraker, *Notes of a Busy Life*, 2 vols. (Cincinnati, 1916), 2:58–59; Luis Machado y Ortega, *La Enmienda Platt: Estudio de su alcance e interpretación y doctrina sobre su aplicación* (Havana, 1922), pp. 102–3; Howard Hill, *Roosevelt and the Caribbean* (Chicago, 1927), pp. 69–105.

25. David Lockmiller, *Magoon in Cuba: A History of the Second Intervention, 1906–1909* (Chapel Hill, 1938), pp. 58–59, 222.

26. Jenks, *Our Cuban Colony*, pp. 97, 126–27; Advisory Law Commission, Report, 15 January 1909, in *Senate Miscellaneous Documents*, 61st Cong., 1st sess., no. 80, p. 23. For an explanation of American motives and accomplishments in the second Cuban intervention, see Allan R. Millett, *The Politics of Intervention: The Military Occupation of Cuba, 1906–1909* (Columbus, Ohio, 1968).

2 • Roosevelt, Taft, and the Search for Central American Stability

1. Philip Jessup, *Elihu Root*, 2 vols. (New York, 1938), 1:468–73; James Brown Scott, "Elihu Root, His Latin American Policy," *Bulletin* of the Pan American Union 71 (1937): 296–304.

2. Thomas Karnes, *The Failure of Union: Central America, 1824–1960* (Chapel Hill, 1961), traces the turbulent history of intra-isthmian rivalries.

3. U.S., Department of State, *Papers Relating to the Foreign Relations of the United States: 1906* (Washington, 1907), pp. 834–46.

4. Charles L. Stansifer, "José Santos Zelaya: A New Look at Nicaragua's Liberal Dictator," *Revista/Review Interamericana* 7 (Fall 1977): 468–85, presents a much more favorable view of the Nicaraguan dictator, whose reputation has suffered severely in Latin American history texts.

5. James Brown Scott, "The Central American Peace Conference of 1907," *American Journal of International Law* 2 (1908): 121–43; Raúl Osegueda, *Operación centroamérica* (Mexico City, 1957), pp. 38–45.

6. Christmas has been immortalized by Hermann B. Deutsch, *The Incredible Yanqui: The Career of Lee Christmas* (London, 1931).

7. Dana G. Munro, *Intervention and Dollar Diplomacy in the Caribbean, 1900–1921* (Princeton, 1964), pp. 157–58; A. Martínez Moreno, *La conferencia de Washington de 1907 y la corte de justicia centroamericana* (San Salvador, 1957).

8. Henry Pringle, *The Life and Times of William Howard Taft*, 2 vols. (New York, 1939), 2:693–99; Walter V. Scholes and Marie V. Scholes, *The Foreign Policies of the Taft Administration* (Columbia, Mo., 1970).

9. Charles L. Stansifer, "José Santos Zelaya: An Interpretation" (paper delivered at the Missouri Valley Conference of Collegiate Teachers of History, Omaha, March 1968).

10. Dana G. Munro, "Dollar Diplomacy in Nicaragua, 1909–1913," *Hispanic American Historical Review* 38 (May 1958): 209–34, contends that American policies were aimed at achieving stability rather than protecting investors.

11. Charles Stansifer has analyzed the fortunes of the nonrecognition clause in "Application of the Tobar Doctrine to Central America," *The Americas* 23 (January 1967): 251–72.

12. Vicente Sáenz, *Norteamericanización de Centro América* (San José, 1925), pp. 45–70. Zelaya published his account in *La revolución de Nicaragua y los Estados Unidos* (Madrid, 1910).

13. Harold Denny, *Dollars for Bullets: The Story of American Rule in Nicaragua* (New York, 1929), pp. 81–83.

14. Scott Nearing and Joseph Freeman, *Dollar Diplomacy: A Study in American Imperialism* (New York, 1925), pp. 151–68.

15. U.S., Department of State, *The United States and Nicaragua: A Survey of*

Relations from 1909 to 1932 (Washington, 1932), includes the Dawson agreements.

16. Munro, *Intervention and Dollar Diplomacy*, pp. 186–204.

17. W. B. Hale, "With the Knox Mission in Central America," *World's Work* 24 (1912): 179–93.

18. U.S., Senate, Committee on Foreign Relations, *Nicaraguan Affairs: Hearings before a Subcommittee . . . to Investigate as to the Alleged Invasion of Nicaragua . . .*, 62nd Cong., 2nd sess. (Washington, 1912), details the military aspects of the rebellion.

19. Scholes and Scholes, *Foreign Policies of the Taft Administration*, pp. 40–44; Luís F. Mejía, *De Lílis á Trujillo* (Caracas, 1944), pp. 76–77, 90–94. For the view of a policymaker under Roosevelt and Taft, see Francis M. Huntington Wilson, *Memoirs of an Ex-Diplomat* (Boston, 1945).

20. Warren Kneer, *Great Britain and the Caribbean, 1901–1913* (East Lansing, Mich., 1975), pp. 134–63.

21. For the Honduran revolution see Deutsch, *The Incredible Yanqui* (London, 1931), pp. 100–175; Ernest Baker, "United Fruit II: The Conquest of Honduras," *Fortune* 7 (March 1933): 31–33.

22. Kenneth Finney analyzes Valentine's fortunes in "Our Man in Honduras: Washington S. Valentine" (paper delivered at the Southern Historical Association Conference, New Orleans, November 1977).

23. Kneer, *Great Britain and the Caribbean*, pp. 188–207.

3 • The Apogee of Caribbean Empire

1. Woodrow Wilson, *United States and Latin America* (Washington, 1913), offers Wilson's views on the eve of his several Latin American crises.

2. Selig Adler, "Bryan and Wilsonian Caribbean Penetration," *Hispanic American Historical Review* 20 (1940): 198–226.

3. The love-hate attitude of Cubans toward Americans had already appeared in Cuban political literature. F. Carrera y Jústiz, *Orientaciones necesarias: Cuba y Panamá* (Havana, 1911), lauded American ways; but J. C. Gandarilla, *Contra el yanquí: Obra de protesta contra la enmienda Platt y contra la absorción y el maquivelismo norteamericano* (Havana, 1903), condemned "North American Machiavellian intrusion."

4. J. D. Frost, "Cuban-American Relations concerning the Isle of Pines," *Hispanic American Historical Review* 2 (1931): 336–50; G. de Quesada, *Los derechos de Cuba á la Isla de Pinos* (Havana, 1909).

5. M. Guiral Moreno, "La intromisión de los extranjeros en nuestros asuntos

domésticos," *Cuba Contemporánea* 7 (February 1915): 137–56; Irene A. Wright, *Cuba* (New York, 1910), pp. 140–55.

6. U.S., Department of State, *Foreign Relations, 1912* (Washington, 1913), pp. 309–22.

7. Rudolfo Z. Carballal, *Estudio sobre la administración del General José M. Gómez, 1909–1913* (Havana, 1915), pp. 48–49, 58; *Foreign Relations, 1912*, pp. 240–56.

8. William Franklin Sands, *Our Jungle Diplomacy* (Chapel Hill, 1944), pp. 37–42.

9. Wayne Bray analyzes the legal presence of the United States in *The Common Law Zone in Panama* (San Juan, P.R., 1976).

10. Frederic J. Haskin, *The Panama Canal* (Garden City, N.Y., 1913), pp. 133–93; Harry N. Howard, *Military Government in the Panama Canal Zone* (Norman, Okla., 1931), pp. 22–23, 58–60; Gerstle Mack, *The Land Divided: A History of the Panama Canal and Other Isthmian Canal Projects* (New York, 1944), p. 563.

11. Lester D. Langley, "The Military Government of the Dominican Republic, 1916–1922" (paper delivered at the Citadel Conference on War and Diplomacy, Charleston, S.C., March 1976).

12. Hans Schmidt, *The United States Occupation of Haiti, 1915–1934* (New Brunswick, N.J., 1971), pp. 42–58.

13. Arthur C. Millspaugh, *Haiti under American Control, 1915–1930* (Boston, 1931), pp. 12–33.

14. Schmidt, *U.S. Occupation of Haiti*, pp. 55–63; Arthur S. Link, *Wilson: The Struggle for Neutrality, 1914–1915* (Princeton, 1960), pp. 516–31.

15. R. B. Davis, Memorandum to Secretary of State, 12 January 1916, in U.S., Department of State, *Foreign Relations, 1916* (Washington, 1925), pp. 311–20.

16. David Healy, *Gunboat Diplomacy in the Wilson Era: The U.S. Navy in Haiti, 1915–1916* (Madison, Wis., 1976), pp. 62–81.

17. Ibid., pp. 155–58.

18. On Butler see Lowell Thomas, *Old Gimlet Eye: The Adventures of Smedley T. Butler as Told to Lowell Thomas* (New York, 1933).

19. Ibid., pp. 201–8.

20. J. H. McCrocklin, comp., *Garde d'Haïti, 1915–1934* (Annapolis, 1956), pp. 90–188; W. H. Posner, "American Marines in Haiti, 1915–1922," *The Americas* 20 (January 1964): 231–66.

21. The constitution is reprinted in U.S., Department of State, *Foreign Relations, 1918* (Washington, 1930), pp. 487–502.

22. Carl Kelsey offers a positive assessment in "The American Intervention in Haiti and the Dominican Republic," *Annals* of the American Academy of Political and Social Science 100 (March 1922): 113–65.

23. Schmidt, *U.S. Occupation of Haiti*, pp. 102–7; Suzy Castor, *La ocupación*

norteamericana de Haiti y sus consecuencias, 1915–1934 (Mexico City, 1971), pp. 113–40.

24. Otto Schoenrich, *Santo Domingo: A Country with a Future* (New York, 1918), pp. 166–67, 218, 232–33, 244–45, 338–39.

25. *Foreign Relations, 1916*, pp. 246–47; Sumner Welles, *Naboth's Vineyard: The Dominican Republic, 1844–1924*, 2 vols. (New York, 1928), 2:797.

26. Samuel Guy Inman, *Through Santo Domingo and Haiti* (New York, 1919), pp. 8–9.

27. Graham Cosmas and Stephen Fuller, *Marines in the Dominican Republic, 1916–1924*; Luís Mejía, *De Lílis á Trujillo* (Caracas, 1944), pp. 156–57; *Literary Digest*, 22 February 1919, pp. 106–7; Bruce J. Calder, "Caudillos and Gavilleros versus the United States Marines: Guerilla Insurgency during the Dominican Intervention, 1916–1924," *Hispanic American Historical Review* 58 (November 1978): 649–75.

28. Marvin Goldwert, *The Constabulary in the Dominican Republic and Haiti: Progeny and Legacy of United States Intervention* (Gainesville, Fla., 1961), pp. 2–3, 8–9, 12–13; Langley, "Military Government of the Dominican Republic."

29. Sarah MacDougall, "Santo Domingo's Second Dawn," *New York Times Magazine*, 10 October 1920, pp. 12, 23; G. W. Brown, "Survey of Santo Domingo," *Journal of Negro History* 8 (April 1923): 138–41.

30. Comm. R. Hayden, "Review of the Reorganization of the Sanitary and Public Health Work in the Dominican Republic under the United States Military Government of Santo Domingo," *U.S. Naval Medical Bulletin* 16 (April 1922): 657–71; U.S., Department of State, *Foreign Relations, 1917* (Washington, 1926), pp. 723–25; Fred Fairchild, "The Public Finance of Santo Domingo," *Political Science Quarterly* 33 (December 1918): 464–69.

31. U.S., Senate, Select Committee on Haiti and Santo Domingo, *Inquiry into Occupation and Administration of Haiti and Santo Domingo: Hearings*, 67th Cong., 1st and 2nd sess., 2 vols. (Washington, 1921–22), pp. 1100–1105; U.S., Department of State, *Foreign Relations, 1920* (Washington, 1936), 2:171–72; Kelsey, "American Intervention in Haiti and the Dominican Republic," pp. 186–87.

32. George T. Weitzel, *American Policy in Nicaragua* (Washington, 1916).

33. Thomas A. Bailey, "Interest in a Nicaraguan Canal, 1903–1931," *Hispanic American Historical Review* 16 (1936): 2–28; G. W. Baker, Jr., "The Wilson Administration and Nicaragua, 1913–1921," *The Americas* 22 (1966): 339–76.

34. Clifford Ham, "Americanizing Nicaragua," *Review of Reviews* 53 (February 1916): 185–91.

35. Harold Denny, *Dollars for Bullets: The Story of American Rule in Nicaragua* (New York, 1929), pp. 171–80.

36. G. W. Baker, Jr., "Woodrow Wilson's Use of the Non-Recognition Policy in Costa Rica," *The Americas* 22 (July 1965): 3–21; A. Gonzáles Flores,

Manifiesto á mis compatriotas, noviembre de 1919 (San José, C.R., 1919), deals with Wilson's non-recognition policy.

37. G. W. Baker, Jr., "Ideas and Realities in the Wilson Administration's Relations with Honduras," *The Americas* 21 (July 1964): 3–19; and idem, "The Woodrow Wilson Administration and Guatemalan Relations," *The Historian* 27 (1965): 155–69.

4 • *A Reassessment of Empire, 1921–1925*

1. Charles Evans Hughes, *Our Relations to the Nations of the Western Hemisphere* (Princeton, 1928), pp. 112–19.

2. Herbert Feis, *The Diplomacy of the Dollar: First Era, 1919–1932* (Baltimore, 1950), pp. 25–29.

3. Joseph Tulchin, *The Aftermath of War: World War I and U.S. Policy toward Latin America* (New York, 1971), pp. 169–71.

4. Ibid., pp. 204–5; Dana G. Munro, *The United States and the Caribbean Republics, 1921–1933* (Princeton, 1974), pp. 152–55.

5. John Blassingame, "The Press and the American Intervention in Haiti and the Dominican Republic," *Caribbean Studies* 9 (July 1969): 28–43.

6. Joseph R. Juarez, "United States Withdrawal from Santo Domingo," *Hispanic American Historical Review* 42 (February 1962): 152–90; Kenneth Grieb, "Warren G. Harding and the Dominican Republic: U.S. Withdrawal, 1921–1923," *Journal of Inter-American Studies and World Affairs* 11 (July 1969): 425–40.

7. Helen Leschorn, "American Atrocities in the Dominican Republic," *Current History* 15 (February 1922): 881–82; U.S., Senate, *Inquiry into Occupation and Administration of Haiti and Santo Domingo: Hearings*, 67th Cong., 1st and 2nd sess., 2 vols. (Washington, 1921–22), 2:1116–21.

8. Maj. Charles F. Williams, "La Guardia Nacional Dominicana," *Marine Corps Gazette* 3 (September 1918): 195–99; "Cutting Santo Domingo's Apron Strings," *Literary Digest*, July 29, 1922, p. 13.

9. Munro, *The U.S. and the Caribbean Republics*, pp. 44–70. The 1922 plan is analyzed in F. E. Mejía, *Alrededor y en contra del plan Hughes-Peynado* (Santo Domingo, 1922).

10. James Weldon Johnson, "Self-Determining Haiti," *Nation* 3, nos. 2878–80, 2882 (28 August–25 September 1920).

11. Hans Schmidt, *The United States Occupation of Haiti, 1915–1934* (New Brunswick, N.J., 1971), p. 123.

12. Arthur C. Millspaugh, "Our Haitian Problem," *Foreign Affairs* 7 (July 1929): 556–70.

13. Arthur C. Millspaugh, *Haiti under American Control, 1915–1930* (Boston, 1931), pp. 99–134. See also Vilfort Beauvoir, *Le contrôle financier du*

gouvernement des États-Unis d'Amérique sur la république d'Haïti (Bordeaux, 1930).

14. Edna Taft, *A Puritan in Voodoo-Land* (Philadelphia, 1938).

15. G. R. Coulthard, "The French West Indian Background of 'Negritude,'" *Caribbean Quarterly* 6 (December 1961): 128–36.

16. Rayford Logan, "Education in Haiti," *Journal of Negro History* 15 (October 1930): 401–60; idem, "The U.S. 'Colonial Experiment' in Haiti," *World Today* 17 (October 1961): 435–46; idem, "The United States Mission in Haiti, 1915–1952," *Inter-American Economic Affairs* 6 (Spring 1953): 18–28.

17. Suzy Castor, *La ocupación norteamericana de Haiti y sus consecuencias* (Mexico City, 1971), pp. 75–94. See also Yvette Gindine, "Images of the American in Haitian Literature during the Occupation, 1915–1934," *Caribbean Studies* 14 (October 1974): 37–52.

18. U.S., Department of State, *Eighth Annual Report of the American High Commissioner at Port-au-Prince, Haiti, 1929* (Washington, 1930).

19. Thomas L. Karnes, *The Failure of Union: Central America, 1824–1960* (Chapel Hill, 1961), pp. 202–10; Kenneth Grieb, "The United States and the Central American Federation," *The Americas* 24 (October 1967): 107–21.

20. James Brown Scott, "The Central American Conference," *American Journal of International Law* 17 (1923): 313–19.

21. Aro Sanso, *Policarpo Bonilla: Algunos apuntes biográficos* (Mexico City, 1936), pp. 447–542; Charles Hackett, "The Background of the Revolution in Honduras," *Review of Reviews* 69 (April 1924): 390–96.

22. Munro, *The U.S. and the Caribbean Republics*, pp. 132–45.

23. L. Mariano Pérez, "Las relaciones económicas entre Cuba y los Estados Unidos," *Cuba Contemporánea* 28 (April 1922): 264–70; Leon Primelles, *Crónica cubana*, 2 vols. (Havana, 1955–57), 1:471–74.

24. David Lockmiller, *Enoch Crowder: Soldier, Lawyer, Statesman* (Columbia, Mo., 1955), pp. 217–22, 228; Primelles, *Crónica cubana*, 2:155–56; U.S., Department of State, *Foreign Relations, 1921* (Washington, 1936), 1:671–87.

25. *Foreign Relations, 1921*, 1:754–61; U.S., Department of State, *Foreign Relations, 1922* (Washington, 1938), 1:1014, 1047–48; Emeterio S. Santovenia, "Experiencia del gobierno propio," in Ramiro Guerra y Sanchez, ed., *Historia de la nación cubana*, 10 vols. (Havana, 1952), 8:59.

26. Manuel Marquez Sterling, *La política exterior y la política nacional del Presidente Machado* (Havana, 1926), pp. 12–13, 23, 26.

5 • *The Empire Embattled, 1925–1933*

1. W. E. Dunn, "The Postwar Attitude of Hispanic America toward the United States," *Hispanic American Historical Review* 3 (1920): 173–83; E. Perry, "Anti-American Propaganda in Hispanic America," ibid., pp. 17–40; J. Fred

Rippy, "Literary Yankeephobia in Latin America," *Journal of International Relations* 12 (1922): 350–71, 524–38.

2. Franklin D. Roosevelt, "Our Foreign Policy: A Democratic View," *Foreign Affairs* 6 (July 1928): 573–86.

3. Harold Dodds, "The United States and Nicaragua," *Annals* of the American Academy of Political and Social Science 132 (1927): 131–41; idem, "American Supervision of the Nicaraguan Election," *Foreign Affairs* 7 (1929): 488–96.

4. William Kamman, *A Search for Stability: United States Diplomacy toward Nicaragua* (Notre Dame, Ind., 1968), pp. 19–68.

5. The Liberals' goals are summarized in H. Osomo Fonseca, *La revolución liberal constitucionalista de 1926* (Managua, 1958). Dennis analyzed the crisis in "Nicaragua: In Again, Out Again," *Foreign Affairs* 9 (1931): 496–500.

6. According to Francisco Cuevas Cancino, *Roosevelt y la buena vecindad* (Mexico City, 1954), p. 163, President Plutarco E. Calles was promoting a Nicaraguan counterrevolution.

7. U.S., Senate, Committee on Foreign Relations, *Use of the United States Navy in Nicaragua: Hearings*, 70th Cong., 1st sess. (Washington, 1928).

8. Henry L. Stimson, *American Policy in Nicaragua* (New York, 1927), pp. 42–89.

9. Neill Macaulay, *The Sandino Affair* (Chicago, 1967), pp. 48–61. See also Joseph Baylen, "Sandino: Patriot or Bandit?" *Hispanic American Historical Review* 31 (1954): 394–419; and Gustavo Alemán Bolaños, *Sandino, el libertador: La epopeya, la paz, el invasor, la muerte* (Mexico City, 1952); and Lejeune Cummins, *Quijote on a Burro* (Mexico City, 1958).

10. Macaulay, *Sandino Affair*, pp. 62–104.

11. Raymond L. Buell, "American Supervision of Elections in Nicaragua," *Foreign Policy Association Information Service* 6 (1930): 385–402.

12. Macaulay, *Sandino Affair*, pp. 185–241.

13. Ibid., pp. 242–56; Joseph O. Baylen, "Sandino: Death and Aftermath," *Mid-America* 36 (April 1954): 116–39.

14. For a summary of the conference see James Brown Scott, "The Sixth International Conference of American States, Held at Havana, January 16–February 20, 1928," *International Conciliation*, no. 241 (June 1928).

15. "The Monroe Doctrine after 100 Years," *Current History* 19 (October 1923): 102–13.

16. Merlo J. Pusey, *Charles Evans Hughes*, 2 vols. (New York, 1951), 2:551–61.

17. Bryce Wood, *The Making of the Good Neighbor Policy* (New York, 1967; orig. pub., 1961), pp. 45–47.

18. Vicente Sáenz, *Rompiendo cadenas: Las del imperialismo en Centro América y on otras repúblicas del continente*, 2d ed. (Mexico City, 1951), p. 216; Charles

Stansifer, "Application of the Tobar Doctrine to Central America," *The Americas* 23 (January 1967): 267–68.

19. L. H. Woolsey, "Recognition of the Government of El Salvador," *American Journal of International Law* 28 (1934): 325–29; Kenneth Grieb, "The United States and the Rise of General Maximiliano Hernández," *Journal of Latin American Studies* 3 (November 1971): 151–72.

20. J. Reuben Clark, *Memorandum on the Monroe Doctrine*, (Washington, 1930).

21. Robert Ferrell, "Repudiation of a Repudiation," *Journal of American History* 51 (March 1965): 669–73; Gene Sessions, "The Clark Memorandum Myth," *The Americas* 34 (July 1977): 40–58.

22. Dana G. Munro, *The United States and the Caribbean Republics, 1921–1933* (Princeton, 1974), pp. 294–302.

23. Robert Crassweller, *Trujillo: The Life and Times of a Caribbean Dictator* (New York, 1966), pp. 63–92.

24. Hans Schmidt, *The United States Occupation of Haiti, 1915–1934* (New Brunswick, N.J., 1971), pp. 154–96.

25. "The Hate of Haiti," *Literary Digest*, 12 December 1929, pp. 6–7.

26. Munro, *The U.S. and the Caribbean Republics*, pp. 309–41; Donald B. Cooper, "The Withdrawal of the United States from Haiti, 1928–1934," *Journal of Inter-American Studies* 5 (January 1963): 83–101.

6 • *Franklin D. Roosevelt and the Meaning of the Good Neighbor Policy*

1. Franklin D. Roosevelt, "Our Foreign Policy: A Democratic View" *Foreign Affairs* 6 (July 1928): 573–86.

2. For a succinct account of Welles's views on Latin America, see Welles, *The Time for Decision* (New York, 1944), pp. 185–241; and the official pamphlets, U.S., Department of State, *The Roosevelt Administration and Its Dealings with the Republics of the Western Hemisphere* (Washington, 1935); and idem, *Two Years of the "Good Neighbor" Policy* (Washington, 1935).

3. Ernest Gruening, "Cuba under the Machado Regime," *Current History* 34 (May 1931): 214.

4. Manuel Márquez Sterling, *La política exterior y la política nacional del Presidente Machado* (Havana, 1926), pp. 15–16; Robert Freeman Smith, *The United States and Cuba: Business and Diplomacy, 1917–1960* (New York, 1961), pp. 113–14.

5. Carleton Beals, *The Crime of Cuba* (Philadelphia, 1933), pp. 244–45; Emilio Roig de Leuchsenring, *Historia de la enmienda Platt*, 2 vols. (Havana, 1951), 1:285; "Where is the Dynamite?" *The Nation*, 14 June 1933, pp. 664–

65; Harry F. Guggenheim, *The United States and Cuba: A Study in International Relations* (New York, 1934), pp. 113, 118–19, 151, 162–66.

6. E. David Cronon, "Interpreting the New Good Neighbor Policy: The Cuban Crisis of 1933," *Hispanic American Historical Review* 39 (November 1959): 538–67.

7. Luis Aguilar, *Cuba, 1933: Prologue to Revolution* (New York, 1974; orig. pub., 1972), pp. 128–32.

8. U.S., Department of State, *Foreign Relations, 1933* (Washington, 1952), 5:283–335.

9. Charles A. Thomson, "The Cuban Revolution: Fall of Machado," Foreign Policy Association *Reports* 11 (1935–36): 250–61.

10. Cordell Hull, *Memoirs*, 2 vols. (New York, 1948), 1:314–15; Aguilar, *Cuba, 1933*, pp. 152–62.

11. Smith, *U.S. and Cuba*, pp. 149–50; Raymond L. Buell et al., *Problems of the New Cuba: Report of the Commission on Cuban Affairs* (New York, 1935), pp. 14–15; Welles, *The Time for Decision*, pp. 198–99; *Foreign Relations, 1933*, 5:441–74.

12. Aguilar, *Cuba, 1933*, pp. 183–99. Grau wrote his own defense, *La revolución cubana ante América* (Mexico City, 1936).

13. *Foreign Relations, 1933*, 5:451, 457, 503, 506, 535–36.

14. U.S., Department of State, *Foreign Relations, 1934* (Washington, 1952), 5:95–97, 349; Manuel Marquez Sterling, *Proceso histórico de la enmienda Platt* (Havana, 1941), pp. 402–4.

15. Paul Varg, "The Economic Side of the Good Neighbor Policy: The Reciprocal Trade Program and South America," *Pacific Historical Review* 45 (February 1976): 47–71.

16. Dick Steward, *Trade and Hemisphere: The Good Neighbor Policy and Reciprocal Trade* (Columbia, Mo., 1975), pp. 210–13.

17. Ibid., pp. 89–122.

18. Carleton Beals, "New Machado in Cuba," *The Nation*, 7 August 1935, pp. 152–53.

19. Ramiro Guerra, "Sugar: Index of Cuban-American Co-operation," *Foreign Affairs* 20 (July 1942): 749–50; J. Gatría, "Los tratados de reciprocidad entre Cuba y los Estados Unidos de Norte América," *América* 9 (January 1941): 59–65.

20. E. Borge González, "Nicaragua por dentro: Una dictadura con el beneplácito del Departmento de Estado," *Combate* 1 (March 1959): 33–42; E. F. Carlson, "The Guardia Nacional de Nicaragua," *Marine Corps Gazette* 21 (August 1937): 7–20.

21. Irwin Gellman, *Batista and Roosevelt: Good Neighbor Diplomacy in Cuba, 1933–1945* (Albuquerque, 1973), pp. 98–99. Batista published his own manifesto in *Cuba, su política interna y sus relaciones exteriores* (Havana, 1939).

22. C. A. Thomson, "The Cuban Revolution: Reform and Reaction," Foreign Policy Association *Reports* 11 (1936), no. 22.

23. Ruby Hart Phillips, *Cuba: Island of Paradox* (New York, 1959), pp. 170–82.

24. Miguel Ángel Campa, *Un año de política exterior cubana* (Havana, 1941), pp. ii, 67; Cosme de la Torriente, "Cuba, America, and the War," *Foreign Affairs* 19 (October 1940); 145–55.

25. C. A. Thomson, "Dictatorship in the Dominican Republic," Foreign Policy Association *Reports* (1936), no. 3.

26. G. Pope Atkins and Larman C. Wilson, *The United States and the Trujillo Regime* (New Brunswick, N.J., 1971), pp. 51–52.

27. Robert Crassweller, *Trujillo: The Life and Times of a Caribbean Dictator* (New York, 1966), pp. 149–63.

28. The account of Roosevelt's Panamanian problems is based mostly on my article, "Negotiating New Treaties with Panama, 1936," *Hispanic American Historical Review* 58 (May 1968): 220–33.

29. Alexander DeConde, *Herbert Hoover's Latin-American Policy* (Stanford, 1951), pp. 60–61; John Biesanz and Luke Smith, "Panamanian Politics," *Journal of Politics* 14 (August 1952): 398–99.

30. Ernesto Castillero Reyes, ed., *Galería de presidentes, 1903–1953*, 2d ed. (Panama City, 1953), p. 56.

31. Quoted in Langley, "Negotiating New Treaties with Panama," p. 232.

32. U.S., Department of State, *Treaty Series 945* (Washington, 1939).

33. After the Spanish-American War, Puerto Rican political leaders assumed that the island would be, briefly, a territory and subsequently be incorporated as a state. See Bolivar Pagán, *Historia de los partidos políticos puertorriqueños*, 2 vols. (San Juan, 1959), 1:45–46.

34. The Insular Cases are reprinted in U.S., Dept. of Interior, *Documents on the Constitutional History of Puerto Rico* (Washington, n.d.), pp. 117–51.

35. Truman R. Clark, *Puerto Rico and the United States, 1917–1933* (Pittsburgh, 1976), pp. 23–30, 56–66, 147.

36. Thomas Mathews, *Puerto Rican Politics and the New Deal* (Gainesville, Fla., 1960).

37. Gordon K. Lewis, *Puerto Rico: Freedom and Power in the Caribbean*, Torchbook ed. (New York, 1968), pp. 68–87.

38. Harold Ickes, *The Secret Diary of Harold Ickes*, 3 vols. (New York, 1954), 1:547.

7 • The Impact of War

1. Donald M. Dozer, *Are We Good Neighbors? Three Decades of Inter-American Relations, 1930–1960* (Gainesville, Fla., 1959), pp. 31–33.

2. Bryce Wood, *The Making of the Good Neighbor Policy* (New York, 1967; orig. pub., 1961), pp. 336–42. For Argentina see Carlos Saavedra Lamas, *La conferencia interamericana de consolidación de la paz* (Buenos Aires, 1938).

3. Alton Frye, *Nazi Germany and the American Hemisphere, 1933–1941* (New Haven, 1967).

4. Stetson Conn, Byron Fairchild, and Rose Engelman, *Guarding the United States and Its Outposts* (Washington, 1964), pp. 4, 301–2.

5. On Ubico and the United States see Kenneth Grieb, "American Involvement in the Rise of Jorge Ubico," *Caribbean Studies* 10 (April 1970): 5–33; idem, "The United States and General Jorge Ubico's Retention of Power," *Revista de Historia de América* 71 (January–June 1971): 119–35; and idem, "The Fascist Mirage in Central America: Guatemalan–United States Relations and the Yankee Fear of Fascism, 1936–1944" (paper delivered at the Conference of the Society for Historians of American Foreign Relations, Washington, D.C., August 1975).

6. David Green, *the Containment of Latin America: A History of the Myths and Realities of the Good Neighbor Policy* (Chicago, 1971), pp. 60–74.

7. Harmodio Arias, Jr., "A Collective Neutrality Front for the Americas," *Inter-American Quarterly* 2 (January 1940): 59–67.

8. Melvin Hall and Walter Peck, "Wings for the Trojan Horse," *Foreign Affairs* 19 (January 1941): 347–69.

9. William L. Langer and S. Everett Gleason, *The Challenge to Isolation, 1937–1940* (New York, 1952), pp. 607–29.

10. John A. Logan, Jr., *No Transfer: An American Security Principle* (New Haven, 1961), pp. 309–45; Donald M. Dozer, "Certain Backgrounds and Results of the Havana Conference," *World Affairs* 103 (September 1940): 164–71.

11. Secretary of War, *Report, 1939* (Washington, 1939), p. 2.

12. Mark S. Watson, *Chief of Staff: Prewar Plans and Preparations* (Washington, 1950), pp. 458–60; Lester D. Langley, "The World Crisis and the Good Neighbor Policy in Panama, 1936–1941," *The Americas* 24 (October 1967): 144–46.

13. Ernesto Castillero Pimental, ed., *Galería de presidentes, 1903–1953* (Panama City, 1953), p. 50.

14. Almon R. Wright, "Defense Sites Negotiation between the United States and Panama, 1936–1948," Department of State *Bulletin* 27 (1952): 212–17.

15. Langley, "World Crisis and the Good Neighbor Policy in Panama,"

pp. 147–52. For the view of a Panamanian diplomat see Ricardo J. Alfaro, *Los acuerdos entre Panamá y los Estados Unidos* (Panama City, 1943).

16. J. P. Humphrey, "Argentina's Diplomatic Victory," *Canadian Forum* 21 (March 1942): 362–64; P. del Rio, "La reunión de Rio de Janeiro y sus consecuencias para la unidad continental," *América* 13 (February 1942): 1–6.

17. C. Moran, "The Evolution of Caribbean Strategy," United States Naval Institute *Proceedings* 68 (1942): 365–73.

18. Conn, Fairchild, and Engelman, *Guarding the United States and Its Outposts*, pp. 423–24.

19. On the OCIAA see Gerald K. Haines, "Under the Eagle's Wings: The Franklin D. Roosevelt Administration Forges an American Hemisphere," *Diplomatic History* 1 (Fall 1977): 373–88.

20. A. Vargas Gómez, "La isla de Cuba frente a la Guerra Europea," *Ultra* 11 (April 1942): 420–29; H. N. Stark, "War Bolsters Haiti's Economy," *Foreign Commerce Weekly* 9, no. 11 (1942): 4–8, 38–40; J. Harding and J. A. E. Orliski, "Dominican Republic Tackles War Problems," *Foreign Commerce Weekly* 10, no. 3 (1943): 6–9, 26–28.

21. Rexford G. Tugwell, *The Stricken Land: The Story of Puerto Rico* (New York, 1947), pp. 212–15; H. N. Stark, "War Poses Problems for British West Indies," *Foreign Commerce Weekly* 9, no. 12 (1942): 8–12, 34–36.

22. Paul Blanshard, *Democracy and Empire in the Caribbean: A Contemporary Review* (New York, 1947), pp. 328–29.

23. Dozer, *Are We Good Neighbors?* pp. 117–20, 127–28.

24. Green, *Containment of Latin America*, pp. 291–97.

25. Wood, *Making of the Good Neighbor Policy*, pp. 329–31.

8 • *The Cold War, 1945–1960*

1. Arthur P. Whitaker, "Latin America and Postwar Organization," *Annals* of the American Academy of Political and Social Science 240 (1945): 109–15; Roger R. Trask, "The Impact of the Cold War on United States–Latin American Relations, 1945–1949," *Diplomatic History* 1 (Summer 1977): 271–84.

2. For the postwar economic relationship see N. P. Macdonald, "Latin America and the United States," *Quarterly Review* 297 (April 1959): 219–331; and Donald M. Dozer, *Are We Good Neighbors? Three Decades of Inter-American Relations, 1930–1960* (Gainesville, Fla., 1959), pp. 226–73; and Stephen G. Rabe, "The Elusive Conference: United States Economic Relations with Latin America, 1945–1952," *Diplomatic History* 2 (Summer 1978): 279–94.

3. Annette Baker Fox, *Freedom and Welfare in the Caribbean: A Colonial Dilemma* (New York, 1949), pp. 3–16, 192–203; J. A. Bough, "The Caribbean Commission," *International Organization* 3 (1949): 643–55.

4. On postwar Haiti the study of the United Nations mission is invaluable:

Report of the United Nations Mission of Technical Assistance to the Republic of Haiti (Lake Success, N.Y., 1949), esp. pp. 25–42.

5. Robert Crassweller, *Trujillo: The Life and Times of a Caribbean Dictator* (New York, 1966), pp. 152–53, 160–63.

6. Rayford W. Logan, *Haiti and the Dominican Republic* (New York, 1968), pp. 146–48.

7. Bernard Diederich and Al Burt, *Papa Doc: The Truth about Haiti Today* (New York, 1969), pp. 52–75.

8. Ibid., pp. 76–104; Gerard Pierre-Charles, *Radiografía de una dictadura: Haiti bajo el régimen del Doctor Duvalier* (Mexico City, 1969), pp. 63–65.

9. G. Pope Atkins and Larman C. Wilson, *The United States and the Trujillo Regime* (New Brunswick, N.J., 1971), pp. 81–87.

10. An account of the kidnapping of de Galíndez and the disappearance of Murphy is contained in Germán Ornes, *Trujillo: Little Caesar of the Caribbean* (New York, 1958), pp. 309–38.

11. Atkins and Wilson, *U.S. and the Trujillo Regime*, pp. 69–78.

12. Hugh Thomas, *Cuba, The Pursuit of Freedom* (New York, 1971), pp. 737–58.

13. Ibid., pp. 759–74; Julián Alienes y Mosa, *Características fundamentales de la economía cubana* (Havana, 1950), p. xv.

14. *Diario de la Marina* (Havana), 11 March 1952, p. 1; William S. Stokes, "National and Local Violence in Cuban Politics," *Southwestern Social Science Quarterly* 34 (September 1953): 61–62.

15. Armando Giménez, *Sierra Maestra: La revolución de Fidel Castro* (Buenos Aires, 1959), pp. 19–20; Batista, *The Growth and Decline of the Cuban Republic* (New York, 1964), p. 261; U.S., Department of Commerce, *Investment in Cuba* (Washington, 1956), pp. 5–6, 17.

16. Ernesto Castillero Pimental, *Panamá y los Estados Unidos* (Panama City, 1964), p. 302; Enrique Jiménez, *Para la historia: Breves capítulos de la gestión política y administrativa de un gobernante liberal* (Panama City, 1951), pp. 25–30.

17. Panama, Ministerio de Relaciones Exteriores, *Memoria, 1950: Anexos* (Panama City, 1950), L/1–L/5; U.S., Department of State, *Treaties and Other International Acts, Series 3297* (Washington, 1955).

18. Mercer D. Tate, "Panama Canal and Political Partnership," *Journal of Politics* 25 (February 1963). 126–27.

19. Thelma King, *El problema de la soberania en las relaciones entre Panamá y los Estados Unidos* (Panama City, 1961), p. 133; *New York Times*, 4, 5 November 1959; *Star and Herald* (Panama), 6 November 1959; *La Hora* (Panama), 5, 11 November 1959.

20. White House Press Release, 17 September 1960.

21. U.S., House, Committee on Foreign Affairs, *Report on United States Relations with Panama*, 86th Cong., 2d sess. (Washington, 1960), pp. 12–15, 38–40.

22. John D. Martz, *Central America: The Crisis and the Challenge* (Chapel Hill, 1959), pp. 181–205.

23. J. Lloyd Mecham, *The United States and Inter-American Security, 1889–1960* (Austin, Texas, 1961), pp. 402–6.

24. Ronald M. Schneider, *Communism in Guatemala, 1944–1954* (New York, 1959), pp. 9–34.

25. Cole Blasier, *The Hovering Giant: U.S. Responses to Revolutionary Change in Latin America* (Pittsburgh, 1976), pp. 152–54.

26. Philip B. Taylor, Jr., "The Guatemalan Affair: A Critique of United States Foreign Policy," *American Political Science Review* 50 (September 1956): 787–806; on the CIA see chapter 11 of David Wise and Thomas B. Ross, *The Invisible Government* (New York, 1964), pp. 165–83.

27. Juan Jose Arévalo, *Guatemala: La democracia y el imperio*, 7th ed. (Buenos Aires, 1964), pp. 26–29.

28. United Nations, Security Council, *Official Records*, 20 June 1954; Dwight D. Eisenhower, *The White House Years: Mandate for Change, 1953–1956* (New York, 1963), pp. 424–25.

29. Gregorio Selser, *Guatemalazo: La primera guerra sucia* (Buenos Aires, 1961), pp. 158–60; Guillermo Toriello, *La batalla de Guatemala* (Mexico City, 1955), pp. 161–91; *New York Times*, 18 July 1954. The role of United Fruit Company in the Guatemalan affair is retold by a former UFCO official, Thomas McCann, in *An American Company: The Tragedy of United Fruit* (New York, 1976), pp. 42–62.

9 • *The Cuban Revolution*

1. On Castro's charisma see Ward Morton, *Castro as Charismatic Hero* (Lawrence, Kans., 1965).

2. Fidel Castro, *History Will Absolve Me* (Havana, 1960), pp. 21, 34–36; Teresa Casuso, *Cuba and Castro* (New York, 1961), pp. 96–99.

3. Herbert Matthews, *Revolution in Cuba: An Essay in Understanding* (New York, 1975), pp. 82–86.

4. Ramon E. Ruíz, *Cuba: The Making of a Revolution* (New York, 1970; orig. pub., 1968), pp. 164–69.

5. Earl E. T. Smith, *The Fourth Floor: An Account of the Castro Communist Revolution* (New York, 1962), pp. 6–7, 20, 29–30, 41, 228.

6. Ruíz, *Cuba*, pp. 141–63; Theodore Draper, *Castro's Revolution: Myths and Realities* (New York, 1962).

7. On 21 January 1959, Castro exclaimed to a Cuban throng: "In Cuba we'll execute some 400 war criminals; one for every 1,000 assassinated in Hiroshima and Nagasaki." Quoted in Maurice Halperin, *The Rise and Decline of Fidel Castro* (Berkeley, 1974; orig. pub., 1972), p. 21.

8. Ibid., pp. 23–25.

9. Dwight D. Eisenhower, *The White House Years: Waging Peace, 1956–1961* (Garden City, N.Y., 1965), p. 523; William A. Williams, *The United States, Cuba, and Castro: An Essay on the Dynamics of Revolution and the Dissolution of Empire* (New York, 1962), p. 100; Rufo López Fresquet, *My Fourteen Months with Castro* (Cleveland, 1966), p. 106.

10. Halperin, *Rise and Decline of Fidel Castro*, pp. 45–54.

11. Philip Bonsal, "Cuba, Castro, and the United States," *Foreign Affairs* 45 (January 1967): 260–76.

12. Philip Bonsal, *Cuba, Castro, and the United States* (Pittsburgh, 1971), pp. 108–9.

13. Ibid., pp. 127–28; on the attitude of the American press toward the Cuban revolution in 1959 see Michael J. Francis, "The U.S. Press and Castro: A Study in Declining Relations," *Journalism Quarterly* 44 (Summer 1967): 257–66.

14. Eisenhower, *Waging Peace*, pp. 613–14; Richard Nixon, *Six Crises* (Garden City, N.Y., 1962), pp. 352–55.

15. U.S., Department of State, *Cuba* (Washington, 1961).

16. Halperin, *Rise and Decline of Fidel Castro*, pp. 74–87.

17. Arthur Schlesinger, Jr., *A Thousand Days: John F. Kennedy in the White House* (Boston, 1965), pp. 226–56.

18. Much of this discussion on the Bay of Pigs relies heavily on Karl Meyer and Tad Szulc, *The Cuban Invasion: The Chronicle of a Disaster* (New York, 1962); and Haynes Johnson et al., *The Bay of Pigs: The Leaders' Story of Brigade 2506* (New York, 1964).

19. Hilton got his information from a Guatemalan paper, *La Hora*, which publicized the training camps. The Guatemalan foreign minister denied the story, but the political opposition demanded an investigation. *New York Times*, 10 January 1961, p. 1.

20. Quoted in Halperin, *Rise and Decline of Fidel Castro*, p. 111.

21. Jerome Levinson and Juan de Onís, *The Alliance That Lost Its Way: A Critical Report on the Alliance for Progress* (New York, 1972; orig. pub., 1970), pp. 64–67.

22. The divergent positions are explored in Charles Fenwick, "The Issue at Punta del Este: Non-Intervention v. Collective Security," *American Journal of International Law* 56 (1962): 469–74; and E. V. Corominas, *Cuba en Punta del Este* (Buenos Aires, 1962).

23. Halperin, *Rise and Decline of Fidel Castro*, pp. 160–64.

24. On Russian motives see Arnold Horelick, "Cuban Missile Crisis: An Analysis of Soviet Calculations and Behavior," *World Politics* 16 (April 1964): 363–89.

25. Robert Crane, "The Cuban Crisis: A Strategic Analysis of American

and Soviet Policy," *Orbis* 6 (Winter 1963): 529; David L. Larson, ed., *The Cuban Crisis of 1962: Selected Documents and Chronology* (Boston, 1963), pp. 3, 11–12.

26. The most convenient summary of the crisis is Robert Divine, ed., *The Cuban Missile Crisis* (Chicago, 1971), pp. 7–57.

27. In *The Cuban Missile Crisis*, pp. 58–246, Divine brings together the divergent, and sometimes bitter, interpretations of the crisis. To his selections should be added Graham Allison, *Essence of Decision: Explaining the Cuban Missile Crisis* (Boston, 1971), esp. pp. 245–77; and Robert Kennedy, *Thirteen Days: A Memoir of the Cuban Missile Crisis* (New York, 1969).

28. Fidel Castro to U Thant, 28 October 1962, in *Política Internacional* 1 (January–March 1963): 235.

29. Halperin, *Rise and Decline of Fidel Castro*, pp. 196–97.

30. On Cuban incorporation into the Soviet "bloc" see Daniel Tretiak, "Cuba and the Soviet Union: The Growing Accommodation, 1964–1965," *Orbis* 11 (Summer 1967): 439–58.

31. Daniel's two articles on the Kennedy-Castro dialogue appeared in the *New Republic*, 7 and 14 December 1963; William Attwood, *The Reds and the Blacks: A Personal Adventure* (New York, 1967), pp. 142–45.

32. Quoted in Halperin, *Rise and Decline of Fidel Cstro*, p. 297.

33. Lynn D. Bender, *The Politics of Hostility: Castro's Revolution and United States Policy* (Hato Rey, P.R., 1975), pp. 26–31. Donald Losman, "The Embargo of Cuba: An Economic Appraisal," *Caribbean Studies* 14 (October 1974): 95–120, argues that the embargo was economically devastating for Cuba but failed politically because Castro drew closer to the Soviet Union.

10 • *The Turbulent Sixties*

1. John F. Kennedy, "Alianza para Progreso," Department of State *Bulletin* 44 (1961): 471–78. See also Ernest R. May, "The Alliance for Progress in Historical Perspective," *Foreign Affairs* 41 (1963): 757–74.

2. Arthur Schlesinger, Jr., *A Thousand Days: John F. Kennedy in the White House* (Boston, 1965), pp. 779–93.

3. Ibid., pp. 774–79; Ronald Radosh, *American Labor and United States Foreign Policy: The Cold War in the Unions from Gompers to Lovestone* (New York, 1969), pp. 393–405.

4. Jerome Levinson and Juan de Onís, *The Alliance That Lost Its Way: A Critical Report on the Alliance for Progress* (New York, 1972; orig. pub., 1970), pp. 83–85.

5. Edwin Lieuwen, *Generals vs. Presidents: Neo-Militarism in Latin America* (New York, 1964), pp. 63–68.

6. Levinson and de Onís, *Alliance That Lost Its Way*, pp. 85–87; see also Juan Bosch, *The Unfinished Experiment: Democracy in the Dominican Republic* (London, 1966; orig. pub., Mexico City, 1964), esp. pp. 146–66.

7. John Bartlow Martin, *Overtaken by Events: The Dominican Crisis from the Fall of Trujillo to the Civil War* (New York, 1966), pp. 547–90.

8. Victor F. Goytiá, *La tragedia del Canal* (Panama City, 1966), p. 5; República de Panamá, *Algunos aspectos de las transacciones en bienes y servicias entre Panamá y la Zona del Canal . . .* (Panama City, 1964), p. 3.

9. Most of this section is from my article, "U.S.–Panamanian Relations since 1941," *Journal of Inter-American Studies and World Affairs* 12 (July 1970): 339–66.

10. International Commission of Jurists, *Report on Events in Panama, 9–12 January 1964* (Geneva, 1964), pp. 12–34.

11. Panama's charge of aggression is disputed by Charles G. Fenwick, "Legal Aspects of the Panama Case," *American Journal of International Law* 58 (April 1964): 436–41.

12. *Report on Events in Panama*, pp. 5–6, 36–40.

13. Panama, Ministerio de Relaciones Exteriores, *Memoria, 1965* (Panama City, 1966), pp. 10–11, 25–27.

14. Daniel Flood, *Isthmian Canal Policy Questions* (Washington, 1966), p. 519.

15. Clippings in Panama Canal Information Office files, Canal Zone Library.

16. On a sea-level waterway see Immanuel J. Klette, *From Atlantic to Pacific: A New Interocean Canal* (New York, 1967).

17. In this section I have relied heavily on Abraham Lowenthal, *The Dominican Intervention* (Cambridge, Mass., 1972).

18. Martin, *Overtaken by Events*, pp. 637–45.

19. Lowenthal, *Dominican Intervention*, pp. 42–61.

20. Ibid., pp. 63–112.

21. Tad Szulc, *Dominican Diary* (New York, 1965), pp. 65–77.

22. Lyndon B. Johnson, "The Dominican Republic: A Target of Tyranny," *Vital Speeches* 31 (15 May 1965): 450–52.

23. Herbert Schoonmaker, "The Role of the U.S. Air Force in the Dominican Crisis of 1965" (Ph.D. diss., Univ. of Georgia, 1977).

24. Gordon Connell-Smith, "The OAS and the Dominican Crisis," *World Today* 21 (1965): 229–36.

25. *Life*, 28 May 1965.

26. Theodore Draper, *The Dominican Revolt: A Case Study in American Policy* (New York, 1968), pp. 183–200. Jerome Slater, *Intervention and Negotiation: The United States and the Dominican Revolution* (New York, 1970), pp. 1–14, criticizes the intervention but disputes Draper's thesis.

27. EPICA (Ecumenical Program for Inter-American Communication and Action), *Puerto Rico: A People Challenging Colonialism* (Washington, 1976), pp. 21–23.

28. Juan Ángel Silén, *Historia de la nación puertoriqueña* (Rio Piedras, P.R., 1973), pp. 326–28; United Nations, General Assembly, 8th period, *Plenary Session, 459.*

29. *Washington Post*, 2 March 1954.

30. Gordon K. Lewis, *Puerto Rico: Freedom and Power in the Caribbean*, Harper Torchbook ed. (New York, 1968), pp. 113–33.

31. Michael Meyerson, "Puerto Rico: Our Backyard Colony," *Ramparts* 8 (June 1970): 50–51.

32. Gordon K. Lewis, *Notes on the Puerto Rican Revolution* (New York, 1974), pp. 202–5.

33. Juan Bosch, *Pentagonism: A Substitute for Imperialism* (New York, 1968), pp. 20–22, 106–7, 108–22.

34. Draper, *Dominican Revolt*, pp. 201–8.

11 • The End of Empire

1. Nelson Rockefeller, *The Rockefeller Report on the Americas: The Official Report of a United States Presidential Mission for the Western Hemisphere* (Chicago, 1969), esp. chap. 1.

2. John Bartlow Martin, *U.S. Policy in the Caribbean* (Boulder, Colo., 1978), pp. 193–97.

3. Gordon K. Lewis, *The Growth of the Modern West Indies* (New York, 1968), pp. 343–415.

4. Gerard Pierre-Charles, *El Caribe Contemporáneo* (Mexico City, 1981), pp. 292–332. In the Jamaican election of 1980 Manley's rickety Jamaican socialist experiment was finally toppled by a resurgent capitalist, Edward Seaga.

5. Martin, *U.S. Policy in the Caribbean*, p. 245.

6. An illustration of the Caribbean's growing identification with the Third World was its *support* of OPEC's 1973 oil embargo, despite the damage inflicted on the region's fragile economies.

7. Ronald Jones, "Cuba and the English-speaking Caribbean," in Cole Blasier and Carmelo Mesa-Lago, eds., *Cuba in the World* (Pittsburgh, 1979), pp. 131–43.

8. Much of this section is based on Walter LaFeber, *The Panama Canal: The Crisis in Historical Perspective* (New York, 1978), pp. 160–227.

9. U.S., Senate, Committee on Foreign Relations, *Background Documents Relating to the Panama Canal*, 95th Cong., 1st sess. (Washington, 1977), contains

the 1977 treaties and more than 180 documents relative to the canal from 1826 to 1977.

10. For a compact summary of the civil war see William M. LeoGrande, "The Revolution in Nicaragua: Another Cuba?" *Foreign Affairs* 58 (Fall 1979): 28–50.

11. Exiled in Florida, Somoza continued to be a nuisance to the Carter administration because the former dictator acted as if he were planning a return to power. Fearing assassination by vengeful Sandinistas, Somoza fled to the right-wing sanctuary of Paraguay, where Argentine terrorists ambushed his car, killing him instantly. "Nobody in Nicaragua would ever believe I wouldn't try to get back in power if I ever quit," he had often remarked.

12. "Communist Interference in El Salvador," Department of State *Bulletin* 81 (March 1981): 1–7. But in summer 1981 Venezuela and Mexico appeared to be dividing on the Salvadoran question, the Venezuelans taking a more cautious approach, the Mexicans (with the French) extending what amounted to recognition to the Salvadoran liberation front.

13. Quoted in Viron Vaky, "Reagan's Central American Policy: An Isthmus Restored," in Robert Leiken, ed., *Central America: Anatomy of Conflict* (New York, 1984), p. 237.

14. A lengthy extract of the Report appeared in the *New York Times*, 12 January 1984.

15. Quoted in the *New York Times*, 23 March 1980, p. 8.

Index